# ADVANCE PRAISE FOR
# *THE STRUGGLE FOR FREEDOM*

*"This is one of the best African American history texts I have seen. The narrative writing style is excellent, the first-person accounts help to grab the reader and humanize the story. The balance between social, political, economic, and cultural history is very good."*

Raymond Frey, Centenary College

*"The use of biographical vignettes allows the authors to explore a number of issues that are often ignored and not well covered in other texts. I was impressed with the way the authors were able to deal with issues of culture (especially music and literature) and gender through the biographical approach."*

Thomas Ward, Rockhurst University

*"The scholarship is thorough and up-to-date, and the authors provide nuanced interpretations of many of the most controversial themes. I believe the text balances all types of history equally well, and I was especially pleased with its emphasis on the cultural history of African Americans."*

Rebecca Woodham, Auburn University, Montgomery

*"The major strengths of this work are the ways in which key figures, many of whom are under-explored in most survey texts, are at the centerpiece of the historical narrative."*

Robert S. Smith, University of North Carolina, Charlotte

*"I see the major strengths of this project as the quality of the scholarship, which includes the use of primary material, the freshness of the material, including the introduction of some heretofore neglected figures, and the readability of the textbook."*

Albert S. Broussard, Texas A & M University

*"This text's inclusive nature and abundance of useful information provide the student with a powerful introduction to African American issues."*

Julian C. Chambliss, Rollins College

# ABOUT THE AUTHORS

## CLAYBORNE CARSON

Clayborne Carson was born in Buffalo, New York. He received his BA, MA, and PhD from the University of California, Los Angeles, and has taught at Stanford University since 1974. Active during his undergraduate years in the civil rights and antiwar movements, Carson's publications have focused on the African American protest movements of the post–World War II period. His first book, *In Struggle: SNCC and the Black Awakening of the 1960s* (1981) won the Frederick Jackson Turner Award from the Organization of American Historians. He has also edited *Malcolm X: The FBI File* (1991) and served as an advisor for the award-winning PBS series on the civil rights movement entitled *Eyes on the Prize*, as well as for other documentaries, such as *Freedom on My Mind* (1994), *Blacks and Jews* (1997), *Brother Outsider: The Life of Bayard Rustin* (2002), and *Negroes with Guns: Rob Williams and Black Power* (2005). Carson is director of the Martin Luther King Jr., Research and Education Institute at Stanford, an outgrowth of his work since 1985 as director of the King Papers Project, which has produced five of fourteen volumes of a comprehensive edition of *The Papers of Martin Luther King Jr.* The biographical approach of *The Struggle for Freedom: A History of African Americans* grew out of Carson's vision. He has used it with remarkable results in his course at Stanford.

## EMMA J. LAPSANSKY-WERNER

Emma J. Lapsansky-Werner received her BA, MA, and PhD from the University of Pennsylvania. From 1973 to 1990 she taught at Temple University, the University of Pennsylvania, and Princeton University. Since 1990 she has been a professor of history and curator of special collections at Haverford College. From her experience with voter registration in Mississippi in the 1960s, she became an historian to try to set the record straight. Her professional and research interests include family and community life, antebellum cities, Quaker history, and religion and popular culture in nineteenth-century America. Lapsansky-Werner has written or edited several volumes, including *Back to Africa: Benjamin Coates and the Colonization Movement in America, 1848–1880* (2005, with Margaret Hope Bacon), *Neighborhoods in Transition: William Penn's Dream and Urban Reality* (1994), and *Quaker Aesthetics: Reflections on a Quaker Ethic in American Design and Consumption, 1720–1920* (2003). She is also a contributor to Yale University Press's *Benjamin Franklin, In Search of a Better World* (2005) and to several anthologies on the history of Pennsylvania. She hopes that *The Struggle for Freedom: A History of African Americans* will help broaden the place of African American history in academia, expanding the trend toward including black Americans as not just objects of public policy, but also as leaders in the international struggle for human justice. Through stories, black Americans are presented as multidimensional, alive with their own ambitions, visions, and human failings.

# GARY B. NASH

Gary B. Nash was born in Philadelphia and received his BA and PhD in history from Princeton University. He taught at Princeton briefly and since 1966 has been a faculty member at the University of California, Los Angeles, teaching colonial American, revolutionary American, and African American history. In 1990 he won the school's Distinguished Teacher Award. Nash's many books on early American history include *Quakers and Politics: Pennsylvania, 1681–1726* (1968); *Red, White, and Black: The Peoples of Early North America* (1974; Fifth ed., 2005, 2000); *The Urban Crucible: Social Change, Political Consciousness, and the Origins of the American Revolution* (1979); *Race, Class, and Politics: Essays in American Colonial and Revolutionary Society* (1986); *Forging Freedom: The Formation of Philadelphia's Black Community, 1720–1840* (1988); *Race and Revolution* (1990); *Forbidden Love: The Secret History of Mixed-Race America* (1999); *First City: Philadelphia and the Forging of History Memory* (2001); *Landmarks of the American Revolution* (2003); *The Unknown American Revolution: The Unruly Birth of Democracy and the Struggle to Create America* (2005); *The Forgotten Fifth: African Americans in the Age of Revolution* (2006); and *The American People* (Seventh ed., 2006). Nash wanted to coauthor this book with two good friends and esteemed colleagues because of their common desire to bring the story of the African American people before a wide audience of students and history lovers. African American history has always had a central place in his teaching, and it has been pivotal to his efforts to bring an inclusive, multicultural American history into the K–12 classrooms in this nation and abroad.

# THE STRUGGLE FOR FREEDOM

*Penguin Academics*

# THE STRUGGLE FOR FREEDOM
## A History of African Americans
## Volume I

**CLAYBORNE CARSON**
Stanford University

**EMMA J. LAPSANSKY-WERNER**
Haverford College

**GARY B. NASH**
University of California, Los Angeles

**PEARSON**
Longman

New York   San Francisco   Boston
London   Toronto   Sydney   Tokyo   Singapore   Madrid
Mexico City   Munich   Paris   Cape Town   Hong Kong   Montreal

Executive Editor: Michael Boezi
Development Manager: Betty Slack
Development Editor: Ann Grogg
Executive Marketing Manager: Sue Westmoreland
Supplements Editor: Kristi Olson
Project Coordination, Text Design, and
   Electronic Page Makeup: Electronic Publishing Services Inc., NYC
Cover Design Manager: Wendy Ann Fredericks
Cover Illustration/Photo: *Preparation for the Enjoyment of a Fine Sunday Evening, Norfolk.*
   By Benjamin Henry Latrobe. Watercolor on Paper. Courtesy Maryland Historical Society.
Photo Researcher: Vivette Porges
Manufacturing Buyer: Roy Pickering
Printer and Binder: R.R. Donnelley and Sons
Cover Printer: Phoenix Color Corporation

For more information about the Penguin Academics series, please contact us by mail at Longman Publishers, attn. Marketing Department, 1185 Avenue of the Americas, 25th Floor, New York, NY 10036, or by e-mail at www.ablongman.com

Library of Congress Cataloging-in-Publication Data
Carson, Clayborne, 1944-
  The struggle for freedom : a history of African Americans / Clayborne Carson, Emma J. Lapsansky-Werner, Gary B. Nash.
     p. cm.
  Includes bibliographical references and index.
  ISBN 0-321-35576-8 (alk. paper : single vol. ed.) -- ISBN 0-321-35575-X (alk. paper : v. 1) -- ISBN 0-321-35574-1 (alk. paper : v. 2)  1. African Americans--History.  I. Lapsansky-Werner, Emma J. (Emma Jones), 1945-  II. Nash, Gary B.  III. Title.
E185.C36 2007
973'.0496073--dc22
                              2006014072

Please visit us at www.ablongman.com

ISBN 0-321-35576-8 (Single Volume Edition)
ISBN 0-321-35575-X (Volume I)
ISBN 0-321-35574-1 (Volume II)

1 2 3 4 5 6 7 8 9 10—DOC—09 08 07 06

# BRIEF CONTENTS

# Detailed Contents

CHAPTER 11 | *POST-CIVIL WAR RECONSTRUCTION: A NEW NATIONAL ERA*  253

APPENDIX  A-1

# PREFACE

*Those who profess to favor freedom and yet depreciate agitation, are people who want crops without ploughing the ground; they want rain without thunder and lightning; they want the ocean without the roar of its many waters. The struggle may be a moral one, or it may be a physical one, or it may be both. But it must be a struggle. Power concedes nothing without a demand; it never has and it never will.*

—*Frederick Douglass*

*The Struggle for Freedom: A History of African Americans* is a narrative of the black experience in America, using a distinctive biographical approach to guide the story and animate the history. This biographical approach places African American lives at the center of the narrative. In each chapter, individual African Americans are the pivot points on or around which turn the historical changes of the era. Life stories capture the rush of events that envelop individuals and illuminate the momentous decisions that, collectively, frame the American past and present.

*The Struggle for Freedom: A History of African Americans* introduces the concepts, milestones, and significant figures of African American history. Inasmuch as that history is grounded in struggle—in the consistent and insistent call to the United States to deliver on the constitutional promises made to all its citizens—this book is also an American history text, weaving into the narrative the milestones of mainstream American history, economy, politics, arts and letters.

The biographical approach of *The Struggle for Freedom: A History of African Americans* uses African American lives and stories as the basis for understanding and analysis not only of the black experience in America but of American history in the whole. Too often, expressions such as *the sweep of history, the transit of civilization, manifest destiny,* and *the march of progress* plant the idea that history is inexorable, unalterable, and foreordained—beyond the capacity of men and women to change. That idea has been used to justify a winner's history—an approach that diminishes the full humanness of those who were captured and traded as slaves. To promote the understanding that no individual is forever trapped within iron circumstances beyond his or her ability to alter, every chapter in this book is grounded in the experience of *people* rather than *forces.*

## BIOGRAPHICAL APPROACH

*The Struggle for Freedom: A History of African Americans* examines the efforts of African Americans to define their own identities; it explores the development of nationalist ideas and rhetoric; it ponders Americans' struggle with the concept of race; and it traces the growth of the politics of race from the Republican Party to the Rainbow Coalition. It tells the stories of the lives of the illustrious (abolitionist Martin Delaney) as well as the ordinary (planter Isaiah Montgomery), exploring both the public and the private perspectives of those who shaped the African American story. Some individuals are famous for their specific contributions; other individuals are representative of a larger idea, a concept of a people who have inhabited the American continent for more than half a millennium.

The human stories in *The Struggle for Freedom: A History of African Americans* demonstrate that in every age, in every part of the country, at every level of society, African Americans refused to allow history to crush them. Whether in the small space of plantation quarters or Harlem walkups, or criss-crossing a nation, or calling for the unity of Africans dispossessed and dispersed around the globe, African Americans have shaped their world even as they contested and transformed their subordinate roles in American society. That often they did not succeed in their plans or could not fully realize their hopes does not diminish their strivings and their struggles. It does not alter the fact that for many, nothing was passively accepted; everything was contested or negotiated.

## COVERAGE AND ORGANIZATION

The distinctive people and events of American history are all present in *The Struggle for Freedom: A History of African Americans*. In these pages, readers will learn of the Europeans' first encounter with new people and a new environment; they will see how the American Revolution shaped humanitarian ideals. They will encounter other pivotal events of American history: the War of 1812, the Missouri Compromise, sectional conflicts, wars from the Civil War through this century's war against terrorism. They will also be able to examine cultural trends throughout American history—from the resistance poetry of revolutionary-era Phillis Wheatley through modern-day hip-hop.

Chapters 1 through 7 of *The Struggle for Freedom: A History of African Americans* explore the period up to 1830, when most Africans in North America were enslaved. The book begins, as all human history begins, in Africa with ancient history and the rise of empires in West and Central Africa during the period American and western historians think of as the Middle Ages. European contact and the growth of the slave trade are followed by an analysis of the new conditions of slavery in the Americas. Because Africans were not all enslaved in the same ways and in the same conditions, the chapters treat the formation of notions about race and how they figured in the descent into slavery in different zones of European settlement—French, Dutch, and Spanish as well as English—in the Americas. The galvanizing effect of the American Revolution and the decades thereafter during which free black people in the North and in the South built families, founded churches, forged friendships and communities, and struggled for autonomy and dignity are central themes.

Chapters 8 through 14 examine pivotal junctures in African American history that parallel the American focus on reform and nationality. The 1830s marked the first years when the majority of black Americans were not forced immigrants but rather were born on American soil. Echoing the religious reawakening that undergirded both abolitionism and a vigorous defense of slavery, slave and free African Americans alike claimed their voice in an international antebellum debate about the future of American democracy. Then, through a long and merciless Civil War, the end of slavery, and the South's attempt to re-create the essence of slavery, black Americans persisted in holding forth, before white Americans and the world, the guarantees of equality and citizenship built into the new constitutional amendments. The post-Civil War dispersal of newly freed African Americans to every corner of North America shows how, in the face of a still-hostile white America that abandoned Reconstruction, black people built families, communities, and viable economic lives; established churches, mutual aid and literary societies, and businesses; launched schools and publishing ventures as they sought to transform themselves from slaves to soldiers and citizens and to wrest equality and justice from white America.

The last seven chapters of the book, Chapters 15 through 21, address African American life in modern America. The narrative explores the increasing diversity of African Americans and examines how—during world wars, the Great Depression, and other momentous national and international transformations—they struggled for full participation in a society still marred by racist attitudes and practices. Throughout twentieth-century scientific, technological, and economic changes, one theme permeates African American strategies for securing justice and equal opportunity: the ongoing struggle for a positive sense of identity amidst racism and destructive racial stereotypes. Whether in fighting the nation's wars; helping build the modern economy; adding to the explosion of cultural creativity through innovations in music, art, film, dance, and literature; or emerging on the political stage at the local, state, and national level, African Americans in the last century are portrayed as the principal innovators of the nation's most important liberation movement.

## SPECIAL FEATURES AND PEDAGOGY

Complementing the multitude of stories connecting African American lives and American history, *The Struggle for Freedom: A History of African Americans* includes several features designed to increase the book's usefulness and enhance its appeal to readers.

- *Chapter-opening Vignettes:* Each chapter begins with a personal story—such as the rebelliousness of Venture Smith (Chapter 4) or the wartime experience of First Lieutenant Thomas Edward Jones (Chapter 14)—that draws the reader into the chapter narrative, illuminates the chapter period, and heralds the chapter's events and themes.
- *Chronologies:* Chapter chronologies, placed at the beginning of each chapter following the opening vignette, alert readers to the significant developments in African American history to be covered in the chapter.
- *Conclusions:* Each chapter ends with a summary of the main ideas and events discussed in the chapter, helping the reader recall the essential points of the narrative. A look ahead to the next chapter prepares the reader for the next installment of the story.
- *Visual History:* The graphic materials and illustrations—maps, charts, photographs, lithographs, and paintings—that enrich each chapter impart an additional dimension to the narrative, allowing the reader to see history as participants saw it. Tables that summarize a sequence of events or milestones—for example, judicial decisions, legislative acts, and protest movement flashpoints—facilitate the reader's comprehension of complex or subtle concepts.

African American history has achieved breadth and depth in recent decades, indeed has become one of the most vibrant components of American history, reshaping the way we understand everything from the American economy to innovations in science, politics, and the arts. Reflecting that dynamism, *The Struggle for Freedom: A History of African Americans* is not a story set in stone. Drawing on both classic and recent historical research, it crafts a new synthesis that challenges our understandings of the past and offers new insights about differing historical possibilities. As it engages the reader in viewing history through the lens of many biographies and through the perspectives of people who lived those struggles, *The Struggle for Freedom: A History of African Americans* seeks to ensure, in the words of Langston Hughes's famous poem, that "America Will Be."

## FOR FURTHER INTEREST

Longman is proud to offer the following enhancements for your African American History course:

**Student Resources CD-ROM**  Available at no additional cost when bundled with *The Struggle for Freedom*, this student CD-ROM enhances students' understanding and appreciation of African American history. For each chapter of the book, this multimedia resource contains audio and video clips, maps and graphs, print documents, and images from African American history.

***Penguin Books*** Longman has partnered with Penguin in order to offer you a comprehensive collection of seminal African-American works, both fiction and non-fiction. All of these titles are available at a reduced price when purchased in conjunction with *The Struggle for Freedom*. Please refer to the end of the book for a complete list.

## Acknowledgments

We gratefully acknowledge the many colleagues who took the time to review our manuscript. Their useful comments and keen insights have made this a stronger book. Thank you: John D. Baskerville, *University of Northern Iowa*; Diane L. Beers, *Holyoke Community College*; Albert S. Broussard, *Texas A&M University*; Julian C. Chambliss, *Rollins College*; Sean Condon, *Adrian College*; Jane Dabel, *California State University, Long Beach*; Maceo Crenshaw Dailey Jr., *University of Texas, El Paso*; Vivian Deno, *Butler University*; Roy E. Finkenbine, *University of Detroit, Mercy*; Raymond Frey, *Centenary College*; Aram Goudsouzian, *University of Memphis*; Kevin Hales, *Parkland College*; John A. Hardin, *Western Kentucky University*; W. Sherman Jackson, *Miami University*; Yvonne Johnson, *Central Missouri State University*; Alan K. Lamm, *Mount Olive College*; Karen K. Miller, *Boston College*; Michelle Rief, *CUNY—Borough of Manhattan Community College*; Albert Smith, *Modesto Junior College*; Robert S. Smith, *University of North Carolina, Charlotte*; Rainier Spencer, *University of Nevada*; Thomas Ward, *Rockhurst University*; Derrick White, *Florida Atlantic University*; Regennia N. Williams, *Cleveland State University*; Rebecca Woodham, *Auburn University, Montgomery*.

This book also owes much to the many conscientious historians who reviewed the manuscript of *African American Lives: The Struggle for Freedom* throughout its many drafts and offered valuable suggestions. We acknowledge with gratitude the contributions of the following: Leslie Alexander, *Ohio State University*; Kwame Alford, *Texas Tech University*; Julius A. Amin, *University of Dayton*; Melissa Anyiwo, *University of Tennessee, Chattanooga*; Joseph Appiah, *J. S. Reynolds Community College*; Felix L. Armfield, *State University of New York, Buffalo*; Charles Pete Banner-Haley, *Colgate University*; Abel A. Bartley, *University of Akron*; Donald Scott Barton, *East Central University*; James M. Beeby, *West Virginia Wesleyan College*; Nemata Blyden, *George Washington University*; Robert Bonner, *Amherst College*; Ronald E. Brown, *Westchester Community College*; Kimm Carlton-Smith, *Ferris State University, Long Beach*; Stephanie Cole, *University of Texas, Arlington*; Bruce J. Dierenfield, *Canisius College*; A. G. Dunston, *Eastern Kentucky University*; Patience Essah, *Auburn University*; Melvin Lee Felton Jr., *James Sprunt Community College*; Paul S. George, *Miami-Dade College*; Brian Gordon, *St. Louis Community College*; Lenworth Gunther, *Essex Community College*; Laura Graves, *South Plains College*; Olivia B. Green, *Miles College*; Carmen V. Harris, *University of South Carolina, Spartanburg*;

James Harrison, *Portland Community College, Cascade*; Sharon A. Roger Hepburn, *Radford University*; Ranford B. Hopkins, *Moorpark College*; Carol Sue Humphrey, *Oklahoma Baptist University*; Creed Hyatt, *Lehigh Carbon Community College*; Eric R. Jackson, *Northern Kentucky University*; Randal M. Jelks, *Calvin College*; Cherisse R. Jones, *Arkansas State University*; Theodore Kallman, *San Joaquin Delta College*; Maghan Keita, *Villanova University*; Ben Keppel, *University of Oklahoma*; Daniel Kilbride, *John Carroll University*; Lisa King, *Morgan State University*; William M. King, *University of Colorado*; Alec Kirby, *University of Wisconsin, Stout*; Anne Klejment, *University of St. Thomas*; Linda Rochell Lane, *Benedict College*; Howard Lindsey, *DePaul University*; Arletha D. Livingston, *Georgia State University*; Elizabeth MacGonagle, *University of Kansas*; Kenneth Mason, *Santa Monica College*; David McBride, *Pennsylvania State University*; Larry McGruder, *Abraham Baldwin College*; Jacqueline M. Moore, *Austin College*; Sheila H. Moore, *Hinds Community College*; Earl F. Mulderink, *Southern Utah University*; Cassandra Newby-Alexander, *Norfolk State University*; Julius F. Nimmons Jr., *University of the District of Columbia*; Phillip Oguagha, *CUNY—Medgar Evers College*; Anthony Parent, *Wake Forest University*; John B. Reid, *Truckee Meadows Community College*; Tara Ross, *Onondaga Community College*; Jerrold W. Roy, *Hampton University*; Paul Siff, *Sacred Heart University*; Bradley Skelcher, *Delaware State University*; Dorothy A. Smith-Akubune, *Lynchburg College*; Melissa Soto-Schwartz, *Cuyahoga Community College*; Darlene Spitzer-Antezana, *Bowie State University*; Donald Spivey, *University of Miami*; Marian Strobel, *Furman University*; Michael David Tegeder, *Santa Fe Community College*; Linda D. Tomlinson, *Clark Atlanta University*; William L. Van Deburg, *University of Wisconsin*; Cheryl R. Vinson, *Miles College*; Melissa Walker, *Converse College*; Irma Watkins-Owen, *Fordham University*; Vernon J. Williams Jr., *Purdue University*; Leslie Wilson, *Montclair State University*; Keith A. Winsell, *Talladega College*; Marilyn Leonard Yancy, *Virginia Union University*.

The authors would like to thank the staff of Special Collections at Haverford College and the Crisis Publishing Co., Inc., the publisher of the magazine of the National Association for the Advancement of Colored People, for the use of material published in the November 1935 and June 1938 issues of *Crisis*. The project also owes a monumental debt of gratitude to Ann Grogg. Ann was by turns editor, counselor, circuit rider, diplomat, and loyal friend. Her broad and subtle knowledge of history and of those who teach and learn it were crucial to our progress. So too was her deft editing without altering the authors' voices or meaning.

Clay Carson offers particular thanks to Damani Rivers and Caitrin McKiernan of the King Papers Project at Stanford University for their exceptional research assistance. Susan A. Carson also helped with editing the manuscript. Tenisha Armstrong, Miya Woolfalk, and other King Project staff members and student researchers offered useful comments on the manuscript at various stages of its development. Emma Lapsansky-Werner extends a special thank you to student research assistants James Chappel, Sarah Hartman, and Caroline Boyd, and to her ever-patient husband, Dickson Werner. Gary Nash thanks research assistants Grace Lu and Marian Olivas for good cheer in carrying out many tasks.

—*The Authors*

# 1

# ANCIENT AFRICA

## AFRICAN STORYTELLING AND AFRICAN AMERICAN HISTORY

The storytellers of the Yoruba people of West Africa, the *griots,* have a saying passed down for generations: "However far the stream flows, it never forgets its source." This wisdom is as fresh today as it was a thousand years ago.

From their first arrival in the Americas, Africans knew that without history they would be water without a source, trees without roots. Those roots derive from oral cultures in Africa, where young people heard adults tell stories about the origins of their own village-based people. Other stories taught children what it means to live properly. Still others "handed on the torch," as many Africans say, by capturing the sweep of a people's long history.

Once they were wrenched from their homelands, enslaved Africans continued to keep ancient traditions alive—passing down to their children the stories, morals, and values of their ancestors. Under slavery, the desire to preserve memory of long-ago traditions, as well as more recent experiences, intensified. As soon as they could, Africans began recounting the horrors of capture and transport to the Americas (the middle passage), the desperate struggle for survival under slavery, and the bravery and resolve of those who struck out for freedom. History could not ward off a brutal master's blows or break slavery's chains. Nevertheless, it sustained Africans' souls and nourished their hopes for a better life.

For many generations, Africans in America nurtured the collective memory of their history through oral storytelling. They had few opportunities to publish written accounts because most of them were in bondage to masters who forbade them to learn how to read and write. That began to change in the era of the American Revolution. Enslaved Africans such as Phillis Wheatley and free black people such as Venture Smith were the first black writers to find white patrons

1

## Chronology

(BCE means "Before Common Era"; CE means "Common Era," with years coinciding with the Christian "BC" and "AD" dates.)

| | |
|---|---|
| 3,750,000 BCE | Ancient ancestors of humans in East Africa. |
| 1,800,000 BCE | The oldest humans, *Homo erectus*, in East Africa. |
| 500,000 BCE | Early human ancestors learn to use fire. |
| 160,000 BCE | *Homo sapiens* migrate out of Africa. |
| 3100 BCE | Pharaohs unify Egypt. |
| 1570–1085 BCE | The New Kingdom in Egypt. |
| 750–670 BCE | Kushites rule Egypt. |
| c. 450 BCE | Nok iron smelting begins. |
| 332 BCE–c. 400 CE | Greece and then Rome control Egypt. |
| c. 100–200 CE | Bantu-speaking people migrate south. |
| c. 500–1100 CE | Rise of kingdom of Ghana. |
| c. 610 CE | Muhammad founds the Islamic faith. |
| 632–750 CE | Muslim faith spreads across North Africa. |
| c. 1000 CE | The kingdom of Benin. |
| 1324 CE | Mansa Musa's pilgrimage to Mecca. |
| c. 1460s–1590s CE | Songhai kingdom controls West African trade. |
| 1235 CE | Mali is the major power in West Africa. |
| 1435 CE | Songhai breaks away from the kingdom of Mali. |
| 1591 CE | Morocco captures Timbuktu and Gao. |

who helped publish their recorded thoughts and experiences. In the decades before the Civil War, a handful of black historians, such as Boston's William C. Nell and Philadelphia's William Douglass, published the first histories of black people in North America. Meanwhile, former bondsman Frederick Douglass wrote an autobiographical account of his travails in slavery and his long walk to freedom. His story carried such power and poignancy that it made him an international figure. A people whose memory had been officially suppressed began to regain their voice.

Most nineteenth-century African American histories did not enjoy a wide readership. White Americans, in particular, ignored them. In recent years, however, these accounts have been republished and attracted a growing audience. They have also inspired contemporary black historians to build on their work. Twentieth-century historians such as W. E. B. Du Bois, Rayford Logan, Carter Woodson, and John Hope Franklin insisted that African American history be included in the American story. A half-century ago, a young preacher named Martin Luther King Jr. prophesied on the night of the Montgomery bus boycott in 1955, "When the history books are written in future generations, the historians will say, 'There lived a great people—a black people—who injected new meaning and dignity into the veins of civilization.'" King's prophecy has come to be.

The story of humankind began several million years ago in East Africa, where, according to archaeologists, humans first made their appearance on Earth. Egypt gave birth to the first great African civilization. That civilization in turn shaped ancient Greece and Rome. The spread of Islam and the emergence of West and Central African kingdoms set the stage for an era in which millions of African people were torn from their homelands and forced across the Atlantic to serve as slaves in the Americas.

This chapter looks at the cultures of these African peoples—and some of the individuals who embodied their ways of life. By understanding the societies these men and women came from, the gods they worshiped, the family traditions they cherished, and the social systems and artistic works they created, we will see them as more than faceless units of labor carried across the ocean. By seeing them as peoples with long, rich histories, we can better understand their—and our own—experiences in the Americas.

# FROM HUMAN BEGINNINGS TO THE RISE OF EGYPT

For generations, Yoruba storytellers told young people how Olodumare, the god of the sky, sent two sons down to Earth with a bag, a hen, and a chameleon. The bag contained soft white sand and rich black soil. One son sprinkled the white sand on the water's surface. From the sand sprouted a palm tree. The chameleon gingerly stepped across the sand, discovering that the grains supported its weight. Seeing this, the other son spread the soil over the sand. Then the hen scratched in the dark earth, scattering it in all directions. Pleased with his sons' work, Olodumare sent Aje—goddess of prosperity—from Heaven to dwell there for the rest of her life. The sky god sent his sons additional gifts: maize to plant for food; cowrie shells for trading; and iron bars for forging hoes, knives, and other tools. In this way, Olodumare created Yorubaland.

Like the Yoruba, every human society has developed creation myths to make sense of its beginnings and to understand the mighty forces of nature. Since the emergence of humankind, a rich array of creation stories has arisen. Around the world, these stories yield many interpretations of the first stirrings of humankind. The Yoruba creation story leads us to consider the long history of ancient Africa—from human beginnings through the flourishing of Egyptian civilization to the Roman and Greek conquest of North Africa.

## HUMAN BEGINNINGS IN EAST AFRICA

Scientists offer several explanations of how the Earth was formed and how human beings came to inhabit it. Though much remains to be discovered, the common scientific understanding is that all humans descended from hominids. These humanlike primates had enlarged brains and could walk upright on two legs. Archaeologists have found the oldest fossilized remains of these hominids in eastern Africa. As early as 1871, Charles Darwin proposed in his *Descent of Man* that Africa was probably the birthplace of humankind. But this notion offended

Europeans, who saw their own race as superior to that of the African. Some Europeans thus maintained that human life began not in Africa but in Europe—specifically in Germany's Neander Valley, where fossil remains of an early human species dubbed *Neanderthal man* were discovered in 1856.

Not until 1925, when an archaeologist found a child's skull in a limestone cave at Taung, in South Africa, did the European origins thesis come under scientific scrutiny. Apelike in appearance, the skull also had human characteristics in its forehead and nose structure. Examination revealed it as the most ancient example of *Australopithecine*—a creature who walked upright around three million years ago. Once again, the notion that humans emerged in Africa gained credence.

Then, in the 1950s, the British anthropologists Louis and Mary Leakey found additional fossils of the *Australopithecine* species in East Africa's Olduvai Gorge. Scholars soon felt convinced that human life indeed began in Africa. In 1961, the Leakeys found confirming evidence of the evolution from primate to human being—fossil bones resting alongside simple stone tools. Dating technology revealed that this first group of human ancestors were toolmakers who lived between 1.5 and 3.75 million years ago in East Africa.

More evidence came to light in 1974 in Hadar, Ethiopia. There, paleoanthropologists (who study human origins) discovered "Lucy," the first example of *Homo erectus*, or upright human. This exceptionally complete skeleton, about $3\frac{1}{2}$ feet tall, dates back about 1.8 million years. Thanks to this finding, scientists now widely accept the idea that the ancient ancestors of all humans originated in Africa about 120,000 to 160,000 years ago. These ancestors are called *Homo sapiens*—meaning "wise human."

Though a small group of dissenters argue that hominids originated in several regions of the world and evolved separately in Africa, the Middle East, Europe, and Asia, new discoveries have consolidated the "out of Africa" scenario. In 2002, for example, three fossilized *Homo sapien* skulls excavated in Herto, Ethiopia, were dated through argon-isotope analysis to about 160,000 years ago, solidly supporting the "out of Africa" theory. Though many African Americans speak of "Mother Africa" to signify the homeland of their forebears, most modern scientists agree that Africa is the mother of *all* humans.

## RISE OF EGYPTIAN CIVILIZATION

By at least 60,000 years ago, humans began to migrate out of East Africa to what we today call the Middle East, Asia, and Australia. About 20,000 years later, they appeared in Europe. There they made spear and harpoon points for hunting large fish and big animals such as the wild ox and hippopotamus, and they crafted thin scrapers for cleaning hides. These nomadic groups discovered ways to increase their food supply by domesticating and herding animals. They also made simple clothing out of hides to protect themselves against the cold. By about 10,000 BCE, some of these groups began settling along the banks of the Jordan River in the Middle East. By 6000 BCE, they were harvesting millet and sorghum (grains used to make bread) as they settled along the Nile, the world's longest river, in today's Egypt. This area became the most densely populated part of the ancient world.

Over the next 4,000 years, Egyptian civilization flourished and spread. Learning to use the predictable flooding of the mighty Nile to irrigate crops in a land of little rainfall, early hydrology engineers transformed Egypt from a sparsely populated and forbidding desert into a thriving civilization. By about 3100 BCE, local kingdoms began to emerge throughout Egypt, led by rulers called *pharaohs*. Over many centuries, rival kingdoms set aside their differences and united along the Nile's 4,000-mile-long banks.

Strong, centralized governments evolved out of these kingdoms, headed by pharaohs who claimed godlike power. These rulers commanded the labor of a vast peasantry. They amassed enough wealth from the production of crop surpluses to erect royal tombs, temples, and pyramids that showcased their power. Pharaohs drew their strength from civil servants who collected taxes and supervised irrigation projects. These same servants also compiled and maintained tax and administrative records. To record information, they used a sophisticated system of writing that consisted of *hieroglyphs,* picture signs that represented concepts and numbers.

In the New Kingdom period (1570–1085 BCE), the pharaohs accumulated large armies and led them into wars of expansion against the peoples of Palestine, Syria, and Nubia. The massive statues and temples built by Rameses II, which visitors to Egypt can view today, testify to the power of the empire forged out of conquered lands. As the realm extended its reach, cultural change accelerated as well. Ancient Egypt became a crossroads for merchants and other enterprising men and women seeking to trade with other societies. Within this vast realm, a composite culture arose that comprised Mediterranean peoples from the west, Semitic nomads from the east, and dark-skinned traders and farmers from Kushite and Ethiopian societies to the south.

The Egyptian civilization dominated the lands bordering the Mediterranean Sea for 3,000 years—from about 3100 to roughly 332 BCE, when the Greeks invaded the kingdom. Indeed, ancient Egypt stands as the longest-lasting civilization in human history. Scholars trace about thirty dynasties during this epoch. Perhaps no dynasty has captured the imaginations of students of history more than that of the female pharaoh Hatshepsut, who reigned during the New Kingdom period. This shrewd and skillful ruler built a great temple on the banks of the Nile and restored numerous old temples that foreign invaders had destroyed. Hatshepsut's successor, Thutmose III, became one of Egypt's mightiest pharaohs. Through military expeditions into the eastern Mediterranean region, he extended his empire into Palestine and Syria. Later rulers continued to enlarge the realm while building impressive monuments at home. For example, the three pyramids at Giza still testify to Egyptian achievements in hydraulic engineering, architecture, and sculpture.

Owing to its location, Egypt played virtually no role in the forced migration of Africans to the Americas that unfolded centuries later. Rather, it became a trans-shipment point for West Africans slated for Muslim slave markets to the east.

## DEBATES OVER BLACK EGYPT

Since the eighteenth century, African Americans have cited Egypt's greatness as a way to counter charges that "the dark continent" was home to "savages" useful only as labor for other, more civilized peoples. Europeans had long recognized ancient Egypt as a cradle of civilization and the source of many ideas that powerfully shaped ancient Greece and Rome. In denigrating African peoples, however, these same Europeans mentally plucked Egypt out of Africa and Africans out of Egypt. Yet as any glance at a world map shows, Egypt is solidly part of the African continent.

For generations, African Americans fought the notion that Egypt was not part of Africa. They referred to Egypt as an African society, and many called the Egyptians "Ethiopians." This name was a reference to nearby Ethiopia, with which Egypt had traded extensively over many centuries. By the 1870s, the first historians who tried to write a comprehensive African American history—such as George Washington Williams and Edward Blyden—pointedly began their narratives with accounts of Egypt (see Chapter 11).

Today, scholars still argue passionately over whether the ancient Egyptians were "black," "white," or racially mixed and the degree to which Egypt influenced ancient Greece and Rome. In 1987, Martin Bernal's *Black Athena: The Afroasiatic Roots of Classical Civilization,* set off a furious controversy. Bernal claimed that dark-skinned Egyptian and Semitic peoples played a significant role in the making of Greek civilization, especially in its mathematics, philosophy, and religion. Modern Western civilization, he concluded, owes a great debt to ancient Africa.

Though many scholars dispute Bernal's findings, few deny that they have inspired much new research on the circulation of ideas throughout the Mediterranean basin. Traditional scholarship on ancient Greece now looks much more carefully at Egyptian influences and at the connections among the ancient peoples living around the Mediterranean Sea. *Black Athena* has also provoked discussions about whether identity is determined primarily by race and whether race should be the basis of political empowerment and entitlement programs. Many scholars argue that the ancient Egyptians had no concept of "race" or even "blackness." Rather, this school of thought holds, white people invented these notions to exclude and exploit people of color.

## EGYPT AND NUBIA

Nubia, the state the Egyptians called Kush, has also caught the attention of modern-day African Americans seeking to reclaim a noble past. In ancient times, Nubia lay to the south of Egypt, along the lower Nile from the first great cataract (waterfall) to below the fifth cataract. For centuries, Egypt's rulers sent ships south along the Nile to trade with the dark-skinned Nubians living in Kush. Both societies benefited from this trade. Still, the pharaohs considered Kush part of their empire, so from time to time they sent armies into the region to maintain their control of its valuable assets.

Although Kush adopted many elements of Egyptian culture, it retained its individual character and political structures. Yet power shifted back and forth between Egypt and Kush. By about 1070 BCE, Egypt fell into decline. Emboldened, the Kushite rulers broke away from Egyptian control. By 750 BCE, the Kushite kings had conquered Upper Egypt and its capital city, Thebes, and seized Memphis, the main Egyptian capital. Later, Shabaka became the first Kushite monarch to control all of Egypt. Yet governing a vast empire is complex, difficult work. The Kushites' rule lasted for less than one hundred years. Slowly, Egypt regained its former stature. During the centuries that followed, the two civilizations—each with its own distinct legacy—remained closely connected. Intermarriage, trade, and the exchange of artistic traditions renewed the fusion of peoples living in the vast Nile River region.

## EGYPT AFTER THE GREEK CONQUEST

In 332 BCE, the twenty-four-year-old Macedonian warrior Alexander the Great swept into Egypt with his armies and added the region to his rapidly expanding collection of conquests. Though the last Egyptian dynasty came to an end, Egypt continued to serve as a cultural crossroads in the ancient Middle East as its Greek rulers spread their influence. For the next three centuries, Alexander's general, Ptolemy, and his successors governed Egypt. As one of their most striking achievements, they founded the city of Alexandria, named after the conquering Macedonian king. A port city on the Mediterranean Sea, Alexandria became a vibrant trading and cultural hub. As a crossroads, the city enabled those who lived around the Mediterranean to exchange goods and ideas with people living in the mineral-rich African interior and in Alexander's conquered lands east into India.

Egypt maintained this central cultural position when, around 500 BCE, the Romans began conquering lands as far west as Spain and dominating the Mediterranean. By about 146 BCE, the Romans had supplanted Greek control in northern Africa. The Roman government made Tunisia and Egypt dependent provinces, extracting from them grain, papyrus for papermaking, and even wild animals that were pitted against one another in the vaunted Roman circus games.

In Roman Africa, trade and periodic warfare accelerated the intermingling of peoples. A new faith, Christianity, spread through the Roman Empire as a result of this intermingling. Christianity sank its roots deep into Egypt in the first century CE. Alexandria, Egypt's commercial center, became one of the most vital hubs of early Christendom. Gradually, Christianity spread west across North Africa among Berber-speaking peoples. It also moved south from Egypt into Nubia where today, in Ethiopia, it still flourishes.

# THE SPREAD OF ISLAM

"The seat of Mansa Sulayman [the sultan] was a sprawling, unwalled town set in a 'verdant and hilly' country," wrote seasoned traveler Abu Abdallah Ibn Battuta in 1351 CE after visiting the capital of Mali, a kingdom in northwest Africa. "The sultan had several enclosed palaces there . . . and covered [them] with colored patterns so that it turned out to be the most elegant of buildings. Surrounding the palaces and mosques were the residences of the citizenry, mud-walled houses roofed with domes of timber and reed. . . . Amongst their good qualities is the small amount of injustice amongst them, for of all people they are the furthest from it. Their sultan does not forgive anyone in any matter to do with injustice. . . . There is also the prevalence of peace in their country, the traveler is not afraid in it nor is he who lives there in fear of the thief or of the robber by violence. They do not interfere with the property of the white man who dies in their country even though it may consist of great wealth, but rather they entrust it to the hand of someone dependable among the white men until it is taken by the rightful claimant."

This vivid excerpt from one of the greatest travelers of pre-modern times opens a window onto the theme of this section: the spread of Islam in Africa beginning in the seventh century. Enslaved Africans later carried this faith to North America. The excerpt's author, Ibn Battuta, embodied the rise of Islam. Born in 1304 CE into a family of Muslim legal scholars in Tangier, Morocco (on the southern shore of the Mediterranean Sea), he came of age as Islam was connecting Europe, Asia, and Africa by dint of religious, cultural, and military force. At age twenty-one, Ibn Battuta made a pilgrimage along well-beaten trading routes to the sacred Muslim city of Mecca in Arabia. For more than twenty years he traveled through much of the eastern hemisphere. He visited territories equivalent to forty-four present-day countries and covered about 73,000 miles—three times the distance covered by the legendary Marco Polo. He recorded the words in the excerpt above as he journeyed in 1351 from Fez across the Atlas Mountains to Sijilmasa, a bustling trade center in southern Morocco. Ibn Battuta's careful recordkeeping provides a rare glimpse into a vibrant era in African history.

## The Origins of Islam

Islam, meaning "submission to Allah," was born in 610 CE. That year, a young warrior named Muhammad began preaching in his Arabian village after he saw a vision of the angel Gabriel. The angel, Muhammad claimed, had commanded him to spread messages from God to peoples throughout the land. A gifted orator, Muhammad attracted numerous followers and became the founder of the new faith. Like Christianity, Islam is monotheistic; it recognizes only one god. Muhammad preached that he was God's final prophet. The Qur'an, he avowed, was God's word revealed to him. According to Muhammad, the messages he received from God completed the earlier revelations of the Hebrew prophets and Jesus.

Muhammad won many converts because his message had great appeal. The theological foundation of the faith he advocated was easily understood; it did not require an exclusive, elite class of priests. All believers, Muhammad preached, were equal in the eyes of Allah. Through private prayer, kindness and generosity, and fasting before the holy feast of Ramadan, anyone could embrace the will of the One True God. Islam also provided a code for right living. For example, the rich must demonstrate compassion, share their wealth with the poor, and contribute to public charities such as hospitals. Every Muslim (follower of Islam) must forswear drinking alcohol and gambling. Adherents to the faith must struggle to resist temptation and overcome evil. Muslims also held scholarship in high regard and established strict rules governing commercial activities such as bookkeeping, credit arrangements, and dispute resolution.

## ISLAM'S GREAT REACH

Like Christians, Muslims believed they had a mandate from God to convert all people to their faith. Within a century of Muhammad's death in 632, his followers had reached out aggressively, often militarily, and established control over regions larger than those making up the Roman Empire. Spreading rapidly in Arabia, the new faith soon extended into Syria and Mesopotamia. It then moved east all the way to China, west across Mediterranean North Africa to Spain, and south along the Red Sea coast of East Africa. Invaded by Arab Muslims in 639 CE, Egypt became Islamized, just as it had earlier been Christianized under Roman influence. By the tenth century CE, Egypt had a predominantly Muslim population. Islam then spread south from Mediterranean North Africa across the Sahara Desert into the savannah region of western Africa, then called the Sudan. (The word *sudan* is Arabic for "black people." Today's Sudan is an East African nation bordering the Red Sea.)

Islam initially made little headway among villagers in the Sudanese countryside because these men and women lived far from the trading routes that accelerated the spread of ideas. But Islam began to build momentum, first along trading routes and in urban commercial centers and then deeper into the countryside. Five centuries later, when Portuguese traders initiated the slave traffic in West Africa, they found that many of the Africans they packed into Atlantic slave ships were devout Muslims.

Along with Muslim conquering armies, relying heavily on camels, came the exchange of Muslim goods, ideas, technologies, and religious belief. With its emphasis on scholarship, the religion fostered the spread of literacy and book-learning throughout West Africa. African rulers began embracing the Muslim faith.

Islam spread much faster in East Africa, the region south of Egypt and bordering the Red Sea and Indian Ocean. From its origins in Arabia, it spread through India, Ceylon, the East Indies, and China. As trading flourished in this region during the tenth century, Arab traders settled in the ports along Africa's east coast and intermarried with native people. A blended culture emerged. Muslim city-states arose across the continent, with Kilwa and Sofala, the southernmost ports on the Indian Ocean trade route, controlling the export of gold and ivory to the east. Visiting the immense palace, vast irrigated gardens, and imposing Muslim mosque in Kilwa in 1331, that avid traveler Ibn Battuta described the city as "one of the most beautiful and well-constructed towns in the world. . . . The whole of it is elegantly built."

# THE KINGDOMS OF WEST AND CENTRAL AFRICA

In 951, a Muslim traveler and geographer named Ibn Hawkal journeyed from Baghdad (in modern-day Iraq) to Sijilmasa, the Moroccan trade center that lay north of the Sahara. There he heard reports that the king of Ghana was the wealthiest of all monarchs on Earth. Traveling south, Ibn Hawkal entered the Ghanaian city of Awdaghost, where he observed a brisk trade in gold. He also learned that the Ghana king's title was *Kaya-Maghan*—Lord of the Gold.

Ibn Hawkal's *Opus Geographicum,* written more than a millennium ago, sheds light on why West African kingdoms proliferated with such energy during the tenth century. The gold trade—and the control of the cross-Sahara traffic it required—united peoples of many cultures living in the grasslands of western Africa. Societies built on the wealth made possible by the gold trade developed along the trading routes. Over time, ambitious local rulers expanded their control to create centralized kingdoms.

By the tenth century, Islam had spread across the Sahara Desert to West Africa, a vast region encompassing desert, grasslands, forests, and woodlands. Like Europeans, most West Africans tilled the soil, developing sophisticated agricultural and livestock management practices. The West Africans' ironmaking skills enabled them to make tools that improved their agricultural production.

Iron production began among the Nok in present-day Nigeria about 450 BCE, long before peoples on the European continent mastered this technology. By crushing iron ore and smelting it in a forced-air blast furnace, these early Iron Age Africans produced molten metal that they forged into finely crafted tools for cultivating and harvesting crops. Their agricultural productivity soared, igniting a population boom. With larger populations came greater specialization of tasks. Some workers became experts in toolmaking, some in leatherworking. Specialization in turn catalyzed greater efficiency and additional technical improvements. This pattern resembled that of the so-called agricultural revolution that independently transformed the Americas, Europe, the Middle East, and elsewhere.

West African societies evolved on the southern flank of the Sahara at different rates. Villages and towns in regions blessed by fertile soil, adequate rainfall, and abundant minerals, as in coastal West Africa, grew rapidly, especially with the advent of interregional trade. Meanwhile, groups living in inhospitable deserts or impenetrable forests remained small and changed slowly.

People tend to migrate when their natural environments changes for the worse. For example, the vast Sahara, once a land of flowing rivers and lush pastures and forests, became uninhabitable to humans owing to climate changes that raised temperatures and lowered rainfall. As the region dried up between about 4000 and 2500 BCE, Saharan peoples moved south in search of more fertile land. First they migrated to oases situated along a strip of grassland, or savannah, on the desert's southern border. Then they headed farther south to the fertile rainforests of the Niger River basin. In these forests, they built some of Africa's greatest kingdoms, all inland civilizations whose trading routes ran overland rather than by sea.

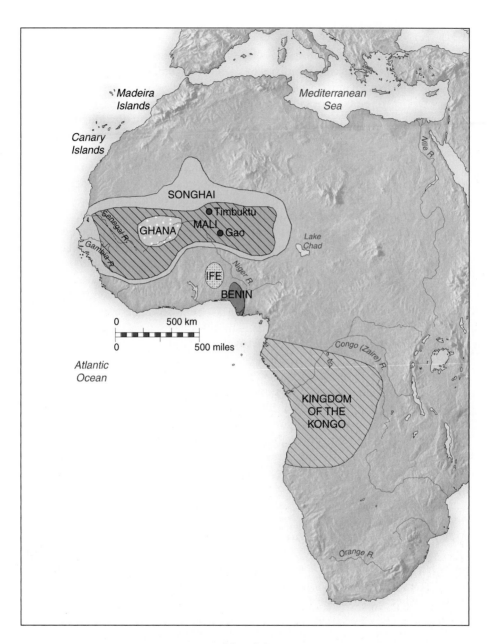

***Map 1.1***
West African Kingdoms, 700–1600

*Through archaeological research, scholars have learned a great deal about the empires of Ghana, Mali, and Songhai in recent years. Still, their main sources consist of the writings of contemporary Arabic historians such as Leo Africanus. This celebrated Moroccan traveled through Songhai in 1510 and 1513 and left a vivid account of the empire at its peak under Muhammad Ture.*

## THE KINGDOM OF GHANA

The first of these inland civilizations was the kingdom of Ghana. Developing between the fifth and eleventh centuries CE (after the Roman Empire collapsed and medieval Europe fell into decline), Ghana occupied a huge territory from the Sahara Desert to the Gulf of Guinea, from the Niger River to the Atlantic Ocean. Ghana evolved from a collection of small villages into a major kingdom noted for its extensive urban settlements, skillfully designed buildings, elaborate sculpture, and effective political and military structure.

The gold trade fueled Ghana's growth and success. The precious metal made Kumbi-Saleh, Ghana's capital, the busiest and wealthiest marketplace in West Africa. The Soninke people of Ghana took advantage of their location just south of the Sahara and north of the Senegal River goldfields to establish trading contacts with Muslim Arabs, who had crossed the Sahara Desert in camel caravans by the eleventh century. In this cross-desert trade, the Soninke exchanged gold for ceramics, glass, oil lamps, and salt from Saharan mines—essential for preserving and flavoring food. From the south, they traded for kola nuts, palm oil, and copper. Their customers carried gold back to Europe, the Middle East, and North Africa, where people used the precious metal to make coins and jewelry.

Gold proved so plentiful that Ghanaian kings devised ways to keep its value high. For example, they maintained a royal monopoly over gold bars, allowing traders to deal only in gold dust. The exhaustion of gold mines in Europe and the Middle East helped boost the value of Ghanaian gold. Even so, salt was so equally coveted that it carried the same value, pound for pound, as gold.

By the time of the western Middle Ages, two-thirds of the gold circulating in the Christian Mediterranean region had originated in Ghana, and Ghanaian gold was the preferred currency throughout the vast Muslim trading network centered in Cairo. The thriving caravan trade spread Muslim influence deep into West Africa, and enterprising Arab merchants came to settle in the empire, especially in Kumbi-Saleh.

With the trading of goods came the exchange of ideas. Arabs brought the first system of writing and numbers to West Africa. The Ghanaian kings adopted Arabic script and appointed Arabs to government positions in charge of trade and taxation. As these Arabs gained influence in Ghana, they spread the Islamic faith. Many Ghanaian rulers kept their traditional religion, however, which emphasized worship of the natural world, and rejected the Muslim principle of patriarchy, whereby royal succession followed the ruling father's lineage. But numerous Ghanaians, especially those living in the cities, converted to Islam. By 1050, Kumbi-Saleh boasted twelve Muslim mosques.

## THE KINGDOM OF MALI

Beginning in the late eleventh century, Muslim Berber warriors swept into Ghana from the north, weakening the realm and sowing religious and political strife. The resulting instability emboldened a ruler of Mali, a state within Ghana, to make war against his overlords. The troops of the Mali king Sundiata crushed Ghanaian warriors in 1235 at the Battle of Kirina, dealing the deathblow to the crippled realm. The Islamic kingdom of Mali, populated primarily by Mandingo people, rose in Ghana's place. The Mandingo quickly mastered agricultural production and seized control of the gold trade. They also cultivated rice and harvested inland deltas for fish, augmenting trade in salt, gold, and copper. Like Ghana before it, Mali grew wealthy from long-distance trade.

Under Sundiata's grandson Mansa Musa, a devout Muslim who assumed the throne in 1307, Mali came to control territory three times as great as Ghana. Young Mansa Musa won fame when in 1324 he began a 3,500-mile pilgrimage across the Sahara, through Cairo, and all the way to Mecca, accompanied by an entourage of 50,000. Dispensing lavish gifts of gold, he made Mali gold legendary. His image on maps of the world for centuries thereafter testified to his importance in promoting West Africa's treasures.

Returning home after several years of pilgrimage, Mansa Musa brought Muslim scholars and artisans with him who helped establish the inland city of Timbuktu, a gateway to the Sahara in the Sudanese region of Songhai. Traveling to Timbuktu in the 1330s, the Arab geographer Ibn Battuta wrote admiringly of "the discipline of [the city's] officials and provincial governors, the excellent condition of public finance, and . . . the respect accorded to the decisions of justice and to the authority of the sovereign."

Noted for its extensive wealth, Timbuktu was also home to an Islamic university with a distinguished faculty who wrote on legal, historical, geographical, and moral topics. Two of the first histories of the western Sudan, both completed in 1665, were written by Timbuktu scholars, Mahmud Kati and Abd al-Rahman as-Sadi. North Africans and southern Europeans flocked to the university to study.

## THE KINGDOM OF SONGHAI

After Mansa Musa died in 1332, his successors could not maintain Mali's dominance in West Africa. The Songhai, a subject people living along the Niger River, saw an opportunity to regain their freedom from the Mandingo. They broke away from Mali in 1435 and began to conquer new territories. Just as Mali had grown out of a state within the empire of Ghana, the new Songhai empire grew out of a region that had once been part of Mali.

In the late 1400s, when Portuguese traders began establishing commercial links with the Kongo kingdom to the south, the Songhai empire reached its peak under the Muslim rulers Sonni Ali (1468–1492) and Askia Muhammad (1493–1528). Yet Songhai, too, collapsed, as some tribes, resentful of Muslim kings, began to break away. But the worst threat came from Morocco, in North Africa. There, rulers coveted Songhai's control of salt and gold—the two critical commodities of African trade. Armed with guns procured in the Middle East, Morocco's ruler captured the major Songhai towns of Timbuktu and Gao in 1591. The North Africans maintained loose control of western Sudan for more than a century as the last great trading empire of West Africa faded into history.

During an era when centralized kingdoms began emerging in Europe, West Africa devolved into smaller states. By the time Europeans reached the continent's Atlantic coast, most Africans resided in states no larger than

Switzerland or Denmark. As the next chapter shows, conflicts among these small states enabled European slave traders to gain a foothold in the region, persuading tribal leaders to send out warrior parties to capture slaves.

## THE FOREST KINGDOMS OF IFE AND BENIN

To the south of Songhai, Yoruba-speaking peoples lived in villages and towns of considerable size. Their territory stretched from the inland savannah woodlands to the long Gulf of Guinea on the Atlantic coast. These peoples—hunters, farmers, and craftsmen—began to cluster in states during the eleventh and twelfth centuries. The kingdoms of Ife and Benin were among the most influential. Here inland cities developed, their rulers governing surrounding peoples. Ife's settlement dates to about the eighth century. It became a religious and cultural center of the Yoruba people.

To the south of Ife stood Benin, which arose about 1000 CE west of the Niger Delta. About 50 miles from the Gulf of Guinea lay Benin City, a major West African center of metalworking and ceramic production. When the Portuguese arrived in Benin in 1485, they found a highly organized society governed by an absolute monarch with an elaborate court of aristocrats, an efficient bureaucracy, and a powerful military force. Benin City was a walled urban complex with broad streets and hundreds of buildings. In 1602, when a Dutch artist visited the city, he compared it favorably to Amsterdam.

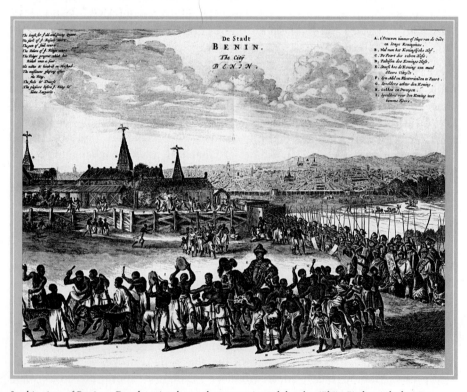

*In this view of Benin, a Dutch artist shows the procession of the* oba *("king") through the city.*

Owing to their location on the African coast and their military might, the leaders of the Yoruba-speaking peoples became powerful slave traders. They captured thousands from the African interior and sold them in Benin City as slaves to the Portuguese. Later, they sold bondspeople (as slaves were also known) to the English at the coastal city of Calabar, the site of a major slave fort.

Both Ife and Benin enjoyed fertile soil and plentiful rainfall. These advantages, along with knowledge of ironworking, enabled the two kingdoms to cultivate surplus cereal and root crops as well as raise domestic animals. This bounty in turn supported trade with outside states. The wealth pouring in from trade freed enough leisure time for some people to explore artistic endeavors such as making jewelry and decorative ceramics.

## THE KINGDOMS OF KONGO AND NDONGO

West Africa became the biggest source of slaves shipped across the Atlantic, but an area farther south along the Atlantic coast, in Central Africa, ultimately became another major source. Hundreds of thousands of modern-day African Americans trace their ancestry to this region, which included the vast kingdoms of Kongo and Ndongo (Angola). The religious, musical, medical, and burial traditions that first emerged in Central Africa still find expression in the United States today.

Kongo, which Europeans first encountered in 1482, was home to the Bakongo people, some two million strong by the 1400s. Their origins trace to Bantu-speaking farmers who began a great migration out of Central Africa in the first few centuries CE. Some traveled east, all the way to the Indian Ocean, while others made their way south to the Kongo Basin. Among those migrating south, the Nok carried with them the knowledge of smelting iron ore and fashioning the metal into spears, axes, fishhooks, and hoes. Thanks to these tools, farmers and fishers could accumulate more food than they needed to survive. So renowned was the Nok's knowledge of ironmaking that one historian has called Kongo "the land of the blacksmith kings." The technology of ironmaking spread from the Kongo Basin through much of West Africa.

The combination of ironworking skills and fertile river valleys enabled the Kongo Basin settlers to flourish in the millennium after the Nok's migration. Ironworking was widespread by the eighth century. Fertile river valleys aided the spread of population. As the centuries unfolded, hunter-gatherer groups who already had been living in the region made permanent homes in agricultural villages. Gradually, strong leaders loosely united these villages into a kingdom that had its royal city at Mbanza Kongo.

Built on a fertile plateau surrounded by rainforests, Mbanza lay 100 miles east of the coast and 50 miles south of the Kongo River. In this lively trade center, artisans, craftspeople, and manufacturers conducted an energetic business. Using the fibers of the raffia palm tree, skilled weavers wove fine cloth, which they traded to merchants from the north for salt and for seashells, used as local currency. From the wheels of hundreds of potters came decorative and functional bowls for carrying water and grain. As will be discussed in Chapter 2, Mbanza also became a slave-trading center after the Portuguese arrived on the Atlantic coast of Kongo in 1482.

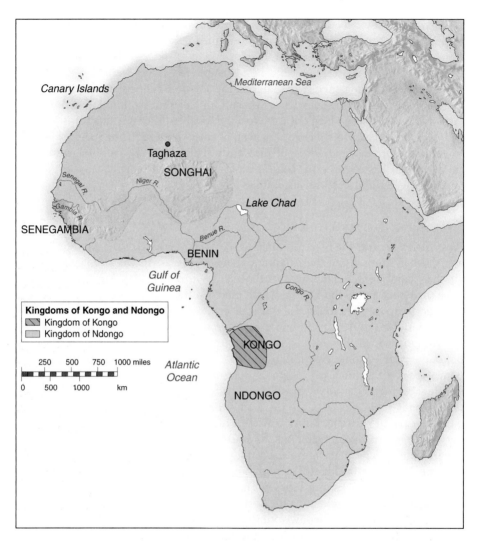

*Map 1.2*
Kingdoms of Kongo and Ndongo

*In 1591, the Portuguese explorers Filippo Pigafetta and Duarte Lopes provided the first European accounts of the densely populated Kongo kingdom.*

South of Kongo, along the Atlantic coast, arose Ndongo (modern-day Angola), which also played a central role in the slave trade after the Portuguese reached Africa. In the 1300s, the Ndongo region consisted of three main chiefdoms—the Pende, Libolo, and Ndongo—but by 1500 the Ndongo chieftains had welded these groups into a unified state. Chapter 2 shows how this centralization enabled the Portuguese to establish solid trade relationships with the kingdom as well as spread their Catholic belief among the Ndongo peoples.

# AFRICAN CULTURE

Many of the peoples of West and Central Africa—Ndongo, Mandingo, Yoruba, Fon, Hausa, Ibo, Bakongo, Whydah, Ga, and others—eventually saw some of their members sent away in slave ships. Though their societies and languages varied greatly, most shared certain ways of life that differentiated them from Europeans. By understanding these cultures, we can better appreciate how Africans refashioned themselves in the Americas and how they built defenses against the cruelties inflicted on them during four centuries of enslavement.

## FAMILY AND COMMUNITY

In ancient and medieval Africa, as elsewhere, the family served as the basic unit of society. Most families lived in villages, though by the 1200s, cities of many thousands dotted the continent. In most villages, people were part of a single lineage—a large, extended family claiming a common ancestor. Thus each person felt closely linked by family ties to others in the village. Individuals defined themselves in terms of their place in a constellation of fathers, mothers, aunts, uncles, brothers, sisters, and cousins. In such close-knit village life, it is not surprising that elders commanded profound respect.

Unlike Europeans, who put fathers and husbands at the center of family life and political power, Africans organized themselves according to a rich variety of kinship systems. Though some were patrilineal, most were matrilineal: property rights and political power descended through the mother rather than the father. Thus, when a chief died, his sister's son claimed the throne. After a wedding, the new husband joined his bride's people. This matrilineal tradition carried over into slavery, as African women continued to wield influence in their families in ways not typically seen in European families.

Regardless of the kinship system they lived by, all Africans emphasized the interdependencies among people over their roles as individuals. Indeed, African languages did not contain a word for *individualism*. When black slaves first encountered the notion of individualism in North America, they found it alien, distasteful, and nearly meaningless. As historian Nathan Huggins has explained, "Alone, a person was nobody. Alone, one was helpless before all that was unknown. The smallest thing could threaten the isolated person—the elements, inanimate objects, animals, and above all, other people."

Many Africans practiced polygamy, so most adult women were co-wives. In many of these family units, one woman ranked as the senior wife and had authority over the others. Outside their dwelling, women cultivated the land and tended the family's livestock and fowls. They also did the marketing, bartering surplus produce such as yams, peppers, rice, chickens, millet, and nuts in return for other produce or household items they wanted.

Many Africans revered female deities. For example, the Yoruba worshiped the river goddess Oshun for giving them life force, fertility, family, power, and wealth. According to legend, Oshun bore twins with a fiery god of thunder, accumulated great wealth, and carried her treasures to the bottom of the Niger River, where she still reigns. Many Yoruba-speaking people today visualize Oshun as wielding a sword, always ready to slay the immoral. They thank her for protecting the people of the Niger River basin from witchcraft.

## RELIGION

As in almost every human society, religious thought and practice in Africa made life's challenges meaningful and bearable. Across Africa, people believed that a supreme being had created the universe. They also associated a pantheon of lesser gods with phenomena they saw in nature, such as rain, animals, mountains, and the fertility of the Earth. Many people considered the Supreme Creator good and merciful. Sayings such as "Rejoice, God never does wrong to people" and epithets like the God of Pity, the Merciful One, and the Kind One reveal the belief in a kind rather than an angry and vengeful god.

Because they believed lesser deities also could intervene in human affairs, Africans honored them with elaborate rituals. West Africans maintained that spirits dwelled in the trees, rocks, and rivers around them. Thus they exercised care in their treatment of these natural objects. For example, men who went fishing in a great river or tried to cross it in a canoe asked for the blessings of the river divinity through offerings or prayers. When drought struck their crops, they implored the rain gods to show mercy.

Africans also believed their ancestors retained a life force after death. Ancestors thus had the power to affect a village's welfare by mediating between the Supreme Creator and the living. Because the dead could exert a significant impact on the living, their surviving relatives held elaborate funeral rites to ensure a deceased person's proper entrance into the spiritual world. The more ancient an ancestor, the greater this person's power became. Therefore, villagers and townspeople invoked the "ancient ones" in prayers and honored them with shrines. Deep family loyalty and regard for family lineage flowed naturally from this reverence of ancestors.

West Africans also believed in spirit possession—gods speaking to men and women through priests, other religious figures, and natural forces and objects. Olaudah Equiano, who wrote an autobiographical account of his enslavement and his later purchase of his freedom, recalled, "Though we had no places of public worship, we had priests and magicians, or wise men . . . held in great reverence by the people. They calculated time, foretold events . . . and when they died, they were succeeded by their sons." In some African societies, evil spirits caused misfortune, sickness, and even death. People beset by an evil spirit often sought the aid of a diviner or medicine man to drive off the troublesome or malicious spirit.

Beginning in the eighth century, the spread of Islam across North Africa into the sub-Saharan Sudan and down the coast of the Red Sea through large regions of East Africa brought thousands of Africans into the Muslim faith. Islam's acceptance of polygamy, which most African societies practiced, facilitated this spread. By the late fifteenth century, as Muslim Arab traders migrated into Africa and believers launched wars of conquest and conversion, Islam had begun displacing traditional African religions in many parts of West and Central Africa, where the Atlantic slave trade began to gather momentum.

This was the complex religious heritage enslaved Africans brought to the Americas. No amount of desolation or physical abuse could wipe out these deeply rooted beliefs. In fact, it was their spiritual traditions that enabled many slaves to bear the hardships inherent in the master-slave relationship.

Yet despite many cultural differences, slaves and their Western owners also shared common ground. For example, people of both cultures recognized a physical world in which the living dwelled and an "other world" inhabited by the souls of the dead. Both believed that this "other world" could not be seen. However, people could come to know it by listening to revelations interpreted by spiritually gifted persons.

These shared foundations of religious belief enabled a hybrid African Christianity to develop in both Africa and the Americas. For example, in the kingdom of Kongo and several small realms close to the Niger Delta, extensive contact between Africans and the Portuguese interwove Christian beliefs with African religious beliefs in the seventeenth century. The worship of the Christian god did not eliminate the reverence for traditional African gods. Although enslavement suppressed some African religious customs, many spiritual beliefs and practices survived and are embraced by some African Americans today.

## SOCIAL ORGANIZATION

When Africans first welcomed Europeans to their lands, they were surprised to discover that Europeans had political organizations as sophisticated as their own. At the top of both European and African societies stood the king. Landowning nobles, military leaders, and priests (usually elderly men) supported the monarch. Beneath them were bureaucrats who collected taxes, kept records, and oversaw commerce. The next layer down was comprised of craftspeople, traders, teachers, and artists of the villages and towns. The broad base of this hierarchy consisted of the great mass of people, most of whom cultivated the soil. "Agriculture is our chief employment," recalled Olaudah Equiano, "and every one, even the children and women, are engaged in it. Thus we are habituated to labour from our earliest years." Equiano continued: "Everyone contributes something to the common stock."

African societies also included slaves—men and the women who had the lowest status and the least freedom. Slavery was not new to Europeans or Africans—or to any other peoples. It had flourished in ancient Greece and Rome, in Russia and Eastern Europe, and in southwestern Asia. Conquering peoples everywhere sold captured enemies into slavery because they could not tolerate holding massive numbers of the enemy in their midst. Selling them to distant lands as slaves neutralized their threat, was more merciful than killing them, and generated profit.

Like peoples living almost everywhere else in the world, Africans accepted enslavement as a condition of servitude and considered slaveholding a mark of wealth. Owning slaves made a person wealthy; trading them boosted his or her wealth. The trade in other humans thus gave upper-crust men and women access to coveted European goods such as Venetian beads, fine cloth, and horses. Equiano described how his tribe traded slaves to "mahogany-coloured men from

A Benin sculptor created this brass bas-relief in the sixteenth or seventeenth century. The work shows a Benin oba, or king, astride a small animal. Attendants shade the royal figure with palm leaves. Such bas-reliefs provide a valuable record of court life and rituals.

the south west" of his village: "Sometimes we sold slaves to them but they were only prisoners of war, or such among us as had been convicted of kidnapping, or adultery, and some other crimes which we esteemed heinous."

In this way, African societies conducted a small but far-reaching slave trade that carried bondspeople across the Sahara Desert to the Christian Roman Europe and the Islamic Middle East. From the tenth to fifteenth centuries, about 5,000 enslaved West Africans each year crossed the Sahara Desert to toil as sugar workers in Egypt, as domestic servants and artisans throughout the Arabic world, and as soldiers in North Africa. These slaves rarely ended up as field hands. Islam facilitated this process by establishing secure trade routes connecting West Africa with the Mediterranean world and the regions to the east. By the time Songhai rose to prominence in West Africa, that kingdom was the major supplier of enslaved captives across the Sahara to North Africa. Songhai warriors especially valued horses, which enabled them to wage war against neighboring peoples and thus capture still more slaves. Though this slave traffic was on the rise, it remained an occasional rather than a highly organized trade.

Africans' conception of slavery contrasted sharply with the notion that developed in European colonies in the Americas during the sixteenth century. Whereas most slaves in overseas European colonies engaged in field labor, generally for life, the majority of slaves within African societies supplied personal

*This rare image of three Africans at a Yemen slave market shows the sale price weighed in gold.*

service to their masters for a limited period. "Those prisoners which were not sold or redeemed," remembered Equiano, "we kept as slaves; but how different was their condition from that of slaves in the West-Indies! With us, they do no more work than other members of the community, even their master. Their food, clothing, and lodging were nearly the same as theirs, except they were not permitted to eat with the free-born and there was scarce any other difference between them, than a superior degree of importance which the head of a family possesses in our state, and that authority which, as such, he exercises every part of his household. Some of the slaves even have slaves under them as their own property and for their own use."

The kind of slavery Equiano described was also well known in Europe. It emerged when Christians and Muslims enslaved one another during centuries of religious wars in the Middle Ages. In these times, some people became slaves by being "outsiders" or "infidels" (nonbelievers) captured in war. Others voluntarily sold themselves into slavery to obtain money for their family. Still others were enslaved as punishment for committing a heinous crime.

Enslavement in Africa or Europe severely restricted a person's rights and prevented that individual from improving his or her lot in life. Yet these slaves still had certain protections. For example, they could obtain an education, marry and raise families, and count on decent treatment from their owners. In fact, some slaves in Africa were so highly trusted that they served as soldiers, administrators, royal advisors, and even occasionally as royal consorts.

But African slavery differed from that in North America in two important ways. First, slavery was not a lifelong condition in Africa. Second, it was not automatically passed down to the children of slaves. Because of these differences, black slaves in North America faced a far bleaker existence than slaves elsewhere.

## MUSIC, DANCE, AND ART

Aesthetics—what a society considers beautiful, moving, and life-sustaining—constituted a core value in traditional African society. People expressed their love of beauty through music, dance, and art as well as through body decoration, hair styling, and the concoction of elaborate, savory meals. Maintaining these expressions helped Africans endure enslavement in North America. Later chapters show how these forms of expression took deep root in African American life and embedded themselves in the larger American culture.

Africans engaged in dance and music-making to celebrate life and wove these activities into communal religious observances and festivals. Most religious gatherings involved *antiphony*—the call of a religious leader and the spoken or sung responses of the worshipers—a practice that prevails today in African American church services. Drums, rattles, flutes, bells, banjoes, other stringed instruments, and the *balafo* (similar to a xylophone) also enhanced religious rejoicing—akin to the ecstatic singing and shouting also a part of African American spiritual services. In addition, Africans engaged in singing and dancing at funeral observances.

Music and dance also served a playful purpose. Ibn Khaldun, one of the first Arab Muslim historians of Islamized Africa, observed of the Africans he encountered in the fourteenth century that "they are found eager to dance whenever they hear a melody." Dancing, singing, and playing instruments enabled Africans to celebrate life together, and entire villages participated. Individual performance for a passive audience, a practice widespread in Europe at the time, was foreign to African village life.

Often dancing and music-making bridged the sacred and the secular. From ancient times, African societies performed ceremonies honoring rain, sun, and other important natural phenomena. For instance, the Dinka people conducted rain ceremonies each year at the start of the rainy season. The purpose of these ceremonies was not to open the skies again; rather it was to celebrate rain as an indispensable force on which life depended.

African music featured antiphony, syncopation, and a percussive style characterized by multiple rhythms unfolding simultaneously. The drum, in its many forms, played an essential part. African musicians also prized improvisation—the continual changing of a piece of music. With improvisation, musicians felt they shared ownership of a musical composition rather than attributing a work to a single creator, as was the case in Europe. This sense of sharing echoed the emphasis on community and interdependence that marked African culture.

African art also involved communal expression. Most traditional African artists created functional objects rather than paintings of scenes or individuals. But some works served the same purpose as European court art. For example, Benin artists carved their kings' likenesses in stone or wood to glorify and commemorate their power.

From Ife, Benin, and other parts of West and Central Africa came a diverse array of sculptures and carvings fashioned from wood, terra cotta, ivory, copper, brass, and bronze. Inheritors of the ancient knowledge of iron production and metal casting from Nok culture, the artists of Ife and Benin were prized for their abilities. Many people believed these individuals possessed spiritual powers that found expression in their work. In other parts of West Africa, craftspeople carved elephant tusks into delicate pedestals surmounted by containers meant to hold salt, a precious commodity. When Portuguese traders first encountered the Sapis in what is now Sierra Leone, they were dazzled by such carvings. Especially intriguing to Europeans was the African ability to carve ivory to a lacelike thinness. In 1520, the German artist Albrecht Dürer purchased two African saltcellars carved in ivory and transported to the Netherlands by a slave ship captain.

African objects worked in brass, wood, and gold were equally impressive. For example, in Senegambia, European traders found elaborately carved antelope headdresses worn by young, masked Bambara men in agricultural rites. On the Gold Coast, they found carved royal stools inlaid with gold and silver. One Frenchman described "very fine gold casting that even a

*A Benin artist carved this saltcellar from an elephant tusk in the early sixteenth century. Europeans were so struck by the virtuosity of Benin carvers that they commissioned ivory pieces, sometimes providing sketches of decorative motifs. This saltcellar features a king or warrior with a spear in one hand, a sword in the other, and a cross hanging from a beaded necklace.*

European artist would find difficult to imitate." In Benin, Europeans encountered impressive bronze funerary portraits depicting the mothers of Benin's kings.

Private collectors and museums around the world now eagerly bid for the art of Africa both for its beauty and sophistication and for what these objects reveal about cultural interchange. Not only were African saltcellars sold in Europe, but Kongo craftsmen working in bronze began to fashion crosses and statues of saints after the Portuguese spread Catholicism in that kingdom.

## CONCLUSION

In ancient and medieval times, a rich variety of African societies arose in the distinct ecological zones that made up the vast and diverse continent. By the fifteenth century, intercultural contacts within Africa—as well as trade among Mediterranean Europe, North Africa, Egypt, and parts of eastern Africa—knit an elaborate web of connections among these diverse peoples. The rise of Islam accelerated this interweaving. By the early fifteenth century, peoples previously unknown to each other began to trade, exchange ideas, and intermingle throughout various parts of the continent. Though the slave trade was a minor part of this mingling and trading, it was to become the most dominant and tragic aspect of African–European–Middle Eastern contact, as discussed in Chapter 2.

# 2

## AFRICA AND THE ATLANTIC WORLD

### KING NOMIMANSA MEETS DIEGO GOMES

In 1456, the Mandingo king Nomimansa welcomed Diego Gomes, a Portuguese ship captain and emissary, into his home. The king was curious about these light-skinned people who called themselves "Christians." A gracious host, he presented them with generous gifts of ivory and gold. Living near the mouth of the Gambia River, the Mandingo people in the Songhai kingdom were eager to establish mutually advantageous trade arrangements like those they had forged with other foreign travelers to their coast. But Nomimansa also knew that during the previous decade, marauding Europeans had made war against Africans on offshore islands and seized some of them. So the king decided to step carefully in cultivating relations with these newcomers.

Nomimansa listened as Gomes explained how his sovereign, Prince Henry, had sent him to negotiate trade. True, the Portuguese had prospered by using the raid-and-trade tactic, Gomes admitted. But now, the captain reassured his host, they wanted peaceful, well-regulated trade. The Mandingo king agreed to a deal. Gomes sealed the commercial treaty by presenting Portugal's new trading partner with damask cloth from Flanders, huge brass pots from Germany, glass beads from Venice, and swords and knives from Spain. Nomimansa understood that his people were about to become participants in a trading network that could bring them valuable goods and luxuries in return for their gold, ivory, and salt.

But that night, King Nomimansa learned his guest's true intentions. As Gomes tells the story, "Twenty-two people were sleeping. I herded them as if they had been cattle towards the boats." Disobeying Henry's instructions, Gomes seized the people of the Gambia River and forced them onto his three ships. "We captured on that day . . . nearly 650 people, and we went back to Portugal, to Lagos in the Algarve, where the prince was, and he rejoiced with us."

## Chronology

**1402** Castile sponsors a permanent colony in the Canary Islands.

**1417** Portuguese seize the Madeira Islands.

**1420s–1430s** Portuguese sailors explore the African coast and engage in raiding for slaves.

**1427** Portuguese seize the Azores.

**1434** Gil Eannes navigates south of Cape Bojardor and returns home.

**1444** The Portuguese work enslaved Africans on the Madeiras' sugar plantations.

**1453** Turks' capture of Constantinople blocks access to traditional slave markets.

**1456** Diego Gomes negotiates agreements with African rulers that initiate the slave trade.

**1460s** Portugal colonizes Cape Verde Islands.

**1492** Ferdinand and Isabella expel the Muslims from Spain and sponsor Christopher Columbus.

**1496** Kongo king converts to Catholicism, which becomes the royal court's religion.

**1498** Vasco da Gama sails around Africa's southern tip.

**1502** First enslaved Africans reach the Americas on the Spanish ship Hispaniola.

**1518** Spain's Charles I authorizes importation of enslaved Africans to overseas colonies.

**1526** Africans first settle in North America as part of Ayllón's expedition.

**1530** Portugal's King John III authorizes transport of enslaved Africans to the Americas.

**1534–1539** African slave Estévan serves in Spanish exploration parties in North America.

**1550** Beginning of Catholic and Protestant Wars in Europe.

**1562** John Hawkins makes first English slave voyage.

Gomes's act prefigured a tragic aspect of European-African relations that would unfold for four centuries to come. From the mid-fifteenth century to the late nineteenth century, European slave traders carried off huge numbers of the most able-bodied members of African societies, especially in West and Central Africa. The Africans' fate? To toil in the new colonies European nations were founding on islands off the West African coast and in the Americas. As it turned out, ship captains who followed Gomes would not find it necessary to kidnap slaves because the Portuguese, and then other Europeans, found willing African trading partners to supply captives. Four years after his first meeting with King Nomimansa, Captain Gomes was trading again near the mouth of the Gambia River. But this time, he complained, "the natives used to give twelve Negroes for one horse, now they gave only six."

This chapter describes the first encounters between the Portuguese and Africans as the former worked their way down Africa's west coast. It examines the impact of the slave trade on both Europeans and Africans. The Europeans transformed an ancient, widespread practice into a harsh, lifelong bondage where skin color and African origins became the distinguishing marks of bondage. Black men, women, and children became commodities—not much different from horses or casks of tobacco. The Portuguese used slave labor first to cultivate sugar on the Atlantic islands off the coast of West Africa, creating what became known as the plantation system. Understanding how this system worked reveals insights into the experience of enslaved Africans in the Americas. A closer look at "the middle passage," the waterborne journey to the Western Hemisphere that huge numbers of Africans endured, sheds additional light on African lives under slavery. Once across the Atlantic, the lives of slaves owned by Spanish explorers differed markedly from those of Africans who worked on Portuguese and English plantations. Many of the Spanish-owned slaves became part of the Spanish conquest of an immense part of the Western Hemisphere in the late fifteenth and early sixteenth centuries.

# AFRICA AND EUROPE: THE FATEFUL CONNECTION

The point of no return was Cape Bojador. Beyond it lay "the green sea of darkness." Cape Bojador, just south of the Canary Islands off West Africa's shore, struck fear into the hearts of European and Muslim sailors riding the Atlantic Ocean current along the Saharan coast from Portugal and Spain. Ship captains dared not venture south of the cape because they had no way of defying the prevailing wind and current to return to their point of origin. But all that changed in 1434, when the bold Portuguese ship captain Gil Eannes sailed south on "seas none had sailed before" and managed to make his way back home. How did Eannes accomplish this feat? He modified Moorish-designed small wooden ships with lanteen (three-cornered) sails. Now he could sail into the wind and return to Portugal.

With Eannes's successful voyage, a new era of high-seas sailing had dawned. The Atlantic basin now lay open to any sailor who had the technology and nerve to navigate it. This revolution in trans-Atlantic navigation would have profound consequences for both Europeans and Africans. Most important, it cast a dark shadow over Africa that has not altogether lifted even today.

## PORTUGAL COLONIZES THE ATLANTIC ISLANDS

Prince Henry, son of Portugal's king João I, earned his name as Henry the Navigator. Politically ambitious, energetic, and experienced on the battlefield, the young monarch brimmed with both business and religious zeal. Henry sponsored improvements in navigation and energetically promoted his kingdom's expansion into the Atlantic Ocean. In 1417, he ordered the seizure of the unoccupied Madeira Islands off the northern part of West Africa. Subsequently, he took the Canaries and the Azores.

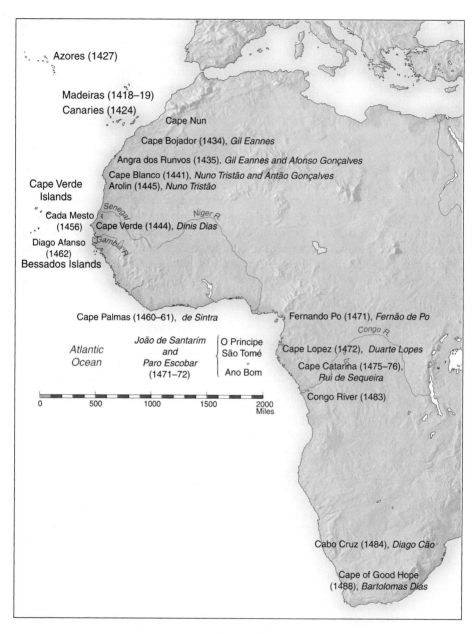

Azores (1427)

Madeiras (1418–19)
Canaries (1424)

Cape Nun

Cape Bojador (1434), *Gil Eannes*

Angra dos Runvos (1435), *Gil Eannes and Afonso Gonçalves*

Cape Blanco (1441), *Nuno Tristão and Antão Gonçalves*

Cape Verde
Islands

Arolin (1445), *Nuno Tristão*

Cada Mesto
(1456)    Cape Verde (1444), *Dinis Dias*

Diago Afanso
(1462)
Bessados Islands

Cape Palmas (1460–61),  *de Sintra*

Fernando Po (1471), *Fernão de Po*

João de Santarím
and
Paro Escobar
(1471–72)

O Principe
São Tomé

Ano Bom

Cape Lopez (1472),  *Duarte Lopes*

Cape Catarina (1475–76),
*Rui de Sequeira*

Atlantic
Ocean

Congo River (1483)

Cabo Cruz (1484), *Diago Cão*

Cape of Good Hope
(1488), *Bartolomas Dias*

Senegal

Niger R.

Gambia R.

Congo R.

0      500      1000      1500      2000
Miles

## Map 2.1
Portuguese Colonization of Atlantic Islands

*The earliest European expeditions took sailors along the eastern shores of the Atlantic and onto the islands off West Africa's coast in the mid-fifteenth century. Europeans would not venture across the Atlantic to the "strange new lands" of the Americas for a few more years.*

The Portuguese put down roots on these islands. At first they gathered treasures from the wild, such as honey and indigenous plants from which they made dyes to trade. Then they began experimenting with growing wheat and grapevines in the islands' rich volcanic soils. Around the same time, they sent infrequent raiding parties to the African coast in search of a few slaves to work the fields on these island colonies. By the 1470s, the Portuguese had sailed farther south to forge trading agreements along the coast of what is today's Ghana. They also struck deals with the African kingdom of Benin, trading in exchange for the "grains of paradise"—high-quality pepper that fetched a handsome price in Europe.

The Portuguese combined their cautious, small-scale experiments on the Atlantic islands with slave raiding on the West African coast. Initially they supplied slaves to Europe, where landowners kept up a modest demand for raw labor. But as populations on the European continent boomed in the late fifteenth century, landowners had plenty of human muscle to work the fields. Demand for slaves in Europe began to dry up, leaving the Portuguese with little reason to continue slave raiding in Africa. But all this shifted when the Portuguese began cultivating sugar on the Madeiras in the 1450s.

## THE PLANTATION SYSTEM: A MODEL FOR MISERY ON THE ATLANTIC ISLANDS

Produced in the temperate Mediterranean region since the eighth century, sugar had long been an exotic and expensive luxury. Only the wealthiest families could afford to sweeten their diets with the precious flavoring. Yet by the mid-1400s, the demand for sugar spread. On islands hundreds of miles from the African coast, Portuguese settlers spotted an opportunity. They experimented with growing sugarcane first on the Madeiras. To their delight, the plant flourished. Now these entrepreneurs needed laborers—not a few, but many. The plantation system they established became the first of its kind. It comprised three interwoven components: large landholding, the forced labor of gangs of enslaved peoples, and a cash crop that commanded steep prices in distant places. The plantation system meshed perfectly with the emerging European notion of mercantilism, whereby overseas colonists combined land and labor to produce wealth for the benefit of their home countries.

On the Madeiras, enslaved Africans initially toiled alongside slaves procured from Russia and the Balkans, where slavery was common. The Portuguese had imported these light-skinned individuals because they had long experience with planting and chopping cane in the sugar fields of Cyprus and Sicily. They also knew how to extract sugar from the cane. But the Portuguese found it far cheaper to import black men and women from the nearby West African coast than from distant Mediterranean locations. Thus the forced migration of Africans started unofficially in the 1440s, when Portuguese ship captains like Diego Gomes started kidnapping them for lifelong labor on the Atlantic islands.

Soon the Portuguese were cultivating sugar on other islands they had claimed, especially São Tomé, off Angola's coast. By 1500, they were importing about five thousand African slaves annually. As sugar production increased, it became more affordable, increasing demand. Soon the Portuguese were using the islands as slave-trading centers. Slave trading became increasingly lucrative after Turks conquered Constantinople in 1453, closing European access to the slave markets in Russia and the Balkans. For generations, Europeans had relied on these sources for domestic and agricultural laborers. It was precisely for these reasons that Prince Henry had sent Diego Gomes to negotiate treaties with African rulers. Though Gomes betrayed his charge—stealing rather than bartering for slaves—the Portuguese entrepreneurs who followed him established a mutually beneficial reciprocal trade with African coastal rulers.

# AFRICA AND THE RISING ATLANTIC WORLD

In 1486, the Spanish king put his seal on a grant to Fernão Dulmo, a military commander with a taste for exploration. The grant entitled Dulmo to all lands he could discover in the vast Atlantic Ocean—including "a great island or islands, or coastal parts of a mainland." European adventurers had no idea where they might find such islands. Moreover, they assumed that the "mainland" referred to in the grant was faraway China, then known as Cathay. Despite his determined forays throughout the Atlantic, Dulmo found nothing. But six years later, in 1492, Christopher Columbus reached what he believed were parts of Asia. Continued improvements in European navigation that for half a century had allowed colonization and trade along the African coast enabled the intrepid Genoese sailor to make his way across the entire Atlantic, an expedition chartered by the king and queen of Spain. In an instant, the momentum of European overseas colonization shifted from the Portuguese to the Spanish. This change would redirect the entire course of African history.

## INITIATING THE ATLANTIC SLAVE TRADE

After 1492, Europeans began settling in the Americas (including the Caribbean), where they cultivated valuable cash crops such as sugar, coffee, tobacco, and rice. Sensing new opportunities, European merchants and investors turned their attention from the Mediterranean Sea in Old World Europe to the Atlantic Ocean in the New World. As investment capital began flowing into the plantations dotting the Americas, a far-reaching new trade network took shape and expanded throughout the Atlantic basin. The continent of Africa provided this network with the labor and agricultural expertise plantation owners in the Americas needed to sell their bounty to the merchant houses of England, France, Spain, Portugal, and the Netherlands. Individuals fortunate enough to hold favored positions in this network—slave traders, shipbuilders, land speculators, and plantation owners—amassed great wealth. Almost every European nation sent ships to trade in Africa for slaves in addition to the usual gold, ivory, and other luxuries.

As Europeans launched themselves across the Atlantic, conquering and colonizing vast territories, their nearly insatiable demand for labor transformed the entire calculus of African trade. Plantations on large tracts of land could be productive only with mass human labor. Soon Europeans began referring to African slaves as "black gold." For almost four centuries after Columbus's voyages to the Americas, European colonizers transported Africans out of their homeland in the largest forced migration in human history. Estimates vary widely, but the number of Africans who survived the trip across to Atlantic to labor in the Americas probably reached more than ten million. Several million more perished during the forced marches from the African interior to coastal trading forts or during the ocean voyage west to the Americas.

In Angola, the Portuguese used their considerable military might to capture and enslave Africans beginning in 1491—a change from earlier policy. Elsewhere in Africa, local rulers controlled the raiding of slaves, marching captives to the coast and selling them to European merchants and ship captains. Coastal political authorities extracted taxes and tolls from the Europeans according to African law and custom. Not every African ruler engaged in the Atlantic slave trade, but over four centuries, the leaders of some two hundred African societies participated.

Why did some African leaders engage in slave raiding and selling? In part, the answer lies in the long history of slave trading among a variety of peoples in West and Central Africa. The tendency of human beings to mistreat those perceived as different from themselves also offers insight. Black rulers and their agents did not think of themselves as Africans capturing and selling other Africans. Rather, they viewed themselves as raiding enemies and members of outside—and thus inferior—societies. There was no unified African identity. The people of Mali or Benin did not identify themselves as Africans any more than the people of France or Portugal identified themselves as Europeans.

Thus Africans felt no moral distaste for the practice of capturing and selling slaves. Indeed, as early as the 1650s, they had been selling captives to Muslim slave traders, who transported them in caravans across the Sahara to slave markets around the Red Sea and Indian Ocean. Estimates suggest that as many enslaved Africans went east by land between the 1650s and 1800 as went west by water from the 1490s to 1800.

The living conditions of slaves sold in Muslim lands differed markedly from those sold in the New World. Because most Muslim societies had large peasant populations, they did not need agricultural laborers. Rather, they needed porters, soldiers, concubines (mistresses), cooks, and personal attendants. Muslim masters did not exploit their slaves but valued them for their personal services. For this reason, slave traders sent roughly two captured African women east for every man—the reverse of the gender ratio for slaves sent across the Atlantic for male-dominated field labor in the plantation system.

Other differences distinguished slavery in Muslim lands from that in European colonies. Whereas their masters in the Americas viewed slaves as nonhuman possessions, Muslim masters saw bondsmen and women as people, though to be sure, they treated them harshly. In the east, slaves had more rights than in the Americas. Some had the right to embrace the religion of their captors, while others were obligated to convert on the pain of death. Muslim masters freed more of their slaves than owners in the Americas did. Once they gained their freedom, many Africans living in Muslim societies had the same rights as non-Africans and blended into the general population—seldom the case in the Americas. A final difference is that Islam emphasized a universal community that transcended race, so former African slaves who had embraced the faith found it easier to feel united spiritually with other Muslims. This was not so in the Americas.

The African rulers who negotiated the first trade treaties with Europeans could not have predicted the damage these new partnerships would ultimately do to their own kingdoms. One example of the slave trade reveals its dire consequences. By the early 1500s, when the Portuguese began pressing their Kongo trading partners for slaves, missionaries had also reached the Kongo court. King Mani-Kongo was receptive to the Catholic religious message, even allowing his son to be baptized with the Christian name Alfonso I. In a spirit of cordiality, the king agreed to an exchange of gold, ivory, and slaves for Portuguese guns, knives, and trade goods. But soon Kongo was engulfed in conflict. By 1526, Portuguese merchants from São Tomé were urging village chiefs to wage war against each other to increase the slave catch, and supplying guns for the task. When Alfonso succeeded his father as monarch, he asked the Portuguese king to ban slave trading in Kongo. "Merchants are taking every day our natives, sons of the land and sons of our noblemen," he wrote. "So great is the corruption and licentiousness that our country is becoming completely depopulated." But Alfonso's request fell on deaf ears. Trapped in a web of guns, slaves, and power, the beleaguered ruler could not find a way out. As slave raiding devastated Africa's heartlands, rebels in Kongo's provinces ignited a civil war.

## SUGAR AND SLAVERY

The African slave trade would never have become more than a minor commerce without the burgeoning labor shortage created by Europe's overseas expansion and the intensifying hunger for sugar. Were it not for Europe's colonization of the Americas, the early slave trade that brought limited numbers of African slaves to southern Europe and the Atlantic islands might have ceased and been remembered simply as a short-lived phenomenon stemming from early European contacts with Africa. Sugar changed all that. When the Spanish and Portuguese stepped up their colonizing in the Caribbean and South America during the sixteenth century, they quickly learned that sugarcane grew just as easily in these lands as it did in the Atlantic islands off the west coast of Africa. Once the newcomers had subdued the native peoples they encountered, they replicated the plantation system they had developed on the Atlantic islands. Now increased demand for slaves came from the Caribbean and South America.

At first, the Spanish and Portuguese looked to the native peoples of the Americas as an obvious source of forced gang labor. In some areas, such as

*Sugar production in Brazil. The demand for sugar led to the cultivation of the crop in the Atlantic islands and in the Americas.*

Mexico and Brazil, the newcomers coerced local men and women into working on plantations and in mines. But diseases to which native Americans were not immune—such as smallpox, influenza, and scarlet fever—soon devastated the local populations. Far more familiar with their surroundings than their white captors, slaves who survived these plagues often escaped back to their villages.

Now in need of a new source of labor, the Europeans turned their attention to the huge supply of labor available in Africa. Whereas they previously traded *with* Africans, they now began trading *in* Africans. By the mid-1500s in Portuguese Brazil, and by the early 1600s on islands throughout the Caribbean, enslaved Africans were hacking out sugar plantations from tropical forest. By the mid-eighteenth century, about nine out of every ten West Africans captured for export across the Atlantic went to labor in New World sugarcane fields. After finding gold and silver mines in Mexico and Peru, the Spanish stepped up their purchase of African laborers. After successfully introducing additional cash crops—coffee, tobacco, rice, and indigo—the Spanish and Portuguese sent thousands of ships to the West African coast and packed them with slaves. Dutch, French, and English vessels followed. Hardly anyone would have disagreed with one seventeenth-century Englishman who called African slaves "the strength and the sinews of this western world."

Once established on a large scale, the Atlantic slave trade transformed slave recruitment in Africa. At first, African leaders had sold criminals or prisoners of war. But the intensifying demand for workers in the New World presented irresistible new opportunities. Now African kings waged war against their neighbors to secure sufficient quantities of the "black gold" for which the Europeans paid so handsomely. European guns perpetuated this shift. By 1730, Europeans were providing about 180,000 arms a year to African slave traders. The availability of guns enabled unscrupulous traders to kidnap slaves and set up paramilitary organizations throughout Africa. Eager to maintain their lucrative commercial relations with European powers, some African rulers declined to stop the kidnapping and organized violence. In several cases, their decision cost them their kingdoms. Others used the situation to strengthen their own militaries.

As the demand for African slaves multiplied in the eighteenth century, the armies and agents of coastal and interior kings repeatedly invaded the hinterlands of western and central Africa. At least half of the slaves transported to

*In 1624, Queen Njinga took the throne of Ndongo (present-day Angola), defying a custom that prohibited women from ruling. She quickly solidified her rule by contesting Portuguese incursions into her domain. When the Portuguese went on the offensive in a series of wars to secure territory as well as access to the slave trade, Queen Njinga led the resistance. Her fierce battle cry, which reportedly could be heard from miles away, established her as a heroic figure who has become an enduring legend. Here, the kneeling Queen Njinga receives a blessing from the standing Portuguese governor with African and Portuguese attendants looking on. Three hundred years after her death in 1663, Angolans fighting for independence from Portugal went into battle inspired by the woman who had come to symbolize resistance to European imperialism in Africa.*

English North America came from the part of western Africa that lies between the Senegal and Niger Rivers and the Gulf of Biafra. Most of the others were enslaved in Angola, on the west coast of central Africa. By the end of the eighteenth century, slaving had devastated these regions' populations.

## EUROPEAN COMPETITION FOR THE SLAVE TRADE

For Europeans, the slave trade generated immense profits. As early as 1550, one chronicler asserted that slaves "will triple your investment." During the sixteenth and seventeenth centuries, European nations warred incessantly for trading advantages and coastal forts on the West African coast. For example, the major Portuguese slaving fort at Elmina on the Gold Coast, constructed by the Portuguese in 1481, was captured by the Dutch and then by the English. By the end of the seventeenth century, European nations were negotiating for the sole right to supply slaves to the plantations in the Americas.

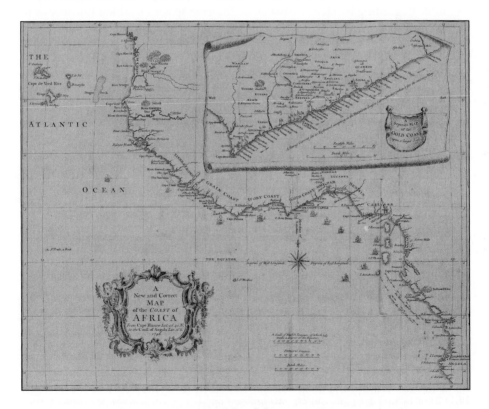

*Map 2.2*
English Slave Trade

*This map appeared in a pamphlet promoting the English slave trade. The pamphlet author described the British Empire in gushing terms as "a magnificent superstructure of American commerce and naval power on an African foundation." The Gold Coast, the Bight of Biafra, and the Bight of Benin—all on West Africa's coast—became major slave-trading centers for English traders.*

The English came late to the slave trade, which was long dominated by the Portuguese. But in 1562, Englishman John Hawkins seized a slave ship, sold the slaves to the Spanish, and returned with a fat profit for Queen Elizabeth I. After this, the English gave priority to supplying the Spanish colonies with slaves. It would be another century before their dominance was secure. Meanwhile the English king Charles II granted a charter to the Royal Adventurers to Africa—a joint-stock company headed by his brother, the Duke of York—giving it the exclusive right to carry slaves to England's overseas colonies. For thirty-four years after 1663, each slave transported across the Atlantic bore the brand "DY" for the Duke of York. Eventually merchants pressured Parliament to end slave trade monopolies. Then the English slave trade boomed—from some 6,000 slaves carried out of Africa per year in the 1680s to more than 20,000 per year in the early 1700s. By the 1790s, England was the foremost slave-trading nation in Europe.

Though the motive for the slave trade was profit, racist sentiment began to build. Regarding black Africans as an inferior species enabled Europeans to rationalize their brutal traffic in human beings. Almost from the start Europeans had thought of their captives as heathen, savage, and deserving of their fate. Notions of African "backwardness" and cultural impoverishment strengthened European justifications. These ignorant heathens, thought Europeans, were better off toiling in the sugar, rice, and tobacco fields of the Americas than living where they were born. In the Americas, Europeans believed, the black "savages" could be "civilized" through exposure to Christianity and European culture.

## THE TRAUMA OF ENSLAVEMENT

"The first object which saluted my eyes when I arrived on the coast [in about 1755]," wrote Olaudah Equiano, "was the sea, and a slave-ship, which was then riding at anchor, and waiting for its cargo." The eleven-year-old had arrived at the old slave fort at Calabar, which still stands, and was about to endure the so-called middle passage across the Atlantic. This journey constituted the second leg of the three-part transit that for captives began in the African interior and concluded with the march to a final destination in the Americas, where they were purchased as slaves.

Equiano's account is the most vivid of the few to survive Africans' centuries-long diaspora. Many enslaved Africans would have told stories different from Equiano's, for each experience was unique. But most who reached the shores of the Americas did not live long enough to record their experiences. On average, they died in just seven years. So Equiano's story, covering fifty-three years, has assumed a place in historical literature far greater than he could have hoped for. Yet even his account cannot fully convey the agony and demoralization of the forced march to the west coast of Africa, the loading of captives onto wooden-hulled ships, the miserable journey across the ocean, and the sale, as chattel, in a new land.

*Nobody has discovered who painted this handsome picture of Olaudah Equiano, completed probably when he was in his forties. Equiano saw nine editions of his* Interesting Narrative of the Life of Olaudah Equiano *published in London, Dublin, Edinburgh, and Norwich before he died in March 1797. After his death, enterprising printers republished his* Narrative *in many cities. Today, Equiano's* Narrative *is republished every several years, is read by thousands of people, and has won widespread recognition as the most compelling first-person story of enslavement and liberation from the pen of an African American or Afro-Briton. Equiano was enslaved a few decades after the map shown on page 35 was drawn, but this map accurately depicts the region where he first saw the slave ship that took him to Barbados and then Virginia.*

## CAPTURE AND SALE IN AFRICA

Born in a village in a "charming fruitful vale," Equiano regarded his homeland as "the most considerable" of a variety of kingdoms in the "part of Africa known by the name of Guinea." European slave traders preferred young men, like Equiano, over women because they knew that buyers on the other side of the Atlantic valued physical strength over everything else. Most captives were in their teens, twenties, and thirties. Only about 10 percent were under ten or elderly.

Once captured, slaves were marched to the sea in "coffles," or trains, or brought by large canoes down the rivers that emptied into the Atlantic. A Scotsman, Mungo Park, described the coffle he marched with for 550 miles through Gambia in the 1790s. In this coffle, seventy-three men, women, and children were tied together by the neck with leather thongs. Several captives attempted to commit suicide by eating clay. Another was abandoned after being badly stung by bees. Still others died of exhaustion and starvation. After two months, depleted by thirst, hunger, and exposure, the prisoners reached the coast. There their captors herded them into fortified enclosures called barracoons.

The forced march was just the first leg of the 5,000-mile journey. On the coast, the captives were brought forth from the enclosures for purchase. Ship surgeons, wrote one slave trader, "examine every part of every one of them, to the smallest member, men and women, being all stark naked." Then the bargaining began. Negotiating the purchase price of slaves proved a complicated, capricious affair, as African sellers were wily barterers. "The natives have a splendid mental capacity with much judgment and sharp and ready apprehension," wrote one slave ship captain. A male slave might bring thirteen bars of iron; a female, nine bars and two brass rings. Often the bargaining dragged on for days. In addition to slaves, ship captains purchased the provisions (such as yams and other foods) that the slaves and crews would consume during the fifty to eighty days it took to cross the ocean.

When the bargaining ended, the slaves were ferried in large canoes, manned by local Africans, to the ships waiting at anchor offshore. Some tried to swallow handfuls of sand in a desperate effort to maintain a link to their homeland. Often branded with a hot iron and shackled in pairs, they huddled on deck, watching other prisoners being hauled aboard. Sometimes weeks passed before the captain had packed the ship with as many slaves as possible. During those weeks, some of the captives succumbed to disease or killed themselves.

Equiano recalled, "When I was carried on board, I was immediately handled, and tossed up, to see if I were sound, by some of the crew; and I was now persuaded that I had gotten into a world of bad spirits, and that they were going to kill me." Frightened by their long hair, their strange language, and their bleached skin, the Ibo youth concluded that "if ten thousand worlds had been my own, I would have freely parted with them all to have exchanged my condition with that of the meanest slave in my own country."

On the slave ship, the bound Africans were thrust below into half-decks with little more than four feet of headroom. If the ship that carried Equiano was typical, he would have been jammed below deck among roughly three hundred other slaves. Like him, about forty-five of them would have been under fourteen years of age. "The stench of the hold while we were on the coast," Equiano recalled, "was so intolerably loathsome, that it was dangerous to remain there for any time. . . . The closeness of the place, and the heat of the climate added to the number in the ship which was so crowded that each had scarcely room to turn himself, almost suffocated us. This . . . produced copious perspirations, so that the air soon became unfit for respiration, from a variety of loathsome smells, and brought on a sickness amongst the slaves of which many died, thus falling victims to the improvident avarice, as I may call it, of their purchasers."

Confined below deck as the ship was readied for sail, the Africans lost all hope of seeing their families and homelands again. As European slave traders knew, this was the moment when the chance of suicide or an uprising was greatest. One slaver warned that "these slaves have so great a love for their country, that they despair when they see that they are leaving it forever; that makes them die of grief, and I have heard merchants . . . say that they die more often before leaving the port than during the voyage."

## THE MIDDLE PASSAGE: A FLOATING HELL

The fear that inspired suicide while still on African land lessened as the ship got under way and the "middle passage" began, but the chance of death by disease or privation increased. Even on the better ships, the shackled Africans found that their cramped quarters made it impossible to walk unless their captors dragged them on deck for exercise. On the worst ships, they could barely turn over in the

*European ships had transported enslaved Africans across the Atlantic for more than three centuries before any European sketched or painted a below-deck scene from such a vessel. In about 1840, an officer of the HMS Albatross—a British Royal Navy ship intercepting Portuguese slave ships carrying Africans to Brazil—painted this haunting scene, which he witnessed on the slave ship Albanez.*

holds. "They had not so much room as a man in his coffin," testified one ship's surgeon. "This wretched situation," Equiano wrote in his narrative, "was again aggravated by the galling of the chains, now become insupportable; and the filth of the necessary tubs, into which the children often fell, and were almost suffocated. The shrieks of the women, and the groans of the dying, rendered the whole scene of horror almost inconceivable."

Even though it was to the advantage of the ship captains to deliver sellable slaves on the other side of the Atlantic, few stocked their ships properly. Pitiful rations led to undernourishment, confinement in leg irons spread disease, and the impossibility of basic hygiene eroded the Africans' self-respect. Equiano explained that "the loathsomeness of the stench and crying together" below decks made him unable to eat, for which he was flogged. Slaves who refused to eat were sometimes force-fed. The ship's crew applied hot coals to open captives' lips or used an instrument, the speculum oris (mouth opener), to wrench their jaws apart.

Dehydration imperiled the captives as well. On one ship, the captain provided just one coconut shell filled with water with each meal—which amounted to less than two pints of liquid a day. On many ships, the slaves had even less water. As their sodium and potassium levels dropped due to dehydration, they lost weight, grew listless, and fell into a dazed state. The slavers called this condition "melancholy" and believed it set in as slaves willed themselves to die. But some perceptive observers, such as the port physician in Charleston, South Carolina, knew otherwise. Recognizing the symptoms of malnutrition and dehydration, he wondered how any incoming Africans "escape with life."

For enslaved African women, the middle passage had one additional terror and humiliation: rape. Slavers of all European nations separated African men and women during the ocean crossing, in part because they feared the women would incite the men to mutiny. But the arrangement also gave sailors access to their female captives, whom they regarded as fair sexual prey. They brought women above deck often only to rape them. Equiano had "even known them [sailors] to gratify their brutal passion with females not ten years old."

Desperate for deliverance from this living hell, some enslaved Africans plotted mutiny. Experienced English ship captains tried to prevent conspiracy by obtaining their human cargo from different regions along the African coast so the captives could not communicate. To stifle insurrection, captains also used stark brutality. Leaders of a suspected uprising were flogged to death or dismembered in full view of the others to send a warning. John Atkins, aboard an English slave vessel in 1721, described how the captain "whipped and scarified" several plotters and sentenced others "to cruel deaths, making them first eat the Heart and Liver of one of them killed." The captain hoisted one female resistor up by the thumbs, then "whipp'd and slashed her with knives, before the other slaves, till she died."

## SALE IN THE AMERICAS

Probably not more than two of every three captured Africans lived to see the Americas. Those who survived were psychologically numb and physically depleted. But stumbling ashore, they had to endure yet another horror: being sold as chattel to a European master and then transported to the place of their labor. For Equiano, this final stage proved as devastating as the physical agony of the crossing. In Barbados, a slave-based English sugar colony in the West Indies, he trembled as merchants and planters clambered aboard ship. He believed that "we should be eaten by these ugly men, as they appeared to us." But the merchants informed the slaves that they "were not to be eaten, but to work, and were soon to go on land, where we should see many of our country people." Taken ashore, Equiano shrank in terror as "the buyers rush at once into the yard where the slaves are confined, and make choice of that parcel they like best. The noise and clamour with which this is attended . . . serve not a little to increase the apprehensions of the terrified Africans. . . . In this manner, without scruple, are relations and friends separated, most of them never to see each other again."

No one bought Equiano; he was too young and weak. So he was shipped to North America. Far up a river off the Chesapeake Bay, the owner of a small Virginia plantation purchased the boy. There, torn from all that was familiar, he had "now totally lost the small remains of comfort I had enjoyed in conversing with my countrymen; the women too, who used to wash and take care of me, were all gone different ways, and I never saw one of them afterwards." Isolated,

Equiano remembered being "exceedingly miserable, and thought myself worse off than any of the rest of my companions; for they could talk to each other, but I had no person to speak to that I could understand. In this state I was constantly grieving and pining, and wishing for death rather than anything else."

From capture in Africa to arrival at the plantation, farm, or city home of a European master may have averaged six months. During this time the African was completely cut off from family, home, and community life. The body was tortured, the spirit, shocked and seared. Now the African had to learn a new language, adjust to a new diet, adapt to a new climate and physical environment, and master new work routines. Most important, he or she had to find a way to live in bondage forever. But for many, "forever" proved short. Every fourth African arriving on American soil died within just four years. 25%,

# EARLY AFRICANS IN NORTH AMERICA

"We commended ourselves to God Our Lord and made our escape. . . . As we traveled that day, in considerable fear that the Indians would follow us, we saw some smoke and, toward the end of the day, reached it, where we espied an Indian who, when he saw us coming toward him, fled without waiting for our arrival. We sent the black after him, and when the Indian saw that he was alone, he waited for him." With these words, Alvar Núñez Cabeza de Vaca, a Spanish conquistador (conqueror), told the story of his epic escape from enslavement by Florida Indians in the 1530s and the start of a five-year journey through the southern reaches of North America. The "black" he referred to was Estévan, also called Estéban, Estévanico, and sometimes "the black Arabian." "The black," continued de Vaca, "told [the Indian] that we were looking for the people who were making that smoke. He replied that . . . he would guide us to them: and so we followed him and he ran to tell the people that we were coming; at sunset . . . we reached them . . . and they indicated that they were happy to have our company; and so they took us to their houses and lodged Dorantes [de Vaca's compatriot] and the black in the house of one medicine man."

This encounter among Spanish explorers, a black Arabian, and Native Americans in the forests of Florida occurred in 1534. Fifty years later, the English would make their first attempt to plant a colony in North America. Nearly a century later, the young Equiano would labor in the fields and houses of Virginia. The incident de Vaca describes shows how cultures converged and the definitions of race blurred in this early era in North American history.

## AFRICANS AND THE SPANISH CONQUEST IN THE AMERICAS

Estévan was the product of three cultures coming together along the western edge of the Atlantic. His experience embodied the beginning of a long process by which the notion of race first emerged in Europe, Africa, and the Americas. The Spanish referred to him as "a black," "a Moor," or "an Arabian." But these words merely described his skin color (dark), his religion (Islam), and his homeland (Morocco). De Vaca never called him a slave—though he was owned by Andrés Dorantes. Nor did de Vaca ever suggest that Estévan was inferior, primitive, or savage. Rather, de Vaca's account described how four men—three Spanish and one African—became the first non-natives to penetrate the vast interior of North America. What mattered in this strange and often hostile land was not Estévan's blackness or even his slave status. It was his linguistic abilities, his fortitude, and his cleverness as a go-between. Estévan was an Atlantic Creole—a person from the eastern shore of the Atlantic who acquired new cultural and linguistic attributes on the western shore. His owner and companions counted on him to help them navigate the challenges of their daunting journey.

Seventy-five years before the English first tried to establish colonies in North America, Africans had been in the Americas. By 1580, 45,000 of them had arrived in the Spanish colonies in Florida and present-day New Mexico. Africans had also come to South America. About 13,000 had been shipped to Brazil, where Portuguese entrepreneurs had set up huge sugar and coffee plantations.

Many Spanish explorers and settlers came to the Americas with enslaved Africans whose ability to soldier and to learn native languages made them valuable negotiators with native peoples. For example, two Africans with Hispanicized names—Juan Garrido and Juan González—were on Juan Ponce de León's expedition to explore and seize Puerto Rico in 1508. By assisting the explorer, Garrido and González obtained their freedom and stayed on to mine gold. Some Africans also aided the Spanish in slaving raids against the Caribs on the islands of Guadalupe, Dominica, and Santa Cruz. In 1513, when Vasco Nuñez de Balboa became the first European to cross the Isthmus of Panama and see the

Born in Africa, Juan Garrido accompanied Juan Ponce de León on his expeditions to Puerto Rico and Florida. This image shows Garrido with de León astride a Spanish horse as the two approach several Indian chiefs in about 1519. The picture appeared in Diego Duran's Historia de las Indias de Nueve España e Islas de la Tierra Firme, published in Spain in 1581.

Pacific Ocean, he had thirty Africans with him. Africans also accompanied Hernán Cortés during his siege of the Aztec capital of Tenochtitlán (in modern-day Mexico) in 1521. Cortés's entourage included Garrido, who later became a gold miner, landowner, caretaker of one of the conquered city's aqueducts, and gatekeeper of its *cabildo* (city hall). Likewise, Africans participated in Francisco Pizarro's conquest of the Incas in Peru in 1532. Later, when local Indians murdered Pizarro, Africans carried his body to the Catholic cathedral that the Spanish had built in Lima. Some historians have claimed that one of Columbus's mariners, Pedro Alonso Niño, was an African, though this is disputed.

## AFRICANS IN EARLY SPANISH NORTH AMERICA

As early as 1513, when the Spanish first set foot on what would become the United States, they had African slaves with them. As in Puerto Rico, Ponce de León included Juan Garrido and Juan González, as well as African scouts and ship handlers, in his expedition to Florida. In 1521, they returned with de León to Florida to help stake Spain's claim to the entire eastern coast of North America. To make good on this claim, 600 Spanish settlers—led by Lucas Vásquez de Ayllón and accompanied by many black slaves—tried to establish a permanent colony in La Florida (as the Spanish called it) in 1526. The group settled near present-day Sapelo Sound in Georgia. When starvation, disease, and a leadership crisis beset the expedition and Guale Indians attacked, some Africans fled and joined the Guale tribe. They married Guales, started families, and began the mixing of Africans and Native Americans that would continue in North America for centuries.

In 1528, Estévan arrived in Florida with his Spanish master as part of Pánfilo de Narváez's expedition. There, the 500 Spanish and Africans settled near the swamplands of Tampa Bay. This colony fared as poorly; only four members survived, including de Vaca and Estévan, and were shortly enslaved by nearby Native Americans. During his captivity, Estévan became a linguist, healer, guide, and negotiator.

Following their escape, the four fled Florida and headed west. Estévan continued to negotiate with the hostile Indians they encountered. In the course of the journey, his status as the slave of a Spanish adventurer all but dissolved. Paddling crude boats across the Gulf of Mexico, the four shipwrecked on the Texas coast, took refuge among merciful natives, and then plunged into the Texas interior. Following Indian guides for the next two years, the four came to be regarded as holy men who possessed the power to heal. Indians in Spanish New Mexico described them as "four great doctors, one of them black, the other three white, who gave blessings [and] healed the sick." On one occasion, Indians gave Estévan a sacred gourd rattle—a rare honor. Making their way southwest, the four eventually met with Spanish settlers in Mexico. Evidence suggests that they reached the Pacific Ocean in 1536.

In 1539, Estévan joined a new Spanish expedition. Departing from Mexico City and heading north into Spanish New Mexico, the group blazed a trail for Francisco Vásquez de Coronado's expedition of 1540. In what would later be Arizona, the Spanish selected Estévan to forge ahead into Zuni country with Indian guides in search of the fabled seven gold-filled cities of Cíbola. He became the first outsider to penetrate the vast Colorado Plateau. Unfortunately for him and his group, the Zuni saw him as an intruder and killed him.

In the same year that Estévan had set out, Hernando de Soto made a further attempt to settle La Florida. Like every other Spanish expedition, this one included free and enslaved Africans. But the search for silver in the country of the Creeks failed, and de Soto perished at the hands of the Indians. Half of his soldiers and the accompanying Africans died as well. Those who survived limped back to Mexico "dressed only in animal skins."

Late in the sixteenth century, the Spanish—again accompanied by free and enslaved Africans—finally established a secure presence in La Florida. When French Huguenots (Protestants) planted a small rival colony near present-day Jacksonville in 1562, the Spanish sent Pedro Menéndez de Avilés, captain general of the Spanish fleets in the West Indies, to crush them. Avilés quickly identified a talented, free mulatto (part European and part African) named Luis living with the Calusa tribe south of St. Augustine. He came to depend on Luis to negotiate with the native people to gain their support. Avilés found other Africans living with Indian tribes as well, many of whom had fled French masters. Avilés destroyed the French outpost and established a Spanish colony in Florida that lasted for two centuries.

Life in La Florida was harsh for Spaniards and Africans alike. But the scarcity of capable workers and skilled linguists gave enslaved Africans a higher status and a greater degree of freedom than they would have after the English set up colonies in North America. By the time the English had mounted their Jamestown expedition in 1606, about one hundred African slaves and a small number of free black people, many of them married to Indians or Spaniards, lived in La Florida.

The role of Africans on these grueling expeditions through mapless territory gave slavery a distinct character in the early Spanish settlements. The slaves did much of the back-breaking work in the fields, on supply trains, and in fort and church construction. But they also served as soldiers, guides, and linguists. Along the west coast, Africans were a significant fraction of settlers in Mexico's northern frontier, including what would become the American Southwest, where they also served in a variety of roles. On both the east and west coasts, Africans forged sexual unions and raised children with Native Americans and Spanish people. This genetic blending blurred the definition of slavery. Officially, the Spanish regarded purity of lineage as the entitlement to elite status and ranked people on a social scale according to their ancestry. But pure lineage meant little on the frontiers of New Spain. There, Spanish, Native Americans, and Africans intermingled so much that traditional social categories broke down. A person's value to the community mattered far more than his or her "race." By the early 1700s, one observer of New Spain's northern frontier remarked that "practically all those who wish to be considered Spaniards are people of mixed blood."

# CONCLUSION

When Diego Gomes first reached the coast of West Africa in 1456 to arrange treaties of commerce with African rulers, he unwittingly formed links between Europeans and Africans that would lock the two in a shameful embrace. Struggling to establish plantations on the islands off Africa's coast, the Portuguese began depending on enslaved Africans to produce highly profitable sugar. By the end of the 1400s, the Portuguese had extended the plantation system to the other side of the ocean. Europe, Africa, and the Americas were now bound together in a vast, Atlantic-wide system of trade and cultural exchange. The system would exert a disastrous impact on the peoples of Africa—not only those left behind but also those who survived the brutal journey to the Americas.

From the mid-fifteenth to the late nineteenth centuries, Europeans tore millions of Africans from their ancestral homelands and shipped them to the Atlantic islands and the Americas to labor in their colonies. No account of the enslavement of Africans can quite convey the demoralization and agony that accompanied the forced march to the coast of Africa and the subsequent loading aboard of the unfortunate captives. One historian has called it "the most traumatizing mass human migration in modern history."

Africans who ended up in North America met with profoundly different experiences, depending on who owned them, when they arrived on the coast, and where they ended up living. In the 1500s, only a few thousand Africans arrived in the Americas in chains. Many of them assumed roles based on their valuable skills, not on their "race." Moreover, they raised families with Native American and Spanish partners, contributing to a blending of cultures that would powerfully shape the New World. But during the 1600s, the trickle of Africans across the Atlantic burgeoned into a steady stream. By the time Equiano arrived in the mid-eighteenth century, it was a torrent. With increasing numbers of slaves, the English entry into the Atlantic slave trade, and English challenges to Spanish, French, and Dutch footholds in North America, came changing attitudes toward Africans and changes in the practice of slavery itself.

# 3

## AFRICANS IN EARLY NORTH AMERICA, 1619–1726

### ANTHONY JOHNSON AND HIS FAMILY IN THE EARLY CHESAPEAKE

Antonio had been in Virginia only a year before a furious assault by Powhatan Indians nearly destroyed Warresquioke, his master's tobacco plantation. The day was March 22, 1622—Good Friday. Antonio survived, along with just four others of the fifty-seven people (mostly field laborers) living on the plantation. Opechancanough, the Indian leader intent on driving the English back into the ocean after fifteen years of clashes, led the well-planned attack. Antonio was no stranger to violence, having been wrenched from his home in Africa. Now he witnessed firsthand the bitter conflicts between indigenous people and Europeans seeking to establish settlements in North America.

Antonio was almost certainly brought to the Americas on a Portuguese slave ship from the Kongo-Angolan region of Africa. Then he was likely captured by a Dutch ship and sold in Jamestown, the center of the Virginia colony the English had founded in 1607. The young African labored on the plantation for nearly twenty years after his owner recovered his losses and replenished his supply of slaves.

After the Powhatan attacks, Antonio found a wife—quite a feat in a colony that now had only a handful of women. He married Mary, an African woman who had just recently arrived in Virginia, and they started a family. The couple lived together for more than forty years. One of their grandchildren honored the family's heritage by naming his 44-acre Maryland farm Angola.

Sometime in the 1640s, Antonio and Mary gained their freedom. They chose the names Anthony and Mary Johnson to signify their new status and made a place for themselves in Northampton County, on Virginia's eastern shore. By

1651, they had acquired 250 acres of tobacco land, built up a small herd of cattle and hogs, and had two black servants. In this corner of North America, where slave status and racial boundaries had not yet hardened in legal terms, the Johnsons were among many small planters scrambling to improve their lot in life. They apparently enjoyed respect from the authorities; in 1653, the county court forgave their taxes after a fire destroyed their dwelling. As Anthony Johnson told the court, "[Our] hard labors and known services for obtaining [our] livelihood were well known."

Both of Anthony and Mary's sons acquired homesteads—one of 550 acres; the other, 100 acres. One of the young men married a white woman. This wasn't unusual at a time when an African man could offer a woman just as decent a life as a white man could.

However, by the 1640s slave status and racial boundaries began to harden. Virginia's planter-lawmakers moved to regulate human bondage and interracial relations. Yet because slavery did not exist in England, they had no laws to copy. They began to create laws of their own, just as English settlers had done in the West Indies. Bit by bit, court judges and legislators established precedents that assigned Africans to lifelong slavery. The newly defined institution contrasted sharply with indentured servitude, an ancient English labor contract into which master and servant entered freely. Most indentured servitude agreements specified terms of five to seven years. During that time, the servant was entirely at the master's disposal but looked forward to regaining his or her freedom at the end of the term.

In 1655, Anthony Johnson himself became involved in distinguishing between servant and slave. A neighboring white planter had taken up the case of John Casor, the Johnsons' servant. The Johnsons, the neighbor argued before the county court, had held Casor beyond the agreed-upon seven years specified in most indentured servitude terms. Johnson retorted that he and Casor had not made an indenture. In fact, he added, neither Casor nor the neighbor could produce the indenture they claimed Johnson had violated. In the end, the court accepted Johnson's argument that he had purchased the lifelong labor of Casor— that, in effect, Casor was a slave. Because Casor had been enslaved in his African homeland, the court decided that anyone who bought him—even a fellow African—could count on his service for life. Losing his case, Casor served the Johnsons for another seventeen years before they gave him his freedom. Eventually, he succeeded in his own right as a tobacco planter.

By 1664, perhaps sensing diminishing opportunities for their children and their mixed-race grandchildren in Virginia, the Johnsons and one son began selling their land to white neighbors. They then moved north to Maryland, a colony founded in 1632 as a refuge for English Catholics. Renting land there, they took up farming and cattle-raising again. Six years later, when Anthony died, Virginia's tightening restrictions on Africans thwarted the execution of his will. A jury of white men declared that because Johnson "was a Negroe and by consequence an alien," the 50 Virginia acres he had deeded to his son Richard before moving to Maryland should go to a local white planter. In a colony filled with

## *Chronology*

1586  Africans help defend Spanish St. Augustine against the English.

1607  First permanent North American English colony at Jamestown, Virginia.

1613  First Africans on Manhattan Island (later New Amsterdam).

1619  Ships deliver Africans to Virginia for sale into bondage.

1620  Pilgrims settle Plymouth Colony in Massachusetts.

1625  Dutch in New Amsterdam begin to purchase enslaved Africans.

1630s  English planters begin importing slaves to the Caribbean.

1630  English Puritans establish colonies in New England.

1637  Puritans trade captured Pequot Indians for enslaved Africans.

1663  South Carolina settlers import slaves from the West Indies.

1664  English seize New Netherlands (now New York) and sanction slavery.

1675  Bacon's Rebellion in Virginia fuels replacement of white servants with African slaves.

1682  The French claim the vast North American interior.

1684  English settlers in Pennsylvania engage in the slave trade.

1690s  Chesapeake planters shift from white indentured labor to African slave labor.

1696  English Parliament opens slave trade to British merchants.

1702  New York passes a slave code.
English marauders burn Spanish St. Augustine, a slave sanctuary.

1712  Slave revolt in New York City sparks executions and brutal punishments.
South Carolina passes a comprehensive slave code.

1715  Yamasee War pits Indians and Africans against English colonists and Africans.

1718  French build New Orleans with the labor of enslaved Africans.

1724  Louisiana's *Code Noir* regulates slavery.

1725–1726  Pennsylvania passes act "for the better regulation of Negroes."

---

unfree laborers of many skin hues, the legal net began tightening around the small number of free Africans and their children.

By the late seventeenth century, enslaved Africans laboring in Maryland and Virginia became trapped in a legal system designed to keep them in perpetual bondage. Those who did manage to win their freedom were forced to the margins of society by whites eager to claim the fruits of former slaves' initiative and hard work. In just this way, Anthony and Mary Johnson's family suffered a slow decline from being landowners to tenant farmers. In the early 1680s, one of the couple's sons, John, moved north into Delaware. There, one of his daughters married a local Indian and became part of a triracial community that survives to the present day. The other son, Richard, stayed behind in Virginia. Stripped of the land left him by his parents, he worked as a carpenter and had little to leave his own sons when he died in 1689. Anthony and Mary Johnson's grandchildren in Virginia worked as tenant farmers and servants, laboring on plantations owned by white people.

The Johnson family's story mirrors the plight of many African newcomers in the seventeenth and early eighteenth centuries. During the first few decades of English settlement along the Atlantic coast of North America, slave status and racial boundaries were fluid. Black people born and enslaved in Africa could marry in the young Virginia colony, earn their freedom, farm "myne owne ground," testify in court, and see a son marry a white woman. But after the mid-eighteenth century, new laws eroded Africans' standing and security and eventually defined slavery solely on the basis of race. In Virginia, Maryland, and the Carolinas, a few Africans captured as slaves initially mingled with white indentured servants and eventually obtained their freedom. Now plantation owners—increasingly dependent on the labor of captives from Africa—had a vested interest in consigning black people to lifelong slavery.

As this momentous change transformed the southern colonies, slavery began to take root in the northern colonies as well, though not on the same scale. The institution also emerged along the boundaries of English settlement, in the Spanish and French colonies of Florida and Louisiana. However, the shape and character of these Afro-Spanish and Afro-French societies contrasted sharply with those of the English settlements. Those differences exerted an impact that persists today.

## THE FIRST AFRICANS IN ENGLISH NORTH AMERICA

"Your country? How came it yours? Before the Pilgrims landed we were here." Thus wrote W. E. B. Du Bois, the pioneering black historian and political leader who in 1895 became the first African American to receive a PhD in history at Harvard University. Du Bois posed this question many decades ago, prompted by history textbooks' near total silence on the subject of Africans' contributions to the building of European colonies in North America. As he rightly pointed out, Africans were present at the beginning of almost every European settlement. Probably 75 percent of all who crossed the Atlantic to take up life in the Americas in the three centuries after Columbus's first voyage in 1492 were Africans. In North America, more than half the newcomers were Africans.

By the end of the 1600s, use of African slaves had enabled plantation owners to make whopping profits. The slave trade also catalyzed exchanges of valuable crops, agricultural techniques, and medical knowledge that redefined ways of life not only in the Americas but also in Europe and Africa. During this period, white indentured labor gave way to slave labor in the English colonies, and colonial legislators created laws to sanction, justify, and administer the emerging slave system.

### THE CHESAPEAKE COLONIES

When Anthony Johnson reached Virginia in 1621, he probably met countrymen and women who had arrived in 1619 from the Kongo-Angola region of West Central Africa. Most had been caught in the slave network operating out of

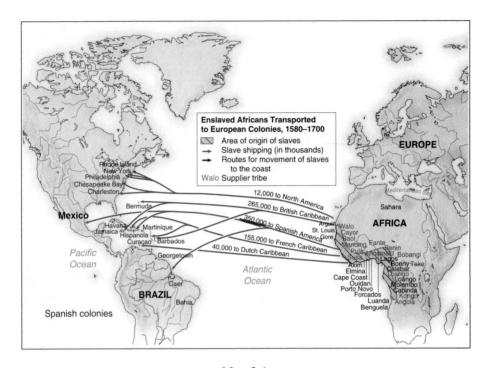

## Map 3.1
### Enslaved Africans Transported to European Colonies, 1580–1700

*This map contrasts the small number of enslaved Africans transported to the North American colonies in the seventeenth century with the number imported to the Caribbean and Spanish America. For example, from 1660 to 1700, about 120,000 Africans arrived in Barbados. During that same time, only about 10,000 came to Maryland and Virginia.*

Luanda, the primary port of Angola, a Portuguese colony in Africa. Luanda shipped about 8,000 slaves across the Atlantic each year. The vast majority were sold in Spanish and Portuguese New World colonies where white settlers had established the plantation system. By 1640, the Spanish had imported at least 335,000 slaves to their colonies in the West Indies and Mexico, while the Portuguese had brought upwards of 215,000 slaves to the coffee and sugar fields of Brazil. Thus, Anthony Johnson was among the handful of Africans forced into North America before the slave trade boomed there.

English plantation owners in Virginia and Maryland, along the Chesapeake Bay, needed field hands to work their tobacco fields. Because they found plenty of white indentured servants and English prisoners eager to contract their labor for passage to the Americas, they had little interest in buying black slaves from Africa. After all, it was much cheaper to transport poor English and Irish laborers in English ships than to purchase enslaved Africans from Portuguese and Dutch slave traders, whose monopoly of the African slave trade allowed them to charge high prices.

By 1650, Virginia's white settlers had weathered early conflicts with Native Americans and had grown to about 18,300 in number—including thousands of white indentured servants. Only about 400 Africans lived in Virginia—a stark contrast to European-African population ratios in the Caribbean and South American colonies. Maryland, England's Catholic colony, also had few Africans. In the Chesapeake region white indentured servants and white convicts planted, weeded, harvested, cured, and packed tobacco.

As late as 1680, when the Chesapeake colonies' populations had swelled to about 57,000 in total, only some 4,600 were slaves (about 8 percent of the population). Despite the boom in tobacco production, indentured white people still made up the majority of the people working the fields.

## THE NORTHERN COLONIES

Anthony and Mary Johnson were among the first of just a few Africans in the English colonies in the early 1600s. But as the century wore on, the number of Africans grew. The Puritans of Massachusetts Bay colony, founded in 1630, first imported Africans in 1637 after enslaving Pequot Indian survivors of the bloody Puritan-Pequot war. Knowing they could not hold the Pequots in slavery in an area the natives knew better than their captors, the Puritans shipped them to Providence Island, off the coast of South America, where Puritan planters had already begun using African slaves. Here, the Massachusetts planters exchanged the captive Indians for Africans.

Even though Massachusetts law books didn't specify slavery terms, buyers expected that Africans brought to the Puritan colony would serve a lifetime in bondage. So did the Rhode Islanders who purchased slaves when they could find them. However, like the Virginians, they employed mainly white indentured servants for most of the seventeenth century. The number of Africans grew slowly in New England, in part because the climate didn't support year-round farming. In addition, most white settlers prized homogeneous Christian communities and had little interest in seeing Africans "do all our business." As late as 1700, slaves made up less than 3 percent of New England's population. Most were domestic laborers in the port towns on the rocky coastline.

Nonetheless, New Englanders did have connections to the slave trade. For example, they supplied grain, flour, wood products, and salted fish to the large slave plantations in the West Indies. Moreover, they constructed and sailed ships to the English-run sugar and tobacco islands, where they dealt in slaves and rum. New Englanders also began consuming slave-produced sugar, coffee, rice, tobacco, and indigo—and prizing these luxuries. Not until the late 1690s did England allow New Englanders to enter the slave trade directly by sailing their ships to Africa's west coast. Nonetheless, New England's economy, almost as much as the Chesapeake's, came to rely on the slave system. By the eighteenth century, many upper-class officials, merchants, and ministers measured their status by the number of slaves they owned.

In the Dutch colony of New Netherlands (later renamed New York by the English) slavery eventually took root more firmly and deeply than it did in seventeenth-century Virginia and Maryland. But at first, some newly arriving Africans had opportunities to build lives based on freedom. For example, Jan Rodrigues—an African probably transported by a Portuguese slaver—was left on Manhattan Island in 1613 by a Dutch ship captain. The first non-Indian resident of the island, Rodrigues learned the Indian language, married a Rockaway woman, and fathered several children. He also initiated trade between the Indians and Europeans, which eventually formed the foundation of the colony the Dutch established eleven years later.

Interest in African slaves intensified as the agricultural families, soldiers, and officials of the Dutch West Indies Company set up farms along the Hudson River. In 1625, the Company purchased sixteen black slaves from pirates who had stolen them from Spanish vessels. Their names—including Paul D'Angola, Simon Congo, Anthony Portuguese, and Anthony Portuguis Gracia—suggest that they had either come from Angola or were captured by Portuguese slavers. The Dutch bought additional captive Africans and set them to work building forts, constructing roads, clearing land, and sawing boards out of trees.

Like Anthony and Mary Johnson, these people were slaves, but not necessarily forever. To be sure, Europeans had begun to consider a person's skin color a mark of slave or free status. However, these Africans with Portuguese names still had opportunities to regain their freedom, accumulate land, and mix with white neighbors. They could also drill with the Dutch militia, sue and be sued in court, and trade independently. Former slave Anthony Jansen van Vaes, for example, took a Dutch wife, joined the Dutch Reformed Church, acquired farmland in Coney Island, and worked as a merchant on Manhattan Island. By 1660, free Afro-Dutch farms were sprinkled along lower Manhattan in the area known today as the Bowery, and a "negro burying ground" served this emerging free black community.

But just as the first Africans in New Netherlands were working their way out of servitude, more and more Africans slated for lifelong bondage began arriving in the colony. By 1650, New Netherlands ranked as the largest slave importation center in North America. The Dutch also moved to control the source of slaves in Africa. In 1637, they captured Castle Elmina, the Portuguese slave trading center on West Africa's Guinea coast, and in the 1640s, they seized Portuguese slaving posts along the coast of present-day Angola and Zaire. Now the Dutch monopolized the flow of slaves up and down Africa's west coast. When the English captured New Netherlands in 1664, one-tenth of the colony's population, and nearly one-quarter of its capital, was African—a far greater black presence than in the Chesapeake.

Small numbers of enslaved Africans arrived in other mid-Atlantic colonies. For example, when the Swedes and Finns established a small colony along the Delaware River in the 1630s, they imported a few Africans. The Dutch seized this colony in 1655 and brought in additional African slaves. After England captured New Netherlands in 1664, English settlers streamed into East Jersey across the Hudson River in search of good land. These settlers included planters from the West Indies island of Barbados seeking larger land holdings, and many brought dozens of slaves with them. They also brought their harsh attitudes

### Table 3.1
### Regional African Population in English America, 1630–1710

*This table reveals that the rate of growth in African populations was four times as high in the southern colonies as in New England. The table also shows that throughout the seventeenth century, slaves in the English colonies lived and worked mostly in the West Indies.*

|      | NEW ENGLAND | MID-ATLANTIC | SOUTH | WEST INDIES | TOTAL | % OF SLAVES IN WEST INDIES |
|------|-------------|--------------|-------|-------------|-------|----------------------------|
| 1630 | —           | 20           | 50    | 10,000      | 10,070 | 99.3 |
| 1650 | 400         | 520          | 700   | 20,000      | 21,620 | 92.5 |
| 1670 | 500         | 800          | 3,400 | 40,000      | 44,700 | 89.5 |
| 1690 | 950         | 2,500        | 13,300 | 90,000     | 106,750 | 84.3 |
| 1710 | 2,600       | 6,200        | 29,000 | 148,000    | 185,800 | 79.6 |

toward slaves, viewing them as chattel no different from horses or oxen. These attitudes soon infected the thinking of European settlers in North America who had not yet seen the harsher slavery practiced in the Caribbean. While Europeans prized the opportunity to acquire land as free men and to control their own labor, they saw no irony in using slave labor to work their land.

In the 1670s, more Europeans came to the mid-Atlantic coast. English, Irish, and German Quakers fleeing religious persecution settled East and West Jersey as well as William Penn's new colony of Pennsylvania. These newcomers found only small numbers of slaves in the Delaware River valley region. But within two years of its founding, Philadelphia became a slave trading and slaveholding hub. When the English slave ship *Isabella* arrived in 1684, 150 dazed Africans staggered ashore. Pioneering Quakers, living in riverbank caves and crude buildings at first, soon put the Africans to work clearing trees and brush, splitting wood and sawing boards, digging house foundations, and laying out streets. In a town comprised of about 800 settlers, these 150 Africans nearly doubled the workforce while relieving white craftsmen of heavy labor.

As members of the Society of Friends, the Quakers followed a "peace testimony" that renounced violence in human affairs. But slave ownership put them in a dilemma: how could they administer physical punishment? One Quaker objected that "Quakers do here handle men" as people in Europe "handle their cattle." And some German Quakers lamented the very nature of slavery and refused to own slaves.

How would the Society of Friends handle an outright slave revolt—the kind that erupted periodically in the English West Indies? Word had already reached Philadelphia of the 1685–1686 revolt in Jamaica, in which slaves had murdered several dozen white people and white authorities had, in retaliation, burned slaves at the stake, had them torn apart by hunting dogs, or ordered them drawn and quartered. In Barbados, too, Quakers learned, slaves had mounted a massive uprising in 1675 and plotted further revolts in 1683 and 1686.

Most Quakers held just one or a few slaves and tried to treat them humanely. Deeply disturbed by antislavery protests, they wrestled with their consciences for many years. But less conscientious Quakers joined other colonists in exploiting black labor, trading beef, wheat, and wood products for slaves, sugar, and rum in the British islands. Gradually, they entrenched themselves in the Atlantic basin human trade network connecting West Africa with the Caribbean and the North American mainland.

# THE FATEFUL TRANSITION

Anthony and Mary Johnson did not live to see what their children witnessed—the emergence of slave societies in which imported Africans performed the majority of field labor. The Johnsons had lived in a place and time in which slavery provided just one of many sources of labor. But their children experienced a pivotal changeover when slavery became the foundation of North America's southern economy—the primary means of producing goods and providing services. In Spanish Mexico, Cuba, and Peru; in Dutch Surinam; in Portuguese Brazil; and in the French Caribbean, European colonists had already seen how consigning Africans to field labor produced cash crops and handsome profits. Soon white planters in North America, inspired by this success, set out to acquire as much land and black muscle as possible.

## ENGLAND CAPTURES THE SLAVE TRADE

The English were the last Europeans to engage in the slave-based plantation system, mostly because they had a late start colonizing the Caribbean. Not until the 1640s did English settlers in Barbados, Jamaica, and the Leeward Islands begin copying their European rivals by purchasing thousands of enslaved Africans, mostly from Dutch ships. Soon they embraced slavery enthusiastically, especially after England's defeat of the Dutch in the commercial wars of 1650–1674 meant that England took over the slave trade itself. As English and New England ship captains brought their human cargoes directly from Africa to British America, Britain's slave population increased exponentially. On tiny Barbados, the population was half European and half African in 1660; two generations later, Africans outnumbered Europeans three to one.

## SOUTH CAROLINA AS A SLAVE SOCIETY

Chartered by the English King Charles II in 1663, South Carolina almost immediately (and to Charles's surprise) became the center of a thriving plantation system. Its first white settlers were well acquainted with slavery. About half came from crowded Barbados, bringing their slaves. For the next two generations, slave-owning English Barbadians controlled South Carolina's politics, commerce, and society. By the early 1700s, these planters relied almost exclusively on slaves to work their rice and indigo plantations. In the eighteenth century, more than half of all enslaved Africans brought to Britain's mainland colonies would flow through Charleston, South Carolina's capital.

Planters wanted slaves with strong backs to do the difficult work of digging ditches and draining the swampy coastal country for rice cultivation. About two-thirds of the Africans they imported were male, most in their teens or early twenties. South Carolinian planters worked these men mercilessly. On average, Africans in this colony died earlier than they did in the Chesapeake. As in the West Indies and Brazil, South Carolina planters treated slaves as replaceable commodities with little regard for how long they lived. The high death rate and need for constant replacements meant that most slaves in this colony had been born in Africa. In the Chesapeake, by contrast, more and more slaves were America-born.

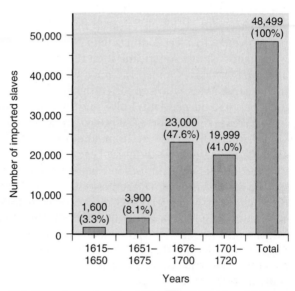

**Figure 3.1**
Number of Slaves Imported from Africa to North America, 1615–1720

*This figure shows the sharp increase in the number of African slaves brought to England's North American colonies after 1675. Births to slaves added to the numbers of those brought from Africa so that by 1720, about 70,000 slaves lived in the English mainland colonies. The numbers suggest that births of slaves greatly outnumbered deaths.*

As the number of slaves rose in South Carolina, the slave system grew harsher. Francis Le Jau, an Anglican missionary, cringed in 1709 to see a slave woman burned alive. Slave masters, he lamented, "hamstring, maim, and unlimb those poor Creatures for small faults." A few years later, South Carolina's legislature sanctioned such grisly punishments and more. A 1714 law made a black person's striking of a white man punishable by death. Other laws permitted retaliations unheard of in other colonies. For example, slave owners could slit the nose or cut the ankle tendons of disobedient slaves.

## BACON'S REBELLION AND SLAVERY IN THE CHESAPEAKE

In 1680, when about 65,000 Africans were laboring in the sugar and coffee fields in the English West Indies, no more than 7,000 slaves toiled in all of England's North American colonies, and in the northern colonies, except where tobacco was cultivated, the number of slaves was small. But in the Chesapeake, the number and proportion of ·slaves increased dramatically after 1680, especially following an uprising by angry, poor white settlers that unwittingly drew the region deeper into slavery. The rebellion started in 1675, when the brash young Nathaniel Bacon, a recent immigrant from England, raised a small army of landless but well-armed poor white people. Mostly former indentured servants, Bacon's followers chafed at their limited opportunities in Virginia's Tidewater region. They were especially enraged that Virginia's governor had closed off frontier settlement to avert conflicts with Native Americans. What began as a frontier war against Native Americans soon turned into a civil war. As free black people and runaway slaves joined the poor white rebels, Bacon's forces turned against planter aristocrats who supported the governor. By the time the violence ebbed, the rebels had burned Jamestown and forced the governor to flee.

Shaken, white planters refrained from recruiting indentured servants, who would eventually secure freedom, and began purchasing slaves, who would constitute a permanent labor force. Fear was not the only driving factor, however. First, economic opportunities in England had improved, so fewer white men and women were venturing to the New World in search of a livelihood. Moreover, those who did come preferred the northern colonies, where terms of servitude were shorter and less harsh than in the Chesapeake. Second, seeking to suppress discontent, Virginia and Maryland clamped down on the shipment of white convicts to the Chesapeake. Finally, just as the supply of indentured servants and convicts in the Chesapeake dwindled, the supply of Africans boomed. England's control of the slave trade caused it to flourish, especially after 1696, when English merchants persuaded Parliament to end the royal monopoly. With hundreds of new merchants now entering the trade, the flow of slaves to North America swelled. And with greater supply, the price of slaves dropped—so southern planters could purchase Africans more easily and cheaply than ever.

## AFRICANS RESIST

As white colonists soon learned, dependence on black labor came at great cost. On a Monday morning in April 1712, white residents of New York awoke to a horrific sight: white bodies bleeding in the streets. Three of the dead were English, three were French, two were Dutch, one was a German, and another was a Walloon (from today's Belgium). Seven others had survived their wounds. The perpetrators were a group of more than twenty Africans who set fire to a building and then lay in wait, with knives and axes, for whites to come extinguish the flames. Some of the attackers were newly arrived African slaves; one was a free black man who claimed mystical powers. "Had it not been for the garrison [of English soldiers] there," reported one New Yorker, "that city would have been reduced to ashes, and the greatest part of the inhabitants murdered."

After quelling the revolt, white New Yorkers took about seventy slaves into custody. They tried forty-three and convicted twenty-five, including three women and several enslaved Indians. Determined to raise the cost of rebellion, white magistrates imposed grisly death penalties: thirteen slaves died on the gallows, three were burned at the stake, one was starved to death in chains, and one was broken on the wheel. Six others killed themselves to escape this kind of retribution.

Though the white leaders hoped to set an example with these punishments, neither they nor the Africans were convinced that fear would suppress revolts.

# Defining Slavery, Defining Race

John Punch stood before Virginia's high court alongside his friends Victor and James Gregory in 1640. Their heads no doubt bowed, the three indentured servants waited anxiously for the judge's decision. They must have suspected that the court would punish them severely for fleeing their Welsh master, Hugh Gwyn, despite their vivid descriptions of his brutality. After escaping, they had managed to reach Maryland, but there they were captured. John Punch, an African; Victor, a Dutchman; and James Gregory, a Scot: they had joined their fates in their escape.

John Punch listened to the bewigged judge read out the sentence: Victor and James were to receive thirty lashes, serve Gwyn an extra year, and then labor three more years for the colony. Next came these astonishing words: "Being a negro . . . John Punch shall serve his said master or his assigns for the time of his natural life here or elsewhere."

John Punch left no testimony revealing his response to being singled out as "a negro." But his unique sentence revealed a profound shift in white people's attitudes toward black people. During the sixteenth and early seventeenth centuries, the English had called Africans and Native Americans "heathens," and Christian tradition had long sanctioned the enslavement of heathen peoples. Until the mid-seventeenth century in Virginia, being a heathen had defined slavery far more than being dark-skinned did.

Yet neither piety nor pigmentation had much to do with a person's ability to cultivate tobacco. So why did Virginia's high court cite John Punch's race to justify handing him a life sentence? Did simple economics lie behind the decision? Was the court acting on behalf of premier planters—seeking to secure Virginia's labor force by converting black servants' transgressions into a lifetime of hard labor? How could Punch have reasoned otherwise, if no other runaway servant had received such a sentence?

A well-known case ten years before Punch's sentencing had made clear that white Virginians viewed Africans as not just different but inferior. In 1630, the court had ordered Hugh Davis, a white man, "to be soundly whipt before an assembly of negroes & others for abusing himself to the dishonor of God and shame of Christianity by defiling his body in lying with a negro which fault he is to acknowledge next sabbath day." By shaming Davis "before negroes and others," the court hoped to stop interracial sex. Social biases were turning into unequal justice. Racial prejudice had begun paving the way for laws defining race-based slavery.

## Laws Defining Social and Racial Relations

The legal decisions in the Punch and Davis cases set precedents defining how people of different races could relate. These precedents eventually influenced how white authorities defined slavery and what kinds of restrictions applied to bondspeople. As Virginia's African population grew slowly between 1640 and 1680, the legislature and courts gradually stripped away their rights and forged the fatal link between slavery and race. Step by step, the terms *English, Christian, white,* and *free* became nearly synonymous in the minds of white colonizers. Meanwhile, the words *African, heathen, black,* and *slave* became equally interchangeable. In gradually associating slavery with race, the English drew from the experience of the West Indies, where English settlers had already worked out definitions of slavery and pieced together a slave code—a comprehensive series of laws regulating the governance of bondspeople.

In Virginia, the slave code developed piecemeal. Race-based punishments and privileges first made their appearance in the 1630 Davis case. Nine years later, white fear of African rebelliousness assumed legal force when the Virginia court ruled that "all persons except Negroes" were to be provided with arms and ammunition for militia duty. Precedents in court rulings and language in legal documents distinguished between white and black, servant and slave. In 1643, the Virginia assembly levied a tax on African women, making it more expensive for Africans to marry, purchase their freedom, and establish independent households. Wills written by white colonists in the 1640s bequeathed Africans and their children "forever."

The earliest Virginian slave owners likely assumed the Africans they imported would serve them for life. But in the 1640s, such assumptions were crystallized in law. As early as 1642, county courts began recording sales of Africans and their children into lifelong bondage to their white owners. In 1660, the legislature implicitly acknowledged the lifelong servitude of Africans when it pinned extra years of indentured servitude on any white servant who ran away with an African— since "Negroes . . . are incapable of making satisfaction by addition of time."

In 1662, the ambiguous legal status of Africans ended. Virginia's House of Burgesses ruled that "all children borne in this country shall be held bond or free only according to the condition of the mother." The legislature passed this law because "some doubts have arisen whether children got by any Englishman upon a negro woman should be slave or free." Here were the two crucial distinctions that set enslavement of Africans throughout the Americas apart from slavery elsewhere in the world: Slave status was lifelong, and it was inherited through enslaved mothers.

While the 1662 law reflected a growing abhorrence of interracial sex, its primary effect was to benefit white slave owners. By declaring that an enslaved black woman's child took the mother's status (the opposite of English legal doctrine in which the child took the father's status), the law ensured that the colony's black labor force would reproduce itself.

Now African women were more vulnerable than ever to white men's sexual exploitation. Every child conceived by a white master, in either a coercive or a consensual relationship with an African woman, added to that labor force—at no extra cost to the master. By extending slave status to the womb, planter-politicians ensured that the *reproductive* as well as *productive* work of black

*The marriage of Anthony and Mary Johnson's black son to an Englishwoman in the mid-seventeenth century occasioned little comment in the historical record. But by 1820, the approximate year this anonymous crude painting was done, interracial sex and interracial violence were seen as two sides of the same coin. Though a new Virginia law forbade interracial marriage in 1691, legal efforts could not stop such relationships.*

women belonged to their master and that a child's paternity had no relevance in the eyes of the law.

Maryland law was much like Virginia's in requiring that "All Negroes" and their children must serve for life. But in 1664, to stop white women from making matches with black men, a new law required that any freeborn white wife of an African slave must serve her husband's master as long as her husband lived and that their children would be enslaved for life. Within decades, nearly every main-land colony had a similar law.

## RESTRICTIONS ON FREE BLACK PEOPLE

These noxious laws may have figured in Mary and Anthony Johnson's decision to move out of Virginia. In 1645, "Anthony the negro" (probably Anthony Johnson) had declared in a Northampton County court: "I know myne owne ground and I will worke when I please and play when I please." But by the 1660s, he would not have been so confident, as new restrictions prevented Africans from acquiring land and intruded on family relations. Mary and Anthony Johnson's new daughter-in-law, wife of their son Richard, was an Englishwoman, but evolving law set out to prohibit such unions. Though nowhere in the Dutch, Spanish, or Portuguese colonies did courts ban interracial marriage, and nowhere else in English America except in Antigua and Bermuda, now courts in Maryland and Virginia—and ultimately more than thirty states—adopted such rulings. These laws remained on the books until as late as the 1970s.

Mary and Anthony Johnson's descendants who remained in Virginia after Anthony's death in 1670 must have felt the impact of Virginia's new restrictions. After 1691, even their marriages were criminalized, as a new law, intended to prevent "that abominable mixture and spurious issue [that is, offspring] . . . by Negroes, mulattoes [mixed-race people] and Indians intermarrying with English or other white women," banished any white man or woman who married an Indian or African person—whether free or enslaved. Like other free black people, the Johnsons' children and grandchildren struggled to navigate around these hardening racial distinctions. Some joined triracial communities in southern Delaware, where Nanticoke Indian, African, and European bloodlines criss-crossed. Others, with white wives or mothers, identified loosely with full-blooded Africans but strove as free, light-skinned Negroes to maintain ties with white neighbors, patrons, and employers.

In basing the definition of slavery on race, Virginia's planters took two additional steps to seal the system. In 1667, the House of Burgesses ruled that "the conferring of baptism doth not alter the condition of the person as to his bondage or freedom." In other words, conversion to Christianity would no longer be an avenue to freedom. Like many black servants who had gained freedom before 1660, Mary and Anthony took Christian vows, baptized their children, and attended church, but now Christian faith offered no protection. The second step came in 1691, when Virginia lawmakers required masters who freed their slaves to transport them out of the colony within six months. This ruling made it clear that only enslaved Africans were welcome in Virginia.

## SOUTH CAROLINA'S SLAVE CODE

South Carolina recognized slavery from the beginning, its Fundamental Constitutions (1669) proclaiming that "every freeman . . . shall have absolute power and authority over Negro slaves, of what opinion or religion soever." Here white planters legislated the most complete deprivation of freedom found in the mainland colonies. South Carolina's slave laws required slaves to carry a pass when traveling on their own away from their owner's plantation. Runaways received brutal punishment—whipping for men for the first offense, branding for the second, mutilation or even castration for the third. Anyone who captured an escaped slave received a reward.

Living among legions of enslaved Africans and Indians, as well as indentured whites, Carolina lawmakers also imposed the death penalty on white servants who ran away with enslaved Africans. This unusual measure reflected planters' fear that cross-color alliances at the bottom rungs of society, such as Bacon's Rebellion in Virginia, might topple the slave system entirely. In 1712, South Carolina brought its scattered laws together in a comprehensive slave code.

Though South Carolina developed the most severe racial code in English North America, the colony displayed a remarkable tolerance for interracial sex between white men and black women specifically. Why? There were few white women in the colony. As on Caribbean islands such as Jamaica and Barbados, South Carolinians accepted sexual relations between white men and enslaved black women as a given, and the rising mulatto population testified to this attitude. But at the same time, South Carolina's lawmakers sought to prevent white women from engaging in sex with black men, consigning any white woman who delivered a child fathered by a black man to seven years' servitude. Her child, if a girl, had to serve eighteen years; if a boy, twenty-one years. To keep white women away from free black men, this 1717 law further provided that any free black father of a child born of a white woman must serve as a slave for seven years. Despite the severity of these laws, South Carolinian legislators never prohibited interracial marriages, nor did they employ the emotionally loaded language used in other colonies, where legal terminology described children of mixed parentage as "abominable mixture," "spurious issue," or "disgrace of the nation."

## SLAVERY AND RACE NORTH OF THE CHESAPEAKE

Black Alice, as she was known, was born in slavery in Philadelphia, in 1686. She died in 1802—at the age of 116—and her story survived not only because of her longevity but because her remarkable character interested white Philadelphians. For forty years she was the toll keeper at Dunk's Ferry on the Delaware River. She herself was a storyteller who, in the tradition of an African *griot*—archivist of a tribe's collective memory—remembered the land on which Philadelphia stood "when it was a wilderness, and when the Indians hunted wild game in the

*Lithographs, paintings, or sketches of Africans in early North America are rare because artists almost always worked by commission. Few black Americans, whether free or slave, could afford to pay for portraits. The visual record of the early black experience is even sketchier than the literary record. This engraving of Black Alice thus provides a unique glimpse into early North American life. At age ninety-six, the redoubtable Black Alice began to lose her eyesight, but her deteriorating vision hardly slowed her down. Frequently she rowed into the middle of the Delaware River "from which she seldom returned without a handsome supply of fish for her master's table."*

woods." She remembered lighting the pipe of William Penn, a slave owner himself. Joining Christ Church, she recalled the first crude sanctuary with ceilings so low "she could reach [them] with her hands from the floor." Until age ninety-five, she rode to church on a horse. "The veneration she had for the bible," claimed one notice after her death, "induced her to lament that she was not able to read it." But when her friends read it to her, she "would listen with great attention, and often make pertinent remarks."

Black Alice's experience was far from typical, but her story reveals the flexible definitions of slavery and race in the northern colonies in this era. Gaining admission to a white Anglican church, working as toll keeper, socializing with important white figures, and winning respect and admiration for her memory of Philadelphia's earliest history, Black Alice had experiences that simply weren't possible in the southern colonies—though she was a slave her entire life.

Unlike Virginia, Maryland, and North and South Carolina, the northern colonies did not make slave labor the main prop of their economy. Nonetheless, white settlers in the North participated eagerly in the African slave trade and created slave codes that remained in force until the American Revolution and beyond.

## SLAVE CODES IN NEW ENGLAND

During the seventeenth century, New Englanders held more enslaved Indians than imported Africans. They never specifically legislated perpetual and hereditary slavery. However, surviving legal documents such as wills show that slave owners regarded their human property as lifelong servants as early as 1641. By at least 1660, many white people living in New England also assumed that children born of slaves would be lifelong slaves themselves.

Yet Africans teetered between extended servitude and lifelong bondage while occupying an indeterminate status between that of property and that of person. Though they associated slavery with African origins, New Englanders gave their bondspeople many privileges that masters in the southern colonies denied them—for example, the right to testify and sue in court, to make contracts, and to bear arms in colonial wars with masters' consent. Northern slaves could also acquire, hold, or transfer property and even petition the legislature for their freedom. Even more significant, slaves working in New England had the right to life: Their masters could not kill them without legal repercussions, as they could in Maryland and Virginia after 1705. New Englanders never passed laws preventing masters from freeing their slaves.

## SLAVERY AND THE LAW IN THE MID-ATLANTIC

The vise of slavery tightened more rapidly around black life in New Netherlands than in the New England colonies, but not nearly as quickly as in Virginia and Maryland. While the Dutch ruled New Netherlands, men who had capital to invest in imported Africans held slaves for life. They also regarded the offspring of enslaved African women as slaves at birth, though no law mandated this condition.

But the legal fog surrounding Africans evaporated when the English conquered New Netherlands in 1664 and named it New York. Within a year, the legislative assembly sanctioned lifelong servitude for black slaves. Another ruling specified that "no Negro slave who becomes a Christian after he had been bought shall be set at liberty." In 1702, after importing substantial numbers of Africans, the English in New York devised a fully developed slave code that stripped away many entitlements slaves had treasured under Dutch rule, including the right to earn money, bear arms, and secure freedom through self-purchase. The English slave code gave masters the right to inflict any punishment they wanted on a slave, short of dismemberment and death. It also outlawed the assembly of more than three slaves without their masters' consent. It prohibited slaves from buying or selling property, and it removed their right to testify in court except when providing evidence against another slave for running away, destroying his or her master's property, or conspiring to revolt.

South of New York, Quakers in Pennsylvania, New Jersey, and Delaware practiced a milder form of slavery than other white colonists did. However, Quakers still feared slave resistance and revolt. Out of this fear came slave codes meant to limit enslaved black peoples' privileges and control their activities. But discrimination was moderated. In the early years, for example, African and European servants received the same penalties for running away, and free black people had equal access to the courts. Nor was interracial sex penalized. To illustrate, Francis Johnson Anthony and Mary Johnson's grandson who moved to Delaware, married a white woman, worked as a free farmer, and, in 1687, sued a white man in court.

Yet even in William Penn's Quaker haven, a slave code slowly took shape, accompanied by discriminatory treatment of free black people. By 1693, Philadelphia forbade slaves from traveling on Sundays without passes from their owners. In 1700, the legislature authorized special courts to try, judge, and convict black persons charged with criminal offenses. Race-based justice made African Americans liable to capital punishment for burglary and to castration for the rape of a white woman—a form of retaliation reserved for them only. In 1725–1726, much later than in other colonies, Pennsylvania passed a comprehensive "act for the better regulation of Negroes." The code placed new restrictions on free African Americans. For example, any free black person convicted of fornication or adultery with a white person could be sold into servitude for seven years.

With rising numbers of Africans in all colonies came laws governing slave behavior and punishment. In general, the higher the proportion of Africans in a particular region, the harsher the code. But codes could not entirely control enslaved Africans. So long as bondsmen and women had the will to resist, slavery remained unstable. White colonists had to constantly negotiate the legal details of the institution as well as continually patrol their human holdings.

## BEYOND ENGLISH BOUNDARIES

Juan Fernandez, a black soldier in the Spanish garrison town of St. Augustine, Florida, awoke one morning in 1586 to see a fleet of twenty heavily armed English ships tacking along the coast. Led by England's famous explorer Francis

Drake, the ships commenced a two-day bombardment of the garrison. Fernandez and other garrison soldiers fled to nearby Indian villages and tried to prevent the English from coming ashore, but in vain. The invaders looted the town, set it aflame, and departed. When the garrison's occupants returned, they found a smoking ruin where St. Augustine had once stood. Determined to persevere, the Spanish and African soldiers rebuilt this small outpost that would plague the English for more than a century, especially when it gained a reputation as a slave sanctuary.

## AFRICANS IN SPANISH AMERICA

By the time of Drake's attack, Africans had lived in Spanish Florida for decades, giving the early Spanish settlements a distinct character. Some Africans were royal slaves, owned by the Spanish king, who put them to work in the garrisons. Others belonged to Spanish settlers. Some had gained freedom in ways not revealed in the historical records. This mixture mirrored Africans' situation in Spain, where Muslim North Africans and black men of the African continent had mingled with the native Spaniards known as Castilians for centuries. In Spain, Castilian law offered many avenues out of slavery, and the Catholic church welcomed Africans.

The character of slavery in Spanish colonies such as Florida has led some historians to see a paradox: Enslaved Africans in autocratically run Spanish colonies seemed to fare better than Africans in English colonies, where white lawmakers emphasized representative government. In Spanish Florida, African slaves did the most backbreaking work—as field laborers, supply train workers, and fort and church builders. Yet they, along with free black men, also served as soldiers, guides, and linguists. Like many Spanish soldiers, black slaves mingled and started families with neighboring Indians so frequently that the Spanish didn't associate slavery with skin color or African heritage in the way that the English did. The Spanish treated slaves more humanely, gave them opportunities for freedom, and permitted freed slaves to become full citizens. Their Catholic priests viewed every slave as a potential soul to be protected and converted, and local officials enforced Catholic protections. Spanish law, inherited from the Romans, defined slaves' rights and masters' obligations. By contrast, the Church of England did not do much to Christianize slaves or demand respect for their souls, and Anglo-Saxon law said nothing on the subject of slavery. Thus English colonists were free to establish slave codes as harsh as they wished. African slaves in England's colonies were at the complete mercy of their masters.

However, unique conditions within the Spanish colonies played just as large a role in shaping slavery as the institutions transported by European settlers from their homelands. Among these conditions, climate, crops, and the size of the slave population had the most decisive impact. In the Caribbean and Latin America, for example, slaves were driven to human limits in the difficult work of cultivating sugar and coffee, which grew only in tropical zones. Also, as slaves vastly outnumbered white settlers, masters treated bondspeople far more harshly than did owners in temperate zones where the white-black ratio was more balanced. Wherever slaves became more numerous than white people, masters' fear of a slave revolt—and their compulsion to crack down on black people—intensified.

But Florida was not quite tropical, and Spanish authorities viewed Florida as a mere outpost on the fringe of Spain's New World empire. Even though St. Augustine recovered from the English assault, its population grew only gradually, and yellow fever in 1649 and smallpox in 1654 claimed numerous African and Spanish lives. Lacking large plantations and the silver and gold mines the Spanish prized, the town was neglected by Spain. Left to their own devices, settlers in Florida established numerous cattle ranches, where some Africans became North America's first black *vaqueros* (cowboys).

After the 1660s, when English sugar planters from Barbados began to acquire land in South Carolina, the slaves they brought with them heard of the freedom Africans enjoyed in Spanish Florida. Catholic St. Augustine, with its massive stone fort and the promise of sanctuary, had a strong appeal. Not surprisingly, the garrison town unnerved English Protestant Carolinians.

Irritated by St. Augustine's presence, the English forged alliances with Indians and began harassing the garrison and surrounding Spanish settlements in the early 1680s. The Spanish governor retaliated in 1686, with a racially mixed militia that included free and enslaved Africans as well as Indians. His strike force even managed to steal several of the Carolina governor's slaves—a particularly humiliating blow. Border warfare between the two colonies raged for years, fueled by a constant flow of Carolinian slaves into Spanish territory. Once they had escaped their masters, many of these slaves requested baptism into the Catholic Church. They knew this sacrament would give them protections and opportunities, such as the right to marry, that the English no longer extended. When in 1693 Spain's King Charles II granted liberty to all enslaved men and women who reached Florida, he set the stage for the formation of a free black community in this Spanish outpost.

Florida grew even more turbulent in 1702, when the War of Spanish Succession (known in North America as Queen Anne's War, after the English queen) erupted in Europe. The English battered the Spanish sanctuary, and South Carolina's governor led a mixed force of Yamasee Indian allies, African slaves, and white settlers to burn St. Augustine for the second time. Two years later, the English destroyed most of the town of Apalachee. These raids devastated the Indian villages and took the lives of many Afro-Spanish, both enslaved and free. The Carolinians also captured some 24,000–50,000 Indians, marched them north to Charleston, and sold them into slavery. Many were shipped to the West Indies and to Boston and other New England towns.

Despite the violence, Africans in English Carolina and Spanish Florida maintained communication, and South Carolina slaves increasingly associated Florida with Catholicism and the freedom and protections it offered. After a triracial Spanish force invaded Charleston in 1706, and former Carolina slaves who had escaped to Florida now attacked the men who had owned them, Carolina slaves were further encouraged to break for freedom. Though Charleston's residents repelled the Spanish assault, they lost slaves to Florida, especially in slave revolts in 1711 and 1714. The next year more slaves defected, joining the Yamasee Indians, South

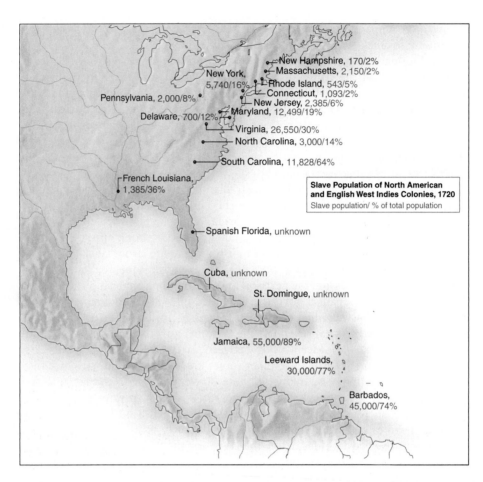

*Map 3.2*
Slave Population of North American and English West Indies Colonies, 1720

*In Virginia and French Louisiana, slaves composed about one-third of the entire population in 1720. In marked contrast, slaves in Jamaica, Barbados, Haiti, and most other West Indian colonies typically made up 75–90 percent of the population.*

Carolina's former allies, in an attack on the English that united remnants of the coastal tribes and the powerful interior nations of Creeks, Choctaws, and Cherokees. Carolina's military leaders found evidence of their presence in the design of an Indian fort that incorporated African defenses. During this Yamasee War, Africans and Native Americans continued a collaboration against white masters that had gone on for years in the borderlands of Spanish Florida and Carolina.

## SLAVERY IN FRENCH COLONIES

While the Spanish quickly incorporated Africans into mission and ranching life in the Southeast, the French settlers who preceded the English in Carolina hardly lasted long enough for Africans to establish a presence there. The small French settlement planted in 1562 near the mouth of St. John's River in Florida crumbled under a Spanish assault three years later. Farther north, in Canada, the French established their main North American base. Initially, they had little use for enslaved Africans because the climate did not support intensive agriculture; their interest was more in fur-trading than raising cash crops. When French explorer Robert de LaSalle canoed through the Great Lakes and down the Mississippi River to its mouth in 1682, the French king claimed for France the vast North American interior stretching from Spanish Florida to the Mississippi River. Hoping to outflank the English colonies—or at least pin them to the Atlantic coast—the French began building trading posts and garrisons in the heart of Indian America. Now they made liberal use of Indian and African slaves to establish settlements in 1699 on the Biloxi and Mobile rivers, which emptied into the Gulf of Mexico east of the Mississippi River.

In 1718, the French stepped up their effort to occupy the immense territory they had claimed, which they called Louisiana. Establishing their capital at New Orleans, members of the French Company of the Indies began building what they envisioned as a tobacco- and indigo-based bonanza port city. In time, they hoped, their presence in New Orleans would enable them to control the vast lower Mississippi Valley. They accomplished this feat of construction almost entirely with coerced labor: 1,900 Africans, some 1,200 *engagés* (criminals emptied from French jails), several thousand indentured servants, fewer than 200 adventurous French settlers, and a garrison of soldiers who held the unlikely mass together.

By 1721, nearly 2,000 black slaves—more than one-fifth of the population—formed the backbone of Louisiana's economy. These skilled rice growers, indigo processors, metalworkers, river navigators, herbalists, and cattle keepers proved indispensable to the French. Like enslaved men in Spanish Florida, African men in Louisiana mingled extensively with Indian women. These couples produced mixed-race children, born into slavery, who were known locally as *grifs*. Few French women ventured to the New World, so many French soldiers had liaisons with enslaved African women.

France's *Code Noir*, introduced in 1724 to regulate the conduct of slavery, forbade interracial marriage. But everyone in Louisiana knew that a law inscribed on the far side of the Atlantic meant little in the wilds of the lower Mississippi. To be sure, Catholic priests did not sanction interracial marriages, but a French man who took a common-law African wife raised no eyebrows in this frontier territory. Moreover, such relations often opened the door to freedom for mixed-race individuals whose white parent, usually the father, did not want his children enslaved. Many Afro-Indian, Franco-Indian, and Afro-French children born into slavery in early Louisiana won their liberty either through manumission or self-purchase. After a decade of colonization, Louisiana was still a lawless frontier zone, but it boasted a more flexible multiracial society than the English colonists had created.

# CONCLUSION

Slavery took only shallow root in the North American English colonies for three-quarters of a century after a Dutch ship delivered a small number of Africans to

Virginia in 1619. In 1637, Massachusetts Puritans traded Pequot captives for Africans enslaved in the West Indies. Because the Dutch controlled the Atlantic slave trade in North America during the mid-seventeenth century, slavery sank particularly deep roots into New Netherlands. But for most of the century, the majority of European settlers in North America satisfied their labor needs with white indentured servants and convicted felons transported from England and Ireland. In the last quarter of the seventeenth century, this pattern shifted, and Europeans began using far more enslaved African workers than indentured white laborers. White planters made this transition in reaction to rebellions instigated by former indentured servants in the Chesapeake and to the dwindling supply of white indentured servants coming from overseas. As European planters resorted increasingly to black labor, the slave-based plantation system began to gather momentum in North America.

From English New York to Spanish Florida and French Louisiana, white people became highly dependent on black slaves by the early eighteenth century. In the northern colonies, that dependence developed more slowly. But no matter where or how quickly slavery took root, this growing dependence redefined the meaning of race. Particularly in the English colonies, skin color determined a person's status as free or slave more than ever before. Most English colonists began considering lifelong servitude the natural condition of black people. They also believed it equally natural that slaves' children should be born into perpetual slavery.

In this new color-coded social system, enslaved black people and their families faced harsh work lives, a degradation of their African heritage, and a violent system of discipline. Most died early, never having escaped bondage. The era when Anthony and Mary Johnson had been free to till their own land, testify in court, and marry as they wished—to "know myne owne ground and . . . work . . . and play when I please"—had all but ended by the 1720s. A cruel new chapter had opened for Africans in North America. As the eighteenth century wore on, blacks had to find new ways to survive and to craft lives of dignity, pride, and hope.

# 4

## AFRICANS IN BONDAGE: EARLY EIGHTEENTH CENTURY TO THE AMERICAN REVOLUTION

### VENTURE SMITH DEFIES THE COLONIAL SLAVE SYSTEM

Eight-year-old Broteer was the son of a king. His world collapsed in 1736 when Bambara slave raiders captured all the members of his village in Anamaboe, Guinea. The raiders killed Broteer's father and then marched the boy, along with the other villagers, to the coast. When a slaver from Rhode Island arrived to pick up the human cargo, Broteer's captors sold him to the ship's steward for "four gallons of rum and a piece of calico." The steward renamed the boy Venture, "having purchased me with his own private venture." The steward intended to sell the youngster for a profit as soon as the ship returned to North America.

Arriving in New England by way of Barbados, Venture was purchased by a Connecticut farmer who gave him his surname—Smith. The farmer promptly set the boy to work combing sheep's wool for spinning, pounding corn for poultry feed, and carrying out household tasks. "My behavior had as yet been submissive and obedient," Smith related many years later. Then, at age nine, he reported, "I began to have hard tasks imposed on me . . . or be rigorously punished."

Smith grew tall and strong in his teens, and began chafing against slave life. He found his master's son James particularly galling. James "came up to me . . . big with authority" and "would order me to do *this* business and *that* business different from what my master had directed me." Tempers flared. When James flew into a rage and attacked Smith with a pitchfork, the young African defended himself and pummeled the white boy until he burst into tears.

By age twenty-two, Venture Smith was a giant by eighteenth-century standards. Over six feet tall and weighing 250 pounds, he built a reputation as a prodigious worker with amazing strength. By day, he labored as a carpenter and farmhand. By night, he worked for himself, catching and selling game and fish with an eye toward purchasing his way out of slavery some day. Shortly after marrying Meg, another African slave, Smith made a break for freedom. Accompanied by three white indentured servants, he stole a boat and provisions from his master's home. The fugitives rowed across Long Island Sound for New York territory. But when one of the indentured servants ran off with the provisions, Smith returned to his master. As frequently happened with runaway slaves, his owner put him up for sale. Fortunately, his new Connecticut master, Thomas Stanton, soon purchased Smith's wife and their baby girl.

Then a battle of wills broke out between Meg and Stanton's wife. In a heated argument, Meg stood her ground and ignored her husband's pleas to apologize "for the sake of peace." When the mistress turned her whip on Smith, he hurled it into the fireplace. At first the master seemed to take no notice of the incident, but "some days after, . . . in the morning as I was putting on a log in the fireplace, not suspecting harm from anyone, I received a most violent stroke on the crown of my head with a club two feet long and as large around as a chair post." Staggering to his feet, the strapping slave threw his master to the ground and dragged him out of the house.

Smith thought himself unjustly attacked and fled to a local justice of the peace to plead his case. The justice "advised me to return to my master, and live contented with him till he abused me again, and then complain." Smith complied, but on the way home he was attacked by Stanton and his brother. The muscular Smith overpowered both men. "I became enraged," Smith recounted, "turned them both under me, laid one of them across the other, and stamped both with my feet." Soon the town constable arrived to restrain Smith, and the local blacksmith fitted the slave with ankle and wrist shackles. When his master threatened to sell Smith to the West Indies—a fate most slaves dreaded—Smith replied, "I crossed the waters to come here, and I am willing to cross them to return."

Venture Smith's owner now knew he could never break this African's will and sold him to a man who sold him again. Smith toiled for this latest master for five years, working on his own time to save money coin by coin. Finally, thirty-six years old, enslaved for twenty-eight, he purchased his freedom. But his wife, daughter, and now two sons remained in bondage, and Smith worked furiously to purchase them, too. "In four years, I cut several thousand cords of wood . . . I raised watermelons, and performed many other singular labors," he recalled. Described as a black Paul Bunyan "who swung his axe to break his chains," Smith "shunned all kind of luxuries" and "bought nothing that I absolutely did not want." By 1768, he had purchased his sons out of slavery and later managed to free his daughter. Another five years passed before he could purchase Meg.

## *Chronology*

**1720s–1730s** Number of African slaves imported to southern colonies soars.

**1720s–1740s** The Great Awakening attracts many slaves to Christianity.

**1728** Runaway slaves form a community near Lexington, Virginia.

**1729** Enslaved Africans join Natchez Indians in an uprising against the French in Louisiana.

**1733** Founding of Georgia, which initially bans slavery but allows it after 1750.

**1736** Venture Smith is captured in Guinea and sold in New England.

**1738** Runaway South Carolina slaves establish as sanctuary called Fort Mose.

**1739** White militia puts down Stono Rebellion of South Carolina slaves.

**1741** A slave conspiracy in New York City ends in multiple executions.

**1753** John Woolman writes *Some Considerations on the Keeping of Negroes.*

**1756** Olaudah Equiano reaches North America and is sold to a master in Virginia.

**1756–1763** The Seven Years' War catalyzes importations of Africans to northern colonies.

**1763** Treaty of Paris ends the Seven Years' War.

Francisco Menéndez leads free Spanish black people to Cuba.

**1764** Venture Smith purchases his freedom.

**1766** Olaudah Equiano purchases his freedom.

---

By the eve of the American Revolution, Smith had a farm, a house, a second dwelling on Long Island, and cash savings. As the war raged around him, he owned and managed a fleet of some twenty small coastal vessels that sold cordwood, fish, and garden produce along the shores of Long Island Sound. One of Smith's sons fought the British in the American Revolution.

Venture Smith was one of about 255,000 slaves to arrive in North America's English colonies between 1700 and 1775, the year the American Revolution broke out. This influx dwarfed the 28,000 slaves who arrived in the seventeenth century. Colonial slavery had reached its peak.

The struggle to survive the system of slavery, itself still in the process of formation, was a great test of human endurance. While liberty-loving European settlers paradoxically constructed law codes, social rules, and attitudes designed to deprive Africans and their descendants of freedom, black slaves did not simply accept enslavement. They made the terms of their bondage a matter of negotiation, defying the system in a continual series of abrasive and often violent encounters with their masters and mistresses.

Slavery took many forms in different English colonies and in the Spanish- and French-controlled regions of North America. Yet no matter its shape, the interactions between masters and slaves led to a gradual merging of African and European cultures. By this process, Africans in America became African Americans, while Euro-Americans adopted elements of African culture.

Embedded within their story is a subplot featuring individuals such as Venture Smith, who worked their way out of bondage and inspired hope in the hearts of those still enslaved. Only a tiny fraction of all black Americans achieved what Smith did in this era. But they had allies: a handful of white abolitionists whose voices gathered strength by the 1770s.

# COLONIAL SLAVERY AT HIGH TIDE

A year after reaching Virginia in 1756, Olaudah Equiano, the much-traveled slave autobiographer, had some good fortune: his Virginia master sold him to an English ship captain who later sold him to a merchant in Montserrat, English West Indies. Traveling as a shipboard slave between Caribbean ports and North American settlements, Equiano saw how slavery functioned differently in various English colonies. In the West Indies and in southern ports, he observed colonial societies that in a single generation made slavery the key to producing goods and services and measuring wealth. In Philadelphia and other northern ports, he saw societies in which slavery was one of many forms of labor and not necessarily a mark of social status for white people. Equiano thus had a broad perspective on the workings of the entire cross-Atlantic economy.

## A RISING SLAVE POPULATION

After Virginia and Maryland's planters replaced white indentured servants with African slave labor in the late seventeenth century, the composition of North America's population shifted dramatically. When some 75,000 slaves, almost all coming directly from Africa, reached the Chesapeake colonies between 1700 and 1750, the agricultural and domestic labor force became mostly black. In 1736, one of Virginia's largest planters already worried that his neighbors "import so many Negroes hither that I fear this colony will be confirmed by the name of New Guinea"—referring to the African region where many of Virginia's slaves originated.

In the Lower South—Georgia and South Carolina—slave importations soared after 1710. By the 1730s, field labor became overwhelmingly black in this region. Almost half of all slaves arriving in the English colonies after 1700 first saw land at Sullivan's Island, a quarantine station in Charleston harbor that has been called the Ellis Island of black America. In 1737, one Swiss newcomer traveling through South Carolina thought the colony "looks more like a negro country than like a country settled by white people."

Georgia, founded by British philanthropists in 1733, followed this pattern, though unexpectedly. Launching the colony as an experiment in settling poor English men and women on small plots of land, Georgia's founders banned slavery. But in 1750, at the insistence of the white settlers there, the colony's trustees abandoned their initial vision and permitted slavery. Now wealthy investors purchased large tracts of land and imported shiploads of Africans. By the time the American Revolution broke out, black slaves in Georgia outnumbered the white settlers.

The slaves flooding into the southern colonies originated in many parts of West and Central Africa. A small number came from Madagascar, an island off Africa's southeast coast. But southern planters were particular about the human merchandise they purchased. Moreover, they held strong—if often misinformed—opinions about which Africans were the best. Equiano claimed that West Indian planters prized "the slaves of Benin or Eboe [Ibo] to those of any other part of Guinea, for their hardiness, intelligence, integrity, and zeal." In Virginia, where Iboes like Equiano made up the largest ethnic group, slave owners echoed this sentiment. But slave buyers in South Carolina and Georgia disdained Iboes as despondent and suicidal. In the punishing climate of the Carolina low country, planters preferred Kongolese, Angolan, and Senegambian people from West Central Africa, many of whom had cultivated rice back home. These slave owners imported roughly three men for every two women, and they especially valued young, strong, and healthy males.

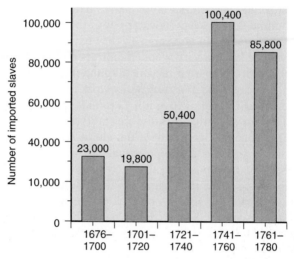

**Figure 4.1**

Importation of Slaves to North America, 1676–1780

*Between 1701 and 1780, ship captains transported about 256,000 slaves directly from Africa to colonial ports, especially Savannah, Charleston, Philadelphia, New York, Newport, and Boston. After the Declaration of Independence was signed in 1776, most states banned the importation of Africans, thus lowering the number of incoming Africans in the 1770s. The disruption of seaborne traffic during the American Revolution further reduced these numbers. But after the war, slavers resumed the traffic, carrying as many as 100,000 slaves to South Carolina and Georgia between 1783 and 1808.*

## SLAVE LIFE IN THE SOUTH

By the early eighteenth century, slavery was embedded in England's southern colonies. Slave importations rivaled those in the West Indies. On South Carolina's coastal lowlands, slave importations and rice cultivation expanded together. Planters in the tidal floodplain relied on African slaves' knowledge about growing rice in such a region. Much of this "African knowledge system," as one geographer has called it, resided within women, who in Africa did most of the sowing and winnowing of rice. Though black families in Africa celebrated rice planting as a time of renewal and promise, rice cultivation in South Carolina—where the whip ruled the fields—meant just another cycle of misery and sickness.

Unlike cultivating wheat or corn in the North, growing rice demanded back-breaking, year-round labor. Slaves had to clear the swampy lowlands in winter, build dykes to keep seawater out of the fields, and plant rice in shallow trenches in the spring. In late summer, they harvested the crop. In the fall, they pounded the rice kernels with wooden mortars and pestles. Come wintertime, they turned the soil to prepare it for a new round of planting.

Rice "is the most unhealthy work in which the slaves were employed," wrote one English visitor to South Carolina, "and they sank under it in great numbers. The causes of this dreadful mortality are the constant moisture and heat of the atmosphere, together with the alternate floodings and dryings of the fields, on which the negroes are perpetually at work, often ankle deep in mud, with their bare heads exposed to the fierce rays of the sun." One-quarter of the Africans imported to the low country in the first half of the eighteenth century died within a year of their arrival—victims of overwork, inadequate nutrition, and respiratory disease. Still, their labor made their owners rich: By the late 1760s, white South Carolina planters were exporting more than 60 million pounds of rice annually.

As South Carolinian planters stepped up rice cultivation, they imported ever larger numbers of Africans. Advertisements regularly announced new arrivals: "A choice cargo of about 250 fine healthy NEGROES just arrived from the Windward & Rice Coast," proclaimed one. Owing to heavy importations, one-third of the slaves in South Carolina were African-born, and they maintained a feeling of close connection to Africa. One visitor to the Carolina low country in 1740 noticed the "many various ages, nations, [and] languages" among the "whole body of slaves"—suggesting that many still spoke their native languages.

In the Chesapeake colonies of Virginia and Maryland, as slave importations grew, Africans also retained native languages. And as masters strived for ever higher tobacco profits, the slaves' working and living conditions worsened. Their workdays were lengthened and their holidays reduced to just three (Christmas, Easter, and Pentecost—the Christian holy day commemorating the descent of the Holy Spirit on the apostles). Whereas masters had previously let slaves rest a bit during the winter, now they ordered them to grind corn, clear stumps, and chop wood in the cold months. They also imposed stricter supervision, cracking the whip and applying the branding iron with more severity than ever.

By the time Equiano arrived in 1756, Virginia had more North American-born than African-born slaves. As large plantations edged out small farms, slaves began living in larger groups, where they found marriage partners more easily, created families, and built the extended kin networks. These factors triggered a natural population increase. By the late colonial period, slaves had ties of kinship and friendship that crisscrossed the countryside, causing southern planters to complain of the "continual concourse of Negroes on Sabbath and holy days meeting in great numbers."

Births in Chesapeake slave families gradually evened out the gender imbalance in slave imports. At the same time, the increase in North American-born slaves gave white planters less reason to import new captives fresh from Africa. Because a more gender-balanced population provided greater opportunity for early marriages, Virginia-born slave women bore children at younger ages than their African-born mothers had. Families thus grew larger. By the 1770s, Virginia's slave population was expanding at the rate of 5,000 per year, but only about 500 to 800 were arriving from Africa. The rest of the increase came from American-born slaves' fertility and the rising ratio of slave births over slave deaths.

In the southern colonies overall, slave fertility exceeded that in the British West Indies. White Caribbean planters imported five times as many slaves in the colonial era as white people in the mainland southern colonies did, yet on the eve of the American Revolution slave numbers in the two regions were roughly the same. In the islands, the brutal sugar work regimen extinguished lives quickly. In the southern colonies, by contrast, there were more than 400,000 slaves by 1770—a whopping increase over the 13,000 slaves in the region just eighty years earlier.

Eighteenth-century plantations were small worlds in themselves. In addition to field hands and house servants, they required the labor of carpenters, black-smiths, bricklayers, weavers, coopers (barrelmakers), butchers, and leatherwork-ers. The male slaves who acquired these artisan skills were highly valued and al-lowed to move around more freely—from home to workshop, plantation to

*This depiction of conical-roofed houses at Mulberry Plantation in South Carolina shows that Africans often built their own living quarters based on designs they knew from their West African home villages. Slave housing improved during the eighteenth century, as sex-segregated barracks gave way to family cabins on many plantations.*

town, warehouse to wharf—than field slaves could. Those who drove wag-onloads of crops to river landings and piloted tobacco- and rice-laden rafts and boats through the inland waterways of the coastal South spent much of their time away from the plantation.

The experience of these slaves resembled that of urban bondspeople, many of whom were also skilled artisans and shopworkers. In visits to Charleston and Savannah, Equiano saw slave women selling goods from street carts and pur-chasing food for the kitchens they ran in their white masters' homes. Most urban slaves had easier lives than plantation slaves because they were spared back-breaking field labor. However, their isolation in white households made it harder for them to form families and friendships with other slaves.

Most bondsmen and -women in the southern colonies labored in the fields. Nearly every black woman on a small farm or large plantation wielded a hoe and sickle as well as tended and butchered livestock, cultivated vegetable gardens, and took care of dairy cows. Slave women who worked in the houses of their masters had a more diverse work routine. They attended the births of the mas-ter's children and fed, suckled, and bathed his infants. As the children grew, slave women rocked them to sleep and supervised their play. They also washed, mended, and ironed clothes; cooked, baked, and canned; served meals and washed up afterward; and spun, wove, and stitched clothing.

## SEXUAL OPPRESSION

Whether in the fields or the master's household, slave women lived under the constant threat of sexual aggression by white men. The rape of an enslaved black woman probably constituted the most destructive means of control in the mas-ter's arsenal. In raping black women, white men also asserted their power over black men. Indeed, to demonstrate their dominance, some white slave owners forced black men to witness their assault on a wife, sister, or daughter. The pain stemming from these attacks disrupted black families and inflicted permanent emotional scars not only on the victims but on all who cared about them.

Interracial rape was the purview of white men. Few black men were accused of raping white women. Indeed, most sexual unions between white women and black men were consensual. Though laws forbade white-black marriages, the scores of white women dragged into court for bearing mulatto children testified to their willingness to choose a black mate.

Some sexual relationships between white men and black women were also consensual. For example, a slave woman might agree to have sex with a white man to gain advantages for herself or her children. In some cases, these relation-ships endured for many decades, but affection was rare. Moreover, these rela-tionships, consensual or not, spawned excruciating tensions among both black and white people. They reinforced the dependency of black women on white men and were a painful reminder that black men had little power or worth in the so-ciety. The aggressions of white men also put their wives in a painful position, en-during silently their husbands' adulterous relations with slaves. When such unions produced children, these youngsters suffered as well. They lived in a kind of social no-man's land. The law said they were slaves because their mothers were slaves. Yet some had the affection of their white fathers. Others received favorable work assignments and their freedom on reaching adulthood. But despite these advantages, they rarely found acceptance in white society.

## SLAVE LIFE IN THE NORTH

North of the Chesapeake, Africans made up only about 5 percent of the population. Still, slave importations directly from Africa continued, increasing the northern black population from 9,000 in 1710 to 32,000 in 1750. When the Seven Years' War (1756–1763) cut off the supply of white indentured servants from Ireland and Germany, it created a labor vacuum that northerners gladly filled with even more African slaves. Their numbers swelled to about 50,000 by 1770.

Like Venture Smith, most slaves in New England and the mid-Atlantic colonies had work lives characterized by variety and seasonal rhythms. Many black men and women also possessed a range of valuable skills—from farming, woodworking, and seafaring to cargo transporting, cattle tending, and cooking. Indeed, numerous slave advertisements spoke of a black man who could "turn his hand at many sorts of trades" or was "fit for town and country." A large

*Venture Smith died in 1805 at age seventy-nine. Four pallbearers struggled to hoist the coffin containing this giant man of more than 250 pounds. Stories about Smith's prodigious strength circulated around Connecticut for years after his death. One man recalled that "a noted wrestler tried his skill in wrestling with Venture but found he might as well try to remove a tree."*

number of black people mingled with white indentured servants and wage labor-ers and hired out their free time to labor for others. Many were sold from master to master, often gaining new skills. In northern cities, most wealthy households had at least one slave. By 1770, nearly one-quarter of white householders in Philadelphia and New York owned slaves—about the same proportion as in North Carolina. Even families only recently advancing to the middle class, such as Benjamin Franklin's, bought slaves to handle domestic chores.

Slaves in the North had easier work lives than those in the South, mostly be-cause the northern climate did not permit year-round farming. But these more tolerable work lives came at the cost of family life. Like Venture Smith, most slaves ate, slept, and lived in their owner's home because slave quarters were un-necessary. Thus slaves lacked the after-sundown privacy, away from the master's watchful eye, that southern slaves prized. Northern slaves were often the only slave in a household, so they were isolated and lacked the sense of community southern slaves treasured. An excess of black men over women prevented many from forming families. Only in Rhode Island's Narragansett area and in New York's Kings and Queens Counties, where dozens of slaves worked large farms, did the black population prove dense enough for slaves to construct durable, ex-tended kin groups. Elsewhere, slaves formed so-called abroad marriages, in which husbands and wives lived in different white households and only occasion-ally spent time together. The children of such marriages were often sold away from their mother at an early age.

African Americans in the North mingled more closely with white people than did slaves in the South. In streets, churches, and taverns, and along ocean-side wharves and river-ferry landings, black and white peoples encountered one another every day as they went about their business. In many households, black slaves took their meals with white masters. One Englishwoman traveling in Connecticut marveled that masters allowed slaves "to sit at table with them (as they say to save time), and into the dish goes the black hoof as freely as the white hand." Yet despite these advantages, many northern slaves endured brutal treat-ment by masters and unequal treatment under the law.

More rapidly than in the South, black northerners became part of the wider emerging American culture. Encompassing English, Dutch, German, Scots, and Scots-Irish elements, this culture had a rich variety not seen in the South. Black people and Europeans borrowed from and adapted one another's practice of medicine and other knowledge. A notable example was the West African knowl-edge of smallpox inoculation, which a slave of Boston's eminent minister, Cotton Mather, demonstrated for his master. The practice spread quickly, and within a single generation, smallpox was no longer a dreaded epidemic.

Though northern colonists had relatively few slaves, they had strong ties to slavery. New England ship captains transported a large portion of the Africans brought to North America. New Englanders built and manned these ships. In them northern merchants sent fish, meat, and grain to feed the huge West Indies slave population; brought back molasses, which they distilled into rum; and shipped the rum to Africa, where they exchanged it for slaves whom they sold in the West Indies or North America. New Englanders consumed slave-produced

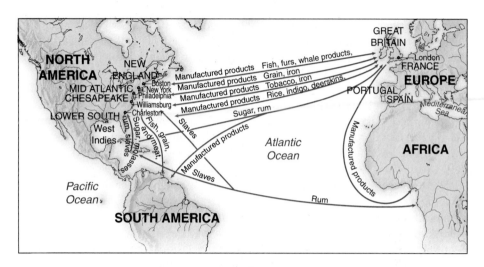

**Map 4.1**
The Commercial Triangle

*Southern colonists had the most extensive daily interactions with slaves, yet northern colonists acquired the most experience in doing business with slave traders in Africa and slave-owning merchants and planters in the West Indies.*

sugar, coffee, rice, and tobacco; they dyed their clothing with slave-produced indigo. It is fair to say that most northern colonists participated in or benefited from slavery directly or indirectly.

## NEGOTIATED BONDAGE

According to white colonists' law books, Africans brought to the colonies in chains had no power. But the day-to-day realities of living with the people they enslaved forced slave owners to admit that absolute control over other humans was impossible. Of this Venture Smith's masters had no doubt. When one of his masters tried to sell Smith to William Hooker of Hartford, Smith said he would refuse to go to northern New York with his new owner. "If you will go by no other measures," Hooker warned, "I will tie you down in my sleigh." Undaunted, Smith replied "that if he carried me in that manner, no person would purchase me, for it would be thought that he had a murderer for sale." That ended the potential sale. "After this he tried no more, and said he would not have me as a gift."

Europeans rationalized their involvement in slavery by maintaining that Africans were subhuman heathens intended to be beasts of burden. To that end, owners sought to convert slaves into mindless drudges who obeyed every command, worked efficiently for the master's profit, and accepted their lowly status. Slave owners used law, terror, torture, and, ultimately, the control of life and death over slaves to preserve this power imbalance. Yet masters never achieved absolute control. Not every slave had Smith's physical strength or defiance, but every master knew that slaves were volatile property. They always had to take into account what a slave might or might not do. Sometimes it was easier to compromise than to insist on total obedience. Slave advertisements give glimpses into this reality: "The cause of his being sold," explained one, "is that he is not inclined to farming."

Slave and master were bound in intimate interdependence. Masters could set the boundaries of the slave's existence—defining physical location, work roles, rations, and shelter. But slave owners depended on slaves to plant, tend, and harvest, to construct buildings, and to care for children. Practical owners knew that if they pushed slaves too far, the work simply would not get done, or not get done right.

In addition, masters had limited power over precisely how slaves did their work. Unless an owner wanted to monitor a slave's every action, he had to accept that the slave would make his or her own decisions about how to approach a task. Nor did masters have much say over whether and how slaves made friends, fell in love, formed kin groups, raised children, worshiped, buried their dead, and spent their scant leisure time.

## RESISTING SLAVERY

Slave owners anticipated resistance from the moment African captives stepped foot on American soil. Most white people agreed that newly imported slaves, known as saltwater Africans, were far more dangerous than "country-born" slaves. "If he must be broke, either from obstinacy, or ... from greatness of soul, [it] will require ... hard discipline," wrote one North Carolina planter. "You would really be surprised at their perseverance ... they often die before they can be conquered." Many also escaped on arrival, as newspaper advertisements testify.

Resistance and the threat of violence pervaded the master-slave relationship. "When you make men slaves, you compel them to live with you in a state of war," wrote Olaudah Equiano. Every slave owner knew this. Surely all who owned Venture Smith dared not relax. One Maryland planter claimed he had "never known a single instance of a negro being contented in slavery." A German minister acknowledged that slaves were "always on the point of rebellion." In every slave-owning region of North America, some bondsmen and women murdered their masters. Such killings kept white people on edge as long as slavery existed.

## CONTESTING LABOR

Labor was the core of the slave's existence. Because their survival—as well as their dignity and self-respect—depended on work, slaves strove to perform their duties on their own terms. They controlled what they could, practicing African work habits in New World fields. For example, they preferred team to individual work and drew on homeland knowledge of rice cultivation to work in familiar ways that made their lives more bearable. All the while, they devised strategies for defying their master's authority. By shamming sickness, breaking hoes, drop-ping dishes, dragging out a job, pretending ignorance, uprooting freshly planted seedlings, and harvesting carelessly, they foiled their master's purpose. A Virginia planter despaired, "I find it almost impossible to make a negro do his work well. No orders can engage it, no encouragement persuade it, nor no punishment oblige it."

In this contest of wills, some masters treated their slaves leniently; others ap-plied the lash with increasing frustration. Slave owners knew that one way to maintain discipline was through terror and torture—legalized flogging, branding, burning, amputation of limbs, and murder. But they also knew that, pushed too hard, slaves would strike back. In 1732, the *South Carolina Gazette* reported "Mr. James Gray worked his Negroes late in his Barn at Night, and the next Morning before Day, hurried them out again, and when they came to it, found it burnt down to the Ground, and all that was in it." A decade later in Caroline County, Virginia, a slave named Phill torched his master's home, corn house, and tobacco house. Though Virginian legislators made arson a capital crime, they could not prevent it.

Savvy masters realized they could get the most out of their human chattel by sharing power. Some owners along the rice coast of South Carolina and Georgia used the tasking system, assigning slaves specific tasks—such as so many bas-kets of rice to thresh—and then allowing them to do what they wanted when they finished. Masters liked the tasking system because it gave slaves an incen-tive to get the work done. Slaves liked it because it permitted them some control over their lives.

Most slaves used any leisure to their advantage. They cultivated garden plots and kept poultry that enriched their diets. Some also traveled to towns and neighboring plantations to market their produce. Eventually, they created their own economy within the master's economy. They saved coins to buy small things or, in rare cases, to purchase their freedom. Owners recognized that slaves who had the right to produce for themselves and barter what they made were less likely to run away. From the slaves' perspective, the arrangement allowed com-panionship and some measure of satisfaction.

Sometimes slaves pilfered chickens, livestock, crops, or tools from their mas-ters and sold the stolen goods in underground market systems spread over con-siderable distances. Domestic slaves took advantage of their station to pinch liquor and pocket household items. Most slaves saw no sin at all in taking crops they had planted, raised, and harvested, even if their master called it stealing. Most masters kept the peace by looking the other way.

## CREATING FAMILY TIES

In the master's view, slave family life was theoretically impossible because alle-giance was supposed to run in only one direction: from slave to master. To that end, the majority of colonies prohibited marriage contracts between slaves. Yet masters also knew that slaves who forged family ties might have children, thus increasing the owner's wealth at no additional investment. As Thomas Jefferson put it, "A woman who brings a child every two years [is] more profitable than the best man on the farm, [for] what she produces is an addition to the capital, while his labor disappears in mere consumption." (When grown, a male slave was typically worth $1,000 in today's currency.) In addition to the profitability of slave families, owners also valued the power of family ties to keep slaves from fleeing. Thus many masters struck bargains with slaves regarding domestic life.

But such bargains always involved tension, especially when slave owners contemplated auctioning members of slave families. Often, slaves were sold after an owner's death to fulfill the terms of the deceased person's will. Aware that shattered families made for unhappy, recalcitrant slaves, a new owner might agree to let slave husbands visit "abroad" wives and children. Refusal could provoke flight, as a slave advertisement from South Carolina in 1749 reveals: Cuffee's escape, said the announcement, was "occasion'd by his Wife and Child's being sold from him." A generation later, not even a spiky iron collar could keep a slave woman named Patt from escaping to find her husband, to whom "she [was] very much attached."

## RUNNING AWAY

For most slaves, running away offered the best hope of resistance. Colonial newspapers recorded thousands of runaway cases, posting notices of fleeing slaves and offering rewards for their capture. Runaway-slave advertisements tell a vivid story about people who used their linguistic skills and knowledge of a region's geography to seize freedom. For example, when twenty-three-year-old Joe, a mixed-race Philadelphia slave, fled his master in 1762, he reinvented himself as Joseph Boudron—because a free black needed a full first name and a distinctive surname. He "speaks good English, French, Spanish, and Portuguese," read the advertisement announcing his escape. Boudron also knew his way around. Born in Guadalupe, a French sugar island in the West Indies, he had already lived in Charleston, South Carolina, and New York—where his Philadelphia master thought he was headed. "A good cook and much used to the Seas," Boudron could pose as a free black mariner or chef.

Many runaway slaves disguised themselves to increase their chances. Some impersonated Native Americans. In 1751, Tom, a thirty-seven-year-old mulatto in East New Jersey, cut his coat short to make Indian stockings, lopped off his hair, and searched for a blanket "to pass for an Indian." He then headed for a Susquehannah Indian village where the German Moravian sect in Pennsylvania had established a mission.

Some slaves ran away knowing they would return, often voluntarily; they just needed the comfort of a loved one, relief from a heartless overseer, or a few days in the woods on their own. But most runaways set out for permanent freedom. Men fled far more often than women, who felt tied to their places of captivity by their children. Yet many women escaped, too, sometimes while pregnant or with small children in their arms.

In the southern colonies, most runaways were recaptured and returned to their owners. A slave had to make it as far north as Philadelphia to find sanctuary in communities formed by freed slaves. A few settlements of escaped slaves survived briefly in the Carolinas and the Chesapeake. At one, near present-day Lexington, Virginia, in 1728, runaway slaves built a small village of huts resembling those they had known in Africa and formed a government under a chief whose father had been a king. But these communities did not last long, as masters were determined to root them out. In a region where there were only one or two free Africans for every hundred slaves, it was next to impossible to masquerade as a free person indefinitely.

Masters did everything they could to discourage slaves from running away. Some chopped off the toes of repeat offenders or hobbled them with heavy ankle chains and iron collars. Others branded and flogged recaptured runaways and punished their families. The first African Equiano saw in Virginia was a woman punished for running away with a lock on her mouth, "so fast that she could scarcely speak; and could not eat nor drink. I was much astonished and shocked at this contrivance, which I afterwards learned was called the iron muzzle." Though such treatment might discourage individuals, it could not vanquish the collective will for freedom.

## REBELLING

For bondspeople, organized revolt was the highest form of resistance. The largest slave uprising in the colonies erupted in 1730 in Virginia's Tidewater. Some 300 slaves, after choosing "officers to command them," fled to the Dismal Swamp "where they commit[ted] many outrages against the [white] Christians." With the aid of local Pasquotank Indians, white Virginians suppressed the insurrection and hanged twenty-nine of the rebels.

Nine years later, an uprising known as the Stono Rebellion broke out in South Carolina. About twenty slaves along the Stono River southwest of Charleston—most newly arrived from Angola or Kongo—seized weapons from their masters. They killed several white people and headed for Florida, where they hoped to find refuge among the Spanish, as handfuls of slaves had done for years. Raising banners and marching to a stirring drumbeat, they burned and plundered plantations as they went. Attracting additional slaves, the small army swelled to about a hundred. But the colonial militia intercepted them and, with Indian assistance, defeated them in a pitched battle. Thirty slaves lost their lives. Shaken, South Carolina's legislature halted imports of Africans for several years and restricted slaves' use of passes. Yet punishments could not prevent slaves from organizing resistance. Southern white authorities squelched several other revolts in the making, including plots in Charleston, South Carolina, in 1730 and in Annapolis, Maryland, in 1740.

Though large-scale rebellions were rare, they occurred often enough to sustain fear. A wave of slave unrest swept the northeastern seaboard in 1740–1741, first erupting as a series of barn burnings in New Jersey. Authorities executed two slaves for the crime. The following year, New York City experienced a rash of thefts and fires. Because England and its colonies were at war with Spain and France (King George's War, 1739–1744), these fires triggered widespread concern.

Then another blaze hit New York City. After authorities overheard one slave muttering "Fire, fire, scorch, scorch a little damn it," they linked the blaze to a white tavern keeper, his wife, and an indentured servant girl, a tavern prostitute. Tortured and promised immunity, the servant confessed that her master was conspiring with several slaves and a Catholic priest to burn the city to the ground, kill all its white people and free all its slaves. This confession led to the arrests and trials of the tavern keeper and his wife and two slaves, all of whom were hanged. As the dragnet pulled in more suspects, officials threatened torture and execution to extract the names of other conspirators. Eventually 150 slaves and twenty-five white people were tried, and seventeen slaves and four white people hanged. Thirteen more slaves were burned at the stake, and seventy-two were transported out of the colony to the West Indies.

## AFRO-FLORIDIANS AND AFRO-LOUISIANANS

Whereas England's North American colonies had an elaborate system of slavery by the mid-eighteenth century, Spain's and France's colonies had a more porous slave system, characterized by racial intermingling and communities of free Africans.

### FORT MOSE: THE FIRST FREE BLACK TOWN

In Spanish Florida, free black people formed a fortified town—the first such community in North America. The town's founder was Francisco Menéndez. Born in a Mandingo village in Africa around 1700, Menéndez was given his Spanish name by his captors and transported to Florida in the 1720s. There his owner freed him for his bravery in a battle against the English in 1728. Menéndez rose to the rank of captain of the free black military unit charged with protecting the Spanish foothold in Florida.

Granted land two miles north of St. Augustine, Menéndez and the rest of his unit built Pueblo de Gracia Real de Santa Terese de Mose, known simply as Mose. The fort consisted of stout walls enclosing thatched huts. Mose's Afro-Spaniards swore they would be "the most cruel enemies of the English" and would spill their "last drop of blood in defense of the great Crown of Spain and the Holy Faith." Their vow reflects their adherence to Catholicism; under Spanish rule, slaves were sometimes released if willing to convert. Thoroughly intermixed with local Indians, the free Africans lived as farmers and militiamen.

In the political turmoil of the eighteenth century, Mose was hotly contested by the Spanish and English. It was also a sanctuary for Africans fleeing South Carolina slavery. Desperate to stanch the outflow of slaves, the English attacked and drove Mose's free black people from the fort several times in the early 1740s, but each time, Menéndez and his people returned to rebuild the fort. In 1763, however, when Spain ceded Florida to England, Menéndez realized that free black people had no future under English rule, and he led Mose's inhabitants to Havana, Cuba.

Now South Carolinians and Georgians took up land grants in northern Florida, and they brought enslaved Africans with them. By the onset of the American Revolution, slave labor had built profitable rice, indigo, cotton, sugar, and orange plantations along the St. Johns and St. Mary's rivers. The free black town was gone, but it remained in memory as a symbol of African freedom, and many black Floridians named their sons Mose.

## FRENCH LOUISIANA: A BLACK MAJORITY

Like the Spanish in Florida, the French in Louisiana treated their slaves differently than the English did. Louisiana was the only North American colony that started out with a black majority. By 1731, Louisiana had about 4,000 slaves—more than two Africans for every white French inhabitant. By 1746, the ratio was three to one. Most slaves were imported directly from Africa, initially from Angola and the Gulf of Benin. By the 1730s, they came primarily from Senegambia, where the French had extensive trading contacts. The majority of these later arrivals were Malinka-speaking Bambaras.

In a raw frontier wilderness, French planters had to make concessions to enslaved Africans and militant Indians, who frequently joined forces against the French. In 1729, African slaves joined Natchez Indians in an uprising that killed more than 200 of the already disease-decimated French. The planters who survived offered freedom to those slaves who would retaliate against the rebels the next year. The French renewed the offer for slaves willing to fight against the Chickasaw Indians allied with the British in the 1730s and against the Choctaws in the 1740s. Taking advantage of black military skills, the French were able to pit Africans against hostile Indians and reduce the likelihood of a disastrous Indian-African alliance. The arrangement gave Africans more privileges, and even opportunities for authority, than slaves had in other southeastern colonies.

Samba Bambara's story provides an example. In the 1720s, Bambara worked in West Africa as a Senegal River boatman and interpreter for France's Company of the Indies. Around 1730, perhaps seeing the usefulness of Bambara's talents, the French enslaved him and shipped him to Louisiana. There, his knowledge of French and several African languages earned him a privileged position as a court translator in Louisiana's legislative and judicial body. Later he became the overseer on the Company of the Indies' huge sugar plantation near New Orleans. But neither privilege nor position made Samba Bambara content; in 1731, he led a rebellion. The French crushed the revolt and executed Bambara and seven other conspirators.

Slave revolts in Louisiana proved rare, but the thick swamps and forests of the lower Mississippi provided cover for villages of escaped slaves. Though the French used black militiamen to ferret out the renegades, they never completely eliminated such villages from Louisiana.

Nor did the French manage to establish a thriving colony. Louisiana's rich soil, plentiful water, and year-round growing climate counted for little because the French focused their resources on the sugar islands of the West Indies. Few French settlers arrived after the frustrated Company of the Indies handed the colony back to the French king in 1731. Only a single slave ship arrived in the next thirty-five years to replenish Louisiana's African population. Consequently, planters tried to preserve what few slaves they had by moderating workloads and encouraging family formation. Catholic priests solemnized slave marriages and baptisms and permitted Africans to participate in church ceremonies. In New Orleans, where most slaves lived, white people valued their bondsmen's artisan skills highly and permitted many of them to live in their own dwellings and hire themselves out in their free time. Even more important, slaves in Louisiana slowly gained the rights to maintain their own garden plots and keep poultry and livestock. By 1763, the end of the French period in Louisiana, slaves had developed an economy of their own. They marketed poultry and produce, gained control over more of their time, and circulated with few restraints. These conditions gave them a crucial advantage: the opportunity to save for self-purchase.

Since Louisiana had never generated a profit for its investors, French diplomats happily unloaded the colony on Spain in 1763 at the end of the Seven Years' War. By that time, because there had been almost no importation of slaves, the black population stood at less than 6,000. By contrast, more than twice as many Africans lived in the New England colonies, and Maryland and Virginia's total slave population had reached 250,000. Spain controlled the territory for only twenty years; at the conclusion of the American Revolution, Louisiana returned to France. Yet during those two decades of Spanish control, Afro-Louisianans acquired unique rights. New doors opened to them when the Spanish set up a black militia to patrol French planters resistant to Spanish rule. Unheard-of in any English colony, the black militia played an indispensable role in colonial defense. Its ranks swelled with former slaves who had exercised the Spanish policy of *coartación* to purchase their freedom.

The French *Code Noir* (like the English slave codes) contained no policy akin to *coartación*. Only slave owners could decide whether to free their human property. Yet in the eighteenth century, law and social custom increasingly discouraged French slave owners from taking that step. The Spanish practice of *coartación*, however, gave slaves the right to initiate self-purchase by agreement with their master. If a master resisted, slaves could petition the governor's court to gain their freedom.

Through *coartación*, hundreds of slaves in Louisiana freed themselves during the Spanish period. Those who had raised and marketed produce for years now had the means to do so. Other masters freed their slaves voluntarily, particularly their slave wives and their mixed-race children for reasons of "love and affection." By the end of the Spanish era, New Orleans had a free black population of over 900—nearly 10 percent of the city's black people, a proportion unequaled in North America.

# BECOMING AFRICAN AMERICAN

What's in a name? For Africans recently torn from their homelands, a birth name provided not just a cherished connection to family and community but a deep mark of identity. Yet even this was stripped from them. The long transition from African to African American often began when a master assigned a slave a new name. Olaudah Equiano remembered vividly how his third master named him Gustavus Vasa. "I refused to be called so," Equiano recounted, "and told him as well as I could that I would be called Jacob," the name assigned by his Virginia master. When Equiano published his autobiography, it was under his African name.

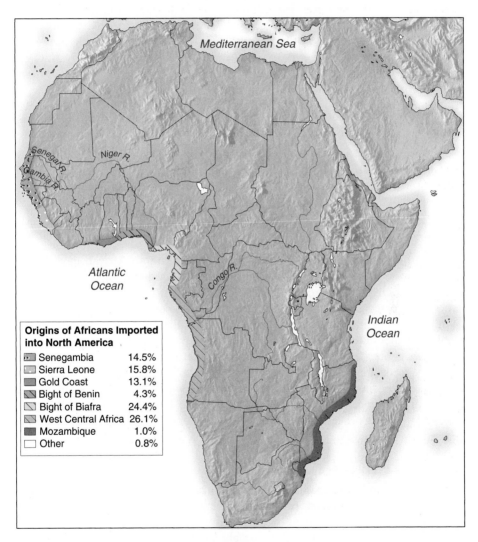

**Origins of Africans Imported into North America**

| | |
|---|---|
| Senegambia | 14.5% |
| Sierra Leone | 15.8% |
| Gold Coast | 13.1% |
| Bight of Benin | 4.3% |
| Bight of Biafra | 24.4% |
| West Central Africa | 26.1% |
| Mozambique | 1.0% |
| Other | 0.8% |

*Map 4.2*
Origins of Africans Imported into North America

*The origins of imported Africans changed markedly during the eighteenth and early nineteenth centuries. Slaves from West Central Africa (Kongo and Angolan peoples) predominated through the 1730s, but thereafter, Ibos from the Bight of Biafra made up the bulk of imported slaves.*

**Figure 4.2**
Percentage of African-born Slaves in American Colonies, 1620–1780

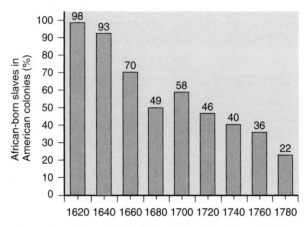

*After the Seven Years' War (1756–1763) choked off slave importations and births to slave couples, the percentage of African-born slaves in the English colonies declined. However, this varied from place to place. South Carolina and Georgia had the largest ratio of African-born to North American–born slaves.*

Acquiring a new name was only one part of being an African in America. The transition from African to African American unfolded gradually, influenced by factors such as the regional population density of the enslaved Africans, the ratio of imported Africans to North American-born slaves, and the type of community (town, plantation, frontier farm). Two parallel processes also shaped the transition: encounters among people from different parts of Africa, and encounters between black slaves and white European masters. The brutal circumstances of enslavement impelled peoples from different homelands to fashion a collective identity. At the same time, all slaves had to adapt to European masters whose culture differed markedly from theirs. Indeed, their lives depended on their ability to adapt. This process fueled a new African American culture that slaves expressed through religious beliefs and cultural practices.

## AFRICAN CHRISTIANITY

In fashioning viable lives and new identities in North America, slaves struggled to clarify their place in the cosmos. Equiano was cut off from the Ibo people's spiritual universe in 1756 when he started his long march to West Africa's coast. Like anyone plunged into harsh circumstances, he sought spiritual solace and, like most slaves, gradually embraced a religion that blended African traditions with Christian practices and beliefs. Purchasing his freedom in 1766, six years after he was baptized, he practiced a Christianity that contained traces of Ibo spirituality.

Until about the time of Equiano's conversion, most Africans in the North American colonies had known little of Christianity. Instead, they clung to the religious practices and values they remembered from their homelands. Their rituals included burying a deceased person so that the body faced east. Africans also placed coins, porcelain plates, shoes, or treasured possessions on the stomach of the deceased to ensure a journey to an afterlife of ease in the African homeland.

With most slaves following African spiritual traditions, Christianity only slowly penetrated slave life. Many bondspeople found little comfort in it. Its spirituality seemed confined to the church, and the highly intellectual Protestant message seemed cold and complex. Slave masters, moreover, did little to promote Christian thinking and practice among slaves. In their view, the religion's emphasis on equality before God and a community of all humankind threatened to undercut their own authority. In 1730, following a period of unusual missionary activity in Richmond County, Virginia, some baptized slaves claimed that their acceptance of Christ entitled them to freedom. When this claim sparked a rebellion near Norfolk, masters cracked down on slave conversions.

Then a movement known as the Great Awakening whipped up new enthusiasm for Christianizing slaves. This wave of evangelical fervor began in the northern colonies in the late 1720s and spread south in the 1740s. In the parish of Williamsburg, the capital of Virginia, Anglican clergymen baptized nearly a thousand slaves in a single generation. Presbyterians began conversions in the southern colonies in the 1750s and 1760s. On the eve of the American Revolution, most urban churches in the northern colonies had black worshipers, who married and baptized their children there.

Why did so many slaves find that Protestantism had something to offer after all? The Great Awakening gave rise to a new brand of religion that appealed strongly to Africans. For example, Methodist and Baptist preachers developed a more emotional, informal preaching style that black people appreciated. During sermons, evangelical clergymen and unschooled lay preachers spoke passionately about personal rebirth. They swayed back and forth, swept up in the power of their message, and invited the dynamic participation of worshipers. Some preachers delivered sermons spontaneously, often in fields and barns, and encouraged ecstatic dancing, chanting, shouting, rhythmic clapping, and singing. Perhaps not surprisingly, followers—black and white alike—found the experience intensely emotional compared to the dry sermons delivered from elevated Protestant pulpits.

For the first time in the North American colonies, slaves encountered a worship style that reminded them of African spirituality. The Awakeners stressed that Christ blessed the weak, the poor, and the humble. In the day of reckoning, "the last would be first, and the first would be last." This was a powerful, comforting message for people who had little hope of freedom in this life. Slave owners, for their part, hoped their human property would embrace the Christian values of meekness and obedience.

Once slaves had experienced Christian teaching, not even the most controlling master could suppress its uplifting message. Visiting Savannah, Georgia, in 1765, Equiano heard the spellbinding English evangelist George Whitefield preach that all souls are equal before God. The church was packed with white and black worshipers. This was a God for everyone.

Africans converted to Christianity for the comfort and hope it promised. But by interweaving their own spiritual practices into the faith, they created a unique manifestation of the religion. They found expression in slave spirituals, or songs, singing Anglo-American hymns with an African rhythm. They also created their own songs about biblical heroes who appealed to them—Daniel, Joshua, Jonah, Moses—men who had resisted persecutors to prevail in this world rather than waiting for justice in heaven. Meanwhile, "sorrow songs" both expressed and eased the pain of enslavement. "We sing," said one slave, "to take away trouble."

Other spirituals asserted individual worth and strength. Historians have no way of knowing when slaves began to sing "We Are the People of God" or "I'm Born of God, I Know I Am," but after the American Revolution slaves found these songs sustaining, suggesting that earlier generations sang songs with similar themes. Challenging white people's discredit of African culture, these songs demonstrate a sense of self-worth, a feeling of fellowship, and a commitment to life purpose.

## AFRICAN MUSLIMS

While some enslaved Africans began to embrace Christianity and blend it with African religious ways, other slaves came as Muslims to North America and continued to practice Islam. The evidence of early Islam in America is fragmentary, as most descendants of Muslim slaves were reluctant to discuss it. But clearly, many slaves came from areas in West and Central Africa—especially Senegambia, Sierra Leone, the Gold Coast, and coastal Benin—where Islam had made extensive inroads. Runaway slave advertisements, especially those in South Carolina and Georgia, mention distinctly Muslim names such as Mustapha, Fatima, and Mamdo.

*When the famous painter of the American Revolution, Charles Willson Peale, sought out Yarrow Mamout in Baltimore, he found the Muslim slave "healthy, active, and very full of fun." Whether Mamout was 134 years old, as he told Peale, cannot be verified. But the descendants of his first American slave master felt certain he had reached at least 100 years of age.*

One such Muslim was Yarrow Mamout, who arrived aboard a slave ship around 1720. Purchased by a Maryland family, Mamout became a skilled brickmaker. He gained his freedom after making all the bricks for his master's new mansion in Georgetown, now part of the District of Columbia. For many years, Mamout lived as a free man and eventually became a property owner of modest wealth. A faithful Muslim, he often strolled Baltimore's streets singing praises to Allah.

Another Muslim, Job Ben Solomon, arrived at Annapolis, Maryland, on a slave ship in 1731. He was sold to a tobacco planter, who found him resistant to field work but of agile mind and princely demeanor. As it turned out, Solomon was the son of a king in the land of Futa, in the Senegal River region. Captured by Mandingo enemies, he had been sold as a slave to an English slave ship captain. After learning of this identity, his master sent him to England. Eventually, Solomon returned to his home in Africa, where he ascended the throne.

## AFRICAN AMERICAN CULTURE: MUSIC, DANCE, AND BODY ADORNMENT

Like their countrymen and women in Africa, black people in the colonies found joy in aesthetic expression. "We are almost a nation of dancers, musicians, and poets," wrote Equiano of his homeland. Music and dance played central roles in black slaves' spirituality and everyday life—in the fields where they toiled, in the quarters where they lived, and in the woods and along riverbanks where they gathered when they could. "Night is their day," one slave owner remarked. When their "day" began at sunset, slaves gathered to create a world that sustained them. Dance, rhythm, rattles, and banjoes (an instrument with direct African antecedents) all testify to Africans' ability to maintain their cherished traditions. Slaves also expressed themselves through fiddling, clapping, and drumming, though some masters forbade drums because they feared slaves used them to send coded messages to each other. Above all, slaves reveled in shout songs and singing—testaments to their African spirit.

In every one of these activities, slaves fused their inherited West African knowledge with new ideas they acquired in North America. They merged what they had experienced through encounters with Native Americans and Europeans with what they remembered from African ways—and developed innovations. How to form a pot from clay, weave a basket from sea grass, style one's hair, arrange fabric over the body, play an instrument, play with words, or use one's voice to sing or one's body to dance all came together in a unique culture developed by people determined to make life worth living.

Though given Western names and coarse clothes, slaves found ways to display their individuality. For example, they experimented with hairstyles. Drawing on homeland fashions and ideals of beauty, they braided their hair with beads, shells, and strips of material. They complemented these styles with turbans and bandanas, highly valued in West African societies. Eventually, they also began wearing beaver and raccoon-skin hats as well as flower-decked Scotch bonnets. Jaunty displays of hats, caps, and scarves cropped up throughout slave quarters in the colonies.

*The artist of this rare watercolor of the* juba, *a West African dance, remains unknown. On the right, a banjo player provides music, while a cross-legged man beats a drum with two twisted leather sticks. The plantation house, outbuildings, and a row of slave cabins loom in the background.*
Source: The Old Plantation, c. 1790–1800. Abby Aldrich Rockefeller Folk Art Museum. Colonial Williamsburg Foundation, Williamsburg, VA.

Though few slaves in North American practiced scarification, a common tradition throughout Africa, some developed other forms of body adornment. White authorities complained about slaves who dressed in apparel "quite gay and beyond their condition" or who dressed "so bold and impudent that they insult every poor white person they meet with." Slaves drew on African knowledge of natural dyes to add touches of color to their clothing. They also found ways to add bright cuffs, patches, and collars to jackets, trousers, and wraparound skirts. They fashioned brass wire earrings, beaded armbands and necklaces, and cloth bands that they draped over or wrapped around the body. These forms of personal adornment were small victories to combat the humiliation of slavery.

As another cultural defense against their plight, slaves embraced humor and playfulness. Skits mimicking masters brought the liberation of laughter, and stories from Africa kept spirits alive. The tale about the trickster spider Anansi who outwits his more powerful captors was a special favorite. In time, this story showed up in the Aunt Nancy tales recounted in Caribbean lore. It also made an appearance in the still later animal tales of Uncle Remus, collected and published in the late nineteenth century.

Slaves sought to maintain African practices even in the way they walked. Runaway slave advertisements describe "stately" or "strutting" gaits, a "proud carriage," a "swaggering knee," or a "remarkably grand and strong" walk—evidence of Africans who refused to adopt postures of defeat.

## MERGING TRADITIONS

By the eve of the American Revolution, Africans had begun to shed some aspects of their individual tribal identities and develop a new, collective identity as African Americans. Slaves in the North, outnumbered twenty to one or more by white people, understandably absorbed more European ways than those in the South. We can see the merging of traditions especially in the Pinkster holiday, an adaptation of Pentecost. Introduced by the Dutch in New Amsterdam and New Jersey, Pinkster became a sacred African and Dutch holy day as well as a joyous festival. On one occasion, slave baptisms were followed by Africans "playing upon several instruments, a dancing and a shouting so loud that they might be heard half a league off." Religious services on Pentecost Monday were followed by a Tuesday holiday during which Dutch and Africans feasted, drank, and danced together.

New England's equivalent of Pinkster Day was Negro Election Day. Like Pinkster, it meshed African and Yankee traditions. These annual celebrations drew slaves from the surrounding countryside for feasting, parading, dancing, and the electing of black kings, judges, and other officials. "All the various languages of Africa, mixed with broken and ludicrous English filled the air," came one report from Newport, Rhode Island, "accompanied with the music of the fiddle, tambourine, the banjo [and] drum." In a ritualized role reversal, African Americans dressed in the clothes of their masters and rode their masters' horses. They extracted money tributes from their owners, drank wine and beer, and danced exuberantly in the streets. For a day, they symbolically ruled the town.

Why did white northerners permit such celebrations? They could afford to take the risk because they vastly outnumbered black people and, like role reversals in ancient times in other parts of the world, Negro Election Day acted as a safety valve. By offering black people a chance to let off steam, the festivals discouraged rebellion. They benefited slaves as well by providing a mechanism for them to choose and honor their own leaders, who acted throughout the year as unofficial mediators of disputes and as counselors. Such festivals did not necessarily appeal to all slaves. For example, Venture Smith shunned "superfluous finery" and "expensive gatherings" and proudly claimed that he was never "at the expense of sixpence worth" of liquor. Nor could such holidays alter the cruel fact of bondage. But they did offer momentary entertainment in an otherwise grim existence.

While Africans were becoming African American, Euro-Americans were becoming Africanized in subtle ways. For all their disparagement of African culture, white colonists knew they needed their slaves' knowledge and skills to prevail in a new environment. Only an impractical South Carolina planter would ignore the rice-growing expertise of West Africans. Similarly, New England Puritans applied African medical knowledge of inoculation for smallpox. In South Carolina, legislators granted freedom and a lifelong pension to an African who knew how to save victims of rattlesnake bites.

Apart from such sensible borrowing of African knowledge, white people became Africanized almost without realizing it. In the South, where black people outnumbered white people in many regions, masters came to appreciate foods of African origin such as barbecued pork, fried chicken, and mustard and collard greens. Black cooks working in their master's kitchen had plentiful opportunities to carry on culinary traditions brought from West and Central Africa.

A cross-pollination of languages also occurred. One commentator reflected that after generations of living in close contact with African slaves, "the language of the common people of [South Carolina] is a curious mixture of English and African." Even masters wove African phrases and tones into their speech. One wealthy plantation owner was described as speaking "like a negro." Whether influenced by African medical practices, speech patterns, music, cuisine, or even notions about death and afterlife, hardly a white colonist in the South remained untouched by African culture.

## BLACK AMERICANS ON THE EVE OF THE AMERICAN REVOLUTION

African-born Olaudah Equiano and Venture Smith worked their way out of slavery with extraordinary perseverance and skill. But few slaves transported directly from Africa won their freedom. Most who gained freedom were North American-born. Many were mixed-race individuals who owed their manumission to a white father.

Slaves who possessed craft skills were the best equipped to escape from bondage. Whether in towns or on farms and plantations, they had greater mobility, more thorough knowledge of the world around them, and often broader linguistic skills that served them well when they encountered patrols or constables. In making a bid for freedom, many impersonated free black sailors and hired themselves out. If they succeeded in this strategy, they hid in towns with other free black people or poor white families.

### CURBING MANUMISSION

In the early eighteenth century, white legislators turned  from controlling slaves to narrowing free black people's privileges, such as the right to hold office or vote, bear arms or serve in the militia, and employ white indentured servants. In many colonies, laws slapped special taxes on free black people and defined unusually severe punishments for crimes committed by African Americans. Only by excluding "free-negros & mulattos . . . from that great privilege of a freeman," declared Virginia's governor in 1723, could whites "make the free-Negroes sensible that a distinction ought to be made between their offspring and the descendants of an Englishman, with whom they never were to be accounted equal."

Beginning in the 1690s, colonial legislators in the South erected legal roadblocks to freedom. One provision abolished slave owners' right to free their slaves without specific legislative approval. Another required slave owners to transport a newly freed man or woman out of the colony, though this ruling was not often enforced. With manumission severely curtailed, the number of free black people in the southern colonies shrank. Only a few thousand free black people lived in the southern colonies amid more than 400,000 slaves.

Beginning in the 1720s, most northern colonies also curbed manumission by requiring slave owners to post hefty bonds guaranteeing the good conduct of those they freed and to maintain those requiring public charity, a provision recognizing that most black men and women released from enforced servitude were old and sickly. Their former owners were just eager to dispose of a "burden." As in the South, lawmakers in the North barred free black people from voting, testifying in court or serving on juries, and serving in the militia.

Yet cracks were appearing in the edifice of slavery. During the Seven Years' War, the need for militia recruits convinced white northerners to set aside the ban against arming black men. Scores of slaves volunteered to fight in the war that drove France from Canada and the western frontier, thereby earning freedom. By the outbreak of the American Revolution, about 4,000 free African Americans lived in northern colonies, a higher proportion than lived in southern colonies.

## PROTESTING SLAVERY

Even as slaves nurtured the hope of liberty and at least some of the privileges white colonists enjoyed, a few white men and women shared their vision. Every generation in North America contained a handful of white people who recognized slavery for what it was: an immoral system designed solely to enrich slave owners through the brutal use of human beings. These white people refused to be swayed by biblical sanctions of the practice or examples of the widespread use of slavery throughout human history. Though slavery may have always existed, they said, that didn't mean decent people could not—and should not—stop it now.

Back in 1688, four Quakers in Germantown, Pennsylvania, had protested slavery. In the 1730s, a new breed of antislavery advocates emerged in the same colony. Whereas earlier protesters occasionally spoke out against slavery, now white men such as Benjamin Lay, John Woolman, and Anthony Benezet dedicated themselves to eliminating it. For many such reformers, their efforts cost them their place in society.

Benjamin Lay was an outsider from the moment of his birth in England, owing to a deformity that left him a hunchback. But his twisted body did not stop his compassion and determination. Immigrating to Barbados, he witnessed the most barbaric manifestation of slavery firsthand. Arriving in Philadelphia in 1731 and seeing slavery taking hold there as well, he initiated a crusade with tactics that attracted attention. In what was later known as the *free produce strategy,* he boycotted slave-produced necessities, made his own clothes from sheep's wool and flax, and publicly smashed his wife's teacups to protest the use of slave-produced sugar. By standing with one bare foot in the snow outside a Quaker meeting, he shamed those who deprived their slaves of boots. He even kidnapped a white Quaker child to teach the Society of Friends about the grief suffered by African families when their children were sold at auctions. Once he spattered red pokeberry juice on startled Quakers, suggesting that Quakers with slaves had blood on their hands.

In the 1750s, a new wave of Quaker reformers set out to cleanse the Society's membership of slave traders and owners. John Woolman, a leader in this effort, had journeyed through the southern colonies, where he witnessed the "many vices and corruptions" created by slavery. In *Some Considerations on the Keeping of Negroes* (1753), he warned that if we "treat our inferiors with rigour, to increase our wealth and gain riches for our children, what then shall we do when God riseth up; and when he visiteth, what shall we answer him?" Like Lay, Woolman earned the resentment of his fellow Quakers who traded or owned slaves.

Another plain-spoken reformer, Anthony Benezet of Philadelphia, echoed Woolman's protests. During the day, Benezet taught poor white children; at night, he taught black children, slave and free, to read. After years of teaching, he concluded that black children were as intellectually capable as white youngsters. His published statement directly challenged the common proslavery argument that Africans were inherently inferior to Europeans, suited only for forced labor. Like Woolman, Benezet published stirring denunciations of slavery in the 1750s, inspiring a growing number of Quakers to organize antislavery blocs at meetings and to promote bans on the importation, sale, and ownership of slaves.

It took reformers a long time to change even Quaker minds, but Quaker leaders in Pennsylvania and New Jersey initiated a crusade that offered hope to thousands of enslaved and free African Americans and laid the foundation for a movement that, within a century, redirected the course of a fledgling nation.

## CONCLUSION

By the eve of the American Revolution, slavery had made violence a way of life in the English colonies. Masters used violence to keep Africans under control, and slaves struck back with violence in protest. Was it true, as the Quaker John Woolman believed, that slaveholding, even among kindly masters, "depraved the mind . . . with as great certainty as prevailing cold congeals water"? If so, many people shuddered at the implications for the North American society that had begun to take shape. Did slaves' outwardly visible degradation stem directly from what Woolman called the white colonists' "inner corruption"?

Despite such anxieties, Europeans had bound themselves to Africans in an economic system that brought wealth to the powerful and pain to the exploited. That same system gradually fused elements of European, Indian, and African cultures into a unique new entity. For their part, Africans were becoming African American. They learned to speak their master's language, acquired knowledge of the local terrain, and even formed emotional attachments to the land. They started families, incorporated elements of Christianity into their traditional religious beliefs, and devised strategies to endure the unendurable. Some ran away, lashed out at masters, or initiated slave revolts—though masters countered with increasingly repressive laws and brutal punishments.

As tensions between white colonists and their British overlords mounted, few slave owners perceived the parallels between their situation and that of their slaves. If the colonists had to resort to violence to keep black people under control, what response might these same white people expect when they tried to break the shackles their British imperial masters imposed on them? Nor did white people see the bitter irony behind their own clamoring for liberty and their subjugation of black people asking for the very same thing.

# 5

—△—

# THE REVOLUTIONARY ERA: CROSSROADS OF FREEDOM

## THOMAS PETERS SEIZES HIS FREEDOM

On a steamy summer day in 1775, Thomas Peters heard rumors of a slave insurrection planned for July 8. Living in the house of his master in Wilmington, North Carolina, Peters was no stranger to feverish talk of rebellion as a way to secure a person's rights. William Campbell, Peters's owner, led Wilmington's Sons of Liberty—a citizens' group protesting the British Parliament's taxation policies. The Sons of Liberty spoke avidly about the natural rights they believed belonged to everyone at birth.

Even before the colonists began grumbling about English tyranny, Peters had fought for his own freedom. He had reached North America in 1760, at about age twenty-two, after slavers snatched him from his Yoruba homeland in what is now Nigeria. Marched to the coast like Olaudah Equiano and millions of others, Peters had been sold to a French slave trader and transported to French Louisiana. Three times he tried to escape—and three times he was recaptured and punished with whipping, branding, and ankle shackling.

Sold from one owner to another, Peters acquired an array of language skills. How he came to Campbell, a Scottish immigrant in North Carolina, we do not know. But in Wilmington, a Cape Fear River town of 200 households, Peters learned his trade as a millwright, making planking and barrel staves from the pines of the coastal forests.

When Wilmington's white citizens discovered the slave plot for July 8, they quickly rounded up suspects, imposed punishments, and redoubled patrols. With American militia units and British regulars exchanging fire at Lexington and Concord in Massachusetts in the spring, the white settlers of Cape Fear worried about slave rebellions more than ever. As the Wilmington Committee of Safety

## Chronology

1770  Crispus Attucks is killed in the Boston Massacre.

1773  Boston Tea Party inflames conflict between England and the colonies.

Phillis Wheatley's poems are published in London.

Slaves in Massachusetts petition for their freedom.

1775  American Revolution opens with battles at Lexington and Concord.

American forces, including African Americans, defend Breed's Hill.

Quakers in Philadelphia establish first abolition society.

Virginia's royal governor offers freedom to slaves who join the British army.

1776  Declaration of Independence asserts "all men are created equal."

1777  Vermont towns write a constitution outlawing slavery.

1778  Americans form an alliance with the French.

1780  Pennsylvania law initiates gradual emancipation of slaves.

1781  Elizabeth Freeman sues for freedom under the new Massachusetts constitution.

British expel thousands of African Americans who had joined them to gain freedom.

The British surrender at Yorktown.

1782  Laws in Maryland and Virginia repeal prohibitions on manumission.

1783  Treaty of Paris ends British rule and acknowledges U.S. independence.

Slaves who gained freedom by serving in the British army resettle in Nova Scotia.

Massachusetts abolishes slavery by judicial decree in Quock Walker case.

1784  Rhode Island and Connecticut begin gradual emancipation of slaves.

1786–1787  Black Bostonians offer to fight Daniel Shays; others fight with him.

1787  Northwest Ordinance bans entry of slaves into the Northwest Territory.

Constitutional Convention in Philadelphia writes a new constitution for the confederated colonies.

1788–1789  Ratified Constitution protects the institution of slavery.

1789  George Washington is first president under the Constitution.

1791  A slave revolution erupts in Haiti.

1792  Former slaves in Nova Scotia return to Africa.

Benjamin Banneker publishes his first almanac.

---

warned, "There is much reason to fear, in these times of general tumult and confusion, that the slaves may be instigated, encouraged by our inveterate enemies, to an insurrection."

The Committee's warning had merit, for British military leaders were inciting black slaves to rise up against their masters. In July, the British commander of the fort at the mouth of the Cape Fear River gave "encouragement to Negroes to elope from their masters" and offered protection to those who escaped. Slaves began fleeing into the woods outside Wilmington, and word spread among them that the British had promised that "every Negro that would murder his master and family . . . should have his master's plantation." Appalled, colonial authorities imposed martial law that gave militia units wide authority to impose curfews and limit the movement of slaves.

Like enslaved Africans everywhere in the colonies, Peters had to weigh his options carefully. He had married Sally, a slave, and in 1771 she had given birth to a girl the couple named Clairy. What chance did Peters's family have of reaching the protection of British forces? If the young father fled by himself, would his wife and child suffer the retaliation white owners and colonial lawmakers threatened on kinfolk left behind? In March 1776, Peters and his family risked all. Slipping away unseen from the Campbell plantation, they headed for the British ships on Cape Fear River. There, Peters signed up with the company of Black Guides and Pioneers, led by Captain George Martin of the British army.

The Peters family had their freedom at last. But for them and half a million other African Americans, the future held opportunity and peril. Colonist rhetoric about unalienable rights and Britain's crackdown on patriots in the 1760s and 1770s suggested that slavery might come to an end. But could slaves count on that? Could they wait for that day? As the American Revolution unfolded, enslaved African Americans faced difficult choices: respond to British offers of freedom, join the white patriots' cause if given the chance, or wait out the war. As this chapter reveals, all three choices brought hope of liberation.

But unlike white colonists, black rebels lacked the luxury of town meetings, countywide gatherings, and state conventions to discuss their options. They had to make these difficult decisions individually or in small groups. All the while, newborn states created constitutions that laid out the terms of how the states would govern themselves—including what they would do about slavery. When a convention met in Philadelphia in 1787 to write a constitution for the new nation, slavery became a major point of contention.

After the Revolution, thousands of African Americans who had been promised freedom by the British had the chance to start new lives. Peters and others went to Nova Scotia, but when life there proved difficult, Peters led 1,200 former slaves back to Africa in an unprecedented return to the motherland.

## BRITISH "TYRANNY" AND A CRY FOR FREEDOM

"In every human Breast," wrote a young New England slave named Phillis Wheatley, "God has implanted a Principle, which we call Love of Freedom." So how can the "Cry for Liberty" be reconciled with "the Exercise of oppressive Power over others"? Her question expressed the sentiments of half a million African Americans caught up in the events leading to the American Revolution. From 1764 to 1776, as white colonists proclaimed their love of freedom yet kept black people enslaved, many, like Wheatley, perceived the hypocrisy.

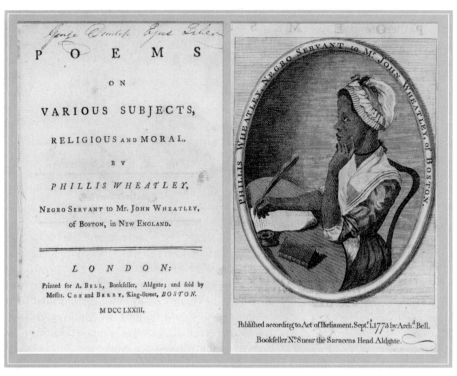

*Frontispiece engraving of Wheatley's* Poems on Various Subjects, *with a pen drawing of Wheatley. Scipio Moorhead, a slave owned by a Boston minister, also wrote poetry and crafted this picture of Wheatley for her anthology of poems—creating the colonies' first identified African American portrait. To show her appreciation, Wheatley wrote the poem "To S. M., a young African Painter, on seeing his Works."*

Born in Gambia in 1755 and abducted by slave traders as a small child, Wheatley arrived in North America in 1764. The slavers named her Phillis, after the vessel that transported her. She ended up in the household of a Boston tailor named Wheatley, who gave her his surname. Just eighteen months later, the nine-year-old girl could read the most difficult biblical passages and every piece of secular and religious literature that Boston clergymen put in her hands. At age thirteen, her first poem was published. At sixteen, she commemorated the Boston Massacre in verse. By 1773, when her poems were published in London, Wheatley created a sensation in the English-speaking world. This frail young African became the first woman in the American colonies to publish poetry about political events. At that time, she was arguably read more widely than any other woman in North America.

## FREEDOM RHETORIC EXPOSES COLONIAL ENSLAVEMENT

African Americans in North America had witnessed the events that led white colonists to declare independence from England. They were aware of the riots and protests touched off by the Stamp Act of 1765 and the Townshend duties of

1767. They knew of the Boston Massacre and the Tea Act of 1773 that provoked Bostonians into dumping tea into the harbor, an event later called the Boston Tea Party. After Britain's Coercive Acts of 1774 further polarized the two sides, armed conflict broke out in April 1775 in the Massachusetts towns of Lexington and Concord.

Each step toward revolution riveted white colonists' attention on the question of Britain's rights and responsibilities regarding its colonies. But arguments about whether Britain had the right to tax colonists who had no representation in the British Parliament or whether royal governors could legally disband elected colonial legislatures mattered little to black Americans. What did capture their interest were the language and methods of protest white colonists used to resist the British government.

As the conflict between the colonies and Britain escalated, Africans in North America saw new opportunities to seize their own liberty. From the first colonial protests against British revenue policy in 1765 to the end of the Revolutionary War in 1783, black people staged the most widespread and protracted slave rebellion in American history. Their efforts exposed a lie that many white people believed—that most slaves were content with their lot. Tens of thousands of slaves fled to the British side to gain freedom. Meanwhile, other black people cast their lot with the Americans in the belief that they would be rewarded with liberation.

Thousands of black Americans overheard their masters' dinner-table conversations and debates, worked in taverns and coffeehouses where colonists argued about revolutionary politics, and listened to white patriots describing Britain's policies as tantamount to tyranny and enslavement. These Africans pondered the notion of inalienable rights—the idea that some privileges are not earned but acquired at birth. Natural rights, political theorists maintained, could not be alienated (separated) from an individual.

Black people applied the ringing phrases of the day to their own situation. And in northern towns and on some southern plantations, they had the support of a few white colonists who recognized the contradiction between natural rights and Africans' enslavement. James Otis, a fervent pamphleteer on the rights of English-born citizens, had asserted as early as 1764 that the "colonists are by the law of nature free born, as indeed all men are, white or black. . . . Does it follow that it is right to enslave a man because he is black?"

Enslaved Africans' spirits no doubt soared as white colonists' rhetoric of freedom and resistance to tyranny heated up. In 1768, the *Pennsylvania Chronicle* urged colonists to ban the African slave trade, "emancipate the whole race" of Africans, and restore "that liberty we have so long unjustly detained from them." In 1773, Nathaniel Niles wrote: "For shame, let us either cease to enslave our fellow-men or else let us cease to complain of those that would enslave us." In 1775, Thomas Paine, author of the incendiary pamphlet *Common Sense*, challenged slaveholders: "With what consistency or decency [do white colonists] complain so loudly of attempts to enslave them, while they hold so many hundred thousand in slavery?"

Such rhetoric ignited Africans' own revolutionary spirit. In northern colonies, where slaves had the right to petition, some black Americans couched pleas for freedom in ways calculated to stir the conscience of their masters. But their language grew bolder after war broke out. "We . . . ask for nothing but what we are fully persuaded is ours to claim," asserted a Connecticut slave petition in 1777, for "we are the Creatures of that God, who made of one blood, and kindred, all the nations of the earth." That same year Prince Hall, a former slave who helped found the first black Masonic lodge in North America, exclaimed that the principles on which Americans had acted "in the course of their unhappy difficulties with Great Britain pleads stronger than a thousand arguments . . . [that black people] may be restored to the enjoyments of that which is the natural right of all men." Rhetoric pressing for the end of slavery provides some of the most compelling language of the revolutionary era.

## FREEDOM FEVER IN THE SOUTH

In the southern colonies, laws forbade slaves from petitioning the courts. Nevertheless, black Americans stepped up demands for their liberty as revolutionary protests escalated. In Charleston, the South's largest city, enslaved Africans chanted "Liberty, liberty" as white colonists celebrated the resignation of the Stamp Act distributor in 1766. Yet the same colonists promptly cracked down on agitating black slaves. "The city was thrown under arms for a week," reported an alarmed white official, and messengers were dispatched throughout the colony to warn of possible slave uprisings.

Still, unrest among African Americans intensified. In Georgia and South Carolina in 1773, groups of slaves fled to the country's interior. The following year, rebelling slaves killed several white people. In August 1775, another slave plot percolated in South Carolina when the free black river pilot Thomas Jeremiah planned to guide the British Royal Navy into Charleston harbor and help bondspeople win their freedom. But officials discovered Jeremiah's scheme, hanged him, and set him aflame on August 18, 1775. As one historian wrote, "Behind the bewitching rhetoric of liberty was the hideous face of slavery."

# AFRICAN AMERICANS
# AND THE AMERICAN REVOLUTION

By its nature, the Revolutionary War opened new doors for African Americans. With the immense movement of both civilian and military populations in and out of nearly every major seaport from Savannah to Boston between 1775 and 1783, urban slaves had unprecedented opportunities for seizing independence and destabilizing the institution of slavery. In the countryside, as British and American forces crisscrossed the land, slaves fled to the British side by the thousands, disrupting plantation work routines. The few free African Americans faced a dilemma: Should they offer to fight with the American rebels in the hopes of improving their image in the minds of white patriots? Should they join the British as a means for overthrowing slavery? Or should they keep their heads down while waiting for the storm to pass? With war swirling around them, black Americans made their choices. For all, the hope of personal freedom guided their decisions.

## CHOOSING THE BRITISH: BLACK LOYALISTS

As Thomas Peters discovered, the British offered slaves their best chance at liberty. In November 1775, Virginia's royal governor, Lord Dunmore, issued a proclamation offering freedom for slaves and indentured servants "able and willing to bear arms" who escaped their masters and joined the British forces. Dunmore's proclamation lifted the hopes of enslaved Africans everywhere. Within just a few months, about a thousand Virginia runaway slaves reached the British lines. Many slaves who were old, infirm, very young, or pregnant decided against traveling such long distances. However, in every region, black women with children ran away from their masters in much greater proportion than they had in the colonial period. They knew that with the British offering refuge, they had a far better chance than ever before of winning—and keeping—their freedom.

Thomas Peters and his family were among those who chose the British and liberty. He fought with the Black Guides and Pioneers for eight years; others formed the Ethiopian Regiment, also led by white British officers. Some inscribed "Liberty to Slaves" across their uniforms. Peters moved north with the British forces to occupy Philadelphia in the fall of 1777 and was in New York City with the British when the war ended in 1783. Twice wounded, he received a promotion to sergeant in recognition of his leadership among his fellow escaped slaves. His family joined him in New York City by the time American and British diplomats were negotiating the peace treaty in Paris in 1782 and 1783.

Peters's wartime service brought him into contact with thousands of other black people who hoped for freedom through a similar route. It is difficult to know how many slaves allied with the British, but Thomas Jefferson acknowledged losing 10 to 20 percent of his slave labor force, and during the southern campaigns, from 1779 to 1782, plantations in South Carolina and Georgia lost thousands of slaves to occupying British forces.

Even in the North, where white masters exercised their rule less harshly than in the South, slaves opted for the British deal. When Thomas Peters was with the British regiments occupying Philadelphia, he observed slaves flocking to British ranks. Surveying Pennsylvania's losses in 1779, one white legislator lamented, "By the invasion of this state, and the possession the enemy obtain of this city and neighborhood, [a] great part of the slaves hereabouts were enticed away by the British army." New York City and its surrounding countryside offered numerous opportunities for slaves to escape because the British controlled the area during most of the war.

Yet British military leaders did not welcome all bondspeople, refusing, in particular, to accept slaves belonging to British loyalists. In 1779, Sir Henry Clinton, British commander-in-chief, issued a more restrictive version of Dunmore's proclamation; he offered freedom only to refugee slaves of rebellious Americans and warned that any African Americans captured in American uniforms would be sold back into bondage. In fact, some British officers claimed captured slaves as property rather than delivering the promised freedom.

One of the most intrepid black men enlisting with the British was the self-named Colonel Tye. A young slave in northern New Jersey, Tye fled when his master refused Quaker appeals for his freedom, and he organized a guerrilla band of other fugitive slaves and free black men. Fighting alongside New Jersey loyalists, they kidnapped farmers, seized crops and cattle, and patrolled border posts. Hiding out in familiar swamps and inlets, Tye gathered runaway slaves wherever he went. He fought many battles before dying of wounds and lockjaw in 1780. A symbol of black rebellion, he inspired awe among New Jersey patriots despite the havoc he created. The first notice of his death in local newspapers described Tye as "justly to be more feared and respected than any of his brethren of a fairer complexion."

Though thousands of black Americans saw the British as liberators, they discovered that fighting alongside them was anything but glorious. The British promise of freedom was more a military strategy, it seems, than a commitment to equality. To the British, black men and women were workers whose recruitment could disrupt the enemy's economy. Only a few, such as Peters, were soldiers; most were laborers, wagon drivers, cooks, and servants. They repaired roads, cleaned camp, hauled equipment, and built fortifications. Rations were short, clothing shabby, and barracks overcrowded. Camp fevers and contagious diseases proved more lethal than warfare, and thousands of black people who joined the British met early deaths.

Though some British royal governors and military officers genuinely believed that slaves deserved freedom, most had decidedly pragmatic interests. During the showdown at Yorktown in 1781, when British troops were surrounded and short of provisions, General Charles Cornwallis expelled thousands of African Americans from his encampments. An embarrassed Hessian officer serving with the British wrote that Cornwallis's officers "drove back to the enemy all of our black friends, whom we had taken along to despoil the countryside. . . . We had used them to good advantage and set them free, and now, with fear and trembling they had to face the reward of their cruel masters."

## FIGHTING FOR INDEPENDENCE: BLACK PATRIOTS

Choosing a different path from that of Sergeant Peters and Colonel Tye, many free African Americans and a few slaves fought for the American cause. William C. Nell, the first black American historian, honored them in the 1850s when, working to advance the abolitionist crusade, he recalled the blood shed for the "glorious cause" by black Americans in the time of the nation's birth. In his *Colored Patriots of the American Revolution* (1855), Nell cited Crispus Attucks as the first person to fall during the Boston Massacre of 1770 and thus the first to lose his life in the Americans' bid for independence.

Half Wampanoag Indian and half African, Attucks had fled slavery twenty years earlier and worked on New England whaling ships. In Boston on the night of March 5, 1770, he led an attack against a contingent of British regulars, brandishing a stout cordwood stick. When the British fired at point-blank range, five Americans perished in what was later called the Boston Massacre. "The first to defy, and the first to die," as a Boston poet wrote a century later, Attucks became a symbol of American resistance to the hated British occupation of Boston.

Salem Poor was another free black patriot. His bravery in the Battle of Charlestown in 1775 inspired fourteen Massachusetts officers to petition the Continental Congress to reward "so great and distinguished a character" and such a "brave and gallant soldier." Poor went on to fight with Washington's army at White Plains, New York, and endured the grueling winter of 1777–1778 at Valley Forge.

Some black patriots were slaves. Peter Salem, for example, a slave from Framingham, Massachusetts, served alongside his master at the Battle of Lexington. At the Battle of Bunker Hill, Salem took aim and killed Major John Pitcairn of the British Marines, the officer who led the attack on patriot fortifications. Salem later fought at Stony Point and Saratoga, New York. Prince Whipple, another slave patriot, pulled the stroke oar in the small boat that carried George Washington across the Delaware River. This crossing, amid a piercing winter storm on Christmas night in 1776, is immortalized in a painting in which Whipple is shown, that today hangs in the U.S. Capitol. The subsequent American attack, which surprised the British at Trenton, New Jersey, handed the patriots their first major victory.

One Virginia slave, James Armistead, served as a spy for the Marquis de Lafayette, the celebrated French nobleman who came to fight with the Americans. Armistead's master, William Armistead, granted his desire to enlist when Lafayette called for the recruitment of black troops in March 1781. Posing as a runaway slave, Armistead infiltrated the British lines at Yorktown, observed the British formations and tactical positions, and returned with crucial information that gave the Americans the upper hand in what became the climactic battle of the war.

Just after the war, Lafayette gave Armistead a handwritten testimonial declaring, "His intelligence from the enemy's camp were industriously collected and more faithfully delivered. He perfectly acquitted himself with some important commissions I gave him and appears to me entitled to every reward his situation can admit of." In 1786, the General Assembly

*This painting of James Armistead shows Armistead fitted out elaborately. During the war, the Marquis de Lafayette developed an antislavery stance and proposed to George Washington that the two men establish a small plantation in South America where Washington's freed slaves and Lafayette's could till the soil as tenant farmers.*

of Virginia responded by emancipating Armistead and appropriating money to compensate his master. Thereafter, Armistead gave up his master's surname and called himself James Lafayette. Nearly a half-century later, when the French hero returned to the United States for a triumphal tour, he visited his namesake. James Lafayette lived poor but proud on a small farm in Virginia, a pensioner of the American Revolution.

Faithful wartime service did not usually earn black Americans freedom or pensions, as William Lee, George Washington's slave, discovered. Like many revolutionary leaders, Washington professed a hatred of slavery but could not bring himself to part with his slaves. He grudgingly agreed to grant Lee's request in 1784 to transport his free black wife from Philadelphia to Mount Vernon, Washington's plantation on the Potomac River in Virginia. "I cannot refuse his request," wrote Washington, "as he has lived with me so long and followed my fortunes through the war with fidelity." The black couple lived at Mount Vernon for fifteen years—the husband a slave, the wife free—until Washington died in 1799.

Most patriot leaders refused to permit African Americans, whether slave or free, to fight on the American side at all. The natural rights principle, which on the eve of the revolution seemed poised to inspire a broad anti-slavery movement, withered once the fighting erupted. By late 1775 and early 1776, the Continental Army and most state militias had banned free blacks and slaves from military service. The idea of putting weapons in the hands of African Americans raised disturbing images of a broad black rebellion and of black men possessing inflated notions of equality.

Yet two years into the war, white patriots changed their minds once more—this time for pragmatic, not moral, reasons. Concerned about a worsening manpower shortage, the states began to accept free black men in militia units in 1777. At the same time, recruiting sergeants quietly accepted slaves in place of their masters, often pri-

In this lithograph, William Lee holds Washington's white horse while the American general accepts the surrender of General Lord Cornwallis at Yorktown.

vately promising them freedom at war's end. As the "spirit of '76" wore off among white people and the war dragged on, militias in the northern states and towns reached deeper and deeper into the reservoir of black manpower. Most African Americans serving in state militias fought alongside white soldiers, although Rhode Island, Connecticut, and Massachusetts created mostly black regiments led by white officers.

Some southern states also began tapping the African American population for military duty. Sorely pressed to fill the state quotas set by the Continental Congress each year, Maryland reluctantly recruited free black men into service and, after the British army came south, slaves—with their masters' consent. Not surprisingly, few slaveholders would give up able-bodied black men. Virginia permitted free black men to enlist, but not slaves.

Legislatures in South Carolina and Georgia, dominated by slave owners, banned any form of black enlistment. If the image of the revolutionary army as a refuge for runaway slaves and agitators alarmed most northerners, it terrified southerners. Especially in the Deep South and along coastal areas, where black people far outnumbered white, the thought of putting guns into the hands of any black—slave or free—struck white southerners as suicidal.

Only 1 percent of the black population was free at the outbreak of the war. Many of these African Americans viewed joining the patriots as a means to advance their place in a new republic. They believed that the patriots' rhetoric about natural rights and personal freedom foretold the end of slavery and the beginning of racial equality.

Consider James Forten of Philadelphia. His great-grandfather had been dragged to the Delaware River Valley in chains, probably by Dutch slavers, even before William Penn's Quakers arrived. His grandfather was one of the first Africans in Pennsylvania to purchase his freedom. His father became a sailmaker in Philadelphia and James was born in 1766. Enjoying the advantages of Quaker schooling and rankling at the British occupation of Philadelphia in 1777–1778, young Forten cast his lot with the Americans and signed on with a privateer—a licensed merchant ship outfitted to capture British vessels. "Scarce wafted from his native shore, and periled upon the dark blue sea," wrote William Nell, "than he found himself amid the roar of cannon, the smoke of blood, the dying, and the dead." Nell was describing a bloody engagement in 1782 in which Forten was the only survivor at his gun station.

But in the next voyage Forten was not so lucky, as his ship was captured by the British in a fierce sea battle. When the British captain's young son befriended Forten, the captain offered the black youth free passage to England and the patronage of his family. "NO, NO!" replied Forten. "I am here a prisoner for the liberties of my country; I never, NEVER, shall prove a traitor to her interests." His offer spurned, the British captain consigned Forten to the *Old Jersey*—the rotting, death-trap prison ship anchored in New York harbor. Thousands of captured Americans died on such vessels, but Forten survived even this ordeal. Released seven months later as the war drew to a close, the sixteen-year-old boy made his way barefoot from New York to Philadelphia.

# RHETORIC AND REALITY
# IN THE NEW NATION

While fighting for independence from Britain, white Americans also established new governments and paved the way for expansion westward. Yet even as they argued that the British crown and Parliament had denied their inalienable rights, most white people who owned slaves exempted their human property from these very rights, and those who did not own slaves felt only a half-hearted desire to abolish the institution. The new state constitutions perpetuated this gap between rhetoric and reality by preserving slavery. Yet African Americans pushed the agenda of freedom forward—achieving success in some states.

## CONTINUED SLAVERY IN THE SOUTH

The fighting between America and England wound down at Yorktown in 1781, and the new nation's independence was guaranteed by the Treaty of Paris in 1783. During these years, enslaved Africans in the South must have hoped the discordance between slavery and a republic founded on inalienable rights would be recognized. And some white leaders did see it. For example, leaders of the fast-growing Methodists wrote in 1784 that "the practice of holding our fellow creatures in slavery . . . [is] contrary to the golden law of God on which hang all the law and the prophets and the unalienable rights of mankind." In 1788 Maryland's attorney general, Luther Martin, declared that slavery was "inconsistent with the genius of republicanism and has a tendency to destroy those principles on which it is supported, as it lessens the sense of the equal rights of mankind and habituates us to tyranny and oppression."

In 1782, lawmakers in Virginia and Maryland repealed prohibitions on masters' right to manumit, or free, their slaves. Consequently, the number of free black people in Maryland soared from about 2,000 on the eve of the revolution to 8,000 by 1790, mainly through manumission. In Virginia, where about half of all American slave owners resided, the number of free black persons expanded from about 1,800 in 1782 to more than 12,000 in 1790. By that year, about 5,000 free black persons lived in North Carolina. Enlightenment ideas about natural rights moved some white owners to release their slaves, but others were practical; by switching from tobacco production to less labor-intensive wheat production, they did not require as many slaves as before.

Despite manumissions, the vast majority of African Americans in the Upper South remained enslaved, and their numbers increased. As slave births exceeded deaths, the slave population grew, even though slave importations during the war had ceased. Virginia's slave population, for example, increased from about 200,000 to nearly 300,000 between 1776 and 1790. Maryland and North Carolina experienced similar trends.

In the Lower South, manumission was rare. While almost one out of every twenty African Americans in the Upper South had gained freedom by 1790, only one in sixty in the Lower South was free. The slave population of South Carolina and Georgia—the two states that resumed importing slaves after the revolution—continued to rise. Switching from enslaved to free labor made no economic sense to planters in these states, and the doctrine of inalienable rights had little meaning for them. Having armed themselves heavily during the war against Britain, white people in the Lower South now had the weapons to crush black rebellion and consolidate their hold on the far more numerous slaves.

## EMANCIPATION IN THE NORTH

At the end of the war, only about one in ten black Americans lived in the North, and most were still in bondage. But they were encouraged when the Green Mountain towns seceded from New York in 1777 and wrote a constitution, as the new state of Vermont (admitted to the Union in 1791) that outlawed slavery.

Other northern states followed suit. In 1780 Pennsylvania passed the first state law mandating the gradual abolition of slavery. Four years later, Rhode Island and Connecticut took similar steps. Yet in New Jersey and New York, where slavery played a major role in the economy, lawmakers declined to eradicate the institution. Moreover, slavery expanded steadily in these states, despite rulings that halted slave importation. Not until 1799 and 1804, respectively, would New York and New Jersey pass gradual abolition laws. Delaware never abolished slavery. White people living in that state could legally own human chattel until the Thirteenth Amendment ended slavery after the Civil War.

Though these new laws must have raised African Americans' hopes, they phased out slavery only slowly. Equally frustrating to black people, abolition laws generated such heated debate that legislators sometimes diluted them. Pennsylvania's abolition law illustrates this point. In 1775, Quakers in Philadelphia organized the Society for the Relief of Free Negroes Unlawfully Held in Bondage. Society members moved rapidly to cleanse themselves of what they saw as the sin of slaveholding. Though not explicitly an abolition society at first, the Quaker organization flowered after the revolution, attracting non-Quakers and becoming the first group in the English-speaking world dedicated to the eradication of human bondage.

The Society's strong stand against slavery influenced many of the state's political leaders. Building on this foundation, Pennsylvania lawmakers believed that the state's 1780 abolition law would gain them the respect of "all Europe, who are astonished to see a people eager for liberty holding Negroes in bondage." Yet the act sparked intense debate. Ground down by vigorous opposition from slave owners, lawmakers amended the proposed law so that it freed no slaves and postponed full emancipation for more than half a century. It specified that all children born before the day the law took effect—March 1, 1780—would remain enslaved. Children born after that date were consigned to twenty-eight years of bondage. Hence, any child born of a slave on the last day of February 1780 could live out his or her life in slavery. If an enslaved black woman bore a child in 1820, her son or daughter would not be free until 1848.

Some African Americans decided not to wait for white legislators and judges to apply the rhetoric of freedom to their own lives. In Massachusetts a slave named Elizabeth Freeman set in motion a chain of events and a judicial decision that ended slavery in her state. Her story shows that in the revolutionary era, even the humblest descendants of Africans could effect profound change.

**Map 5.1**
Free and Enslaved African Americans in 1790

*Because many northern states abolished slavery only by degrees, a few African Americans remained in bondage until the mid-nineteenth century. For example, the federal census showed 1,129 slaves still living in northern states in 1840; 262 in 1850; and 64 in 1860.*

In 1781, with the war nearing its end, Freeman and her sister served a wealthy family in Sheffield. After a blow from her mistress left Freeman with a scar that "she bore to the day of her death," Freeman stalked from the house and refused to return. When her master appealed to the court for her recovery, Freeman asked lawyer Theodore Sedgwick to test whether the language of Massachusetts's new state constitution, with its statement that "all men are born free and equal," applied to her. Arguing the case in 1781, Sedgwick convinced an all-white jury that it did, and Elizabeth Freeman was freed. Freeman then worked as a housekeeper for the Sedgwicks for many years. As a noted midwife and nurse, she was revered for her skills in curing and calming her patients. After her death in 1829, Sedgwick's son commemorated Freeman's strength: "If there could be a practical refutation of the imagined superiority of our race to hers, the life and character of this woman would afford that refutation. . . . She uniformly

*Susan Sedgwick, daughter of Theodore Sedgwick, painted Elizabeth Freeman's watercolor portrait in 1811 when Freeman was sixty-seven years of age. Eighteen years later, Freeman died. She left a will bequeathing to her daughter gowns belonging to Freeman's African-born parents. Freeman was buried in the Sedgwick family plot in the Stockbridge, Massachusetts, burial ground.*

... obtained an ascendancy over all those with whom she was associated in service. . . . She claimed no distinction but it was yielded to her from her superior experience, energy, skill, and sagacity."

The Freeman decision set a precedent. In a similar case two years later, a runaway slave named Quock Walker sued for his freedom. The state supreme court upheld the county court jury decision, striking down 150 years of slavery in Massachusetts with these stirring words: "Is not a law of nature that all men are equal and free? Is not the laws of nature the laws of God? Is not the law of God then against slavery?"

## THE NORTHWEST ORDINANCE OF 1787

Four years after war's end, the Second Continental Congress passed the Northwest Ordinance to provide for the political organization of the vast region beyond the Appalachian Mountains. With land-hungry Americans heading west in droves, many accompanied by their slaves, Congress had to decide what role, if any, slavery would play. The resulting decision—the Northwest Ordinance—banned slaveholders from taking slaves north of the Ohio River but allowed slaveholders already in the region to keep their human property.

When a proposal banning slaveholders from taking slaves south of the Ohio River failed, white people in the South got what they wanted most: permission to extend slavery into a region where plantation agriculture would be profitable. This area ultimately comprised the states of Kentucky, Tennessee, Alabama, and Mississippi. But antislavery northerners also got some of what they wanted:

prohibition of slavery in a specified territory, which later consisted of Ohio, Indiana, Illinois, Michigan, and Wisconsin. The Northwest Ordinance was thus the first of many compromises by which leaders of the new nation determined where slavery could spread as Americans flooded west to set up homesteads.

# THE CONSTITUTIONAL SETTLEMENT

After the revolution, some Americans viewed the emerging political landscape with deep concern. Could the newly independent republic survive, they asked, if one-fifth of its people were in chains? Though the prospect of abolition loomed large at war's end, it vanished in a few sorrowful years. Reform-minded white Americans confronted two main problems in advancing their agenda: How would the nation compensate slave owners for the immense investment they had made in their human chattel? How would free African Americans fit into the social fabric? Solutions to both problems hinged on a willingness to make economic sacrifices and to envision a biracial, republican society. To the crushing disappointment of hundreds of thousands of African Americans, white America lost its commitment to the vision. By the time members of the revolutionary generation lay in their graves, the United States had sacrificed its best opportunity to eradicate human bondage.

## ROADBLOCKS TO ERADICATING SLAVERY

Two cases illustrate the economic and social roadblocks to abolition. In 1773, Dr. Benjamin Rush of Philadelphia had predicted an end to slavery. "National crimes," he stated in his antislavery pamphlet, "require national punishment" to be imposed on high unless "God shall cease to be just or merciful." But three years later, Rush purchased a slave, showing that a public antislavery stance did not keep men from enjoying the private advantages of a household slave. Even after joining the Pennsylvania Abolition Society in 1784, Rush refused to release his slave.

Rush was aware of the hypocrisy involved in publicly attacking slavery while personally owning a human being, and his problem was a microcosm of the nation's problem. Everyone who wanted to abolish slavery knew that slave owners would have to be compensated for the loss of their human property. Some called for a compensated emancipation scheme—a plan for raising taxes with which to pay slave owners to free their slaves. But like Rush, the nation's leaders ultimately put economic interest above moral commitment and shied away from this tax burden.

Like Benjamin Rush, Thomas Jefferson knew that slavery compromised Americans' attempt to create a liberty-loving republic. Also like Rush, Jefferson could not bring himself to part with his slaves. Yet unlike Rush, Jefferson regarded black people as innately inferior to white people. Africans were "inferior to the whites in ... mind and body," he contended in his widely read Notes on the State of Virginia (1782) because they were "originally a distinct race, or made distinct by time and circumstances." In particular, Jefferson wrote that an end of slavery would mean a mixing of the races that would threaten racial purity. As early as 1776, he argued that the abolition of slavery would have to be followed by the recolonization of freed slaves in Africa or some remote region of the western United States. In *Notes on the State of Virginia,* he asserted that freed Africans must be "removed beyond the reach of mixture."

Jefferson never overcame his "aversion . . . to the mixture of colour." In the early 1790s, he advocated banishing white Virginia women (but not black women) who bore "mulatto" children. The Virginia legislature defined the term as anyone "who shall have one-fourth part or more of Negro blood." Near the end of his long life, Jefferson maintained that "nothing is more certainly written in the book of fate than that the two races, equally free, cannot live in the same government." Yet Jefferson had an intimate relationship with his slave Sally Hemings. Hemings was the half-sister of Jefferson's deceased wife, and her father was Jefferson's father-in-law. Hemings bore five children whose descendants trace their lineage to Jefferson. Recent DNA analysis has confirmed Jefferson's sexual liaison with his light-skinned slave.

## BLACK GENIUS AND BLACK ACTIVISM

Jefferson's staunch view of Africans as an "inferior" and "distinct" race blinded him to the examples of black genius that surfaced in the revolutionary era. He dismissed the talent evident in Phillis Wheatley's poetry and denigrated the almanac of Benjamin Banneker, who used spheroid trigonometry to chart the heavenly bodies. The son of a freed slave from Guinea who married a mixed-race woman, Banneker grew up near Baltimore, where his

*Benjamin Banneker, pictured here in a woodcut from his* Almanac, *for many years kept a journal in which he recorded details about the natural world. One young white contemporary of Banneker's remembered that "he was very precise in conversation and exhibited deep reflection. . . . He seemed to be acquainted with everything of importance that was passing in the country."*

English grandmother taught him to read. At age twenty-two, he used a pocketknife to carve a wooden clock that kept accurate time and struck the hours for the next half-century. In his fifties, Banneker took up astronomy. He published almanacs with calculations charting the movement of the sun, moon, and planets throughout the year. Surmising that Banneker must have received help from a white patron, Jefferson concluded that Banneker "had a mind of very common stature indeed." But Philadelphia's David Rittenhouse, the nation's foremost astronomer, thought differently, praising Banneker's first almanac, published in 1792, as a "very extraordinary performance."

In the postwar turmoil, some African Americans found themselves once again on opposing sides, much as they had been during the war. This time the issue was economic. A postwar economic downturn, combined with stiff taxes levied to pay off the revolutionary debt, drove small farmers to the brink of bankruptcy. Deeming the taxes unfair in 1786, Daniel Shays led the farmers of western Massachusetts in armed protest against the court proceedings. Some free black farmers, also staggering under a grievous tax load, fought alongside the white rebels. Moses Sash, for example, served as an officer and was a member of Shays's council. Meanwhile, other African Americans from Boston sided with the government in this standoff. For instance, Prince Hall offered the support of Boston's black Masons, who, he wrote Governor James Bowdoin, "are willing to help and support . . . in this time of trouble and confusion, as you in your wisdom shall direct us."

Governor Bowdoin did not accept the black Masons' offer but encouraged Hall to petition the Massachusetts legislature to support a plan for their return to Africa. This ignited the first black-inspired recolonization movement in the new American republic. The movement, in turn, revealed African Americans' view of the young nation as irreparably divided by race. In a lengthy address to legislators, seventy-three "African Blacks" explained that only by finding a place of their own, beyond the reach of white power, could black people achieve dignity and fulfillment. The petitioners added that they wished "earnestly . . . to return to Africa, our native country . . . where we shall live among our equals and be more comfortable and happy, than we can be in our present situation." The state legislature refused financial support for this scheme. Nevertheless, the petition planted the seeds for a black nationalism that resurfaced again and again in later decades.

## A MORE PERFECT UNION?

In the torrid summer of 1787, the revolutionary generation received another chance to turn the rhetoric of liberty and equality into reality for African Americans. Meeting in Philadelphia, fifty-five delegates representing all the states except Rhode Island wrote a new constitution designed "to create a more perfect union." What emerged, however, was a compromise between large states and small states, between North and South, and between slavery opponents and slavery advocates. Many delegates who attended the convention owned human property and considered slavery a necessary evil. But others believed the time had come to put an end to the practice. For them, the question was not whether to do so, but when and how. Gouverneur Morris, representing Pennsylvania, stated his preference for "a tax paying for all the Negroes in the United States." This plan, Morris believed, would be a far better alternative to "saddl[ing] posterity" with a constitution that preserved slavery. But northern leaders, unwilling to shoulder financial responsibility for a compensated emancipation, rejected Morris's idea. Southerners concluded that the matter merited no further discussion.

Indeed, the delegates from South Carolina and Georgia exploded at the suggestion that the nation could uproot slavery from its economy and society. The "true question," argued South Carolina's John Rutledge ominously, "is whether the southern states shall or shall not be parties to the union." Was Rutledge bluffing? Georgia and South Carolina faced a precarious situation in 1787. Their white population was just one-twentieth of the nation's total, but their black population constituted about one-third of the national number. With the powerful Creek Indian confederacy and the Spanish in Florida threatening them militarily, no two states needed a strong national government more.

But no one called Rutledge's bluff. Many years later, James Madison, principal author of the Constitution, told his friend Lafayette that to try abolishing slavery in 1787 would have been akin to setting "a spark to a mass of gunpowder." Unwilling to create a national plan for freeing slaves, northern leaders simply ducked the issue.

As a result, the delegates designed a document that never explicitly mentioned slaves or slavery. Instead, they filled the Constitution with compromises designed to satisfy southerners' desire to preserve the institution. First, to determine the number of seats each state would have in the House of Representatives (which was based on a state's population), Congress decided to count three-fifths of all slaves (called "other persons") in the population calculation. This method guaranteed southern states many more votes in the House and in the Electoral College (which elected the president) than if slaves had not been counted. Second, a fugitive slave clause forbade the states from emancipating anyone who had fled bondage. The clause also required states to return runaways to their owners. Third, another clause prohibited Congress from banning the importation of slaves (called "such persons as any of the states now existing shall think proper to admit") for twenty years. In 1807, Congress would decide whether or not to allow the slave trade to continue.

Together, these provisions protected the interests of slave owners and their allies. In the South as well as in northern states such as New York, New Jersey, and Delaware, slaveholders acquired more and more human property. North and South Carolina, along with Georgia, kept the Atlantic slave trade open. Thus, as the new nation conducted its first experiments with democracy, slave ships continued disgorging thousands of African captives on American shores.

Under the Constitution, ratified in 1788, millions of newborn Americans entered the world as lifelong chattel. Runaway slaves—even if they managed to flee to a non-slave state—were forcibly returned to their masters if captured. A half-century later, Frederick Douglass reflected, "The Constitution of the United States—What is it? Who made it? For whom and for what was it made? Liberty and Slavery—opposite as Heaven and Hell—are both in the Constitution; and the oath to support the latter is an oath to perform that which God has made impossible. . . . If we adopt the preamble, with Liberty and Justice, we must repudiate the enacting clauses, with Kidnapping and Slave holding."

Historians have used the phrase "the compromise of 1787" to justify the revolutionary generation's accommodation of slavery. In explaining the failure of the new nation to come to grips with the institution, many historians point to the vulnerability of the newly forged union. The northern and southern states, they maintain, made a compromise in order to secure the cohesion of a constellation of states that had previously been separate colonies with distinct practices and beliefs.

But some historians argue that a national abolition plan might have strengthened rather than weakened that cohesion. Ending slavery, they contend, could have helped create a truly united nation out of loosely connected regions by eliminating a rankling sore on the body politic and enabling the United States to practice the ideological principles on which its birth was founded. Any society in which a people's behavior aligns with their principles and values is far stronger than one in which practice and principle are at odds. Moreover, those who assumed the new nation could *not* have abolished slavery make the all-too-common error of inevitability. Often, people who argue that certain regrettable historical events were inevitable are the same individuals who contributed to those events—not those who suffered their consequences.

In the end, all Americans paid a high price for the compromises that sullied the Constitution. Slavery continued to pose a painful dilemma for the new nation. Both advocates and opponents of the institution continued to cast about for a solution. When the "solution" finally came, it cost 600,000 soldiers their lives—one for each of the 600,000 black Americans whose inalienable rights the Constitution had ignored to create a more "perfect union."

Long before the Civil War broke out, some Americans continued to propose ways to end slavery. Ferdinando Fairfax, a man with ties to Virginia's largest planters, published a plan in 1790 for phasing out the institution. A protégé of George Washington, Fairfax claimed that many slaveholders were ready to release their slaves voluntarily and that many others could be induced to do so with compensation. But these planters, Fairfax said, would never agree to equal rights for free black people. Therefore, newly liberated slaves would have to be repatriated to Africa.

In 1796, St. George Tucker, another prominent Virginian, laid before the state legislature a full plan for the gradual abolition of slavery. Tucker voiced alarm over the first federal census of 1790, which showed Virginia's slave population rising rapidly. He expressed fear that the massive slave revolt that erupted in Haiti in 1791 might spread to the southern states. He also quoted the French philosopher Montesquieu that "slavery not only violates the Laws of Nature and of civil Society, it also wounds the best Forms of Government; in a Democracy, where all Men are Equal." Tucker's comments fell on deaf ears. But a few months later, Jefferson prophetically wrote that "if something is not done, and done soon, we shall be the murderers of our own children . . . ; the revolutionary storm, now sweeping the globe, will be upon us."

# THE RESETTLEMENT OF AFRICAN AMERICAN LOYALISTS

For those African Americans who had joined the British side in the revolution, the Constitution mattered little because the United States was no longer their home. In 1783, just after England and the United States signed the Treaty of Paris, the British had to resettle thousands of former slaves, refusing to return them to former masters. Yet where would England send the free black loyalists? Its West Indies sugar islands, built on slave labor, were no place for a large community of free black people. Nor was England, as officials in London and other cities were already lamenting the number of impoverished black people seeking public support. Instead black loyalists were sent to Nova Scotia, the easternmost province of Canada and, unlike all other English colonies in the Americas, a free labor agricultural society.

## BLACK NOVA SCOTIANS

Thomas Peters and his family were among the 3,000 black persons evacuated from New York City for relocation to Nova Scotia in late 1783. The journey was grueling. Gales blew the ship off course; not until the following spring did the exiles reach their new home. Peters led his family ashore at Annapolis Royal, a small port on the east side of the Bay of Fundy, across the water from the Maine coast. In this raw, remote corner of the earth, the former American slaves sought to establish new lives based on freedom.

But their dream of life, liberty, and the pursuit of happiness soon turned into a nightmare. The refugees were segregated in impoverished villages and given scraps of rocky land impossible to till. Deprived of the rights normally extended to British subjects, they were forced to work on road construction in return for provisions. With few resources and scant support from the British, they sank into poverty. Soon British soldiers resettling in Nova Scotia attacked the black villages, burning, looting, and pulling down residents' houses.

Peters became a leader of the exiles in Digby, near Annapolis Royal, where some 500 white and 100 black families competed for land. Discouraged, he traveled across the bay to St. John, New Brunswick, in search of unallocated tracts. Working as a millwright, he struggled to feed his family and to find suitable homesteads for other black settlers. He also had to ward off so-called bodysnatchers already at work re-enslaving blacks and selling them in the United States or West Indies. To worsen matters, crop failures brought a punishing famine in 1788.

## RETURN TO AFRICA

By 1790, after six years of hand-to-mouth existence, Peters concluded that his people needed to move and seek true independence elsewhere. Representing more than 200 black families in St. John and Digby, he composed a petition to the Secretary of State in London. Then, despite the risk of re-enslavement that accompanied any black person who braved an ocean voyage, he sailed from

Halifax to the English capital with little more in his pocket than the fragile piece of paper. In the document, the petitioners asked for fair treatment in Nova Scotia or resettlement "wherever the wisdom of government may think proper to provide for [my people] as free subjects of the British Empire."

The black leader could not have chosen a better time to head for London. English abolitionists such as Granville Sharp, Thomas Clarkson, and William Wilberforce had stepped up their activism. Though they had failed to force through Parliament a bill abolishing the English slave trade, they did win passage of a bill to charter the Sierra Leone Company for thirty-one years. The deal included a grant of trading and settlement rights on the African coast. Even better, the recruits for the new colony would consist of the former slaves from North America now living in Nova Scotia.

Peters returned to Nova Scotia a year later. There, he spread the word that the English government would provide free transport for any black exiles who wished to journey to Sierra Leone. Once on the African coast, he explained, they would receive plots of land. John Clarkson, the younger brother of one of England's best-known abolitionists, traveled with Peters to oversee the resettlement plan.

This opportunity to return to Africa excited the former slaves, but some white Nova Scotians were now reluctant to let them leave. The governor saw their emigration as an indication of his failure to provide adequately for them in Canada. Others protested that they would thus be deprived of customers. Still others had forged indentures and work contracts they claimed bound black people to them. Some even refused to settle back wages and debts in hopes of discouraging the Sierra Leone venture. "The white people . . . were very unwilling that we should go," wrote one black minister, "though they had been very cruel to us, and treated many of us as though we had been slaves."

But neither white officials nor white settlers could stem the tide of black enthusiasm for resettlement to Africa. Working through black preachers—the principal leaders in the black communities—Peters and Clarkson spread the word of the Sierra Leone plan. The telling soon took on overtones of the Old Testament story about the delivery of the Israelites from bondage in Egypt. Some 350 blacks trekked through the rain to Birchtown, a black settlement near Annapolis, to hear their blind and lame preacher, Moses Wilkinson, explain the Sierra Leone Company's terms. Ultimately, almost 1,200 black people chose to return to Africa. By the end of 1791, they had made their way to the port of Halifax, some trudging 340 miles around the Bay of Fundy through dense forest and snow-blanketed terrain.

Peters and Clarkson inspected each of the fifteen ships assigned for the return to Africa, ordering some decks removed, ventilation holes fitted, and berths constructed. Remembering the horrors of his own middle passage thirty-two years before, Peters resolved that the return trip would be different. As crew members prepared the fleet, the recruits talked of how they would soon "kiss their dear Malagueta," a reference to the Malagueta pepper, or "grains of paradise," that thrived in West Africa.

Setting sail on January 15, 1792, the ships held men, women, and children whose collective experiences in North America ran the gamut of slave travail.

The African-born Charles Wilkinson, a former soldier in the Black Guides and Pioneers, made the trip with his mother and two small daughters. Also on board were religious leaders such as David George, founder of the first black Baptist church in North America in Silver Bluff, South Carolina, in 1773; Moses Wilkinson, who had escaped his Virginia master in 1776; and Boston King, who had converted to Methodism in New York while serving with the British. The oldest voyager was a woman whom Clarkson described in his shipboard journal as "104 years of age who had requested me to take her, that she might lay her bones in her native country." Young and old, African-born and American-born, military veterans and those too young to have seen wartime service—all shared the dream of finding a place where they could govern themselves and live in freedom. This was to be their year of jubilee.

But they had to endure additional perils before reaching Africa. Boston King recorded that the winter gales were the worst in the seasoned crew members' history. Two ship captains and sixty-five passengers died en route. Snow squalls and heavy gales scattered the small fleet, yet after two months all the vessels reached Africa. The ships had crossed an ocean that for nearly 300 years had borne Africans in the opposite direction, as shackled captives bound for the land of misery.

Legend says that Thomas Peters, sick from shipboard fever, led his shipmates ashore in Sierra Leone singing, "The day of jubilee is come; return ye ransomed sinners home." Yet despite their joy at returning to Africa, the settlers encountered difficulties. Provisions ran short. Diseases claimed lives. Land distribution proceeded slowly. British councilors sent from London to supervise the colony acted irresponsibly. Racial discord reigned. As the elected speaker-general for the black settlers in their dealings with the white governing council, Peters tried to stem the spreading frustration. Some settlers spoke of replacing the councilors appointed by the Sierra Leone Company with an elected black government. This incipient rebellion never came to pass, but Peters remained the leader of the unofficial opposition to the white government. He died in the spring of 1792—less than four months after stepping foot on Africa's shores. His family and friends buried him in Freetown, where his descendants live today.

# CONCLUSION

Thomas Peters lived for fifty-four years. For most of his adult life, he struggled for both survival and freedom. He crossed the Atlantic four times. He lived in Yorubaland, French Louisiana, North Carolina, New York, Nova Scotia, New Brunswick, Bermuda, London, and Sierra Leone. He worked as a field hand, millwright, ship hand, laborer, soldier, and community leader. He also struggled against slave masters, government officials, and hostile white neighbors. He worked to secure political rights, social equity, and human dignity for himself and other former slaves.

Peters's story provides a glimpse at black Americans' lives during a pivotal time in history. When war broke out between Britain and its colonies, white revolutionaries' rhetoric about British tyranny and inalienable rights spread quickly among enslaved men and women. Taking the white colonists' cries for freedom at face value, black people petitioned for the end of slavery. Many joined white colonists who themselves lamented the contradiction between white planters' freedom claims and their continued enslavement of half a million human beings.

Thousands of bondspeople who fled their masters to claim the freedom promised by the British made the American Revolution the first large-scale slave rebellion in North America. Other enslaved blacks joined the American cause, believing their decision would win them their freedom as well. Thousands of individual acts of defiance and courage created a collective legend of black struggle, testified to black strength, and set forth a black vision of a better future.

For Peters and thousands like him, war's end meant finding new homes as British subjects—first in Nova Scotia and then in Sierra Leone in what became American slaves' first return to the ancient homeland. But back in the newborn United States, a far greater number of African Americans faced a future made uncertain by the compromise-riddled Constitution of 1787. Slavery stood on the brink of extinction in the northern states but in the South, where most bondspeople lived, black people had scant hope of regaining their freedom when George Washington assumed office in 1790 as the nation's first president.

# 6

## AFTER THE REVOLUTION: CONSTRUCTING FREE LIFE AND COMBATING SLAVERY, 1787–1816

### RICHARD ALLEN AND ABSALOM JONES LEAD CHURCH WALKOUT

"**M**eeting had begun, and they were nearly done singing, and just as we got to the seats, the elder said, 'Let us pray.'" Former slave Richard Allen was remembering a momentous day in 1792 at St. George's Methodist church in Philadelphia. "We had not been long upon our knees before I heard considerable scuffling and low talking," Allen related. "I raised my head up and saw one of the [white] trustees . . . having hold of the Rev. Absalom Jones, pulling him up off of his knees, and saying, 'You must get up—you must not kneel here.' Mr. Jones replied, 'Wait until prayer is over.'" Allen was thirty-two when he witnessed this scene, and seventy when he recounted it. When prayer was over, he recalled, "we all went out of the church in a body, and they were no more plagued with us in the church."

At St. George's, white church officials had abruptly decided to relegate black worshipers to a segregated section. The incident Allen described was a defining moment in African American history because it initiated the formation of independent northern black churches. It also sounded a foreboding note for racial tensions in Philadelphia and proved a crucial moment for the nation, whose course Congress charted at Independence Hall, only a few blocks from St. George's. Worried about a tremendous black rebellion brewing on the Caribbean island of St. Domingue (now Haiti), legislators viewed the confrontation at St. George's as ominous for similar tension in the United States.

Even before the incident at St. George's, Allen had faced a series of tests. In 1779, his Delaware master, convinced by Methodist preachers that slaveholding was a sin, offered to free him and his brother for 60 pounds of gold or silver, to be paid in installments. The brothers agreed, and Allen found work sawing cordwood and hauling salt for the patriots during the American Revolution. But already he had a different life's work in mind, inspired by Methodist meetings at a nearby farm. "One night I thought hell would be my portion," Allen remembered. "I cried unto Him who delighteth to hear the prayers of a poor sinner, and all of a sudden my dungeon shook, my chains flew off, and, glory to God, I cried. My soul was filled." From this point on, Allen later wrote, "my lot was cast."

For the duration of the war, Allen worked to pay off his purchase price. At the same time, he began to preach the Methodist faith. By 1783, when the Treaty of Paris concluded the American war for independence, the twenty-three-year-old former slave was delivering rousing sermons. Believing "it to be his Duty to Travel abroad as a Preacher of Righteousness," he traveled thousands of miles from New York to South Carolina, spending two months preaching among Native Americans. Then in the autumn of 1785, he headed north to a village west of Philadelphia, where local Methodist leaders asked him to preach to the small group of black Methodists attending services there.

Richard Allen was one of the numerous visionaries who emerged to lead the free black communities taking shape in the 1780s. The largest of these communities arose in maritime cities, from Boston to New Orleans, where free black men and women found work, companionship, and independent black churches. Most sizable towns between Maine and Louisiana also had communities of free African Americans.

In Philadelphia, Allen lifted the spirits of hundreds of black people. "I preached in the commons, in Southwark, Northern Liberties, and wherever I could find an opening," he remembered. "I frequently preached twice a day, at 5 o'clock in the morning and in the evening, and it was not uncommon for me to preach from four to five times a day." But that was before the white Methodists at St. George's demanded that Allen and other black worshipers sit in a separate section of the church.

Even as black worshipers endured this assault on their dignity, two profound transformations were overturning the Atlantic world. Both took inspiration from the American revolutionary ideology that all men are created equal and entitled by birth to certain rights. The first transformation, the French Revolution, erupted in Paris in 1789. The second, a slave rebellion in 1791 on the French sugar and coffee island of St. Domingue, compelled Americans to consider whether their experiment in democracy would include *racial* equality.

In the United States, the questions and passions stirred by these revolutions played out at the individual level. Though the Constitution preserved the institution of slavery, antislavery sentiment continued to percolate. The rebellion in St. Domingue demonstrated that slaves would not necessarily accept perpetual bondage. Though slavery was dying in the North, questions remained about how

## *Chronology*

1787 Richard Allen and Absalom Jones establish the Free African Society of Philadelphia.

The U.S. Constitution protects slavery.

1789 The French Revolution breaks out.

1791 Slaves in St. Domingue precipitate a violent revolution.

1792 Black worshipers in Philadelphia establish separate black congregations.

Former American slaves settled in Sierra Leone under Britain's protection.

1793 Allen and Jones appeal for an end to slavery.

Fugitive Slave Act strengthens the Constitution's fugitive slave clause.

Eli Whitney invents the cotton gin.

1794 France abolishes slavery in all its colonies.

1795 Spain cedes territory east of the Mississippi River to the United States.

Slave rebellion in Pointe Coupée, Louisiana, is crushed.

1798 Congress establishes the Mississippi Territory.

1800 Gabriel's Rebellion in Richmond, Virginia, fails.

1803 Louisiana Purchase vastly increases the size of the United States.

1804 Haiti is the first republic of African people in the Western Hemisphere.

1805 Peter Spencer establishes the Ezion Methodist Episcopal Church.

1808 Congress ends U.S. participation in the Atlantic slave trade.

1811 Paul Cuffe of Massachusetts sails for Africa to promote black emigration.

1812 The United States declares war on Britain.

1813 The Ezion Church becomes the first fully independent African American church.

James Forten challenges attempts to prohibit free black people from entering Pennsylvania.

1814 British offer freedom to slaves, some of whom participate in burning Washington, DC.

1815 War of 1812 ends.

1816 Mother Bethel church in Philadelphia breaks from the Methodist Conference.

---

free black people would fit into the dominant white society there. Would northern states confer equal rights on black citizens—as their state constitutions implied? Could black and white people live together as fellow citizens in integrated neighborhoods, churches, workplaces, and marketplaces? How would black Americans define themselves as a people? In the South, would slavery wither away as the slave trade ended, as many white leaders believed? Would Congress listen to petitioners urging the end of slavery? If the new nation became a republic for white men only, how would slaves and free black people respond?

Despite these questions, black Americans moved energetically to enhance the quality of their lives. In this chapter, we see how the expanding free population of African Americans constructed vital communities and churches of their own as part of their struggle for respect and equality. We also examine how the American revolutionary ideology of inalienable rights fueled revolution in France, which ignited the slave rebellion in St. Domingue and inspired similar uprisings in Virginia. Yet twin strivings—to overthrow slavery in the South and obtain political and social equality in the North—could halt neither the expansion of slavery nor intensifying white hostility toward dark-skinned Americans. Watching revolutionary egalitarianism fade, African Americans had little choice but to explore fresh options and forge new identities for themselves.

# THE EMERGENCE OF FREE BLACK COMMUNITIES

"Men are more influenced by their moral equals than by their superiors" and "are more easily governed by persons chosen by themselves for that purpose than by persons who are placed over them by accidental circumstances." Richard Allen and Absalom Jones spoke these words when they set out to establish an all-black congregation in Philadelphia shortly after the U.S. Constitution was ratified. Such democratic thoughts about self-governance strongly shaped African American community life as the ranks of free black people began to swell in the new republic. The creation of free black communities during the nation's early decades laid the foundation for the urban experience of future African Americans.

## AN EXPANDING FREE BLACK POPULATION

Only a few thousand African Americans had their freedom on the eve of the American Revolution. But after the war, their numbers swelled—to nearly 60,000 by 1790, to 108,000 by 1800, and to more than 233,000 by 1820. Several forces fueled this growth. Some African Americans purchased their freedom or sued for it in court, while others won freedom by escaping. Some slave owners freed their bondspeople, and several state legislatures abolished slavery. Finally, immigration of liberated people from places such as St. Domingue further expanded the ranks of free black Americans.

During the early years of the new republic, roughly 60 percent of the nation's free black people lived in the South and 40 percent in the North. However, in the South, free black people were a minority of all people of color. By contrast, freed black people in the North far exceeded the dwindling number of slaves. Free black people tended to live in the Upper South. About eight of every ten lived in Delaware, Maryland, Virginia, and Louisiana (see Figure 6.1). In 1810, for example, only 14,000 free blacks lived south of Virginia (more than half of them in Louisiana). That same year, 94,000 resided in Virginia, Maryland, Delaware, and the District of Columbia. Overall, the proportion of African Americans who were free inched upward in the South—to 5 percent in 1790, 7 percent in 1800, and 8 percent in 1820.

Everywhere, free African Americans congregated in the cities, where they could find friends, marriage partners, and work. By 1820, nine cities each had

**Figure 6.1**
Free Black Population by Region, 1790–1820

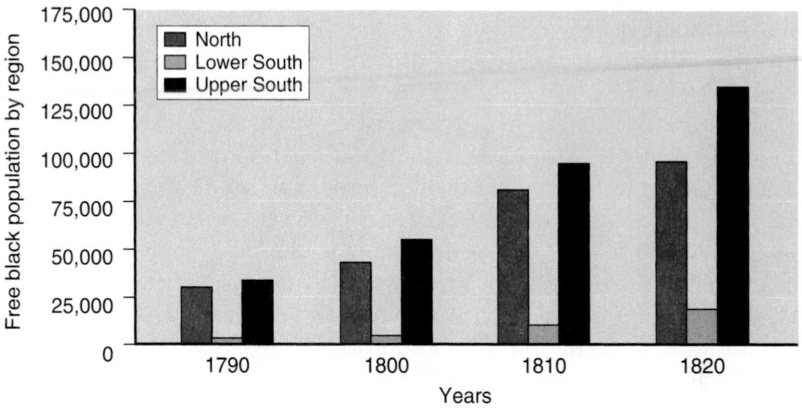

The Upper South includes Delaware, Maryland, Virginia, District of Columbia, Kentucky, Missouri, Tennessee, and North Carolina. The Lower South is comprised of South Carolina, Georgia, Alabama, Mississippi, and Louisiana.

more than 1,000 free African Americans, and New York, Philadelphia, Baltimore, and New Orleans each had more than 6,000.

## FREE BLACK WORK LIVES

Liberated African Americans took steps to establish fulfilling home and work lives in the cities. The rise of industrialization, which depended on power-driven machinery more than human labor, might have afforded them employment, but many owners of textile mills, machine foundries, and boot and shoe factories refused to hire black workers. These employers preferred native-born and immigrant whites, whom they considered as more reliable and educable. Thus, most free black people had to toil at unskilled labor. Black men typically worked as stevedores loading and unloading cargo on the wharves; as cellar-, well-, and gravediggers; as chimneysweeps and ash haulers; and as construction workers, ragpickers who collected discarded clothing, bootblacks, stablehands, and woodcutters.

Black women worked as washerwomen or domestic servants for white families. Many lived in their employers' households. But every city also had independent black seamstresses, cooks, basketmakers, confectioners, and street vendors—women who hawked pies, vegetables, fruits, fish, clothing, and handmade items from small stands. Other African American women operated small shops, boardinghouses, and oyster cellars; some worked as midwives, teachers, and nurses. Because these women's earnings were indispensable to their families' survival, their lives were different from the lives of white women, who increasingly withdrew from work outside the home.

Even in lowly occupations, however, free African Americans sustained independence and a sense of dignity, setting their work schedules when they could. In some occupations, such as oyster selling, carriage driving, and hairdressing, they developed near monopolies. Most opportunities for black self-employment lay in service positions or the skilled crafts. Every city had black shoemakers, tailors, and bakers. These men and women provided valued services and much-needed articles.

The free black Philadelphian James Forten, whom we met in Chapter 5, is an example of the rise of African Americans in certain industries. Forten joined the patriot cause as a teenager. After the war he took to sea as a deckhand on a merchant ship bound for London, where for a year he sewed canvas sails on the Thames River docks. He returned to Philadelphia and apprenticed himself to white sailmaker Robert Bridges. Soon he was a foreman. When Bridges retired in 1798, Forten took over the enterprise. Business proved so brisk that by 1805 he was employing a racially mixed crew of twenty-five apprentices. His workers made sails for many of the city's largest merchant ships.

Though racism kept most free blacks from the most promising occupations, it could not stifle ambition. Richard Allen exemplifies this drive. Best known as a religious leader, Allen was an entrepreneur from the day of his release from slavery. He took up shoemaking and wagon-driving before moving to Philadelphia, where, in 1792, he purchased his first piece of property. In the following years he bought and sold real estate frequently. His household almost always included several servants and apprentices. To supplement his minister's salary, he worked as a shoemaker, houseware dealer, shoe store proprietor, and chimneysweep supervisor. In 1794, he attempted to establish a nail factory with his friend Absalom Jones. Though the project never materialized, it reflected Allen's ambitious spirit—one shared by many free African Americans in their first generation of liberty.

Of all the black-dominated occupations, seafaring had special importance for free African

*Richard Allen's earnest demeanor shows in this portrait by an unknown artist. His reputation for honesty spread just after he purchased his freedom in 1779. Finding a trunk with a small fortune in silver and gold, Allen placed newspaper notices advertising his discovery. He refused to accept a generous reward from the grateful owner who claimed the trunk. Finally, he accepted a new suit of coarse cloth.*

Americans. From almost the moment the Atlantic slave trade brought the first Africans to the Americas, merchants and ship captains took enslaved African men and boys—such as Olaudah Equiano—to sea with them. After the revolution, black freedmen sailed before the mast in large numbers. As hard and dangerous as the work was, life at sea was more free of discrimination than life ashore, as ship captains prized any man, regardless of color, who could splice rope properly, haul down canvas in a sudden storm, or scramble aloft to handle the topsails. Though only a handful of black mariners became captains, they usually received pay equal to that of white mariners. Nearly one out of four mariners sailing out of New York, Philadelphia, Baltimore, New Orleans, and Newport, Rhode Island, was an African American. In some cases, white captains sailed with all-black crews.

As free black communities burgeoned in the North and in southern seaports such as New Orleans and Charleston, cadres of professionals and entrepreneurs created the nucleus of a black middle class. These cities had a small but influential number of landlords, doctors, ministers, musicians, and teachers. Eleanor Harris, for example, was described at her death in 1797 as a "woman of character," a "well qualified tutoress of children." James Derham, once owned by a Quaker doctor in Philadelphia, became an accomplished physician in his own right in New Orleans. Samuel Wilson was so highly regarded for his skill in treating cancers that white Philadelphians readily sought his help. In the same city Robert Bogle, a former slave, turned the idea of contracting food services at funerals, weddings, and parties into a profession, as did enterprising free black people in Charleston, South Carolina.

## FAMILY LIFE

In leaving slavery behind, free African Americans put a priority on reuniting families or creating new ones. Neither proved easy. The profound dislocation caused by the Revolutionary War, the migration of free black people north and west afterwards, and the scourge of poverty made household formation difficult. Many black men and women postponed marriage until they could gain their financial footing; thus, black families tended to be smaller than white families in this era. Most families shared housing. In the cities they lived in narrow courts and blind alleys, the poorest in attics and cellars. Though African Americans competed with Irish and German immigrants for jobs, they often shared space with these struggling immigrants. These were "walking cities," where people lived near to their work. Neighborhoods were not segregated by race or even class, and black and white people of all backgrounds and classes interacted daily.

Accommodating themselves to stark reality, most free African Americans built their households step by step. For at least a few years after emancipation, many had little choice but to remain in white households. They saved their earnings, and many indentured their children to white masters and mistresses to save on food and clothing. Eventually, some could afford to do domestic work in white households by day and then go home to relatives, friends, and boarders by night. With some luck, they could establish individual households of their own.

In Boston and New York, for example, about one-third of all free black people lived in white households in 1790, but thirty years later, only one-sixth did so. In southern cities, establishing independent black households took longer.

By 1820, three-quarters or more of the free black households in most major cities contained at least one adult male and one adult female. These numbers suggest that the female-centered form of slave family life—unavoidable owing to the sale and early death of many enslaved black men—gave way to the two-parent family form as African Americans gained freedom.

Prominent African American families emerged in every city and set standards that others sought to emulate. Again, the Forten family in Philadelphia is an example. The Fortens were unusual in many respects, especially in their success and accomplishments. But in their family life, they demonstrated widespread black values. As a young man, James Forten supported his widowed mother and the family of his sister, which had only her husband's mariner wages. His sail-loft business flourishing, Forten married in 1803 at age thirty-seven, but his wife died within the year. A few months later, when his sister was widowed, Forten opened his three-story home to her four children and put two of his nephews to work in his sail loft. A year later, Forten married Charlotte Vandine, a twenty-one-year-old woman with Indian, European, and African ancestors. Between 1808 and 1823, they raised a family of nine children.

The Forten household included an assortment of relatives, apprentices, and boarders, along with children of deceased friends for whom James Forten served as guardian. Census takers recorded that Forten presided over a household of fifteen people in 1810, eighteen in 1820, and twenty-two in 1830. Sometimes the number decreased as a son or daughter reached marriageable age and moved out—but then it grew again if the newlyweds came back to live and work in the household. With frequent comings and goings, the Forten home bustled with activity. Its members also played music, read poetry, and received instruction in French as well as traditional subjects such as literature and mathematics. One of James Forten's daughters described the household as a "happy family circle." Of course, most free black families did not live as comfortably and graciously as the Fortens. But examples of this kind gave hope to those less fortunate.

## New Orleans: A Unique City

While free black communities developed mostly in the North, one also thrived in New Orleans, at the outlet of the Mississippi River. New Orleans became a city in 1803, the year the United States purchased the immense Louisiana Territory from France. When Americans began pouring into the city to pursue new opportunities, they found a unique configuration of races. In the early nineteenth century, slaves living in Louisiana were more linguistically and culturally African than anywhere else in the United States. Yet the population of free people of color was larger, better established, and more racially mixed than in other parts of the country.

Louisiana's free black population had roots reaching back to rule by the French and the Spanish, who tolerated dark-skinned peoples more than Europeans elsewhere in North America did. Since the late seventeenth century,

*With its large free black population, New Orleans had more black artisans, shopkeepers, and street vendors than any other U.S. city. This 1819 painting by Benjamin Latrobe portrays "market folks" in colorful headgear and garments.*

the French explicitly endorsed mixed-race marriages in their overseas colonies. Many French soldiers and colonists married female slaves, and the children of these liaisons often were freed. After the Spanish acquired Louisiana in 1763, the system of slave self-purchase called *coartación* ensured that the free black population would continue to grow. By 1803, New Orleans had 1,800 free black people; by 1809, 3,000, many of whom had fled revolution in Haiti. By 1810, African Americans constituted two-thirds of the city's population of 17,000, and two-thirds of them were free.

Unique among U.S. cities, New Orleans had a hierarchical society with white people at the top, free people of color in the middle, and slaves at the bottom. Over time, free people of color in Louisiana became increasingly urban, lighter-skinned, and disproportionately female. Those released from slavery were mostly black women—the wives or mistresses of white masters. Their mulatto sons and daughters were also freed. By 1791, nearly two-thirds of all free black people in New Orleans were mulatto.

## INDEPENDENT INSTITUTIONS

Finding comfort and inspiration in numbers in the cities, African Americans founded their own churches, schools, and community organizations. "We went out with our subscription paper and met with great success," wrote Richard

*Richard Allen's first church, known as Mother Bethel, was a blacksmith's shop hauled to the lot he purchased in Philadelphia and then refurbished as a place of worship. Methodism's evangelical fervor and simplicity appealed to freed and fugitive southern slaves who reached northern cities.*

Allen, recounting how he and Absalom Jones collected $360 on the first day of their quest to create a separate black church. This was in 1787, shortly after they launched the Free African Society of Philadelphia (FAS), a mutual aid association that used member dues to assist needy free people.

From the beginning, the FAS had religious overtones, and soon its leaders devised plans for a black church of their own. But Allen's fervent Methodism diverged from those who wanted a nondenominational "union" church. So while Jones worked to create the African Church of Philadelphia, later St. Thomas's African Episcopal Church, Allen worked to establish a black Methodist church. Yet both churches had the same guiding idea: that black Americans emerging from slavery required independent black houses of worship. As Jones and Allen explained in their subscription paper, there was a "necessity and propriety of separate and exclusive means, and opportunities, of worshiping God, or instructing their youth, and of taking care of their poor."

## THE RISE OF BLACK CHURCHES

The creation of "separate and exclusive" black churches expressed emancipated slaves' desire to stand on their own as a distinct *African* people. As one historian explains, the black church in these years became "the one impregnable corner of the world where consolation, solidarity, and mutual aid could be found and from which the master and the bossman—at least in the North—could be effectively barred." Black churches became seedbeds of black consciousness. As focal points for social and political organization, they also served as neighborhood centers where free black people could celebrate their African heritage without intrusion by white detractors.

The impulse to form all-black churches originated in the desire for self-government and self-expression. Yet often, white discrimination in interracial congregations provided just as powerful an impetus. In Wilmington, Delaware, for example, the congregation of Asbury Methodist Church was already one-third black at its founding in 1789. By 1802, it was nearly half black. The gifted young preacher Peter Spencer held separate meetings in the homes of free black worshipers or in shady groves at the city's edge, but he was not allowed to preach from the church's pulpit. Black church members were denied communion, barred from ordination, and segregated during worship services, permitted to sit only in the gallery. In 1805, when they were ordered to hold their weekday religious class meetings in the gallery rather than on the sanctuary floor, Spencer and others left to found their own church. They named their all-black church Ezion Methodist Episcopal, after the port where biblical King Solomon kept his warships.

White people often resented independent black churches and mutual aid societies. In their view, free black Americans should remain subservient instead of founding their own organizations. "Their aspiring and little vanities," sneered John Fanning Watson, Philadelphia's first historian, "have been rapidly growing since they got those separate churches. [Before], they were much humbler, more esteemed in their places, and more useful to themselves and others." Comments such as these reflect a disturbing paradox facing African Americans at the end of the eighteenth century: As they extricated themselves from white supervision and the benevolence that came with heavy obligations by founding their own religious and educational institutions, white charges about innate black inferiority intensified. According to Allen and Jones, many white people viewed African Americans as "men whose baseness is incurable." The two ministers freely admitted that "the vile habits often acquired in a state of servitude are not easily thrown off," but they thought it unrealistic to expect too much from people who had been bent and broken by slavery. "Why," they asked, "will you look for grapes from thorns, or figs from thistles?" But, they insisted, as they spoke to white audiences, that black children who were born free and enjoyed "the same privileges with your own" would flourish.

In their independent churches, black Christians heard from their preachers that God had not made them inferior, but had made them a chosen people. When Absalom Jones built his African Episcopal Church, he chose these words from St. Peter (1 Peter 2:9) to be inscribed on the side wall: "But ye are a chosen generation, a royal priesthood, and an holy nation, a peculiar people; that ye should shew forth the praise of him who hath called you out of darkness into his marvelous light; which in time past were not a people, but are now the people of God."

Free African Americans in the new territory of Louisiana tended not to form separate congregations but to stay within the interracial Catholic churches, where they married, baptized their children, and marked other turning points in their lives. Several realities prompted these differences from the experiences of African Americans in the North. First, church authorities in Louisiana never segregated black worshipers or made them feel unwelcome. Second, New Orleans was still strongly Catholic, as the Methodist and Baptist evangelical churches that thrived in the North had not yet brought diverse religious expression to this southern city.

## AFRICAN AMERICAN SCHOOLS

After building their own churches, free African Americans felt emboldened to organize schools. In an era when public schools existed only in New England, black parents had to create educational institutions for their own youngsters. Richard Allen organized the first black Sunday school in America at Philadelphia in 1795, and five years later, Absalom Jones and others established a school for black youth. In 1807, Allen set up the Society of Free People of Color for Promoting the Instruction and School Education of Children of African Descent. Black schools also emerged alongside, or within, black churches in other parts of the country. In 1790, the Brown Fellowship Society in Charleston founded a school for black children, and in 1797 the Baltimore African Academy opened its doors.

Other emerging free black communities established separate churches and schools as well. By the early nineteenth century, black schools operated in all cities with sizeable free black populations.

Like white Americans, black Americans regarded education as the surest path to economic success, moral improvement, and personal happiness. For men and women recently released from slavery, education offered special benefits. It could restore self-confidence and undermine white claims that people of African descent were inherently inferior intellectually. But although they prized education, most black parents—like most white working-class parents—could afford little schooling for their children. Most indentured their children at an early age to reduce household expenses. Children fortunate enough to stay at home had to contribute to the family income by working instead of going to classes. Only the sons and daughters of the black middle class had the luxury of studying through their teenage years.

## AN INDEPENDENT BLACK DENOMINATION

In his attempts to build his African Methodist congregation, Richard Allen had long met with bitter resistance from white Methodist authorities. They controlled the appointment of the preacher, the licensing of lay preachers, and the administration of baptism and communion. To be sure, Allen's church's trustees were African American, and he himself occupied the pulpit at African Methodist. But he and the trustees had agreed to articles of incorporation, necessary to receive monetary support, without realizing that this action made their church the legal property of the white Methodist Conference.

Uncomfortable with the growing independence of Allen's church, white Methodists forced the issue in 1805. Allen vividly remembered the moment when a Methodist elder "waked us up by demanding the keys and books of the church, and forbid us holding any meetings except by orders from him; these propositions we told him we could not agree to." In response, the white elder threatened to expel the entire black congregation from the Methodist Conference. "We told him the house was ours," Allen replied, for "we had bought it, and paid for it." The struggle continued for more than ten years, until the determined white Methodists laid claim to the church itself and ordered it put up for auction. Allen foiled them by outbidding white Methodists at the auction, paying more than $10,000 for the brick church he had built in 1805. Then, on New Year's Day in 1816, the Supreme Court of Pennsylvania ruled that Mother Bethel was an independent church not subject to the authority of the Methodist Conference. Black Philadelphia Methodists had finally seceded from the white Methodist church.

Allen's success in achieving full independence for the African Methodist Episcopal Church exemplified a broader rise of independent black denominations in the first quarter of the nineteenth century. The movement revealed a quest for autonomy fueled by the poisonous racial relations besetting free black communities. Even before Allen's victory, the black preacher Peter Spencer in Wilmington, with forty of his parishioners, created the Union Church of Africans—the country's first fully autonomous African American church. Additional independent black denominations soon appeared in New York, Baltimore, and other cities.

After a generation of tension with white coreligionists, African Americans decided, as one historian has said, "to elect and be elected to church office, to ordain, and be ordained, to discipline as well as be disciplined, to preach, exhort, pray, and administer sacraments—in sum, to have their gifts and graces acknowledged by the whole community." But in asserting black autonomy, black leaders also wondered if they were thereby increasing white antagonism. Still, by the early nineteenth century, urban black leaders took that chance. Their personal emancipation from slavery had catalyzed a psychological rebirth. The collective emancipation of black worshipers from white ecclesiastical bondage enabled them to pursue their vision of a better future. By 1816, as Allen later recalled, his congregation was finally able "to sit down under our own vine and fig tree to worship, and none shall make us afraid."

# BLACK REVOLUTION IN HAITI

In 1791, a white American writer reflecting on the astounding news of a mass slave revolt in French St. Domingue connected it to "that insurrection of Americans which secured their independence." Another urged Americans who had fought their own revolution to "justify those who in a cause like ours fight with equal bravery."

## SELF-LIBERATION IN THE CARIBBEAN

The drama unfolding in the Caribbean captured the imagination of all Americans, but black Americans had particular interest in the massive uprising in

St. Domingue against the most brutal slave system in the Americas. Half a million Africans toiled on the French-owned western half of this Caribbean island (Spain controlled the eastern half), a number approaching the total number of slaves in the United States. St. Domingue also had about 50,000 free people of color (mostly biracial), who occupied a middle caste. The 32,000 white French colonists—a significant minority—maintained an uncertain grip on power. Enslaved Africans outnumbered their masters fifteen to one.

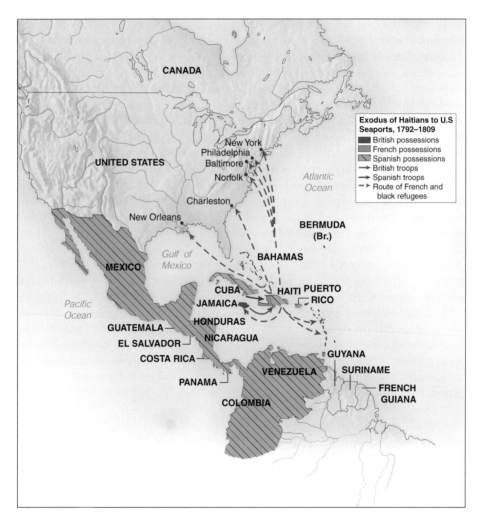

*Map 6.1*
Exodus of Haitians to U.S. Seaports, 1792–1809

*French slaveholders fleeing the slave revolution in 1792 (along with small numbers of free gens de couleur) brought thousands of slaves to U.S. coastal cities. Roughly 3,000 slaves and 3,000 free mulattoes flocked to New Orleans, further enriching that city's linguistic and cultural mix.*

When revolution broke out in France in 1789, the restive free black people on St. Domingue claimed the same "rights of man" as the French revolutionaries. Then, in 1791, a slave named Boukman led a rebellion that attracted the support of white French colonists, who now pitted themselves against French royalists. By the following year, the island was engulfed in violence. In June 1793, self-liberated slaves overran the main seaport of Le Cap Français. Panicked, thousands of French planters and merchants fled to the United States. More than 3,000 reached Philadelphia, while thousands more poured into Norfolk, Baltimore, Charleston, New Orleans, and New York.

Many Americans who initially endorsed the toppling of the brutal slave regime changed their minds when they heard firsthand stories of the

*This image of Toussaint L'Ouverture appeared in* An Historical Account of the Black Empire of Hayti, *published in London in 1805. The book spoke of the black leader's "prepossessing suavity" and remarked on his "astonishing horsemanship" and ability to travel "with inconceivable rapidity."*

bloodbath from the French refugees. Would the fever of black rebellion spread to the United States, they wondered? In 1793, newspapers reported that three slaves in Albany, New York, had set a fire that destroyed twenty-six houses. People along the eastern seaboard soon associated black arson with the overthrow of white rule on St. Domingue. A wave of fires in 1796–1797—including one that burned two-thirds of Savannah—intensified fear of a black uprising.

But black Americans had a different view, sensing a worldwide movement against slavery. They privately applauded the victories of Haitian slaves under the leadership of Toussaint L'Ouverture, formerly a trusted plantation steward. They celebrated again when black Haitians defeated the combined French, English, and Spanish armies sent against them. On January 1, 1804, Haiti proclaimed its independence as a republic of African people. Its revolutionaries had launched the first anticolonial racial war and achieved the first mass emancipation by slaves.

## REVERBERATIONS IN THE UNITED STATES

The revolution of Haiti cast a long shadow across the United States. In Philadelphia, the latest news of Caribbean black rebellion came with yellow fever on a French ship in 1793. The virus spread, claiming 5,000 lives and turning Philadelphia into a morgue. Richard Allen and Absalom Jones mobilized black nurses, death-cart drivers, and gravediggers to deal with the crisis. Charged with profiteering, they produced the first African American attack on slavery after the American Revolution. *A Narrative of the Proceedings of the Black People, During the Late Awful Calamity in Philadelphia* asserted that the "dreadful insurrections" in Haiti should "convince a reasonable man, that great uneasiness and not contentment, is the inhabitant of their [the slaves'] heart." Take notice, Allen and Jones implored. "If you love your children, if you love your country, if you love the God of love, clear your hands from slaves, burden not your children or country with them."

Self-emancipation in Haiti continued to shape African American thought about a worldwide movement against slavery. In 1797, Allen, Jones, and James Forten carried a petition to Congress through the streets of Philadelphia that called for repudiation of the Fugitive Slave Act of 1793. This act, which strengthened the Constitution's fugitive slave clause, permitted southern slave owners and agents to seize free black people they suspected of being runaways. An African American seized as a fugitive slave had no right to prove his or her status as a free person. Could African Americans not expect "public justice" from the national government, the petition signers asked? When would the government end the "unconstitutional bondage" that was a "direct violation of the declared fundamental principles of the Constitution"? With a hint of irony, Jones addressed the petition to "the President, Senate, and House of Representatives of the most free and enlightened nation in the world!!!"

In 1799, Allen and Forten composed a new petition to Congress. "Though our faces are black," they wrote, "yet we are men, and . . . are as anxious to enjoy the birth-right of the human race as those who [are white]." If the Declaration of Independence and the Bill of Rights "are of any validity," then black Americans should "be admitted to partake of the Liberties and inalienable Rights therein held forth." In other cities, African Americans began using the petition and other political means to hold white legislators to the standards of their founding documents. In Boston, Prince Hall, who had led the petition-writing campaign against slavery during the American Revolution, condemned slavery again before the African Masonic Lodge in 1797. While applauding the black rebellion in St. Domingue, Hall denounced "the daily insults" suffered by black citizens on Boston's streets.

The growing self-awareness of free black people sometimes surfaced in unexpected ways. One such occasion occurred in Philadelphia on July 4, 1804, seven months after black Haitians had declared independence. For years, on the Fourth of July, Philadelphians of all classes and colors had gathered in the square facing Independence Hall, where the Declaration of Independence was signed. There they feasted, toasted, and listened to stirring speeches about the blessings of liberty and the prospects of national greatness. But in 1804, several hundred black Philadelphians also celebrated Haitian independence. Organizing themselves into military formations, electing officers, and arming themselves with bludgeons and swords, they marched through the cobblestone streets, attacking white people who crossed their path. The next night, they marched again. Venting their anger over growing white hostility, they terrorized the city, "damning the whites and saying they would shew them St. Domingo."

By 1808, when American participation in the Atlantic slave trade ended officially on January 1, black ministers in many cities turned New Year's Day into the black equivalent of the Fourth of July. African Americans needed a national day of thanksgiving and celebration that had relevance to their lives. New Year's Day served well because it marked both the legal death of the slave trade and the birth of the free black republic of Haiti. Many of the New Year's Day sermons delivered by Richard Allen and other black ministers connected religion and politics. They denounced white leaders for not extending to black people the same rights the Declaration of Independence and many state constitutions had called inalienable. Black preachers repeatedly invoked the elevated phrases of the revolutionary era, confronting white Americans with the hypocrisy of adhering to slavery when their sacred texts prohibited it. "If freedom is the right of one nation," Absalom Jones asked, "why not the right of all nations of the earth?"

## THE FURTHER SPREAD OF SLAVERY

The congressional prohibition of the Atlantic slave trade in 1808 did not eradicate traffic in human beings. Defying the law, slave traders in the Lower South continued to import slaves while the internal slave trade—the selling of human property from region to region within the United States—actually intensified.

In one of the greatest ironies in American history, the revolution in Haiti inadvertently aided the spread of slavery in the United States. Having lost Haiti, France's largest source of wealth in the Americas, Napoleon no longer needed the crops produced in the lower Mississippi Valley to feed the Caribbean island's slaves. Desperate for new income, he agreed to sell the Louisiana Territory (recently acquired from Spain) to the United States for $15 million. The Louisiana Purchase in 1803 doubled the size of the United States and vastly increased the area into which slavery could spread.

As we saw in Chapter 3, slavery had deep roots in Louisiana and Florida, which Spain had turned into a slave-based plantation zone. In 1795, Pinckney's Treaty settled a boundary dispute by recognizing U.S. commerce rights at the port of New Orleans and U.S. control of what later became the states of Mississippi and Alabama. With the Louisiana Purchase, the Lower South became a center of slave trading and slave-based cotton production.

After Congress established the Mississippi Territory in 1798, an immense new region opened for settlement. White Americans, with their slaves in tow, streamed into the sparsely populated but racially diverse region. To carve cotton and sugar plantations out of raw land, planters imported slaves directly from Africa. When the slave trade became illegal in 1808, they smuggled in thousands more Africans. Between 1790 and 1820, the slave population of the lower Mississippi Valley increased tenfold—from 15,000 to 146,000.

The U.S. purchase of Louisiana transformed black life in the South. Infusions of northern and southern capital and the invention of the cotton gin accelerated the transition from an economy based on tobacco, indigo, and rice to one based on sugar and cotton. These changes launched a massive transfer of slaves from the Old South to the sugar and cotton lands of the lower Mississippi Valley. With Americans taking over the Spanish legal system and abolishing slaves' right to self-purchase in 1807, the number of free black people leveled off. Now masters found it difficult to manumit slaves, and the law forbade entry of free African Americans into Louisiana from other states. Between 1810 and 1860, Louisiana changed from a territory where free black people represented 13 percent of the black population to a cluster of states in which they constituted just 1 percent. By sharply restricting opportunities for release from slavery, the laws eroded the relative freedom slaves had enjoyed under the French and Spanish.

Even so, enslaved Louisianans continued to have some advantages over slaves in other parts of the new nation. Living among large numbers of free African Americans inspired hopes of freedom. In addition, many slave masters in New Orleans permitted slaves to hire out their own time and thereby earn money. Some slaves even maintained their own quarters and cultivated close contacts with free African Americans. One observer noted just after the Louisiana Purchase that slaves and dark-skinned free black people "never approach each other without displaying signs of affection and interest, without asking each other news of their relations, their friends, or their acquaintances."

Yet not all relations between free and enslaved blacks were so positive. Light-skinned free people of color were "uncomfortably sandwiched," one historian has written, "between white free people and black slaves"—a "third caste in a social order designed for but two." Often these free people of color saw their well-being as dependent on white patronage, so they aligned themselves with white people in business transactions. Some even owned human property themselves, regarding slave ownership as proof of their social and political solidarity with whites.

# SLAVE RESISTANCE

While some slaves hoped to win their freedom in the new nation through self-purchase or manumission by white masters, others made their bid for liberty on their own terms. The Haitian Revolution inspired many of the rebellions that struck fear into the hearts of slave owners everywhere in the American South.

## FUGITIVE SLAVE SETTLEMENTS

The swamplands in the southern states were good hiding places for escaped slaves. Those who fled their masters headed for swamps, where they formed settlements that plagued slave owners and threatened the slave regime. In North Carolina and Virginia, fleeing slaves established a community in the Great Dismal Swamp in the late 1780s. There they built cabins, planted crops, and governed themselves for many years. Farther south, former slaves who called themselves the King of England's Soldiers (indicating they had gained freedom during the American Revolution by joining the British) also used swamps as staging grounds for resistance. Setting up runaway camps in the Savannah River swamplands, slaves known as Captain Cudjoe and Captain Lewis attracted new refugees in the 1780s. With weapons acquired during the Revolutionary War, they led one hundred men in plundering river plantations just before the Constitutional Convention met in Philadelphia in 1787. When Georgia militia units finally destroyed their encampment, the refugees melted into the wilderness. Similarly, in the Cypress Swamp of Louisiana, black communities in the 1780s drew runaways who fended off periodic attacks by militia units and free African Americans working as slave catchers.

In 1795, slaves organized an uprising at Pointe Coupée, Louisiana. Inspired by the success of the black revolutionaries in Haiti and hoping to ignite a general insurrection, dozens of slaves (aided by three whites, a few Indians, and several free black men) prepared their strategy. But white authorities, alerted to the plot, seized the rebels before they could strike. A white court convicted twenty-three of them and ordered them hanged, their severed heads nailed to posts along the Mississippi River from Pointe Coupée to New Orleans as a warning. But such punishments did not prevent slaves from planning another uprising a year later. Frustrated, the Spanish halted imports of West Indian slaves, whom they considered prime rebels.

## GABRIEL'S REBELLION

No severed heads or brutal crackdowns could suppress slave insurrection. That became apparent in the summer of 1800, when a twenty-four-year-old enslaved blacksmith prepared a strike at the heart of American slavery. Gabriel's Rebellion in Virginia proved the largest slave plot in the republic's early decades.

Born in the year the Declaration of Independence was signed, Gabriel acquired his name from the slave midwife who felt the shape of the baby's head and predicted he would be bold. So the infant's parents named him Gabriel, after the angel who appeared to Old Testament prophets and to the Virgin Mary. In his youth, this choice of name seemed prophetic. Growing up among more than fifty slaves owned by Thomas Prosser, a tobacco planter and merchant in Richmond, Gabriel had the good fortune to learn to read and to master blacksmithing. By the mid-1790s, when Prosser hired him out in Richmond, Gabriel gained a measure of freedom. As his access to the wider world expanded, he learned about the Haitian Revolution. Reported in the Richmond newspapers, the uprising was also recounted by Haitian slaves brought into American port cities. Inspired by the successful slave rebellion, Gabriel developed a scheme to end slavery in the American South.

The young man planned carefully, quietly gathering recruits in Richmond and surrounding counties. Governor James Monroe—a future U.S. president— later maintained that the conspiracy included most of the slaves in the Richmond area and "pervaded other parts, if not the whole, of the State." He was probably right. Gabriel and his lieutenants found the slaves they approached willing to fight for their freedom. When asked "if he thought he could kill White people stoutly," a slave named Jacob answered: "I will fight for my freedom as long as I have breath, and that is as much as any man can do." Another said simply, "I will kill or be killed." Gabriel's brother Martin, a preacher, worked to overcome the fears of those slaves who were hesitant by quoting the Bible: "five of you shall conquer a hundred & a hundred thousand of our enemies."

Gabriel's plan centered on seizing Richmond. On August 30, 1800, 1,000 followers were to meet, divide into three columns, and enter the capital after midnight under a banner inscribed "Death or Liberty," the Haitian revolutionaries' battle cry. The first column would torch Richmond's wooden warehouse district. The second would seize 4,000 rifles from the state arsenal, and the third take Governor Monroe hostage. As white residents rushed out to fight the fires, freshly armed black insurgents would cut them down, sparing only poor women without slaves, Quakers and Methodists, and known opponents of slavery. Once in charge of Richmond, Gabriel's rebels intended to demand their freedom and the abolition of slavery. If slaves in Haiti had done so, they reasoned, why not slaves in Virginia?

But nature conspired against the rebels. As Gabriel's army gathered, a violent storm dumped torrential rain on the region, washing out the bridges by which they had planned to enter Richmond. White Virginians later regarded this downpour as providential, but authorities also knew of the plot from a few slaves who had declined to join. Twenty slaves, including Gabriel's two brothers, were quickly arrested. Gabriel himself slipped away to Norfolk, but was captured when two black sailors betrayed him for a $300 reward and their own freedom.

Using testimony from the informers, the courts tried the rebels for conspiracy and insurrection. Gabriel and his brothers were hanged in October. In all, white authorities executed twenty-six conspirators and transported dozens of others out of state, selling them into slavery in French New Orleans and the West Indies.

Still, Gabriel's Rebellion survived long in the memories of Virginians. In court testimony, one of Gabriel's associates left much to ponder: "I have nothing more to offer than what General Washington would have had to offer, had he been taken by the British and put to trial. I have adventured my life in endeavouring to obtain the liberty of my countrymen, and am a willing sacrifice in their cause." Appalled by the conspiracy and dreading a Haitian-like outbreak in the United States, white Virginians were forced to recognize, as one put it, that "there have never been slaves in any country, who have not seized the first favorable opportunity to revolt." Virginia's nervous governor, James Monroe, agreed: "Unhappily, while this class of people exists among us we can never count with certainty on its tranquil submission."

## OTHER UPRISINGS

Less than a year after Gabriel's Rebellion, a slave named Sancho proved Monroe correct. A ferryman who knew upcountry Virginia well, Sancho was one of Gabriel's followers who had escaped capture. Now he plotted an "Easter rebellion"—a revolt to take place on Good Friday in 1802. By torching houses and fields, his men hoped to precipitate the collapse of slavery. They believed that a "great conflagration of houses, fodder, [hay] stacks, etc. will strike such a damp on their spirits that [white people] will be . . . willing to acknowledge liberty and equality." Word spread of an Easter uprising, even into North Carolina. But again, someone leaked news of the plan, and it quickly unraveled. White militia patrols arrested the plotters, and in 1802 thirty slaves were hanged, Sancho among them. As in Gabriel's scheme, the rebels had not managed to strike that all-important first blow.

Southern planters who hoped that hangings and deportations would end slave resistance were wrong. In 1811, a slave named Tom, arrested in Henrico County, Virginia, confessed that his murder of his master was part of a larger plan to kill slave owners. Slaves "were not made to work for the white people," asserted Tom "but [white people] are made to work for themselves; and [enslaved Africans] would have it so." Later that year, one of North America's largest slave uprisings erupted near New Orleans. Led by Charles Deslondes, a biracial slave from Haiti, about 500 escaped slaves marched on the city, "colors displayed and full of arrogance." Following a battle with white troops, in which two white people and sixty-six rebels died, twenty-one slaves were executed.

White southerners managed to avert or defeat slave revolts, but they did not consider ending slavery. Instead, slave rebellion prompted tighter restrictions on free black people. In 1806, Virginia ordered all newly freed slaves to leave the state within one year or risk re-enslavement.

# BLACK IDENTITY IN THE NEW NATION

In summer 1792, a procession of Philadelphians filed behind the casket of Widow Gray, wife of an African American fruit seller. What distinguished the marchers, said one newspaper, was the "pleasing indifference to complexion," for white and black people alike paid homage to the deceased. This was "a happy presage of the time, fast approaching, when the important declaration in *holy writ* will be fully verified that 'GOD hath made of one blood, all the nations of the Earth,'" the newspaper observed. But those who believed a new era of racial unity had dawned soon saw their hopes dashed.

At the end of the eighteenth century and beginning of the nineteenth, growing hostility toward free blacks led to new restrictions on people of color. Increasingly, white Americans regarded freed African Americans as more dangerous than slaves and less useful for building the new nation. Once again, black people had to rethink their options, including a return to Africa. The War of 1812 raised further questions about their place in America.

## RISING RACIAL HOSTILITY

George Washington had only recently become the nation's first president when Congress began restricting the rights of black people. In 1790, the Naturalization Law limited citizenship to immigrants who were "foreign whites." In 1792, enlistment in the state militias was limited to white men. In 1810, African

Americans were banned from working in the U.S. postal system. States and cities added more restrictions. In the states carved out of the Northwest Territory, laws limited the entry of free black people into the region. In 1807, for example, Ohio required incoming African Americans to post a $500 bond to demonstrate their ability to support themselves. In 1815, Indiana imposed a $300 annual poll tax on all adult black and mulatto men. Even Methodists and Baptists revoked their rule prohibiting slave ownership among members in 1793.

Philadelphia, a center of humanitarian reform, also endured racial conflicts, as working-class white people resented black newcomers from the South who competed for jobs and housing. At a Fourth of July celebration in 1805, white people drove black people from the square facing Independence Hall. A few weeks later, a pamphlet described the city as overrun by black migrants "starving with hunger and destitute of employ."

The racial fear of white Americans dovetailed with the rise of scientifically based racism. Previously, many white intellectuals believed that black people were less capable than white people owing to the degradation of slavery rather than inherent inferiority. "Nurture," not "nature," they maintained, had made black people useless. As we saw in Chapter 5, Thomas Jefferson was among the first to revive the old argument about the supposedly immutable inferiority of people of African descent. By the early nineteenth century, some of the nation's most respected thinkers agreed with Jefferson, attacking the "nurture" theory by contending that Africans had been an inferior race even *before* slavery. In 1811, Charles

*Racist caricatures such as the one shown here lampooned free African Americans in the North. In this image, Governor John Hancock of Massachusetts welcomes Cuffe to "the celebrated Equality Ball given to the Negroes of Boston." In mocking free African Americans, cartoons of this kind made them seem unsuitable for citizenship rights.*

Caldwell, a doctor on the medical faculty at the University of Pennsylvania, argued that the social mixing of the races would lead to disaster—a mixed assortment of individuals with debased abilities who would not fit anywhere.

African American leaders tried to counter these assaults on egalitarianism. James Forten put aside his usual reserve to publish a scorching indictment of the expulsion of black Philadelphians from the July Fourth celebration at Independence Hall Square. Forten also decried proposed laws that would forbid free black people from moving into Pennsylvania.

## NEW ORGANIZATIONAL AND FAMILY NAMES

Following ratification of the Constitution, free African Americans struggled to define their identity in the expanding white nation. Were newly freed people *African* Americans? Did they have a future where they toiled if their culture remained African? Or were they Americans with dark skin who should quickly assimilate into the dominant white society? Or should they regard themselves as Africans living in a strange, hostile land—a displaced people who should return to the realms of their ancestors?

Though the rising generation of free African Americans distanced themselves from the bondage of the past, they titled their churches, schools, and social organizations in ways that suggested a shared heritage. Memories of the African homeland still stirred those who had been born there, and the idea of Africa stirred those who had never seen it. In 1903, the pioneering black historian W. E. B. Du Bois would call this phenomenon "double-consciousness." The black American, Du Bois observed, "ever feels his twoness—an American, a Negro; two souls, two thoughts, two unreconciled strivings; two warring ideals in one dark body, whose dogged strength alone keeps it from being torn asunder."

The African half of this double consciousness showed itself plainly in the way freed people named organizations and churches. The Free African Society in Philadelphia and Newport made its members' identity clear: "We, the free *Africans* and their descendants," stated their articles of incorporation. Black Philadelphians also organized under Africa-inspired names such as Daughters of Ethiopia, Angola Beneficial Society, Daughters of Samaria, Sons of Africa, Daughters of Zion Angolan Ethiopian Society, and the African Friendly Society of St. Thomas. Independent black churches were unvaryingly called "African": the African Baptist Church of Boston, the African Presbyterian Church of New York, the African Union Methodist Church of Wilmington, the First African Church of Augusta. Years later, in the face of mounting white hostility, some black leaders urged followers to remove the word *Africa* from their organizations' names, but for now, free black people embraced connections with African ancestors.

Free black people also grappled with their identity at a personal level: what to name themselves, what to name their children. Inventing a family name—a surname, which most slaves did not have—enabled them to demonstrate their independence. Just as Gustavus Vasa became Olaudah Equiano and James Armistead became James Lafayette, thousands of freed people symbolically left the slave past behind by choosing a new name. Most disposed of their slave names altogether. These names, such as classical names like Caesar and Pompey or mythological names such as Jupiter and Mars, had been conferred by slave masters. Instead newly freed people chose plain Anglo-American names such as John or Mary or biblical names such as Isaac or Ruth. In Philadelphia, the slave Caesar became Samuel Green and Pompey became James Jones. Some freed people chose a surname that announced their new identity, for many Freemans and Newmans are found in church and census records. Others celebrated freedom with a flourish, as did Richard America in Philadelphia and Hudson Rivers in New York City. Still others took names from defining moments in their lives. A slave-born mariner who signed aboard John Paul Jones's ship *Bonhomme Richard* during the Revolution renamed himself Paul Jones. In Baltimore, John Fortune and Elisha Caution selected names that expressed their thoughts about the future. In contrast to practices farther north, freed blacks in New Orleans, Charleston, and other southern cities often tried to preserve ties with white patrons by adopting their masters' surnames.

## THE BACK-TO-AFRICA MOVEMENT

While most northern black leaders chose to stand and fight for their rights in the young nation, others considered a return to Africa. Feeling strong emotional ties to the homeland and desiring to carry Christianity to Africa, these people had few hopes for a decent life in the United States. As we saw in Chapter 5, the back-to-Africa impulse first welled up in Boston only a few years after the American Revolution. In the late 1780s, it surfaced in Newport, where free African Americans reported that they were "strangers and outcasts in a strange land, attended with many disadvantages and evils which are likely to continue on us and our children while we and they live in this country."

At the same time, some white leaders eagerly promoted emigration. The wealthy Quaker William Thornton, for example, garnered the support of Boston's Samuel Adams and Virginia's James Madison for a plan to resettle freed slaves on the coast of Guinea. But Thornton's plan never materialized, as he found few free African Americans willing to leave the United States.

Paul Cuffe was the strongest proponent of emigration in the early nineteenth century. Cuffe, son of an African father who had purchased his freedom and married a Wampanoag woman in Massachusetts, went to sea at age sixteen. Captured by the British in 1776, he was sent with his shipmates to a New York prison ship. Even before the war ended, Cuffe and his brothers asked why free black men—who had no vote and could not hold office—were required to pay taxes. After the war, Cuffe married a Wampanoag woman and prospered in New Bedford, Massachusetts, as a master mariner, ship owner, and merchant. He was distinctly American, even joining the New Bedford Society of Friends.

Yet disillusioned with the treatment of free black people in the North, Cuffe urged an exodus to Africa. In part, he hoped to bring Christianity to Africa, where repatriated free black people would be the principal missionaries. Supported by Philadelphia Quakers, Cuffe organized a trial voyage to West Africa in 1810 to carry out this work. He left from Philadelphia on New Year's Day in 1811 with an all-black crew. Fifty-two days later, he recorded in his ship's journal, "the dust of Africa lodged on our riggings." His voyage stirred debates about whether black Americans best future lay in Africa, America, or both—a debate that lasted for decades.

## THE WAR OF 1812

Even as Cuffe navigated his ship across the Atlantic to West Africa in early 1811, new tensions between Britain and the United States were about to break into hostilities. British cruisers had been seizing American seamen for service on British vessels in an escalation of a long dispute between the two nations. Like other seafaring captains, Cuffe hoped the United States could remain neutral while France and England clashed in the Napoleonic wars. Like other Americans, Cuffe paid the price when Congress, in 1807, passed an embargo on American shipping that threw eastern seaports into a severe depression. Two years later Congress repealed the embargo and reopened trade with all nations except Great Britain and France. But repeal did not stop British and French attacks on U.S. ships. Nor did it stop U.S. customs officials from seizing Cuffe's ship in early 1812 after he returned from West Africa. Charged with possible violations of the most recent maritime trade law, Cuffe managed to repossess his ship and its valuable cargo only by traveling to Washington. He was back in New Bedford by June 1812—the month Congress declared war on England to protect U.S. trade links to Europe. Cuffe now had to postpone his back-to-Africa movement.

The War of 1812 gave free black men and women a chance to prove their allegiance to the new nation and slaves an opportunity to shake off their shackles. Even before war was declared, African Americans had been swept up in the conflict, as black sailors had been among those seized into service by the British. Now free black men enlisted and served in both black regiments and racially mixed regiments. At least one-tenth of the sailors who fought the British on the Great Lakes were African Americans. After the Battle of Lake Erie, Captain Oliver H. Perry declared that his black sailors "seemed absolute insensible to danger." In the summer of 1814, when the British captured and burned Washington, DC, many free black men volunteered to fortify seaport defenses against the marauding British. In September, as the British moved toward Baltimore, William Burleigh of Philadelphia positioned himself in the thick of the Battle of North Point. In early 1815, at the Battle of New Orleans, several free black Louisiana militia units held a strategic position near General Andrew Jackson's main forces and played a gallant role in the U.S. victory.

Later, to promote the antislavery cause, abolitionists celebrated African American contributions to the American effort during the War of 1812. But in truth, many more African Americans served with the British than with the Americans. Just as in the American Revolution, many slaves seized the promise of unconditional freedom in return for joining Britain's cause. When the British fleet conducted hit-and-run raids in the Chesapeake Bay in 1813, Marylanders and Virginians feared a wave of slave rebellions. Rather than rising against their masters, however, slaves simply fled to British ships and bases, where many served as spies, messengers, and guides. U.S. Brigadier General John Hungerford lamented that "these refugee blacks" could "penetrate [these regions] with so much ease."

Refugee slaves' knowledge of the landscape stymied American efforts to defend the nation's capital. The British troops who sailed up the Patuxent River and debarked to march on Washington, DC, were accompanied by at least one hundred newly liberated slaves who served with the Eighty-fifth Regiment of the British Colonial Marines. These were the troops who left the capital a smoking ruin.

Before the war ended, 3,000 to 5,000 slaves of the Upper South, nearly one-third of them women, had fled to the British. Thousands more failed in the attempt. When the British invaded New Orleans in 1815, hundreds of Louisiana slaves fled to them as well. But because the British occupied areas in the South only briefly in the War of 1812, far fewer slaves fled to them than had done so during the American Revolution. Still, the exodus represented the largest act of slave resistance between the American Revolution and the Civil War. In 1815, at war's end, the British faced the same problem they had in 1783: what to do with the escaped slaves who had gained their freedom by reaching British lines. Most went to Nova Scotia; others, to Bermuda or Sierra Leone.

# CONCLUSION

In the late eighteenth and early nineteenth centuries, free black leaders established autonomy for African Americans by setting up independently managed black churches, schools, and other organizations. They built free black communities from Massachusetts to Louisiana, in which many black people made the transition from chattel property to propertied families. But how would black men and women translate that autonomy into equality in the workplace, in politics, and in social life?

How could African Americans continue the fight to end slavery when so many white people believed that black people should remain subordinate and deferential? Despite African American gains, slavery was still spreading geographically, and the number of slaves was soaring—even after the slave trade officially ended in 1808. The antislavery movement was losing steam. Even slave rebellions in Haiti and Virginia—the first successful, the second failed—had not persuaded southern slaveholders to phase out slavery.

Like the American Revolution, the War of 1812 gave free African Americans another chance to win white people's acceptance by showing their willingness to shed their blood for the new nation. For those still in chains, flight to the British lines offered a release from bondage. As peace returned in 1815, as Americans surged west in search of new land in recently established U.S. territories, and as tensions mounted between the North and South, what would happen to the growing population of enslaved African Americans? Bondspeople in the United States numbered about 1.3 million when James Monroe was elected president in 1816. Would they follow the examples of the Haitian black insurrectionists and black rebels in the American South such as Gabriel Prosser and Charles Deslondes? Or would they continue toiling in the fields, sorrowfully bringing children into a world of enslavement—all while hoping that new white political leaders would finally set them free?

# 7

## AFRICAN AMERICANS IN THE ANTEBELLUM ERA

### JAMES FORTEN ON REPATRIATION TO AFRICA

On a wintry January evening in 1817, James Forten squeezed his way forward to the pulpit through nearly 3,000 black men who had thronged Philadelphia's Mother Bethel Church. They packed the main floor, overflowed the balcony, and spilled into the street in an assemblage such as the city had never seen. Representing nearly three-quarters of all African American men in Philadelphia, they had gathered to speak their minds on a hotly debated issue: a campaign initiated by white leaders to repatriate free black people to Africa.

The city's most respected black businessman, Forten opened his heart to his fellow African Americans. He recalled what recent years had been like for the nation's more than two million slaves and several hundred thousand free people of color. The antislavery movement had lost momentum since the slave trade was outlawed in 1808. In the northern cities, white hostility blocked the advancement of free black people, while the federal government restricted their job opportunities. While Forten maintained a workforce of black and white craftsmen in his thriving sail loft, most white craftsmen refused to take black apprentices and pushed skilled black artisans out of the trades. Free black Americans had struggled mightily, but the road forward seemed more difficult than ever. Earlier hopes for racial equality—and an end to slavery—were fading in what African Americans increasingly saw as a white man's country.

A year before, white political leaders had founded the American Colonization Society (ACS) in Washington, DC. Led by outgoing president James Madison and incoming president James Monroe, and including such prominent figures as Chief Justice John Marshall, Kentucky's Henry Clay, South Carolina's

John C. Calhoun, and Francis Scott Key, author of "The Star Spangled Banner," ACS members aimed to resettle free African Americans on Africa's west coast. White northerners endorsed the scheme for various reasons. Some believed white prejudice and the scars of slavery doomed any dream of racial equality in America. Many northern Protestant church leaders saw repatriation as a chance to Christianize the African continent. White southerners saw free African Americans as a threat to the continuation of slavery (and thus to their economy). In their view, free black people's emigration to Africa would remove this threat.

Long before the founding of the ACS, Forten and other northern black leaders had supported colonization. The notion appealed to those African Americans who doubted the United States would ever give up slaveholding. The vast new cotton lands opened to settlement in the Lower South and the Louisiana Territory had fueled the spread of slavery. In the North, white people prejudiced against free African Americans denied them citizenship and equal protection under the law. In a letter to Paul Cuffe, Forten worried that African Americans "will never become a people until they come out from amongst the white people." The idea of returning to Africa was Cuffe's dream, and he had already organized in support of it. In 1811 he had transported thirty-eight black settlers to West Africa.

Chairing the meeting at Mother Bethel, Forten asked the city's three notable black ministers—Richard Allen, Absalom Jones, and Peter Gloucester, of the African Presbyterian Church—to explain the advantages of returning to Africa. Forten added his support. Then it was time to vote. Forten called first for "ayes," those who favored colonization. Not one person spoke up or lifted a hand. Then Forten called for the "nays." The response, he recalled, was one tremendous "no" that seemed "as if it would bring down the walls of the building. . . . There was not a soul that was in favor of going to Africa."

Why did free black people oppose a plan that, on its surface, held so much promise? Ordinary black men and women understood what their leaders did not: that whatever the sincerity and good will of some ACS leaders, the repatriation project would almost certainly be controlled by southerners eager to deport free black people to protect the institution of slavery. Black Philadelphians, Forten reported, were "very much frightened . . . that all the free people would be compelled to go." They could not believe that whites wanted to do "a great good" for a people they hated. Rather, they were certain that "the slaveholders want to get rid of [free blacks] so as to make their [slave] property more secure."

The emotional meeting at Mother Bethel proved a defining event for black Americans. The black men who poured out of the building afterward carried with them a new commitment to the abolition of slavery and a new feeling of unity with dark-skinned peoples of different classes and religious affiliations. The resolutions they endorsed in January 1817 rejected the claim of Henry Clay that free black people were "a dangerous and useless part of the community" and expressed their determination to fight for freedom and equality on U.S. soil. "Whereas our ancestors (not of choice) were the first successful cultivators of the wilds of America," they announced, "we their descendants feel ourselves entitled

## *Chronology*

1816 Richard Allen establishes the African Methodist Church.

Northern and southern political leaders establish the American Colonization Society.

1817 Morris Brown forms a new African Methodist Episcopal congregation in Charleston.

1820s Newly independent republics in Central and South American abolish slavery.

1820 Congress passes the Missouri Compromise.

1821 The American Colonization Society establishes Liberia.

1822 Denmark Vesey plans a slave rebellion in Charleston.

1824 A white mob devastates the black community in Providence, Rhode Island.

1825 Andrew Jackson assumes presidency.

1827 Samuel Cornish and John Russwurm launch *Freedom's Journal*.

1829 David Walker publishes *An Appeal to the Coloured Citizens of the World*.

A white mob pillages a free black community in Cincinnati.

1830 The American Society of Free People of Colour forms in Philadelphia.

1831 William Lloyd Garrison launches *The Liberator*.

Nat Turner leads a slave rebellion in Virginia.

1832 Virginia legislators decide not to abolish slavery.

A South Carolina special convention declares the 1828 tariff null and void.

---

to participate in the blessings of her luxuriant soil, which their blood and sweat manured; and that any measure . . . having the tendency to banish us from her bosom, would not only be cruel, but in direct violation of those principles which have been the boast of the republic. We never will separate ourselves voluntarily from the slave population of this country, . . . our brethren by the ties of consanguinity, or suffering, and of wrong."

So the old battle against prejudice was rejoined. From the founding of the ACS in 1816 to a momentous Virginia slave rebellion in 1831, black Americans across the nation waged a common struggle. Free African Americans looked to build viable communities within a white-dominated land. By establishing independent religious denominations, starting newspapers, and convening national conferences, they hoped to unite dozens of flourishing black communities to fight slavery and its expansion. For the vast majority of black Americans still trapped in slavery, life had grown more difficult than ever. The Louisiana Purchase and the Missouri Compromise triggered a massive transfer of slaves south and west.

Yet black people's dreams of freedom endured. Some African Americans in the South, both enslaved and free, challenged slavery through compelling words and deeds. Three inspirational figures—Denmark Vesey, David Walker, and Nat Turner—led attempts to end slavery, even as southerners stepped up their defense of the practice. Thomas Jefferson's 1814 letter to a friend proved predictive: "The hour of emancipation is advancing in the march of time," he wrote. Jefferson wondered if emancipation would be "brought on by the generous

*This drawing of James Forten, by an unknown artist, is the only known image of the African American leader. Paul Cuffe's reply to Forten's letter quoted on p. 148 was the last he wrote. The New Bedford ship captain died on September 7, 1817.*

energy of our own minds" or perhaps would occur "by the bloody process of St. Domingo"—that is, the slave uprising in Haiti. Full of premonitions, the aging author of the Declaration of Independence could not decide. It "is a leaf of our history," he wrote, "not yet turned over."

## BLACK RELIGION IN THE ANTEBELLUM ERA

The black church was the rock on which all black struggles for freedom and equality rested. The more white hostility intensified, the more black people needed an independent church as a bastion of strength. In the early nineteenth century, separate black churches arose wherever a few hundred free black people lived. The next logical move was to connect these churches in regional networks.

### THE AFRICAN METHODIST EPISCOPAL CHURCH

Richard Allen had such networks in mind when he called a meeting of black Methodists in April 1816. "Taking into consideration their grievances, and in order to secure their privileges, promote union and harmony among themselves," he wrote, black ministers from Maryland, Delaware, New Jersey, and Pennsylvania resolved to "become one body under the name of the African Methodist Episcopal Church" (AME). Thus would they escape the "spiritual despotism which we have so recently experienced." The AME became the largest denomination of black Christians in the United States and spread around the world. Allen was its first bishop.

Black independence offended white Americans who wanted black subordination, not black self-assertion. Years later, one of Allen's successors as AME bishop explained the importance of separate black churches. Taking his cue from the scriptural passage "Stand up, I myself am also a man," Daniel Payne described the psychological and political transformation that came with their creation. When white religious leaders controlled black churches, said Payne, "The colored man was a mere hearer." The point of this paternalism, he believed, was "to prove that the colored man was incapable of self-government and self-support." Founding the AME was "a flat contradiction and triumphant refutation of this slander, so foul in itself and so degrading in its influence."

## CHARISMATIC PREACHERS

One of Allen's first challenges as bishop was to deal with a member of his church who had a mission of her own. Jarena Lee had been born free in New Jersey, but like the children of many poor free black people, she was apprenticed to a white family as a child. Coming to Philadelphia as a teenager, she was transformed by a passionate sermon Allen delivered at Mother Bethel. "That moment, though hundreds were present," she later wrote, "I did leap to my feet and declare that God, for Christ's sake, had pardoned the sins of my soul."

*This image of Jarena Lee was not included in the first edition of her* Life and Religious Experience of Jarena Lee *(1836). The several editions of her book made her one of the first women of the nineteenth century to reach a wide audience through print. In 1844 and 1852, women unsuccessfully petitioned the AME General Conference to allow ordination of black women.*

In 1811, seven years after joining Mother Bethel, she married Joseph Lee, a black minister. Soon she heard a voice telling her, "Go preach the Gospel! Preach the Gospel; I will put words in your mouth." Then, one night in a dream, "there stood before me a great multitude, while I expounded to them the things of religion." Startled by her ability to preach in the dream (a power few expected women to possess), Lee told Allen that God had spoken to her and had commanded her to preach. But Allen said she could not preach from Mother Bethel's pulpit because Methodism had no provision for women preachers. Lee did not back down. "If the man may preach, because the Savior died for him, why not the woman, seeing he died for her also? Is he not a whole Savior, instead of a half one?" Allen still refused, but suggested she hold prayer meetings in her home.

Eight years later Lee arose during a Sunday service at Mother Bethel when the preacher seemed to lose the spirit. Words tumbled from her mouth, and the crowded church fell under her sway. "God made manifest His power in a manner sufficient to show the world that I was called to labor according to my ability," she recalled. Then Allen opened Mother Bethel's pulpit to her. Thereafter, Lee crisscrossed the country, turning fields, farms, and city streets into sacred spaces when she could find no consecrated church in which to preach. Convinced she had divine protection and favor, she often spoke to interracial gatherings. Traveling as far north as Canada and as far south as Maryland, she reached thousands. In one year, she journeyed more than 2,000 miles on foot and by steamboat, delivering 178 sermons.

Though never ordained, Lee served as an inspiration to AME women. Like white women in evangelical denominations, black women did the church's work: teaching in church schools, leading prayer meetings, and organizing church programs. In gaining the pulpit, Lee broke a barrier women did not surmount in other denominations, black or white, for many decades. Across the remnants of this barrier strode other spiritually gifted Methodist women, such as Rebecca Cox Jackson, sister of a lay preacher at Mother Bethel.

## THE EXPANSION OF SLAVERY

"This man came up to me, and, seizing me by the collar, shook me violently, saying I was his property, and must go with him to Georgia. . . . [W]e must set out that very day for the south. I asked if I could not be allowed to go to see my wife and children, . . . but was told that I would be able to get another wife in Georgia." With these words, Charles Ball described the heartache he experienced when he was sold in 1805 by his Maryland master. Nearly a million slaves suffered this agony as slavery expanded to the new cotton frontiers of the South. The Missouri Compromise only worsened the plight of black Americans by facilitating the spread of southern slavery. Native Americans suffered as well. By the 1830s, land-hungry cotton planters had removed Cherokees, Creeks, Choctaws, Chickasaws, and Seminoles from their homelands to territories west of the Mississippi River.

## KING COTTON

The shipment of slaves from the Upper to the Lower South was triggered by the invention of a disarmingly simple machine that processed as much cotton in a single day as fifty slaves cleaned by hand. In 1793, Connecticut schoolteacher Eli Whitney had constructed an engine, or "gin"—a wooden box with a roller and wire teeth—that stripped the sticky green seeds from cotton bolls. Whitney's cotton gin was operated by hand, but when built on a large scale with a giant roller driven by horses or waterpower, the machine could be tended by a single laborer. Before 1793, the time-consuming work of cleaning cotton had limited its profitability. With the gin, cotton cultivation took off.

For landowners, Whitney's invention promised enormous benefits. In Britain and New England, new textile factories turned cotton into cloth coveted around the world. For southern planters, many chronically in debt, the invention slashed the costs of processing cotton and boosted profits to unprecedented heights. Southerners, along with some northerners, headed for the new frontier in the Old Southwest and Louisiana Territory to jump into the cotton business. After the War of 1812, the exodus of white planters from the seaboard states resembled a gold rush. By 1838, slaves in Alabama and Mississippi were producing half the nation's cotton.

But for the 800,000 slaves sold south, Whitney's invention brought heartache. Slave manumissions decreased because masters saw new ways to make slavery profitable. As in Africa centuries before, slave coffles trudged south from Virginia, Maryland, Delaware, and North Carolina. Thousands more slaves were loaded onto ships in ports such as Baltimore and Norfolk and transported to Lower South ports, especially New Orleans. There, strange new masters bought them at auction and took them even farther from family and friends.

The sharp rise in cotton production marked a turning point for the South and the nation. A minor commodity in 1790, cotton became an engine of economic development. As production of cotton soared, so did the southern slave population (see Figure 7.1). "To sell cotton in order to buy negroes—to make more cotton to buy more negroes ad infinitum is the aim and direct tendency of all the operations of the thorough-going planter," wrote one traveler in the South. "His whole soul is wrapped up in the pursuit. It is, apparently, the principle by which he lives, moves, and has his being."

## THE MISSOURI COMPROMISE

Cotton cultivation propelled slavery west across the Mississippi River. When, in 1819, the Missouri Territory applied for statehood with explicit guarantees for slaveholding, Congress could not duck the slavery issue. Admitting Missouri as a slave state would tip the balance in the Senate—so carefully maintained to this point—to the South. For nearly three months Congress debated whether to sanction slavery in this new state. The implications for rising regional tensions filled many with foreboding. "This momentous question, like a firebell in the night," wrote Thomas Jefferson, "awakened and filled me with terror."

**Figure 7.1**
Slave Population and Cotton Production, 1790–1860

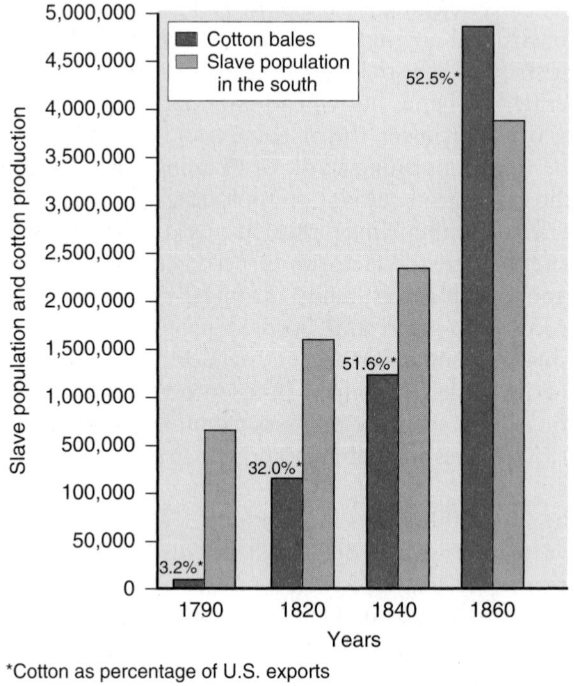

*Cotton as percentage of U.S. exports

*This chart shows why the term "King Cotton" came into use, as it became the nation's most important export.*

Both houses divided sharply on two northern proposals for the gradual abolition of slavery after Missouri gained statehood. The first proposed that slaves born in Missouri be freed at age twenty-five; the second that no new slaves be brought into the state. Both passed the House of Representatives, where free African Americans in the gallery listened with approval, but were defeated in the Senate, where northern and southern states had an even number of seats. The economic necessity and moral uncertainty of slavery was clearly a political flashpoint, preoccupying political leaders and adding fuel to regional conflicts that had been simmering for years.

By March 1820, Congress had hammered out a compromise. It admitted Maine, until now an adjunct of Massachusetts, as a free state to counterbalance the admission of Missouri as a slave state, thus maintaining the North-South balance in Senate seats. It also drew an east-west line along Missouri's southern border (lat 36° 30′) that divided the rest of the Louisiana Territory into future slave and free states.

But there was a second issue. The Missouri constitution forbade free black people from entering the new state. Were free black people not at liberty to go

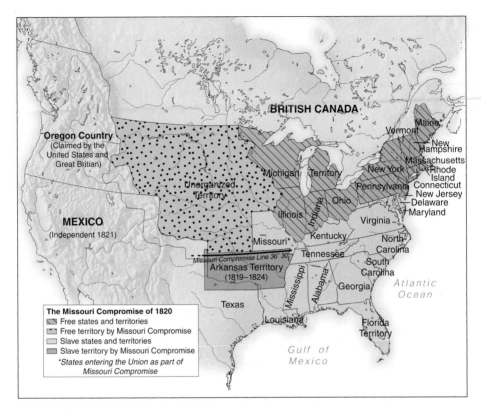

## Map 7.1
### The Missouri Compromise of 1820

*Most southerners were pleased with the Missouri Compromise because it sanctioned slavery in an area where slave labor was most profitable. Out of the Arkansas Territory below the 36° 30', shown on this map, the new slave state of Arkansas was admitted to the Union.*

where they wished? Were they U.S. citizens, or not? Many northern congressmen argued that Missouri's constitution deprived free black people of constitutional rights, including the right to acquire property and the right to religious freedom. But southern congressmen defended this constitution because, in their view, free black people were *not* U.S. citizens. Southerners pointed out that many northern states denied free black people the rights to vote or hold office, give evidence in court, and serve in the militia. Why should a southern state recognize the citizenship of free black people when northern states, as a Delaware congressman put it, treated African Americans as "a weaker caste" that could not "assimilate" with white Americans any more than "oil with water"?

Bringing the pivotal question of African American citizenship to a head, the debate embarrassed the North and heightened regional animosity. In the end, lawmakers added a vague clause to the Missouri constitution that left the legal status of free African Americans for local, state, and federal courts to decide.

Citizenship was not defined. When the Missouri legislature later banned the entry of free black people into the state, Congress remained mute.

The Missouri Compromise temporarily shelved the issues of slavery's expansion and free black people's rights, but these would resurface and spark more violent confrontations between pro- and antislavery Americans.

## THE INTERSTATE SLAVE TRADE

The expansion of slavery across the South stimulated the interstate slave trade, which boomed between the early 1800s and the Civil War. Large slave trading firms, such as Franklin and Armfield of Virginia and Woolfolk and Slatter of Maryland made huge annual profits. Refitting stables and warehouses into slave pens, they herded bondsmen and -women purchased from owners into the enclosures like cattle. From 1810 to 1860, an average of 15,000 slaves a year made the forced journey by ship or on foot through raw country to the Deep South. An estimated 300,000 Virginia slaves were sold "down the river," many from Alexandria, within view of the nation's capital, to a large depot near Natchez, Mississippi.

This vigorous commerce brought new turmoil and terror for slaves, who now faced the nightmare of being sold south. Human misery swelled in the slave pens and on the auction blocks of a country on the move. "I joined fifty-one other slaves," remembered Charles Ball, "thirty-two of these were men, and nineteen women. . . . A strong iron collar was closely fitted by means of a padlock around each of our necks. . . . We were handcuffed in pairs, with iron staples and bolts, with a short chain, about a foot long, uniting the handcuffs and their wearers in pairs. . . . The poor man to whom I was thus ironed wept like an infant when the blacksmith, with his heavy hammer, fastened the ends of the bolts that kept the staples from slipping from our arms." Such episodes reminded slaves that they were commodities to their masters and to the buyers who inspected and haggled over them, as though they were cattle.

The spread of cotton production south and west shattered slave families and separated kinfolk as never before. Enslaved families had never been secure, but in earlier decades they were usually broken up only on the death of an owner, when they were parceled out among heirs or sold to satisfy debts. Painful though the separation was, families in neighborhoods could maintain some contact. But with the rise of the interstate slave trade, husbands were now sold from wives, and children, especially boys, were torn from parents they never saw again. The records of Franklin and Armfield show that, from 1828 to 1836, three-quarters of all slaves sold south were sold as singles; four-fifths of the women sold with children were shipped off without their husbands; of the single males sold, three-quarters were under age twenty-five, and of these one-third were under seventeen. During the antebellum era, probably one-third of all Upper South young black men and boys were sold south.

# SLAVE LIFE AND LABOR

"We were worked in all weather. It was never too hot or too cold; it could never rain, blow hail, or snow too hard for us to work in the field. Work, work, work, was scarcely more the order of the day than of the night." So remembered Frederick Douglass, the most important African American abolitionist and auto-biographer of the antebellum years. "It was—'Fred, come help me to cant this timber here,'" he continued. "'Hurra, Fred! Run and bring me a chisel.' ... 'Come here!—Go there!—Hold on where you are! Damn you, if you move, I'll knock your brains out!' This was my school."

Douglass's words capture the essence of slave life: the expropriation of labor from all those enslaved—young as well as old, women and children as much as men. While northern free black people struggled for their place *in* the sun, a vastly larger number of slaves struggled *under* the sun in lifelong labor. During the antebellum era, the population of enslaved Americans skyrocketed, mostly through natural increase. About 697,000 in 1790, the number of slaves reached nearly 1.2 million in 1810, more than 2 million in 1830, and 3.2 million in 1850.

## Sunup to Sundown: Working for the Master

Slave labor took many forms depending on the region and the crop. Slaves working in the less labor-intensive tobacco- and wheat-growing regions of the Upper South fared better than those in the snake-infested, swampy rice and indigo fields of South Carolina and Georgia. Those who worked in the city enjoyed more advantages than plantation laborers, especially slaves whose masters permitted them to hire themselves out on their own time. Yet plantation labor also varied depending on whether a person worked as a field hand, an artisan, or a domestic servant in the master's house. Men's, women's, and children's work differed markedly as well.

But despite all these differences, three-quarters of all slaves in the South cultivated cotton by the eve of the Civil War. In the cotton fields of Georgia, Alabama, and Mississippi, and even in upcountry Tennessee and Kentucky, slaves endured the harshest possible working conditions. Year-round, they hacked down trees and cleared land. During harvest time, they worked sixteen to eighteen hours a day. At any moment, a man, woman, or child could suffer the lash of the master's whip.

Solomon Northup never forgot the cruel cotton fields. During the hoeing season, "the overseer or driver follows the slaves on horseback with a whip. . . . The lash is flying from morning until night." During picking season, from "day clean to first dark," with just minutes "to swallow [an] allowance of cold bacon," slaves lived in fear that they would not meet their picking quotas. The lash came down hard on those who failed.

In part, the number of slaves living on a plantation shaped their quality of life. Where there were fewer than twenty slaves, most had to labor in the fields. But on the few plantations that had more than twenty slaves, there were more opportunities to work as craftsmen or servants in the big house. Many slaves gladly exchanged the backbreaking repetition of cotton and rice cultivation for the more creative tasks of carpentry, blacksmithing, wagoning, livestock tending, housekeeping, cooking, sewing, and childrearing. The most fortunate slaves had masters who not only trusted them but relied on them to supervise a farm or plantation, carry goods to market by wagon or boat, manage the master's affairs at the marketplace, or oversee other bondspeople's labor.

Slave women's work was sometimes distinct from men's work, but often not. On farms and plantations, as one slave remembered, "women who do outdoor work are used as bad as men." Enslaved women picked cotton, plowed with mule and ox teams, hoed endless rows of corn, dug ditches, spread manure fertilizer, and cut sugarcane. In the evenings, in the slave quarters, they prepared meals for their families, washed and sewed clothes, and cleaned the cabin. Women also worked in groups apart from men, spinning, weaving, and quilting. Elderly women had special responsibilities as nurses, midwives, and caretakers of a slave community's children.

But slavery held distinctive horrors for women. One Virginia slave remembered what thousands of others knew: that an attractive black girl or young woman could be taken into "the big house where the young masters could have the run of her." "Slavery is terrible for men," wrote Harriet Jacobs in *Incidents in the Life of a Slave Girl*, "but it is far more terrible for women." "Superadded to the burden common to all," she explained, "they have wrongs, and sufferings, and mortifications peculiarly their own." In the delicate language of the day, Jacobs tried to convey the frequent sexual abuse white masters inflicted on enslaved women. She revealed that her master, an Edenton, North Carolina, doctor who had fathered eleven children with slave women, began tormenting her as soon as she reached adolescence. "He peopled my young mind with unclean images, such as only a vile monster could think of," she explained. "I turned from him with disgust and hatred. But he was my master. . . . He told me I was his property; that I must be subject to his will in all things." Jacobs was one of the few black women in that household to fend off the master's sexual advances and escape to the North.

In southern cities, where about one-tenth of all slaves and at least one-third of free black people lived, work regimens were more varied than on the plantations, and life was more tolerable. Frederick Douglass believed that "a city slave, in Baltimore, is almost a free citizen compared with a slave on [a] plantation. He is much better fed and clothed, is less dejected in his appearance, and enjoys privileges altogether unknown to the whip-driven slave on the plantation." Slaves in cities also had greater opportunities to gather and exchange news; to participate in races, fairs, and gambling; and to find companionship with fellow African Americans, largely beyond the masters' control, on evenings, Sundays, and holidays.

Nonetheless, urban slaves worked hard: stevedoring on the docks; chopping and hauling wood; digging wells, cellars, and graves; and laboring in construction. In the 1820s, manufacturers began shifting from paid white labor to slave labor, largely to avoid the threat of strikes. In Richmond, for example, the Tredegar Iron Company shifted to slave laborers after an 1847 strike by white ironworkers. Most workers at the city's thirty tobacco-processing plants were slaves, one-third of them children. In Charleston, slaves and free African Americans were more than half the workforce, skilled and unskilled.

Central to a slave's existence, labor was the pivot point of frequent, tense negotiations between master and bondsperson. Though slaves had limited power to negotiate the terms of their lives, they demanded customs governing work hours, holidays, and the right to maintain their own gardens. A master who made no concessions on such customs risked crop sabotage, arson, and poisoning.

This tension also characterized the system of slave hiring common in southern cities. For masters, "leasing" slaves to other white people meant income. Frederick Douglass described the system and its advantages: "After learning to caulk," he wrote, "I sought my own employment, made my own contracts, and collected my own earnings, giving Master Hugh no trouble in any part of the transactions to which I was a party." Self-hiring became so prevalent by the 1840s that brokers and newspaper advertisements began managing arrangements. Longstanding experience, advised one Kentucky broker, "renders us competent of judging and picking good homes and masters for your negroes." Yet self-hiring also had disadvantages. Slaves who leased themselves out were often resented by white laborers, especially in skilled work. Douglass experienced this problem firsthand when he was beaten by a white coworker who, Douglass concluded, "was robbed by the slave system of the just results of his labor because he was flung into competition with a class of laborers who worked without wages."

Urban slaves also frequently came into contact with free African Americans, for every southern city had sizable populations of former slaves who had struggled out of bondage. By the 1830s, in Upper South cities such as Baltimore and Washington, DC, free black people outnumbered slaves. The changing ratio made bondage all the more galling even as it nourished dreams of freedom. But tensions sometimes marred relationships between enslaved and free black people. Some freedmen and women protected their legal advantages by distancing themselves from slaves. For the majority of freed people, who were mulattoes with white fathers, maintaining privileges depended on preserving white relationships.

Regardless of where they worked and what kind of work they did, slaves knew that masters held arbitrary power over most aspects of their lives. Yet the rise of evangelicalism put constraints on masters' exercise of that power. Members of evangelical churches in the South no longer advocated ending slavery, but they did urge masters to treat slaves humanely. Thrown on the defensive, many southern slave masters pointed to their paternalism, conceiving slavery as a system of mutual obligation in which masters housed, fed, and looked after their slaves, who dutifully served their masters in return. "Inspire a negro with perfect confidence in you," wrote one planter, "and learn him to look to you for support & he is your slave." Slave owners also used the idea of Christian stewardship to describe the master-slave relationship. But these concepts of mutual obligation prevailed only in settled regions like Virginia and Maryland. In raw rural states, such as Alabama and Mississippi, masters exercised their arbitrary power without qualms. Moreover, white men's sexual assaults on enslaved women belied all talk of mutual obligation.

Physical, psychological, and legal cruelty held the slave system in place. Whipping was the most common means by which masters battered slaves into compliance. Not every slave was beaten, but all knew that at any moment they *could* be beaten, and all had seen a parent, spouse, or friend subjected to the public bloodying and humiliation that was the mainstay of slave discipline.

Crueler masters advocated routine flogging. "The best plan," said one from South Carolina, "would be to give them 25 or 30 lashes a piece every Saturday night anyhow, which will probably keep them straight until Monday morning." The most effective psychological weapon for controlling slaves was the threat of auction. "In Maryland," recounted Charles Ball after he escaped slavery, "it had always been the practice of masters and mistresses, who wished to terrify their slaves, to threaten to sell them to South Carolina." Every slave knew that a change in the master's moods or fortunes could mean instant—and permanent—separation from family.

In addition to the inherent cruelty of slavery, the close daily interactions of white and black people powerfully influenced the master-slave relationship. This was especially true for southern farmers with fewer than five slaves. Struggling to make a decent living, they shared their housing and meager diet of cornmeal, rice, peas, and salt pork with their slaves. On the new cotton frontiers, master and slave, side by side, put broadax and saw to timber, built log houses, slept on dirt floors, trapped and hunted, and hacked a new life out of the wilderness. But the fruits of this labor fell almost entirely into the master's hands. The "casual intimacies that had sustained them in the leaner times," one historian writes, gave way to separate slave cabins and an impressive house inhabited by only the master and his family.

Yet no matter how vast the social and psychological distance between slave and master, cultural exchange continued. The food on planters' tables blended African and European cuisines. Agricultural techniques reflected mutual knowledge of farming. Herbs and healing remedies used by black women, such as for rattlesnake bites, found their way into the world of white people. Trust and distrust, intimacy and hostility, tenderness and antagonism—these paradoxes marked the master-slave relationship. At one extreme, such relations could be cordial or even affectionate. At the other extreme, they could explode into raw hatred, violence, and murder.

## Sundown to Sunup: Slaves on Their Own Time

When Frederick Douglass was just thirteen, longing "in my loneliness and destitution" for "a father and a protector," a Methodist minister "was the means of causing me to feel that in God I had such a friend." "Though I was a poor, broken-hearted mourner traveling through doubts and fears," Douglass continued, "I finally found my burden lightened, and my heart relieved. . . . I saw the world in a new light." Douglass's words affirm that the life of a slave was much more than endless travail. Though bondspeople might toil all day, they nourished their souls and maintained their dignity, creating "room for the human spirit to live." They took pleasure, as one historian explains, in "something good to eat, a splash of color to wear, the joy in one's body, the delight of dance and music, the ability to find love in another and to create space in which the personal self could exist and breathe." In this personal space, family and religion provided an indispensable sense of meaning, purpose, and joy.

In the face of huge obstacles, slave men and women made marriage commitments, brought children into the world, raised them as best they could, and maintained family connections. Men hired out or sold away from the plantation maintained "abroad" marriages, walking long distances to be with their families on holidays. Slaves authorized to travel delivered messages that kept family and friendship ties alive. In naming children, parents remembered parents and grandparents, brothers and sisters, aunts and uncles. Children sold away from parents were welcomed into new families, though no bloodline existed—gaining fictive aunts and uncles in the process.

The effort to stay in touch with family and friends was extraordinary. Lucy Tucker, born in Virginia and sold into Alabama, managed to send a letter to her mother after a separation of more than ten years. "I received a letter some year or two after I came to this country. . . . My son Burrel . . . has been absent from me nine years. He is now grown, but I have not seen him since he was a boy though I hear from him now and then."

Most slave women became mothers. Masters encouraged childbearing, whether a slave woman was married or not, because each birth constituted a capital gain. Records show that enslaved women typically had their first child at age nineteen, about two years before white women did. Most gave birth to an additional four or five babies. For slave mothers, childbearing provided emotional sustenance. "When I was most sorely oppressed," Harriet Jacobs wrote of her son, "I found solace in his smiles. I loved to watch his infant slumbers; but . . . I could never forget that he was a slave. Sometimes I wished that he might die in infancy." Despite such moments of sadness, raising a family reaffirmed slave women's life force and creative power, giving them a measure of satisfaction in a world of cruelty.

Enslaved black children's lives differed sharply from those of white youngsters. The passing down of property from parent to offspring, so vital to white families, was irrelevant for people who were themselves property. Slave parents had to raise their children under very different circumstances. At age seven or eight, typical childhood games of running and hiding and rhythm and rhyme gave way to carrying wood and water, cleaning cabins, tending gardens, and helping in the kitchen. At this early age, African American youngsters also had to learn how to survive in a white-run world. Mastering the rules governing black-white encounters counted among life's most crucial lessons. Every slave parent knew their children would soon see loved ones whipped, humiliated, maimed, killed, or sold away. Children had to be prepared for this cruel world or they could not survive it.

Survival also meant knowing how to manage white people—how to play on their vanity, feign ignorance, or talk their way out of punishment. These practices became ingrained as enslaved girls and boys grew to young adulthood. Over and over in slave cabins, children heard stories about how to outwit masters or cruel overseers. Often these stories were animal tales, such as the one featuring the trickster Brer Rabbit, who outmaneuvered his stronger foes. Meant to educate and inspire, trickster tales taught important lessons about how to survive.

Next to family, slaves found their greatest support and solace in spirituality. Afro-Christianity took many forms and expressions. In rural areas, where most slaves lived, churches and trained black ministers were rare, so slaves gathered in a forest clearing, a slave cabin, or even a cornfield to sing, pray, and worship. In the antebellum era, more and more masters instructed their slaves in Christianity, hoping to ensure compliance.

But slaves did not necessarily practice the religion their owners taught them. Many adapted Christianity to African spiritual ways that had survived passage across the Atlantic. Throughout the South, slaves believed in the supernatural, especially ghosts ("haunts")—spirits of the dead who returned to make trouble for the living. Many plantations had slave conjurors, revered for their ability to cast spells on enemies and ward off evil spirits.

Slaves and masters viewed bondage through different religious lenses. White masters used Christian teachings to encourage slaves to accept their lot. They drew from the Gospel of Matthew, in which the Sermon on the Mount promises heavenly rewards for obedience. They also emphasized Genesis, in which God makes a contract to protect the heirs of the slaveholding Abraham. African Americans, in contrast, identified with the Old Testament story of Exodus, in which Moses leads the Chosen People out of bondage in Egypt. They also identified with young David, who overcame the giant Goliath, and they longed for the new world order promised in Revelations.

*In this painting of an African American burial in a clearing of a Louisiana cypress forest, the black preacher, wearing a coat, conducts the service. An overseer and his horse stand at the left; white owners of the slaves watch from the right, suggesting a paternalistic plantation owner.*
Source: John Antrobus, Plantation Burial, Oil Painting, The Historic New Orleans Collection.

As a slave in Arkansas observed after hearing a white preacher: "All he say is 'bedience to de white folks, and we hears 'nough of dat without him telling us." Most slaves believed "God never made us to be slaves for white people," as a domestic servant told her mistress. In fact, no Christian idea had more resonance for slaves than divine justice. Charles Ball, for example, believed that in the Kingdom of Heaven "all distinctions of colour, and of condition, will be abolished" and that "Heaven will be no heaven" unless "those who have tormented [slaves] here will most surely be tormented in their turn hereafter."

In southern cities, where a minority of slaves but a majority of free African Americans lived, African Baptist and African Methodist churches grew rapidly, attracting the bondspeople living in the area. Though many urban black people maintained some West African religious practices, they tended to adopt evangelical Christianity more fully than slaves living on plantations did. In the early nineteenth century, the frequent naming of slave children after Old Testament figures—for example, Abraham and Isaac for men, Hagar and Sarah for women—reflected the spread of evangelical Christianity.

In almost all church congregations, women outnumbered men, often two to one. Male preachers played key roles in black communities. Andrew Marshall, for example, who ministered the First African Baptist Church in Savannah for more than three decades, was invited to preach in white Baptist churches and even addressed the Georgia legislature. Founding schools and mutual aid societies, he built a congregation of nearly 2,500 free black people and slaves by the mid-1830s. Like other black ministers, he had to strike a delicate balance, remembering that white people regarded church-organized education and religion as potentially subversive, while simultaneously inspiring his congregants.

Sometimes black religious and secular agendas overlapped. In one example, slaves used songs about gaining freedom in the next world to urge seizing freedom in this world. Music, like spirituality, provided crucial sustenance. Though "the songs of the slave," Douglass explained, "represent the sorrows of his heart," music also expressed faith in deliverance and triumph. The mournful tone of "Nobody knows the trouble I've seen" was balanced by a refrain about berries "sweet as de honey in de comb." The song that began with "Sometimes I feel like a motherless chile" ended with "Sometimes I feel like a eagle in de air, gonna spread my wings an' fly."

Spontaneity characterized slave music. Using animal hides and gourds to fashion drums and banjoes, slaves improvised tunes and created dances. They did the cakewalk or Charleston, or dances like the buzzard lope that featured moves by animals. An English musician traveling through Mississippi in the 1830s marveled at how Vicksburg slaves changed the tempo of a "fine old Psalm tune" into "a kind of negro melody." "Us old heads," a former slave explained about how to create song, "use ter make 'em up on de spurn of de moment. . . . We'd all be at the 'prayer house' de Lord's day, and de white preacher he'd splain de word and read whar Ezekial done say. . . . And, honey, de Lord would come a'shinin' thoo dem pages and revive dis ole nigger's heart, and I'd jump up dar and den and holler and shout and sing and pat, and dey would all cotch de words and I'd sing it to some ole shout song I'd heard 'em

*In this painting of a slave wedding in White Sulphur Springs, Virginia, in 1838, a black fiddler and a bone player provide the music for the festive nuptials of the resort's well-dressed domestic slaves.*

sing from Africa, and dey'd all take it up and keep at it, and keep a'addin' to it, and den it would be a spiritual."

## RESISTANCE AND REBELLION

In 1822, a Charleston slave recalled a pivotal event from that year: "Denmark read at the [church] meeting different chapters from the Old Testament" and spoke of Moses' admonition that whoever steals a man "shall be put to death." White authorities later conceded that Denmark Vesey, a free black carpenter, had indeed mastered the books of the Old Testament and could "readily quote them to prove that slavery was contrary to the laws of God." Here was tangible evidence of a major new development: Black churches had become seedbeds of resistance to slavery as well as houses of spiritual solace.

During the 1820s, free and enslaved African Americans found a call to arms in religion. During this volatile decade, reformers across the nation, often inspired by the evangelicalism of the Second Great Awakening, launched a dizzying array of crusades—for temperance, free public education, and asylums for the poor. All these efforts interested African Americans, but crusades for the abolition of slavery drew their deepest commitment.

## DENMARK VESEY'S REBELLION

Historian Vincent Harding called black Christianity a "liberation theology," one that furnished a biblical and theological justification for challenging slavery and race-based discrimination. This notion became apparent in Charleston, where black Methodists greatly outnumbered white Methodists. Here free and enslaved African Americans who had attended the white Methodist church began, by 1815, to act independently—controlling their own Sunday collections, disciplining errant members, and holding separate black conferences.

Suspecting that even a small congregation of slaves meant trouble, slave owners found this independence alarming. White religious leaders tried to curb black ministers' autonomy and restrict their conduct of services. Black Methodists responded by launching a secession movement in 1817. Led by Morris Brown, a shoemaker and minister who went to Philadelphia to meet with Richard Allen in 1816, more than 4,300 black worshipers, enslaved and free, resigned from the old Methodist church. They soon formed the new African Methodist Episcopal Church in Charleston's Hampstead district.

The leaders of this movement included a brooding free black man named Denmark Vesey. At age twenty-two, he had won $1,500 at a lottery and purchased his freedom from his ship-captain master. He was familiar with slavery in the West Indies and had witnessed the black rebellion in Haiti. Literate in French, Spanish, and English, the tall, bearded Vesey became a respected carpenter, one of the wealthiest black men in Charleston, and a leader at the Methodist church.

Following the black secession from the white Methodist church, Vesey's tolerance for racial abuse wore thin while his anger mounted. He must have fumed in 1818 when white authorities raided the black church, jailed 143 free black and slave worshipers, sentenced Brown and four other church leaders to a month's imprisonment, and ordered others to pay heavy fines or receive ten lashes each. Their crime was educating slaves and holding what white authorities saw as disorderly after-dark religious meetings. Vesey certainly bristled at new South Carolina laws in 1820 that defined teaching slaves to read or write as a crime. These laws also prohibited manumission, forbade free African Americans from entering South Carolina once they left the state, and slapped stiff special taxes on free black householders such as Vesey. This harsh treatment culminated in 1821, when white authorities shut down the AME Church altogether.

Anger turned to resolve. Vesey convinced his most trusted friends that the time was approaching when the deliverance of the children of Israel from Egyptian bondage—a story told many times among black Americans—would play out in the American South. In Charleston and the surrounding areas, Vesey and his comrades preached redemption and divine justice: "Behold the day of the Lord cometh . . . and the city shall be taken . . . and they utterly destroyed all that was in the city, both man and woman, young and old, and ox and sheep, and ass, with the edge of the sword." These Old Testament stories of deliverance inspired listeners, who connected them with the African cultural practices kept alive by "Gullah Jack" Pritchard, a Vesey lieutenant and conjuror well known among Charleston slaves.

In 1822, Vesey and his supporters developed a plan for capturing Charleston and conquering the nearby countryside. Testimony obtained after his capture suggests that he aimed to set fire to the town, seize the armory, overpower white resistance, and perhaps flee by ship to Haiti. The day chosen for the uprising was July 14, the day African Americans in Massachusetts celebrated their emancipation and French republicans celebrated the fall of the Bastille. Further, with many white people out of the city on summer retreats, its 12,000 slaves and some 3,600 free black people would outnumber white people nearly two to one. Most important, on July 14, the moon would be dark, allowing armed slaves from nearby plantations to enter Charleston unseen.

But as Vesey recruited supporters, the risk of betrayal increased. In May risk became reality, as the plan was leaked to white authorities. Rounding up suspects, officials began holding trials. In the end, thirty rebels were executed; all but Vesey were slaves. Thirty-seven others, including Brown, were condemned to die but were pardoned and transported out of state. Later, a letter found in the trunk of one slave who was executed revealed the plot's biblical inspiration: "Fear not, the Lord God that delivered Daniel is able to deliver us."

White authorities considered black rebellion suicidal. After all, white people had managed to suppress black revolts—from the Stono Rebellion of 1739 to Gabriel's conspiracy of 1800—and execute the rebels. Nor could white people understand why well-to-do free black people as well as slaves who belonged to "the most humane and indulgent owners" would conduct vicious assaults on Charleston. "It is difficult to imagine what *infatuation* could have prompted you to attempt an enterprise so wild and visionary," lectured the judge who sentenced Vesey to death. "You were a free man; were comparatively wealthy; and enjoyed every comfort, compatible with your situation. You had therefore, much to risk and little to gain. From your age and experience you *ought* to have known, that success was impracticable." Vesey remained silent, apparently seeing no need to explain why freedom did not mean turning one's back on those still enslaved.

As with earlier slave conspiracies, South Carolina's authorities cracked down on African Americans after suppressing Vesey's Rebellion. Charleston's city council stiffened patrol regulations. The legislature prohibited black crew members whose ships arrived in port from coming ashore. It also criminalized efforts to teach even free black people to sign their names and forbade slaves from hiring themselves out. Even more hurtful, authorities razed the African Church in Hampstead—the heart of black religious, social, and political life. Until the end of the Civil War, black worshipers had to conduct prayer meetings and services secretly. But in 1865, Denmark Vesey's youngest son rebuilt the church.

## DAVID WALKER'S *APPEAL*

A thousand miles north of Charleston, another free black man insisted that the fates of enslaved and free African Americans were entwined. "They think that we do not feel for our brethren, whom they are murdering by the inches, but they are dreadfully deceived," said David Walker. Born free around 1795 in North Carolina, Walker had a white mother and enslaved black father. He traveled to

Charleston in 1822, just before Vesey plotted his rebellion, but headed north. What he saw and heard along the way fortified his hatred of slavery and his anger at a republic that did not live up to its founding principles. Like other African Americans, he knew about the national tumult over the Missouri Compromise. The idea of slavery spreading across the continent further disheartened him.

Reaching Boston in 1825, Walker became a used clothing dealer, a worshiper at the black Methodist church, and an agent for the country's first black newspaper, *Freedom's Journal.* There in the shadow of Bunker Hill, where an early battle for American independence had raged, he penned one of the nineteenth century's most provocative and prophetic essays. In his *Appeal to the Coloured Citizens of the World,* published in 1829, Walker challenged free African Americans to see themselves as part of a worldwide movement for freedom. "Your full glory and happiness," he advised, "shall never be fully consummated, but with the *entire emancipation of your enslaved brethren all over the world.* . . . There is great work for you to do."

Like Denmark Vesey, Walker regarded armed struggle as divinely sanctioned. The God he knew from the Bible hated injustice and oppression of the weak. To resist slavery violently demonstrated obedience to God: "The man who would not fight . . . in the glorious and heavenly cause of freedom and of God . . . ought to be kept with all of his children or family, in slavery, or in chains, to be butchered by his cruel enemies." Knowing the reprisals that followed black rebellion, Walker urged, "If you commence, make sure work—do not trifle, for they will not trifle with you—they want us for their slaves, and think nothing of murdering us in order to subject us to that wretched condition—therefore, . . . kill or be killed."

Walker also intended his *Appeal* to reach the consciences of white Americans and to demolish support for the gradualist approach, which assumed moral suasion would prompt slave owners to release their slaves. Walker also condemned the unprovoked white attacks on free black neighborhoods in Providence, Rhode Island, in 1825; in Boston in 1826; and in Cincinnati in 1829—the first wave of race-based riots in the nation. "Did not God make us all as it seemed best to himself," he asked. "What right, then, has one of us to despise another and to treat him cruel on account of his colour . . . ? Can there be a greater absurdity in nature, and particularly in a free republican country?" "I tell you Americans!" Walker warned, "that unless you speedily alter your course, *you* and your *Country are gone*!!!! For God Almighty will tear up the very face of the earth!!!!"

Grounded in Scripture, Walker's messianic advocacy of armed black resistance had never before appeared in print. White northerners who believed fervently in God and preached the glory of America's republicanism found Walker's words shocking. Black northerners found them inspiring. Christians were hypocrites, Walker insisted, when they condemned intemperance, infidelity, and even Sunday mail deliveries while shutting their eyes to slavery and confining black Christians to "nigger pews." Mocking Jefferson's belief that black people were born mentally inferior, Walker said white people were born *morally* inferior but, led by black Americans, could enter heaven by cleansing themselves of the national sin of slavery.

*Appeal to the Coloured Citizens of the World* affected Boston exactly as Walker had hoped. "It is evident," an evening newspaper reported, that African Americans "have read this pamphlet, nay, we know that the larger portion of them have read it, or heard it read, and that they glory in its principles, as if it were a star in the east, guiding them to freedom and emancipation." To white southerners, the *Appeal* was printed poison. Authorities tried but failed to suppress it. Some black mariners who sailed out of Boston for southern ports sewed copies inside their trousers for safekeeping. "Why do the Slave-holders or Tyrants of America and their advocates fight so hard to keep my brethren from receiving and reading my Book of Appeal to them?" asked Walker in a third edition of his treatise. "Perhaps . . . for fear they will find in it an extract which I made from their Declaration of Independence, which says, 'we hold these truths to be self-evident, that all men are created equal.'"

In July 1830, a few months after the *Appeal* was published, Walker died in Boston, probably of consumption. He was just thirty-three years old. Knowing that Georgians had put a price on his head and that friends had urged him to flee to Canada, many Bostonians believed that he had been poisoned. "I will stand my ground," he had replied to those begging him to go into hiding. "*Somebody must die in this cause.*"

Five months later another Bostonian stepped forward to demand an immediate end to slavery. Twenty-six years old, William Lloyd Garrison had joined the cause in Baltimore, where he had worked with Benjamin Lundy, Quaker publisher of the radical newspaper *Genius of Universal Emancipation,* which exposed the abominable internal slave traffic. Back in Boston, Garrison launched *The Liberator.* Its first issue hit the streets on January 1, 1831, after James Forten loaned Garrison start-up money. In the premier issue, the fiery editor promised to be "as harsh as truth, and as uncompromising as justice. On this subject [of slavery], I do not wish to think, or speak, or write, with moderation. . . . No! No! Tell a man whose house is on fire to give a moderate alarm . . . but urge me not to use moderation in a cause like the present."

## NAT TURNER'S INSURRECTION

A few months after the first issue of *The Liberator* appeared, a slave in Southampton County, Virginia, witnessed an eclipse of the sun and decided that God had called him to lead a rebellion. Nat Turner may have known that slavery was collapsing in other parts of the world. Newspapers reported its abolition in the new Central and South American republics that had wrested independence from Spain. They also reported that Parliament was debating the emancipation of the millions of slaves in Britain's West Indian colonies. A Bible-conscious man and local Baptist lay preacher to fellow slaves, Turner felt certain that an avenging God would punish white oppressors and bring divine judgment to the American republic.

In his youth, Turner had taught himself to read. For years he had searched the Bible for divine inspiration. Around 1830, he had apocalyptic visions of

Christ crucified against a night sky and found what he believed was Christ's blood in a cornfield the following morning. "While labouring in the field, I discovered drops of blood on the corn as though it were dew from heaven," he recounted later. Gathering a trusted group of slaves around him, Turner revealed his vision that the day of judgment was near. God had commanded him to take up the sword.

Turner first chose the Fourth of July, 1831, to launch his uprising, but postponed the date after taking ill. When an atmospheric condition caused the sun to appear bluish green, he and his followers agreed the time was near. Just before dawn on August 22, Turner put his religious mission into action. According to black oral tradition, he told his followers, "Remember, we do not go forth for the sake of blood and carnage; but it is necessary that, in the commencement of this revolution, all the whites we meet should die, until we have an army strong enough to carry out the war on a Christian basis. Remember that ours is not a war for robbery, nor to satisfy our passions; it is a *struggle for freedom.*"

Sixty avenging slaves struck down Turner's master and his family. Then they marched toward the small town of Jerusalem, where they hoped to seize a cache of arms. Storming every house in their path, they slaughtered fifty-five men, women, and children with axes and clubs. Part prophet, part general, Turner soon came upon white militia groups who rushed to the scene as the chilling word of black rebellion spread. Heavily outgunned, the rebels scattered. Most were hunted down, captured, or killed in the woods. By the next day, only Turner and three companions remained at large. Eluding a massive manhunt, Turner was not captured until October 30. He went to the gallows a month later, the last of eighteen slaves executed. Black insurrection had again failed.

But Turner failed only in an immediate sense. Before his death he related his "confessions" to a white slave owning lawyer. Widely circulated as a pamphlet, *The Confessions of Nat Turner* stunned white southerners. Once regarding him as a crazed fanatic, they now found him highly articulate and rational, a man who felt no guilt for pursuing the retributive justice of a Christian God. "Do you not find yourself mistaken now?" asked the white lawyer in Turner's jail cell where he was shackled. "Was not Christ crucified?" replied Turner. Like David Walker and Denmark Vesey, Turner had embraced Christianity and then used it to challenge white America's Christian conduct. Claiming himself a messenger of God, he warned Americans that slavery would destroy their empire of liberty. Slave owners who read Turner's *Confessions* saw that kindness was no protection; Turner himself had a "kind master." Though in no mood to appreciate Turner's messianic message, white southerners feared "that the same bloody deed could be acted out at any time in any place, that the materials for it were spread through the land and always ready for a like explosion." After the carnage, one Virginia legislator suspected there was "a Nat Turner . . . in every family."

Thus Virginia's legislature debated abolishing slavery, but when motions for ending it failed, punishing reprisals were passed instead. To prevent black slaves from hearing the radical message of literate black preachers, enslaved and free African Americans were forbidden to spread the Christian word. Other

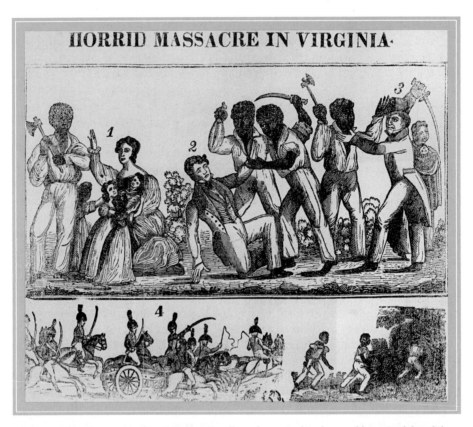

*Abolitionists tried to use Turner's Rebellion to tell southerners what they could expect if they did not end slavery. In this sketch, Turner attacks a white mother and her children (#1); other slaves attack Turner's master (#2); Captain John T. Barrow, a militia captain, defends himself while his wife and child retreat (#3); and the uniformed militia track down the rebels (#4).*

mandates prohibited the teaching of slaves to read and forbade them to assemble in groups of more than two or three.

Yet beyond the reach of law was memory. A new generation of black leaders knew of Turner. Growing up free in Pittsburgh, Martin Delany drew inspiration from him. Harriet Tubman, a Maryland slave, asked herself how she might continue his legacy. In 1833, white men broke up the black Sunday school class that the eighteen-year-old slave Frederick Douglass was organizing. If he "wanted to be another Nat Turner," they warned, he would suffer Turner's fate. In every place where slaves toiled, Turner's visionary quest for liberation lived on.

## FREE BLACK ORGANIZING

"Ought we not to form ourselves into a general body, to protect, aid, and assist each other to the utmost of our power?" asked David Walker four years before Nat Turner's insurrection. Black leaders in the northern cities knew they faced an urgent task in coordinating resistance to colonization, the expansion of slavery, and discriminatory treatment and laws. In their view, organizing nationally offered the best hope of achieving these goals. By the late 1820s, an urban-based network of educated and accomplished black leaders had taken steps to unite black leaders across the nation so all could speak with one voice.

The printed word became a powerful tool in this effort. The first black newspaper, *Freedom's Journal,* was printed in New York City in 1827. Edited by Samuel Cornish, a black Presbyterian minister, and John Russwurm, a recent graduate of Bowdoin College, the publication attacked the American Colonization Society (ACS). It attracted writers and subscribers from all over the North, the Upper South, and the Midwest, including James Forten and Richard Allen from Philadelphia, and David Walker from Boston. The journal became a clearinghouse for black people's exchange of news about the founding of new churches, schools, Masonic lodges, and mutual aid societies. Most important, it served as a forum for discussing the major problems facing African Americans. After Russwurm began promoting emigration and took a post in the new country of Liberia on Africa's west coast, founded by the ACS, *Freedom's Journal* stopped publication. But it was soon replaced by *Rights for All* and later by other newspapers. Clearly, African Americans could now count on a vigorous press aimed at solidifying black opinion while tying communities together in a national network.

As black leaders stepped up organizing efforts, they envisioned a national meeting of free African Americans. In 1829, a vicious attack by white people on black neighborhoods in Cincinnati accelerated plans for the national gathering. Meeting in Philadelphia in 1830, delegates from Pennsylvania, New York, Delaware, Maryland, and Virginia formed the American Society of Free People of Colour. They shared ideas and strategies for fending off white violence, for building educational and vocational institutions, for nurturing moral uplift and self-reliance, and—most essential—for confronting slavery. Seventy-year-old Richard Allen held forth as the patriarch of the 1830 gathering. Drawing on a lifetime of experience as the founder and leader of the AME Church, Allen worried about the personal and regional tensions he observed among African Americans. But he recognized that disputes and competing agendas signaled the coming of age of a new generation. Dozens of black communities were blossoming, he noted, each with its own experiences, accomplishments, problems, and leaders.

Under Allen's leadership, the delegates decried the repatriation of free black Americans to Africa but endorsed emigration to Canada. African Americans, they reasoned, shared a common language with the Canadians, and British authorities in Canada had promised "all the rights, privileges and immunities of other citizens"—exactly what African Americans sought but could not acquire in the United States. Encouraged, many free African Americans began immigrating to Ontario, where they formed new communities.

By the time black delegates arrived in Philadelphia for a second convention in 1831, slaveholders had a strong grip on the nation's economy and political system. Congress routinely rejected antislavery petitions. White southerners advocated seizing Mexican Texas—where lawmakers had abolished slavery—and adding it to the American republic as a slave state. Andrew Jackson was the fifth slaveholder president of seven, and his vice president, John C. Calhoun, was crafting doctrines that recognized state legislatures' right to void federal laws believed adverse to a state's vital interests.

In 1828, matters had come to a head with a new tariff that imposed heavier duties on manufactured goods imported from abroad. Southerners called this the Tariff of Abominations, believing that it enhanced the North's economic power and hurt their own ability to export slave-produced tobacco and cotton. Animosity between northern and southern congressmen escalated into a fiery debate in the summer of 1830. Calhoun's doctrine that states could nullify national action only intensified the conflict, as everyone knew Calhoun had more than tariffs in mind. The doctrine sent the ominous signal that if the national government ever tampered with slavery, southern states could act to protect slavery.

Amid these gathering storm clouds, black leaders accused the American Colonization Society of "pursuing the direct road to perpetuate slavery." Leading African Americans recalled that "many of our fathers, and some of us, have fought and bled for the liberty, independence, and peace which you now enjoy and, surely, it would be ungenerous and unfeeling in you to deny us a humble and quiet grave in that country which gave us birth!"

Members of the American Society of the Free People of Colour sensed that worldwide sentiment was turning sharply against slavery. Delegates to its convention pointed to Denmark's recent abolition of slavery in its West Indies colonies and Britain's plans for a general emancipation in its Caribbean colonies. Encouraged, they called for the removal of the foul "stain upon . . . this great Republic." For many years, the Society met annually to debate strategies for reforming the North and ending slavery in the South.

# CONCLUSION

As the delegates of the American Society of Free People of Colour left Philadelphia in 1831, they knew the generation that had come of age in the republic's early years—most of them born into slavery—was passing on. Many of the founding black ministers were dead or frail, including New York's Peter Williams, Philadelphia's Absalom Jones and Richard Allen, Wilmington's Peter Spencer, and Charleston's Morris Brown. Of the three great secular leaders—Prince Hall in Boston, Paul Cuffe in New Bedford, and James Forten in Philadelphia—the first two had died and the third struggled with ill health. The three great rebels—Gabriel, Denmark Vesey, and Nat Turner—had all been executed. The mightiest pen of the era, held by David Walker, would write no more.

But in many ways, these leaders had already passed the torch to the free black men and women spread across the expanding nation. These African Americans—many born into freedom—were better educated and connected than the previous generation, thanks to the printed word and national networks. These advantages enabled them to resist the ACS's back-to-Africa movement.

As free black communities proliferated during this era, slavery also expanded—as measured by the number of bondspeople and the number of states and territories whose economies depended on slavery. Earlier hopes that slaveholding would wither away with the halt of the slave trade faded. In fact, as cotton slavery spread throughout the Lower South and west into Texas, white slave owners subjected their human chattel to more brutal treatment than before. At the same time, free African Americans were finding white abolitionist allies who yearned to end slavery. This development heightened tensions between northerners and southerners. The work of dismantling slavery and discrimination now lay in the hands of a new generation of black leaders who faced mounting challenges in an increasingly divided nation.

# 8

## AFRICAN AMERICANS IN THE REFORM ERA, 1831–1850

### JAMES FORTEN ADVOCATES AN IMMEDIATE END TO SLAVERY

"The spirit of freedom is marching with rapid strides, and causing tyrants to tremble," wrote James Forten in December 1830 to his friend, fellow abolitionist William Lloyd Garrison. Forten, a free black Philadelphian, was among many reformers exhorting Americans to renew their religious faith and moral leadership. Such efforts, these reformers felt, were necessary to topple the slave regime and end racial hostility.

Like many abolitionists during this era of reform, Forten believed the movement required new goals and strategies. Northern states had all but eradicated slavery. However, a half-century of abolitionist efforts had yielded scant returns in the South, where the slave population was continually expanding. Moreover, the growing number of free African Americans, mostly in northern cities, faced increasing oppression. "That we are not treated as freemen, in any part of the United States, is certain," Forten wrote to Garrison. "This usage . . . is in direct opposition to the Constitution; which positively declares that all men are born equal and endowed with certain inalienable rights."

Although some African Americans over the years promoted colonization in Africa as the only chance for black people to find freedom, Forten opposed this strategy. In the mid-1820s, he had considered a plan to help free black people resettle in the black republic of Haiti. But Forten—whose children counted among the first generation of African Americans born after the American slave trade ended in 1808—soon realized he was American to the core. "To separate the blacks from the whites is as impossible as to bale out the Delaware [River] with a bucket," he wrote Garrison. He would remain in America, Forten assured Garrison, and struggle in the country where his family had toiled for more than a century.

As Garrison prepared to publish the first issue of a radical newspaper entitled *The Liberator* on January 1, 1831, Forten purchased subscriptions for his likeminded Pennsylvania friends. He believed strongly in the *The Liberator's* mission: an immediate end to slavery. *The Liberator* spoke for reform and for abolitionists who would not equivocate. The time of reasoning with slaveholders had ended, abolitionists agreed; the moment for direct confrontation, perhaps even violence, had arrived.

In August 1831, *The Liberator* published a piece by Forten entitled "Men Must Be Free." Forten wrote that a recent outbreak of mysterious fires in Fayetteville, North Carolina, represented a "visitation from God"—a divine warning to slaveholders. "When we . . . hear of almost every nation fighting for its liberty, is it to be expected that the African race will continue always in the degraded state they are in?" Forten asked. "No," he answered. "The time is fast approaching when the words 'Fight for liberty, or die in the attempt' will be sounded in every African ear." Shortly after these words were published, Nat Turner led Virginia slaves in a bloody rampage to gain their liberty. Clearly, some were willing to affirm that the moment had already arrived.

In the mid-nineteenth century, two currents were sweeping the nation. One carried Americans, in day-to-day mingling of peoples and cultures, toward a racially blended melting pot. As white immigrants—especially from Ireland and Germany—settled in the urban North, they toiled alongside free black people in factories and shipyards and lived in the same neighborhoods. In the rural South, slaves continued to live in intimate circumstances with their masters, serving as housekeepers, valets, and nursemaids. The second current involved intense fear and hatred, as immigrants and free African Americans swelled urban populations and caused native-born white Americans to feel overwhelmed.

Both currents reflected the new nation's complex and dynamic economic and geographic expansion. By the mid-1840s, a New York journalist declared that Americans had a "manifest destiny to overspread the continent." Americans of all backgrounds responded to the lure of the West, encountering new peoples and developing new ways of life.

In this era of expansion and reform, black leaders looked to strengthen free African American communities in order to demonstrate their right to full citizenship. They preached self-improvement and education as the best means of building their communities, finding work, and proving their worthiness. Nationwide, the African American population jumped from 2.3 million in 1830 to 3.6 million in 1850. Within this population, however, the percentage of free African Americans dropped from 15.9 to 13.6 percent. The resulting demographics meant 1.3 million more slaves and fewer than 120,000 additional free black people.

The question of citizenship, then, concerned only the shrinking proportion of black Americans who were free. The plight of the ever-increasing slave population

## *Chronology*

**1831** William Lloyd Garrison establishes *The Liberator.*

**1832** New England Anti-Slavery Society forms in Boston.

Maria Miller Stewart's public lecture is the first published speech by an American woman.

Philadelphia experiences the first in a series of race riots.

Florida's Seminole Indians and black comrades begin resettling west of the Mississippi.

**1833** Abolitionists establish the American Anti-Slavery Society.

**1836** Gag Rule allows U.S. Congress to ignore antislavery petitions.

Americans in Texas secede from Mexico to declare an independent republic.

**1837** *The Colored American* publishes Lewis Woodson's blueprint for progress.

**1838** Philadelphia mob destroys abolitionists' Pennsylvania Hall.

**1839** Antislavery groups organize the Liberty Party.

**1840** White abolitionist James G. Birney runs for president.

**1842** Second Seminole War erupts in Florida.

*Prigg* v. *Pennsylvania* rules state officials are not required to capture fugitive slaves.

Second Seminole War ends.

**1843** Martin Delany begins publishing *The Mystery.*

**1844** In a second presidential campaign, Birney receives 60,000 votes.

**1845** United States annexes Texas, including more than 50,000 slaves.

**1846** Mexican-American War breaks out.

Wilmot's Proviso that slavery be prohibited in territory acquired from Mexico is defeated.

**1847** Frederick Douglass, Martin Delany, and William C. Nell establish *The North Star.*

**1848** Mexico cedes a large expanse of territory to the United States.

Gold is discovered in California.

Frederick Douglass speaks at the Women's Rights Convention at Seneca Falls, New York.

**1850** In the Compromise of 1850, Congress admits California to the Union as a free state, allows slavery in other parts of the Southwest, outlaws the slave trade in the District of Columbia, and tightens fugitive slave laws.

was of far greater concern. Among the manifold reforms under public discussion—temperance, woman suffrage, legal punishment, and public education—African Americans focused most strongly on abolition. Always a small minority, outspoken abolitionists faced scorn, violence, and the suppression of their literature. They also struggled with dissension deep within their ranks that splintered friendships and alliances. Yet for all of this, free African Americans continued the struggle.

# BLACK AMERICANS IN AN EXPANDING NATION

Martin Delany, a black leader in the generation before the Civil War, had always been restless. Born in 1812 in Charles Town, Virginia, Delany grew up in Pennsylvania. After studying at a black church school, he worked as a barber and a cupper and leecher—a medical practitioner who treated illness by drawing blood from the patient. In 1843, he married free-born Catherine Richards, who was from a family of well-to-do Pittsburgh cattle farmers. She shared her husband's hatred of racial injustice, for she had seen her family cheated out of land by white neighbors.

A curious man, Delany traversed the country in 1839. In Philadelphia, he visited the Quaker-run Institute for Colored Youth (ICY). Established as an agricultural training school with white teachers, the ICY soon developed an academic curriculum and hired some black teachers at the insistence of black parents. In New York City, Delany encountered James McCune Smith, a black doctor who provided much-needed services to the city's free black community. Smith had earned a medical degree in Scotland because medical schools in the United States refused to accept him. In Boston, Delany met black abolitionist Charles Remond, whose home was a popular destination for abolitionists of all skin colors.

Delany then turned south. Earning his passage by stoking fires on Mississippi River steamboats, he traveled through Mississippi and witnessed slaves' backbreaking labor. Journeying into Louisiana, where earlier French masters had introduced the tradition of black mistresses, he found many mixed-race people, some of whom were free owners of businesses and property.

Next, Delany visited Texas, where a local slave warned him that white Texans would "as like kill you as not, and they feel the same way about Mexicans and Indians." An independent republic, Texas had recently seceded from Mexico and was attracting slave-owning planters from the tobacco-worn soil of Virginia and North Carolina who now turned to cotton. Texas also had free black people, whom white Texans had invited there to help outnumber Mexicans and Indians. Delany continued into Arkansas and the Indian Territory of Oklahoma, where Indians and black refugees had settled in the 1830s.

## BLACK POPULATION GROWTH

In his lifetime, Delany witnessed an explosion in the nation's black population. The southern slave population grew by about 25 percent every decade from 1820 to 1860. The number of free African Americans grew more slowly; thus, while the *number* of free black people increased somewhat, the *proportion* of free black people dropped dramatically after 1830. Why were slaves an ever-larger proportion of the African American population? The decrease in manumissions is a key reason. The freeing of slaves had nearly ceased across most of the South. Only in the border states of Delaware, Maryland, and Kentucky could slaves gain liberty after 1820. Also, high fertility rates of enslaved women swelled the slave population; the average black woman bore seven children. Although infant mortality rate was high (27 percent of black children died in the first year of life) and life expectancy was low (in 1840, life expectancy was only thirty-three years for black males and thirty-five for black females), the high birthrate helped overcome these factors. Also, illegal importation of slaves continued.

In both the South and North, Delany saw that free African Americans preferred cities. More plentiful jobs and established black communities made urban centers attractive. Southern black people, drawn to cities like Charleston and New Orleans, were more than twice as likely as white Southerners to live in urban areas. By mid-century, Baltimore had the nation's largest black community—over 20,000 free African Americans. Black Northerners were even more urbanized. Philadelphia and New York, for example, with about 14,000 and 16,000 free black people, respectively, became thriving centers of black religious and intellectual life.

In the cities, especially in the South, both enslaved and free women outnumbered men. This imbalance resulted from urban employers' and slave owners' greater reliance on women for domestic labor, while in rural areas black men shouldered most of the farm labor. This gender imbalance made it difficult for black women and men to find partners or sustain families.

Meanwhile, during the 1830s and 1840s, slavery spread west of the Appalachians. In 1825, the majority of black Americans lived within a hundred miles of the ocean their ancestors had crossed on slave ships. But thirty years later, most slaves lived deep in the southern interior, thousands of miles from free-state borders, far from easy contact with abolitionists and with the network of reformers known as the Underground Railroad, which helped slaves escape north to freedom. Mild climate and the labor-intensive cotton crop meant a longer and more brutal work schedule. A few of the boldest slaves escaped into Mexico, and there were rumors of aborted slave revolts, but for most, slavery in the Lower South was relentless.

*Figure 8.1*
Free and Enslaved Black People, 1820–1860

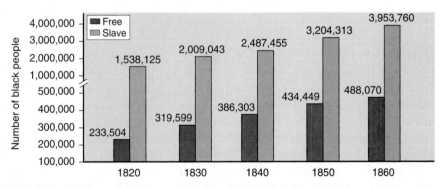

*Though the free black population more than doubled in four decades, the number of slaves, six times greater than the free population in 1820, also more than doubled, dwarfing the growth in free black communities.*

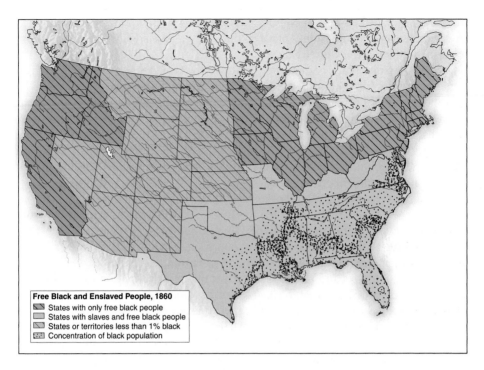

*Map 8.1*
Free Black and Enslaved People, 1860

*By 1860, the presence or absence of slaves defined not only the labor force but also the politics of a given region. The North and Northwest, with few slaves, harbored abolitionists. The Upper South, phasing out slavery, had mixed loyalties to the institution, while the states of the Lower South, where cotton demanded large field crews, based much of their public policy on bound labor.*

## RACIAL SEPARATION

Although free black Americans were decreasing as a proportion of the total population of African Americans, free black people maintained tightly knit communities where they owned land and businesses and learned practical skills. Pittsburgh's Lewis Woodson embodied this community spirit. A slave until purchased by his father at age nineteen, Woodson helped form the Pittsburgh African Education and Benevolent Society, which aimed to educate young black people. Woodson used the classroom to preach religion, industry, thrift, and temperance. The Society assembled a library and subscribed to abolitionist newspapers like Garrison's *The Liberator* and *The Colored American,* which, in 1837, published some of Woodson's prescriptions for black progress. Woodson urged free black men and women to learn artisan and farming skills, purchase land and tools, and get involved in the political process. He also urged them to establish their own settlements in sparsely populated areas where, he believed, they could build safe communities and offer sanctuary to fugitive slaves. He resisted arguments that free black people should settle in Africa, for he thought they would thereby be abandoning slaves who needed their help and protection. Black Americans need "a colony in a place of our choice," insisted Woodson, and that place should be in the United States.

Some separate black communities arose in the South, under white patronage. One was Nashoba, established in 1826 near Memphis, Tennessee. Inspired by European idealists who promoted communal living, British actress and reformer Frances (Fanny) Wright purchased 300 acres for a cooperative farming community that hosted manumitted slaves whose masters hoped to educate them before sending them to Africa. Despite insufficient funds, poor management, and local hostility, Nashoba survived for about five years. When it collapsed, Wright shipped its black members to Haiti.

Meanwhile, a different kind of experiment, aimed at promoting black autonomy, emerged. Congregations of white Quakers and Methodists relocated from North Carolina to the free states of Ohio, Illinois, and Indiana, where they hoped to insulate themselves from slavery and offer asylum to fugitives. From the 1820s through the 1850s, individuals and communities in these states helped thousands of fugitives and manumitted slaves make the transition to freedom.

Free black people also established separate communities. In 1832, 300 black Virginians settled on land in Ohio that their master, John Randolph, had willed to them along with their freedom. In 1836, Frank McWhorter, who had purchased his freedom and that of his family, bought land in Pike County, Illinois. There he founded New Philadelphia, the first of twenty settlements in Illinois and Ohio started by free African Americans. Too isolated to attract many settlers, such towns served mostly as way stations for fugitive slaves traveling to Canada.

Most of these towns disappeared after the Civil War, but Brooklyn, Illinois, 20 miles southeast of New Philadelphia, survived into the twentieth century. Brooklyn grew out of a settlement started about 1830 by eleven families from Missouri. By 1840 it had an African Methodist Episcopal church, a Baptist church, and a railroad connection. In 1873, Brooklyn's few hundred black residents incorporated to become America's first majority-black town.

## BETWEEN SLAVE AND FREE

Martin Delany's national tour introduced him to people of both African and Native American heritage. John Horse, sometimes known as John Caballo (Spanish for "horse"), was one individual who combined both heritages. He was about five years old when Andrew Jackson's troops tried to seize sections of Spanish Florida where fugitive slaves found sanctuary among Seminole Indians. The Seminoles themselves owned black slaves, and John Horse was probably the son of a black slave woman and her Seminole master. However, the Seminoles allowed their slaves to form their own villages, armed them as warriors, and prized them as translators. As black fighters joined the Seminole warriors in resisting U.S. troops, Jackson's officers described the battles as waged "by the negroes."

Despite Jackson's determination, Seminole communities in east Florida survived. When, as president, Jackson signed the Indian Removal Act, some Seminoles agreed to move west to Indian territory in regions that are now Louisiana and Oklahoma. But others resisted, in the First Seminole War in 1835. For more than five years they held off American soldiers. Resistance later continued in a Second Seminole War. When it was over, all the Florida Seminoles had been removed or subdued.

Through these years, John Horse shifted his loyalties. Sometimes he helped the Seminoles battle white soldiers. Other times he aided the U.S. army, serving as a well-paid guide, interpreter, and soldier. By 1840, he had married Susan, a Seminole woman, and soon the couple started a family. As the child of a slave mother, John Horse was not free, but as a slave in the Seminole community he straddled the lines between black and Indian, and between slave and free. His participation in the U.S. army's campaign against the Indians indicates the instability of such things as racial loyalty.

Meanwhile, deep in the South, some slaves managed to carve out a degree of freedom. Benjamin Thornton Montgomery exemplified this situation. Though never free, he enjoyed many privileges usually reserved for white Americans. In 1836, Montgomery was purchased from Virginia by Joseph Davis, owner of Hurricane Plantation near Vicksburg, Mississippi. Davis, a southern reformer experimenting with crop rotation and labor management, believed that treating workers with dignity, and offering them skills and responsibility, would prove more profitable than harsh discipline. No Hurricane slave was ever punished without a hearing before a jury of peers. Davis fired overseers who violated this policy.

Soon after arriving at Hurricane, Ben Montgomery ran away. When he was captured, he negotiated an agreement that made staying more palatable. The literate Montgomery persuaded Davis to lend him books and, eventually, to give him control of the plantation store—including part of the profits. Encouraging Montgomery to master surveying, drafting, and mechanical skills, Davis put him in charge of Hurricane's construction projects and machinery, including several steam engines.

With thrift, discipline, and his master's indulgence, Montgomery amassed broad knowledge and considerable savings. Married in 1840 to another slave, Mary Lewis, he fathered four children. He bought books, paid tutors to educate his children, and purchased his wife's time so she could stay at home to care for their family. Montgomery's family life, with his wife and children sheltered from a bruising work regimen, mirrored the middle-class white ideal. His relationship with his white owner may have come as close to friendship as was possible within slavery. Indeed, Montgomery's children recalled that whenever their father entered a room, Davis pulled a chair up to the table and invited his slave to sit.

Apparently Montgomery never sought legal freedom, and Davis never offered it. Montgomery's situation was enviable compared to the other 100,000 Mississippi slaves. Still, Montgomery was constrained by a society where white people controlled black people's opportunities, and Davis's blueprint for human dignity and an efficient workplace did not include black liberation.

# BLACK AMERICANS AND REFORM

"As Christ died in vain for those who will not accept his offered mercy, so will it be vain for the advocates of freedom to spend their breath in our behalf, unless [African Americans] make some mighty efforts to raise your sons and daughters from the horrible state of degradation in which they are placed." Speaking in Boston in 1832, African American Maria Miller Stewart displayed the religious, intellectual, and political energy that made her one of the era's most dedicated reformers. Though her public speaking was short-lived, she was influential, using religion to inspire broad political and social action.

Building on the reform spirit, free African Americans sought to gain skills and resources to shield themselves from racism and exploitation. They established schools and literary societies for both children and adults. They boycotted slave-produced goods. Black ministers preached about humility and patience. Some also taught rebellion.

## RELIGION AND REFORM

Maria Miller Stewart's early experiences helped mold her ideas. Born to free black parents in Connecticut in 1803 but orphaned by age five, she became a servant to a white minister who taught her to read. Through this early training, she was introduced to the Second Great Awakening, a wave of religious energy that swept America in the 1820s, inspiring leaders to try to cleanse the country of sin.

In 1818 Stewart moved to Boston, working as a domestic until she married James Stewart, a well-to-do black shipper whose income afforded her several years of leisurely reading. But her comfortable life did not last. In 1829, Maria Stewart was widowed. Her husband left her an inheritance and a soon-to-be-born son. But the white executor of the estate swindled Stewart out of her bequest.

To support herself, Stewart turned from reading to writing and speaking. She had applauded the fiery *Appeal to the Coloured Citizens,* published in 1829 by her friend David Walker. Walker had hinted that God might instruct slaves to violently overthrow their masters, and upon Walker's death in 1830, Stewart took up his mixture of religion and revolution. In this she was encouraged by William Lloyd Garrison, who in 1831 helped her publish a pamphlet that caught the attention of Boston's literary circles. This pamphlet, "Religion and the Pure Principles of Morality, the Sure Foundation on Which We Must Build," promoted thrift and sobriety as a means for earning citizenship and stressed the importance of religious faith. "It is the religion of Jesus alone that will constitute your happiness here," she wrote.

Garrison supported Stewart's advocacy of rights for black women. She argued that discrimination against women and African Americans were entwined, preventing black women's full development and mocking Christian virtue. Claiming that black men contributed to the oppression of black women, she warned African American women not to be subservient to them. "How long," she asked, "shall a mean set of men flatter us with their smiles, and enrich themselves with our hard earnings?" Women, she concluded, must "promote and patronize each other," with a spirit that is "bold and enterprising, fearless and undaunted." Stewart urged black women to work together to end their oppression: "How long shall the fair daughters of Africa be compelled to bury their minds and talents beneath a load of iron pots and kettles? Until union, knowledge and love begin to flow among us." With barely 2,500 African Americans living in Boston in 1830, few black women heard Stewart speak. But *The Liberator*'s 3,500 subscribers helped spread her ideas. Inspired, black New Englanders formed the Female Anti-Slavery Society of Salem, Massachusetts, in 1832.

The first female public speaker in America whose speeches were published, Stewart set an example for black women of her day. However, the hostility she encountered wore her down. She left Boston in 1833. "I am about to leave you, for I find it of no use to me to try to make myself useful among my color in this city. God has tried me as if by fire. I can now bless those who have hated me, and pray for those who have used and persecuted me." Stewart moved to New York to teach in a colored school.

## SELF-IMPROVEMENT AND EDUCATION

"Instead of drinking grog or smoking tobacco, we should read the newspaper." Thus did Pittsburgh teacher Lewis Woodson implore his students to use their time and money for self-improvement. Maria Stewart shared this commitment to self-discipline and thrift. "I would implore our men," she admonished, "and especially our rising youth, to flee from the gambling board and the dance hall; for we are poor, and have no money to throw away." Free black Americans like Woodson and Stewart hoped self-improvement would convince white Americans that black people could be responsible and productive citizens. They believed African Americans should learn to read and write, to work outside of slavery, and to lead lives of Christian virtue.

The Pittsburgh African Education Society adopted this blueprint. "The intellectual capacity of the black man is equal to that of the white," said its constitution, "and he is equally susceptible of improvement, all ancient history makes manifest; and modern examples put this beyond a single doubt." Persuaded that "ignorance is the cause of the present degradation and bondage of the people of color in these United States," the Society erected a building to house a school, library, and lecture hall, open to all black people, enslaved and free.

The American Moral Reform Society (AMRS) also promoted black self-improvement. Established in Philadelphia in 1835, it aimed to reform all American society. At age sixty-nine, James Forten became the AMRS president. Less than half Forten's age, the eloquent William Whipper was its spokesman, exhorting "every *American*," regardless of race, to commit to "EDUCATION, TEMPERANCE, ECONOMY, and UNIVERSAL LIBERTY."

The reform spirit fostered many self-help societies. The Afric-Female Intelligence Society of Boston, the New York Female Literary Society, and others met regularly to read and debate history, science, and current events. In Philadelphia, dozens of black organizations modeled responsible citizenship by providing musical, educational, recreational, and burial services.

While self-help societies played a vital role, schools for black children proved even more crucial. During the 1830s, urban public schools excluded black students, so dedicated teachers founded separate schools for them. Most were, of course, in the North. These included Margaretta Forten's school in Philadelphia, Charles L. Reason's Free African School in New York, and the New England Union Academy in Providence, Rhode Island. Even in the South, a few free black children—often the biracial offspring of white masters—studied with black teachers, such as Daniel Payne in Charleston.

Some philanthropic white people set up schools for black children. In Philadelphia, the Quaker-run Institute for Colored Youth opened in the 1830s, becoming the nucleus of a teachers' college that still survives. In 1832, white reformer Prudence Crandall opened a school for black girls in Canterbury, Connecticut. White townspeople, however, harassed Crandall and torched the school. Despite such incidents, teachers persevered.

## From "African" to "Colored"

Working for better lives, free African Americans also focused on self-identity. Black communities traditionally honored their origins by using *African* in naming their organizations. By the 1830s, however, some black leaders suggested discontinuing this practice in order to remind their white neighbors that they and their children were Americans, not Africans.

During these years, many Americans—regardless of skin color or region—were reassessing the meaning of the word *American*. Across the nation, with new canals and railroads transporting citizens, immigrants, printed materials, and fugitive slaves to frontier communities, Americans increasingly encountered people different from themselves. As the new wave of European immigrants increased the number of Catholic congregations and Jewish synagogues, it also intensified native-born white Americans' resistance to newcomers' customs. Anti-immigrant tensions rose, so many black Americans sought to remind white Americans that they were not newcomers. Rather, they were "*colored* Americans."

## Names with Meaning

Free African Americans enjoyed a luxury unavailable to most slaves: choosing their children's names. Maria Stewart named her son after white abolitionist William Lloyd Garrison. The Montgomerys bestowed the Old Testament names Rebecca and Isaiah on two of their children; they named their youngest son for abolitionist William Thornton.

The Delanys also chose names reflecting black concerns as well as Christian values. In 1846, they named a son Toussaint L'Ouverture, honoring the Haitian revolutionary leader. Another son, Charles Lenox Remond, was named for the Massachusetts black abolitionist. Other sons' names were similarly chosen: Alexander Dumas for the black French author; St. Cyprian for the third-century black religious leader; Faustin Soulouque for a Haitian emperor; and Ramses Placido for ancient Egyptian monarchs and a Cuban revolutionary poet. Knowing the biblical promise that, in praise for liberating enslaved peoples,

Ethiopia will "stretch forth her hands to God," the Delanys named their only daughter and last child Ethiopia.

Thus, as parents have done throughout time, the Stewarts, Montgomerys, and Delanys expressed their hopes and values through their children. Earlier generations of African Americans had selected names reflecting their new status (Freeman, Newman, or Trusty) and confirming their American-ness (John, James, or Mary). Reform-era black names bespoke knowledge of literature, history, and current events stretching far beyond the limits of a slave world.

# THE ABOLITIONIST MOVEMENT

Recounting his life story in 1845, Frederick Douglass recalled the day he decided he would never be whipped again. "Whence came the daring spirit . . . I do not know. The fighting madness had come upon me, and I found my strong fingers firmly attached to the throat of the tyrant, as heedless of consequences as if we stood as equals before the law." Douglass's narrative of resistance, escape, and transformation from slave to abolitionist lecturer is among America's most celebrated stories. It chronicles a man's life as well as the subtleties of black-white abolitionist relationships. It also highlights African Americans' sharpened political consciousness and will to resist oppression.

## RADICAL ABOLITIONISM

By 1830, the abolitionist movement turned radical as reformers vowed to break laws, confront slaveholders, or commit violence, if necessary. Though the antislavery movement was not new, the mood of urgency was, as symbolized by *The Liberator*'s strident masthead: "I will not retreat a single inch, and I WILL be heard." Editor William Lloyd Garrison meant to provoke Americans into imagining a radically reformed society.

Radical abolitionism solidified with the 1833 founding of the American Anti-Slavery Society (AAS) in Philadelphia. Garrison led a white delegation to the first meeting that included Arthur and Lewis Tappan from upstate New York and a group of religious revivalists from Ohio. Meeting with James Forten and other influential

*Frederick Douglass was twenty-nine when this daguerreotype was taken. Abolitionists displayed such images in their homes for inspiration.*

black Philadelphians, these men shaped AAS's mission: to complete the abolition begun in some northern states during the American Revolution. The AAS
took particular offense at the Constitution's implication that a black person was
only three-fifths of a citizen. That clause, they said, was "a criminal and dangerous relation to slavery." The AAS promised to organize "in every city, town and
village in our land," to send agents, enlist the press, and circulate literature to
show "the guilt of the nation's oppression" against African Americans.
Members also sponsored lectures where ex-slaves gave firsthand accounts of a
plantation system most northern white people—and many free black people—
had never seen.

Much leadership for the abolitionist movement grew out of the black
churches, particularly the African Methodist Episcopal Church, the largest black
denomination. AME membership soared from 7,000 in 1836 to 20,000 by the
1850s. AME congregations, already strong in Philadelphia and Baltimore, soon
arose in dozens of southern cities. Black Baptist and Presbyterian congregations
also flourished. Although manumissions decreased, the natural increase in black
births resulted in a growing number of free black people in the South—from
180,000 in 1830 to 240,000 by 1850—to fill these churches. Small but tenacious
Catholic, Episcopal, and Moravian congregations took root as well. The
churches became the hub of black community life, offering friendship, education,
entertainment, and, sometimes, information about gaining freedom.

Sending hundreds of organizers across northern and western states to link
2,000 affiliated groups, the AAS had 150,000 members by 1840. The traveling
organizers preached to massive audiences, barraged Congress with antislavery
petitions, and printed volumes about the immorality of slavery. Their most
widely read literature included Garrison's *The Liberator* and Lydia Maria Child's
*An Appeal in Favor of That Class of Americans Called Africans* (1833). Child,
from a white New England family actively involved in reform, decried slavery
and the difficulty free black people had in finding work: "We made slavery, and
slavery makes prejudice." Echoing Garrison, her mentor, she insisted that free
black people were "more temperate and more industrious" than the "foreign
[white] emigrants who are crowding our shores."

In addition to white reformers like Child, Garrison helped recruit African
Americans—including Frederick Douglass—to abolitionism. Born on a Maryland plantation in 1817, Douglass was the son of a slave woman and a white
father he never knew. The planter's wife helped him learn to read as a child.
Though a fight with his overseer crystallized Douglass's intent to escape, it took
three years and two tries before he broke free. Finally, in 1838, disguised as a
sailor, he made his way to New Bedford, Massachusetts. There he married
Anna, a free woman he had met in Baltimore, where she was a domestic servant. In New England, Douglass worked closely with Garrison, describing his
"education" at "Massachusetts University, Mr. Garrison, President." To avoid
capture, the fugitive Douglass spent two years in England while American abolitionists raised funds to purchase his freedom. Free by 1845, Douglass regularly traveled on abolitionist lecture tours and spoke at Conventions of Free
People of Color.

The urgent abolitionist mood generated a wave of antislavery activity. Almost every northern community formed a Vigilance Committee of black people and a few white allies who harbored fugitives in their homes and circulated antislavery petitions. Their connections in ports and along inland trade routes

### Table 8.1
### Abolitionist Organizations

| ORGANIZATION/ YEAR FOUNDED | BLACK LEADERS | WHITE LEADERS | GOALS | STRATEGY |
|---|---|---|---|---|
| American Colonization Society/1816 | Paul Cuffe (died before its founding), Edward Blyden, Robert Campbell | James Madison, James Monroe, Henry Clay | Gradual abolition; black education and resettlement outside the U.S. | Encourage southern manumission; establish schools for free black people. |
| American Anti-slavery Society (AAS)/1833 | James Forten, John B. Vashon, Charles Remond | William Lloyd Garrison, Arthur and Lewis Tappan | Immediate abolition | Petition Congress to broaden the Constitution to outlaw slavery; circulate antislavery literature. |
| Salem Female Anti-slavery Society/1832; Philadelphia Female Antislavery Society/1833 | Sarah Remond, Margaretta Forten, Sarah Mapps Douglass | Lydia Maria Child, Angelina Grimké, Lucretia Mott | Support AAS; encourage black education; pursue women's rights. | Raise money for AAS and for schools; confront AAS on its gender exclusion. |
| Philadelphia Free Produce Society/1838 | Robert Purvis | James Mott, Isaac T. Hopper | Freeze slaveholders out of the American economy. | Produce and sell cotton cloth and sugar from free-labor growers. |
| American and Foreign Anti-slavery Society/1840 | Henry Highland Garnet, Samuel Cornish | Arthur and Lewis Tappan, James G. Birney | Agitate Congress for abolition; mount an antislavery presidential campaign. | Protect American morality by denouncing slavery and refusing to have men and women work together. |
| Liberty Party/ 1840 | Frederick Douglass, Martin Delany | James G. Birney | Establish an antislavery political party. | Challenge traditional presidential candidates. |
| American Missionary Association/ 1846 | Henry R. and Tamar Wilson | Lewis Tappan | Purge white churches of the sin of slavery. | Dispatch missionaries to start black schools and churches. |

helped runaway slaves stay in touch with those left behind. Finally, they supported free produce stores, which sold only products made with non-slave labor. In 1838, several dozen black and white Philadelphians founded the American Free Produce Society, which encouraged consumers to substitute local honey for slave-grown sugar and to shun slave-grown cotton. Following *The Liberator*'s call to be "as uncompromising as justice," they were determined to drive slave owners out of business.

## DIVISIONS AMONG ABOLITIONISTS

Abolitionists agreed on their primary goal: ending slavery. But beyond this there was little unity of motivation or strategy. The primary concern of some white reformers, like the Tappans, was that slavery degraded white Americans' morality. The Tappans would not rent to black tenants or live near African Americans; like many reformers, they hoped free black people would go to Africa. Garrison, by contrast, confessed shame at being part of the white race, socialized with black friends, and published their writing. He also envisioned a society in which all races lived harmoniously. But he could be high-handed with abolitionists—especially black ones—who resisted doing things his way. In 1848, when he discouraged Frederick Douglass from starting a newspaper, Douglass concluded that Garrison resented black leaders and wanted to make decisions for them. Finally, there were white antislavery activists like Gerrit Smith, who embraced black Americans. In the 1840s, Smith donated a large tract of land in northern New York to start a black community, and chose to live there. In 1849, John Brown— who later tried to ignite a slave rebellion in Harpers Ferry, Virginia—moved his family to Smith's black settlement.

Even among free African Americans, there was little unity. Some black entrepreneurs in the North, perhaps wanting to protect thriving businesses or avoid reprisals from white people, remained silent. Others were too focused on mere survival to involve themselves in protests. Only gradually did these black Americans come to see their fate as intertwined with that of slaves.

Gender became another source of division among abolitionists. AAS leaders excluded women from decision making. Like most men of their time, they believed proper ladies should abstain from "promiscuous" gatherings—groups comprising both men and women. Thus, many AAS groups were founded specifically for women, such as the Philadelphia Female Anti-Slavery Society. Women's groups raised funds for black schools or established schools of their own. But they also joined public protests: Women constituted almost half the signers of an 1837 petition to abolish slavery in the District of Columbia.

Appreciating that abolitionist men like Garrison and Douglass believed women's voices should be heard, some women's groups also raised money for *The Liberator*. In 1848, when radical women gathered at Seneca Falls, New York, to write a declaration of women's rights, Douglass was a featured speaker. Though such male support was rare, many women found ways to make a difference. Lydia Maria Child went on the abolitionist lecture circuit, as did Sarah Remond, a black middle-class woman. Frederick Douglass's wife Anna took a

*The Pennsylvania Anti-Slavery Society Executive Committee, shown in this 1851 photograph, included both free African Americans and women. Quaker minister Lucretia Coffin Mott (front row, second from right) provided an important link between abolition and women's rights. Robert Purvis (at Mott's right) was one of Philadelphia's best-known black leaders.*

job in a shoe factory to support her husband's travels. Other women taught children, organized women's literacy programs, and attended political education meetings. In Boston, black women petitioned against segregated schools. In Salem, Massachusetts, they wrote a constitution "associating ourselves for our mutual improvement and to promote the welfare of our color."

Many black women now found a new platform to celebrate both race and gender. Elleanor Eldridge's *Memoirs* (1839), describing her grandfather's noble West African heritage and her brother's leadership among black New Englanders, set an inspiring example. Jarena Lee, whom Philadelphia AME bishop Richard Allen had refused a regular pulpit, became a traveling missionary for Allen's church (see Chapter 7). In 1839, Lee published her story, then joined the AAS, which now provided an outlet for black women's aspirations.

But the appointment of Abbey Kelley to the AAS executive committee in 1840 caused a rupture among abolitionists. Kelley was a tireless lecturer who advocated women's equality, exhorting abolitionists to "take a stand for all truths." Following Garrison's lead, she insisted that "moral suasion" to stir the public conscience was the only sure way to achieve equality. But her appointment alienated many male abolitionists who felt women should not be public leaders. The AAS splintered. Lewis Tappan led a walkout to establish the American and Foreign Antislavery Society, which rushed delegates off to London to persuade the AAS international convention not to seat women.

Sharing Tappan's conviction that women should play a subservient role, ex-slave Henry Highland Garnet became one of only six black men—all ministers—to join the American and Foreign Antislavery Society. Over Garrison's objections that prejudice against women was no better than prejudice against slaves, male delegates banned women from policy-making sessions, consigning them to attend only social events.

This controversy in London crystallized abolitionist divisions. The movement fractured over questions of gender, leadership, the role of free African Americans, and expectations for black people's fate should abolition succeed. After 1840, abolitionists' only common ground was the ending of slavery.

## VIOLENCE AGAINST ABOLITIONISTS

The AAS's confrontational posture drew violent reactions from Southerners and Northerners who feared abolition might dislodge white people's superior social status. Yet many abolitionists welcomed public attacks, feeling they gained publicity and sympathy that ennobled their cause. When Lydia Maria Child's abolitionism drove subscribers away from her children's magazine, she started a sugar-beet farm to promote alternatives to slave-grown sugar. As Garrison was preparing to speak before the Boston Female Antislavery Society in 1835, a white mob that feared black labor competition looped a rope around his neck and dragged him through the streets. He survived only because he was arrested for inciting a riot. The martyrdom pleased Garrison, who viewed the antislavery cause as holy and deemed it better to "have brickbats [thrown at him] in the cause of God than to have wedges of gold in the cause of sin [slavery]."

Elijah Lovejoy was not so lucky. A New England teacher who embraced gradual emancipation, Lovejoy settled in Alton, Illinois, where he founded an abolitionist paper. But local white residents, worried that the newspaper would attract abolitionists to Alton, destroyed his printing press. Infuriated, Lovejoy vowed to defend his constitutional right to free speech. Several times the AAS replaced his equipment; several times angry mobs destroyed it. Finally, in 1837, Lovejoy's opponents destroyed his press and murdered him. Intending mostly to defend free speech, Lovejoy became what a New York black man called "the first martyr in the holy cause of abolition in the nation."

In Philadelphia, barred from meeting in most public buildings, a committee of black and white women who supported the abolitionist cause raised money and built Pennsylvania Hall. It opened in May 1838, with speeches by William Lloyd Garrison and Angelina Grimké, who two days earlier had married Presbyterian minister Theodore Weld. Outraged that black guests had attended the wedding, a white crowd mobbed the building. The following day, the crowd burned the empty building to the ground while the mayor and neighbors stood idly by.

Similar reprisals menaced free black people who agitated for citizenship. Between 1833 and 1838, more than three dozen race riots in northern cities targeted symbols of black independence: churches, businesses, meeting places, and prosperous black families. Often the instigators were white laborers who resented black workers' successes. But some were what one historian called "gentlemen of property and standing"—owners of banks, transportation, and commerce that depended on southern cotton to keep northern textile mills profitable. White clergymen and intellectuals, armed with new pseudoscientific theories about black deficiency, added to the racist chorus. They contended that black Americans lacked the moral character or mental capacity to function as equal citizens.

In the wake of Nat Turner's Rebellion in 1831 (see Chapter 7), southern abolitionism dissolved. A handful of planters quietly continued manumission, but most vocal southern white abolitionists, afraid for their lives, abandoned the South. A few became northern abolitionist leaders. James G. Birney, a slaveholder who helped to develop a manumission policy, left Alabama and in 1837 became AAS's executive secretary. Sarah Grimké, sister of Angelina Grimké Weld and daughter of a prominent South Carolina slaveholding judge, moved to Philadelphia in the 1820s, breaking ties with the South and with her family.

By 1840, few remembered that U.S. presidents Jefferson, Madison, and Monroe—all three from the South—had suggested freeing slaves. The battle lines were drawn: Abolition was a northern movement; Southerners who sympathized had best keep quiet or leave the South.

## NORTHERN BLACK PRESS, SOUTHERN WHITE PRESS

"The *Advocate* will be like a chain, binding you together as ONE," proclaimed New York City's *Weekly Advocate*, an antislavery newspaper, in its inaugural issue of January 1837. "We . . . are opposed to colonization [and] we hold ourselves ready to combat with opposite views," it continued, promising to "contain the news of the day and a variety of scientific and literary matter."

Other black entrepreneurs and communities launched black newssheets. These publications railed against slavery and debated emigration to Africa. Bolstered by the loyalty of their mostly black readers and the increasing reliability of mail delivery, more than a half-dozen black publications appeared by the 1840s. The earliest was John Russwurm's *Freedom's Journal,* begun in 1827. When Russwurm promoted relocating to Liberia, his partner, Samuel Cornish, established an alternative publication, *The Rights of All,* against relocation. Cornish's paper asserted that while a few African Americans might benefit from relocating to Africa, they would be abandoning defenseless slaves. The *Colored American,* begun in 1837, also discouraged black Americans from going to Africa.

Martin Delany's southern travels reinforced his commitment to the black press. In 1843, he launched *The Mystery,* dedicated to "the moral elevation of the Africo-American and African Race." Celebrating African heritage, its masthead proclaimed "all the wisdom of the Egyptians." The newsweekly brimmed with essays, reports from national correspondents, black merchants' advertisements, letters to the editor, and, of course, tirades against slavery. Delany even publicized his support for women's education. From the start, *The Mystery* was both a source of pride, and a drain on Delany's resources. While it boasted more than 1,000 subscribers, Delany often could not collect the subscription fees.

While the mainstream white press lamented depressed cotton prices and an economic downturn that began in 1837, the white-owned *Anti-Slavery Standard* and the black-run papers covered debates important to black reformers. The *Standard* encouraged reformers to unite behind Garrison. But other black newssheets argued for racially separate organizations. Some black reformers echoed Douglass's concern over white abolitionists' efforts to control black people. So black publications like the *Advocate* and *The Mystery* tried to remain independent of white influence.

After several years of struggling with *The Mystery,* Delany joined Douglass and black Boston historian William C. Nell to launch *The North Star.* The new partnership proved just as frustrating as working alone. The newssheet's provocative writing attracted a following, but the paper struggled financially. Yet Delany believed in the power of the press. In 1848, he took to the road again, leaving his ailing wife and his children as he traveled through Maryland, Pennsylvania, Ohio, and Michigan seeking subscriptions.

Proslavery Americans also understood the power of the press. Southern post offices refused to deliver abolitionist tracts, sometimes burning them. Meanwhile, southern periodicals like the widely heralded *DeBow's Review* focused on agricultural management—but all discussions were shaped by proslavery arguments. These periodicals reminded readers that "slave labor is the source of all our wealth and prosperity . . . the basis of the most desirable social and political system the world has ever seen."

Through such publications, southern planters exchanged advice on maximizing the value of their human property. One planter likened his slaves to livestock. Noting that cattle "well cared for in winter were in better condition all the year," he was "cautious of exposing my Negroes in the winter" and recommended providing them with "good houses, good clothing, and good food." Other planters stressed careful attention to daily work schedules, discipline, diet, housing, and religious training. With good management, advised the press, a planter could avoid such pitfalls as *drapetomania*—a mental illness they believed caused slaves to run away—and *dyasthenia aethiopica*, which they said caused slaves to become careless and break tools. Still other planters offered advice on controlling slaves. Some slaves, they explained, "require stirring up, some coaxing, some flattering, and others nothing but good words."

## THE GAG RULE AND LANDMARK LEGAL CASES

Tension over slavery underlay every congressional discussion. Though the Missouri Compromise of 1820 temporarily suppressed debate about whether slavery should spread to western territories, the controversy still percolated, bubbling up as senators Henry Clay of Kentucky, Daniel Webster of Massachusetts, and John Calhoun of South Carolina debated land policy in the West, banking issues in the East, and the division of authority between federal and state governments. Voters watched anxiously as these political stalwarts struggled over concerns.

Meanwhile, the burgeoning northern population foretold a decline in the political power of the South. As immigrants flooded northern cities, the balance in the House of Representatives tipped toward the North. Radical abolitionists, though never more than 5 percent of the North's population, were a strident minority. Many Southerners feared that if abolitionists were elected to Congress, they would limit or end slavery. Surveying their worn-out fields, southern planters yearned to take their slaves farther west, where they might establish new slave states and reclaim their congressional majority.

Fearing incendiary debate about antislavery petitions, Congress instituted the Gag Rule in 1836, consenting to receive antislavery petitions but agreeing to ignore them. Though free speech advocates like former president John Quincy Adams (now a representative) decried this ban on public discussion, the Gag Rule remained in effect for eight years.

In 1839, debate polarized around a dramatic court case after slave captives seized the *Amistad,* a Spanish slave ship. Though the mutiny occurred in international waters near Cuba, it became an American *cause célèbre* when a U.S. naval ship commandeered the vessel. Charged with piracy and murder, the slaves were imprisoned, awaiting settlement of the competing claims of the *Amistad* crew, the American navy, and the Spanish government.

Garrison, proclaiming that the case should awaken the "sympathy of all true-hearted, impartial lovers of liberty," insisted that the slaves had done what Americans had done in their own revolution: defended their rights and liberty. Abolitionist newspapers also decried Spain's disregard for 1818 international laws banning the slave trade.

Over several years, the *Amistad* case slogged through the American legal system. On appeal to the U.S. Supreme Court, John Quincy Adams came to the defense of the mutineers. Though not an avowed abolitionist, he opposed slavery and wanted international law upheld. In 1841, the Supreme Court agreed that the *Amistad* captives should be freed but not that the federal government should transport them to Africa. So abolitionists paid the captives' passage. In November 1841, from Sierra Leone their leader Sengbe Pieh (Joseph Cinque) "thanked all Merica people, for them send Mendi people home."

The *Amistad* episode was followed by a similar case two years later. This time, the outcome disheartened abolitionists. An American ship, the *Creole,*

*To raise funds for the* Amistad *Africans' defense, abolitionists distributed lithographic copies of this painting of Joseph Cinque, leader of the mutiny, for one dollar apiece.*

transporting slaves along the coast, was seized by the slaves and sailed to the Bahamas, where the slaves declared themselves free and under British protection. Daniel Webster, now U.S. Secretary of State, claiming the ship's deck was an extension of American soil, insisted that Britain compensate the owner for his loss. Northern abolitionists felt betrayed by their government. By extending American protection for slaveholders beyond U.S. borders, the federal government, they declared, implicated an unwilling North in the slave trade. Garrison urged northern states to secede from the Union—a "peaceable separation for conscience sake." To slaveholders, this call was further evidence that slavery was under siege.

Historians view the *Amistad* and *Creole* cases as landmarks, setting a precedent for extending abolitionism beyond individual conscience and into the courts, the constitution, and international law. The *Amistad* case also inaugurated the American Missionary Association (AMA), a Christian abolitionist organization that supported schools and missions for black people in Africa and the United States. The organization urged member churches to "purify" themselves by denying membership to slaveholding "sinners" and refusing to do business with them. The AMA did not aim to deprive southern planters of their property. Rather, it sought to cleanse Americans of the sin of slavery, sending missionaries to the American West to preach against it. But the AMA had an additional mission: ridding America of free black people.

## LIMITATIONS AND OPPORTUNITIES

"The heart of the whites must be changed, thoroughly, entirely, permanently changed," wrote New York black physician James McCune Smith to Gerrit Smith in 1846. Otherwise, the black man insisted, racial discrimination would never end. Growing restrictions on free African Americans in the South and new laws denying them the vote in the North made it clear that not enough white hearts were being changed by abolitionist agitation.

Meanwhile, as white Americans streamed across the Appalachian Mountains and the Mississippi River, the slavery issue and racial discrimination accompanied them. In midwestern states like Ohio, Indiana, and Illinois, the 1787 Northwest Ordinance prohibited slavery. But individual state laws often barred black people from entering the state unless they could prove they had money. Some local laws prevented them from owning land. The sparsely populated West seemed to offer greater freedom than the South or the North. The Republic of Texas offered free land to any American—black or white—who would homestead there and help outnumber Mexicans.

### DISFRANCHISEMENT IN THE NORTH

When the Liberty Party nominated abolitionist James A. Birney for president in 1840, Martin Delany and Frederick Douglass campaigned for him. Developing from the AAS division, this was the first antislavery political party. One *Colored American* commentator wrote of the 1840 election: "We ought and must vote for the Liberty Ticket, with James G. Birney at the head, a gentleman, a philan-thropist and a Christian." But only a small number of black men could vote, and the 7,000 votes cast for Birney merely underscored the irony of support from black leaders.

By the 1840s, black political power and participation had all but disap-peared. It had not always been this way. Following the Revolution, as northern states phased out slavery, free black property owners became eligible to vote. But because few black men owned land, most could not exercise this right. Still, in New York, Pennsylvania, and the New England states, the presence of a few hun-dred black voters raised the possibility that eventually black voters could influ-ence elections.

But even as many states began allowing men without property to vote, black men saw their access to the polls narrow. New York, for example, instituted in 1821 a property requirement for black voters only. In 1838, Pennsylvania re-voked the black franchise, despite impassioned entreaties from black leaders who presented evidence of free black people's economic and social stability. Three years later, disfranchisement was narrowly defeated in Rhode Island. In Ohio, Michigan, and Wisconsin, black residents repeatedly—and unsuccessfully—peti-tioned state representatives for the franchise, reminding legislators that the Constitution prohibited taxation without representation.

## THE TEXAS FRONTIER

With increasing limits in the North and South, some African Americans looked west. Greenbury Logan, for example, headed for Texas. Injured in military ser-vice to the Republic of Texas, Logan asked for tax relief in 1841: "I came here in 1831 invited by Col. [Stephen] Austin," explained Logan. "Having no family with me I got one quarter league of land instead of a third, but I love the country and did stay because I felt myself more a freeman than in the [United] states. I am . . . permanently injured and can barely support myself now."

Logan was a free man in a territory severed from Mexico but not yet part of the United States. Indeed, Texas had a unique history. Many southern planters were among the 20,000 white Americans who accepted Mexico's invitation in the 1820s to settle Texas. These planters brought 2,000 slaves with them. When Mexico achieved independence from Spain in 1821 and began abolishing slavery, Texas became a pivotal part of U.S. politics. President Andrew Jackson's unsuc-cessful attempt to buy Texas from Mexico led the Mexican government to retract its invitation to American settlers in 1830. In turn, the Americans already living in Texas seceded from Mexico, inviting more Americans to help resist Mexican control. In 1836, Texans gained independence and set up the Lone Star Republic.

Fighting for Texas secession, Logan also unwittingly helped ensure the en-trenchment of slavery. American planters petitioned Congress to annex Texas as a slave state, and the question of annexing Texas dominated the 1844 U.S. presi-dential election. Capitalizing on northern opposition to another slave state, the Liberty Party drew increased support from abolitionists and others who resented southern aggressiveness. Its 60,000 votes worried proslavery Americans, though

Southerners continued to argue that most Americans favored annexing Texas. In 1845, Congress granted Texas statehood and allowed slavery there. In pursuit of regional compromise, it stipulated that as many as four more states might be carved from Texas, and in some of those states slavery would be prohibited.

As many feared, Mexico retaliated, sparking a two-year war, beginning in 1846. In 1848—only a few days after gold was discovered in California—Mexico capitulated. The Treaty of Guadaloupe Hidalgo gave the United States more than a million square miles that eventually became Texas, Arizona, New Mexico, Utah, and California. Overnight, Greenbury Logan was demoted from a citizen in an independent republic to free black non-citizen in a slave society.

The annexation of Mexican territories had profound consequences. First, Texas's admission to the Union augmented slaveholders' representation in Congress. Second, with fertile soil for growing cotton, corn, sugar cane, and cattle, white Texans prospered, their exports contributing to a flourishing American economy. Third, slaves provided a stable workforce, distant from abolitionist agitation.

But many Americans—black and white, northern and southern—believed the slavery issue could tear the United States apart. As early as 1837, *The Colored American* warned "should Texas be admitted into the Union, farewell to the union of the States. Ten thousand discordant clashing elements and interests will be stirred up, that will only subside with a division of the Union. . . . From the Potomac to the extreme Southern boundaries, anarchy, [and] bloodshed [will] deluge the country."

Radicals like Garrison may have welcomed such discord as a way to dramatize the evils of slavery, but most Americans hoped to avert a clash. Pennsylvania Congressman David Wilmot tried to stop the spread of slavery, proposing in 1846 "neither slavery nor involuntary servitude shall ever exist" in any territories gained from Mexico. Known as the Wilmot Proviso, the measure passed in the northern-dominated House but was defeated in the Senate, where the South retained strength. The defeat of the Wilmot Proviso guaranteed the continuation of the controversy over extending slavery.

While war and rhetoric raged, hundreds of free black Texans worked as skilled artisans in sawmills and brickyards and as blacksmiths, tailors, tavern-keepers, and house servants. A few acquired substantial agricultural holdings. But slavery was the foundation of Texas agriculture. Ten years after Greenbury Logan's plea for tax relief, the slave population in Texas had swelled to nearly 60,000; by 1860, it had more than tripled again.

## THE MOUNTAIN WEST

Texas was just one western destination for African Americans. Lured by wagon trains or the promise of gold in California, some free black people chose the new frontier, while slaves had little choice but to accompany owners who migrated west. Hence, many free and enslaved black Americans ended up in the Rocky Mountain region—Utah, Oregon, and California—as slaves to Mormons or as free explorers, ranchers, or entrepreneurs. James Beckwourth is an example. Born in the South in 1798 to a slave mother and a white father, Beckwourth apprenticed with a blacksmith, then signed on with the Rocky Mountain Fur Company. A skilled scout and translator, he moved easily between local Indians and white settlers. He was adopted into the Crow Indian community, living with them for several years. Later he assisted U.S. troops against the Seminoles in Florida. In 1845 he joined rebel Mexicans in an abortive attempt to wrest California from Mexico. Moving to New Mexico, he joined the U.S. Army's campaigns against Mexico in 1847. He married four times—twice to Indian women, once to a Spanish woman, and finally, at age sixty-two, to an African American woman in Denver, Colorado. With this last

JAMES P. BECKWOURTH IN HUNTER'S COSTUME.

*Trapper James Beckwourth's discovery of an obscure northern California pass through the Sierra Nevada Mountains resulted in the establishment of a town that still bears his name.*

wife, he returned to the Crow community, where he died four years later.

George Washington Bush went west hoping to gain political rights. A free man, he had served under Andrew Jackson in the War of 1812. In 1844, he was a cattle trader in Missouri when a wagon train bound for the Oregon Territory lumbered through town. With his wife, children, and four other families, Bush joined the expedition. Years later, a fellow traveler remembered Bush's concerns: "It was not in the nature of things that he should be permitted to forget his color. He told me he would watch, when we got to Oregon, what usage was awarded to people of color, and if he could not have a freeman's rights he would seek the protection of the Mexican Government in California or New Mexico."

In Oregon, Bush's companions had to help him get an exemption from local anti-black laws in order to receive his 640-acre homestead. Once over this hurdle, Bush put down roots. He introduced the region's first sawmill, gristmill, mower, and reaper, and fathered a dynasty of local leaders known for their generosity to less well-off neighbors.

The discovery of gold in California in 1848 occasioned an influx of black easterners seeking riches. Here, gold dust—not skin color—defined a man's worth. By 1850, nearly a thousand African Americans—mostly single men—were among the fortune-seekers. Even those who did not work directly in mining gained from the booming economy. As cooks, waiters, laundresses, tavern-keepers, and dockworkers in Sacramento, San Francisco, and many small towns, black newcomers enjoyed economic prosperity, even if they lacked citizenship privileges.

## THE COMPROMISE OF 1850

The gold rush brought 80,000 Americans to California, which qualified for statehood by 1850. But admitting California as a free state would upset the regional balance in the U.S. Senate. Thus, proposed statehood for California touched off a bitter congressional debate over whether slavery would extend to the newly gained territory. The controversy resulted in the Compromise of 1850, the last congressional attempt to ease regional tensions by giving something to both North and South.

The compromise contained four momentous provisions. First, California entered the Union as a free state, upsetting the balance of free and slave states. Second, the government authorized the creation of territorial governments in New Mexico and Utah, letting the settlers there decide whether to permit slavery. Third, legislators abolished the internal slave trade in the District of Columbia, but not slavery itself. The compromise's fourth provision, the Fugitive Slave Act, generated the most controversy. It denied accused fugitive slaves a jury trial, leaving their fate to federal commissioners, who were compensated for each fugitive slave case they adjudicated. When the commissioners ruled in favor of the fugitive, they received $5, but they received $10 for ruling in favor of the owner. The Fugitive Slave Act also compelled northern citizens to help apprehend runaways. Now it was not only illegal to assist a fugitive slave; anyone who refused to assist slavecatchers could be prosecuted.

Stephen Douglass, one of the main architects of the Compromise of 1850 in Congress, saw the ruling as the "final settlement" of the slavery question. As we will see in Chapter 9, he was gravely mistaken.

## CONCLUSION

When Thomas Jefferson heard about the 1820 Missouri Compromise—Congress's first attempt to balance slave states and free states—he reacted by being "filled . . . with dread." Jefferson's anxiety was well founded. In the three decades between the Missouri Compromise and the Compromise of 1850, the controversy over slavery followed American settlers into every region of the continent and every aspect of public life. Many Americans sought reform, and for reformers, slavery was often a top priority. Shut out from public life, white and black women stepped forward not only to defend slaves but also to fight for their own rights.

During the reform era, African Americans sought ways to improve their own lives. Some negotiated a bit of latitude within the slave system; others escaped slavery altogether. Some free black people, like Martin Delany and James Forten, assumed leadership in the abolitionist struggle. Other free people sought to educate themselves, choose their own names, and shape their own communities on American soil or elsewhere. Still others, like John Horse and

James Beckwourth, shifted their loyalties between enslaved people and a government that protected slavery.

Both white abolitionists and slaveholders defined black people as different from themselves, and William Lloyd Garrison was one of the few who could envision an interracial society as a positive thing. But for now, the possibility of a harmonious black and white society seemed remote. With the Compromise of 1850, the nation neared a crisis point.

# 9

<br>

# A Prelude to War:
# The 1850s

## Tragedy and Triumph at Christiana

Early on the morning of September 11, 1851, Joshua Kite and six other African American rebels crouched by the windows of a small stone farmhouse on a hill near Christiana, Pennsylvania. Kite was poised to resist his former owner, Edward Gorsuch. Accompanied by federal marshals, Gorsuch had journeyed more than 70 miles from Maryland to take his "boys" back "home."

Two years earlier, rather than awaiting the manumission promised by their master, twenty-one-year-old Kite and several other slaves had escaped from Gorsuch's farm. Crossing the Chesapeake Bay, they headed north. Arriving in Christiana, where they blended into a region populated by 3,000 free and fugitive African Americans, they found refuge among black neighbors, and sympathy from white antislavery Quakers.

Gorsuch had hired slave-hunters to help him locate the fugitives. But by the time he arrived in Christiana, the town had been alerted to his approach. Kite and dozens of his black neighbors stationed themselves at the home of local residents William and Eliza Parker. When a federal marshal challenged him, Parker dismissed the marshal's authority: "I told him I did not care for him nor the United States." Parker's wife threatened the escaped slaves with a corn cutter lest they attempt to surrender. Within minutes of Gorsuch's arrival, he had been shot to death, and his son was badly wounded. White onlookers offered water to the injured and then left them to their fate. Kite, Parker, and a few others escaped to Canada.

The Christiana Riot, as it came to be known, struck terror in the hearts of slaveholders while inspiring hope and pride in African Americans. For once, it was black men—not white—who had prevailed. Southerners demanded hangings, hoping that public executions of black fugitives and their white supporters

# *Chronology*

**1849** Harriet Tubman escapes from slavery.

**1850** Fugitive Slave Act requires private citizens to help capture runaways.

The Underground Railroad steps up its efforts.

Sojourner Truth publishes her life story and begins to lecture on abolition and women's suffrage.

**1851** Joshua Kite and William Parker lead a standoff in Christiana, Pennsylvania.

William and Ellen Craft's narrative of their escape is published.

**1852** Harriet Beecher Stowe's *Uncle Tom's Cabin* is a bestseller.

**1853** Mary Ann Shadd becomes the first female newspaper editor in North America.

**1854** The Kansas-Nebraska Act establishes popular sovereignty.

Fugitive Anthony Burns stands trial in Boston, a test case of the Fugitive Slave Act.

Antislavery groups form the Republican Party.

**1856** Popular sovereignty precipitates open warfare in "Bleeding Kansas."

**1857** In *Dred Scott* v. *Sandford,* the Supreme Court rules that slaves are property protected in every state, that slaves are not entitled to use the courts, and that slaves and their descendants can never be citizens.

Hinton Rowan Helper publishes *The Impending Crisis of the South.*

George Fitzhugh publishes a defense of slavery.

**1858** Lincoln-Douglas debates dramatize regional crisis.

**1859** John Brown leads raid on a federal armory in Harpers Ferry, Virginia.

would deter further rebellion. Officials arrested nearly three dozen people, white and black. A recent law provided that aiding runaway slaves rather than turning them over to authorities was a federal crime, so the detainees were charged with conspiracy and treason—the latter punishable by death. Still, white jurors in Pennsylvania, where the trial was held, acquitted one man and dropped the charges against the rest. They viewed the slave hunt and the trial as a battle between states' rights and the federal government's attempts to erode those rights, and thus they had no interest in assisting slave hunters.

The episode dramatized the regional and racial tensions tearing at American society in the 1850s. The tensions were heightened by the Fugitive Slave Act of 1850, which required individuals to capture and return escaped slaves. Many white Northerners who had been undecided or indifferent about slavery now associated antislavery action with the right to make their own laws. Meanwhile, abolitionist sentiment in the North was growing. Newspapers regularly published harrowing accounts of slavery and daring escapes—many written by escaped slaves.

In contrast, white Southerners increasingly felt outnumbered in the federal government. With their slave-based economy and social system under attack by abolitionists, even white Southerners who did not own slaves often felt duty-bound to defend the institution. Only a few white Southerners viewed the slave system as a drag on the southern economy and a cancer on the nation.

The new militant mood of many African Americans reflected a mixture of defiance and fear. No black person, slave or free, could ignore slavery. The Underground Railroad, which provided a means of escape for slaves in the South, offered some hope to those who were enslaved, as did the growing abolitionist movement. Still, opportunities were limited even for those who were free. In Canada, former slaves could find freedom but few jobs. The American West offered dreams of gold and jobs, but efforts to extend slavery westward made it a risky place to settle. Even as reformers increased efforts to sway America's conscience, political and legal efforts tightened the grip of slavery. Convinced that Americans would never give up slavery peacefully, the boldest abolitionists encouraged a messianic figure, John Brown, who attempted to ignite a slave rebellion at Harpers Ferry, Virginia, in 1859.

# CONTROVERSY OVER THE FUGITIVE SLAVE ACT OF 1850

The Compromise of 1850, passed by Congress in that year, included a Fugitive Slave Act that strengthened federal regulations for apprehending runaway slaves. The new policy raised tensions for many Americans, northern and southern, white and black. The issues included federal authority versus state powers, constitutional protections of private property, individuals' protests against federal power, and black fugitives' security. Both Southerners and Northerners feared capture of federal power by the other. Southern planters increasingly worried that if the federal government acquired too much power, it might ban slavery. Northerners feared that if the federal government could legislate how they treated fugitive slaves, it might begin controlling other facets of their lives. And the prospect of abolishing slavery caused everyone to worry about property rights. If slaves were freed and slaves were property, wouldn't this amount to government seizure of property? If owners were compensated by the federal government, wouldn't this amount to Northerners being implicated in the purchase of slaves?

The rising regional tension was also felt in southern slave quarters, where masters' growing anxiety about rebellion often meant increased repression. And repression, combined with the increasing frequency of slave sales from the Upper South into the Lower South, spurred a dramatic rise in the number of escapes. As the slave grapevine reported growing defiance among northern white abolitionists, greater numbers of slaves became willing to risk all for freedom.

Controversy between the North and South also grew with the widening gulf between their economies. Many northern states had developed mills, factories, and extensive canal and railroad systems to move manufactured goods west and to transport raw materials to eastern cities. Southerners had extended their plantation system, which required many workers and vast stretches of land. People in both regions wanted to make sure their interests were adequately represented in Congress. But through the 1850s, as immigration swelled the North's population, its growing number of congressmen tipped the balance in Congress to the North.

## FEDERAL POWER VERSUS STATES' RIGHTS

The U.S. Constitution protected the rights of slaveholders by providing that any person escaping bondage should be returned. Federal laws passed in the 1790s also required local officials to return fugitives to owners. But in 1826 Pennsylvania reformers had passed a "personal liberty" law banning the forcible return of slaves. In 1842, the U.S. Supreme Court upheld personal liberty laws in *Prigg* v. *Pennsylvania,* ruling that individual states were not obliged to help enforce these federal laws. Several northern states took this decision as permission to pass personal liberty laws *prohibiting* state officials from aiding slavecatchers.

These Northerners resented the Fugitive Slave Act provision whereby citizens who refused to help apprehend slaves could be charged with treason. This provision, they felt, overstepped federal authority. Now, as would-be fugitives could not find safety by crossing into a northern state, their desperation increased, as did the risks associated with escape. Fugitives would have to leave the country or find support in standing their ground in northern states, hoping local resistance to federal authorities would work in their favor. The standoff at Christiana was among the most dramatic of such clashes.

Westward expansion also raised the question of states' rights, specifically whether new territories would be slave or free. As we saw in Chapter 7, Congress approved the Missouri Compromise in 1820, dividing the 1803 Louisiana Purchase into a northern section without slaves and a southern section where slavery was allowed. In 1848, just as Mexico was ceding to the United States new territory that included California, Utah, and New Mexico, the discovery of gold in California sparked a rush westward. Congress responded by designing the complex Compromise of 1850, whereby California entered the union as a free state while the other territories acquired from Mexico might become slave states if their citizens so chose. Thus the compromise established the principle of popular sovereignty: the right of local residents to decide whether their state would be slave or free.

Statehood for California gave the free states a 16–15 edge in the U.S. Senate, worrying Southerners, who got a more stringent Fugitive Slave Act in return. But ultimately the Compromise of 1850 only intensified conflict between North and South. Even white Northerners without strong abolitionist sympathies became convinced that resisting slave-hunting federal marshals was an act of patriotism. Some northern state legislatures broadened personal liberty laws to include the right of state courts to override *any* federal legislation. Massachusetts boldly nullified the Fugitive Slave Act. This was the most flagrant attack a state could make on federal power: to instruct its citizens to ignore or defy a federal law.

Despite northern fears of a "slaveocracy," in which Southerners would spread guarantees for slavery throughout the country, many Southerners in Maryland and Virginia, like Edward Gorsuch, had been preparing to release slaves: As the region's economy shifted from tobacco to grain farming, hiring seasonal field hands was far cheaper than clothing and feeding slaves all year. Nonetheless, Gorsuch's slaves represented more than a financial investment (though a single slave might represent an investment of $2,000). To him slaves embodied the principles of property rights and personal honor. For Southerners

THE CHRISTIANA TRAGEDY.

*First published in 1859 , this engraving of the Christiana incident remained popular for decades.*

like Gorsuch, slaves themselves were less important than the right of a man to maintain control of his property.

## THE UNDERGROUND RAILROAD

In 1849, the same year Joshua Kite fled, another twenty-one-year-old slave escaped from Maryland. After a brief rest on the free soil of Pennsylvania, Harriet Tubman retraced her steps to escort some of her family and friends over the same ground. Soon known as "Black Moses," Tubman made as many as three dozen trips into slave territory, leading hundreds of slaves to freedom, including her own parents. She seemed fearless. Armed with a pistol, she made it clear that she would use it on anyone, white or black, who threatened to sabotage her mission. Slaves revered her. Slaveholders feared what she represented: a new posture of black defiance. Some put a price of $40,000 on her head—equivalent to more than $1 million today. But she was never captured.

Tubman was among the best-known members of the abolitionist network known as the Underground Railroad, a community of African Americans and their white allies, called "conductors." Originally, the Underground Railroad used secret routes along rivers, seaports, and northern border communities to transport slaves from the South to freedom in Ohio, Pennsylvania, and New York. By 1830, conductors were taking a few runaway slaves as far as New England, Canada, Europe, and Mexico. Supported by Vigilance Committees—secret local networks—the Underground Railroad was at its most active during the 1850s as the national upheaval over slavery came to a boil. Of the estimated 100,000 slaves who escaped in this way, probably three-fourths did so after the 1850 Fugitive Slave Act intensified their desperation and their conductors' commitment.

William Still, a black Philadelphian, discovered that a fugitive he "conducted" was his own long-lost brother. Still's coded records of runaways and those who helped them are invaluable to historians working to reconstruct this secret network. Levi Coffin, a white Quaker from North Carolina, moved to Indiana to better position himself to help. John Brown, a white New Englander, relocated to Kansas to further the abolitionist cause.

Fugitives escaped by various methods. Oriented by the North Star of the Big Dipper constellation in the night sky and guided by moss on the north sides of trees, perhaps as many as 8,000 slaves per year fled the South on foot, horseback, or hidden in wagons. Some escaped by sea. Others stowed away on ships going as far as Canada and Britain, or as near as Cincinnati, Detroit, and the northern Mississippi River. Some journeyed on to California, the Pacific Northwest, and Texas. Others joined Native American communities in remote places like Nacimiento, across the Rio Grande in Mexico, where Seminole leader John Horse established a refugee outpost in 1849.

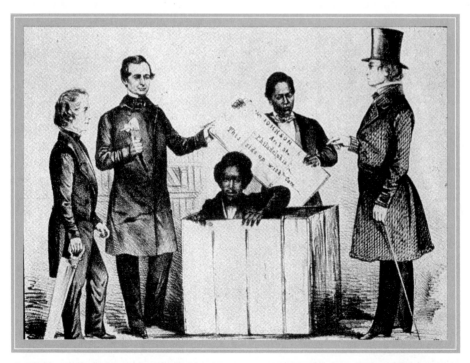

*With help from a northern Vigilance Committee, Henry "Box" Brown was shipped to William Johnson, a Philadelphia black abolitionist. This triumphant portrayal, using the biblical reference of "resurrection" to underscore the righteousness of Brown's escape, was published in 1854.*

## THE ESCAPE AND TRIAL OF ANTHONY BURNS

The experience of Anthony Burns, a slave who escaped to Boston in 1854, exemplifies how the Fugitive Slave Act played out in the North. Learning to read at a young age, Burns became a preacher in his local Baptist church in Virginia, where black and white congregants worshipped together. Hired out by Charles Suttles, his master, to work in Richmond, Burns escaped on a boat bound for Boston. Befriended by a white Quaker abolitionist, he quietly worked in a clothing shop. But he missed his family and could not resist sending a letter to his brother on the Suttles plantation. Suttles intercepted the letter and contacted Boston authorities. Burns was arrested and placed in leg irons in a federal courthouse.

Boston's abolitionists sprang to action. Lawyer Richard Henry Dana, condemning the Fugitive Slave Act as "the devil's license for kidnapping," called a protest meeting that drew several thousand angry people, including hundreds of black residents from the whaling town of New Bedford. In a frenzy, the crowd stormed the courthouse to free Burns, killing one federal official and wounding others. President Franklin Pierce sent troops and authorized "any expense" to uphold federal law. The next day, the abolitionists raised $1,200 to purchase Burns's freedom. But federal officials persuaded Suttles not to sell Burns; it was vital, they said, to use his case to test the Fugitive Slave Act in court.

Dana attempted to prove that Massachusetts's personal liberty law superseded the Fugitive Slave Act. But after the judge ruled that Burns must be returned, armed troops escorted him through an aisle of sobbing abolitionists who had draped buildings in black. By the time Burns was loaded onto a boat for Virginia, more than $100,000 had been spent to uphold Southerners' constitutional right to federal protection of their property.

Anthony Burns's story had a happy ending, as the Boston Vigilance Committee soon purchased his freedom. But his trial deeply affected abolitionists. Charlotte Forten, a seventeen-year-old black Philadelphian, attended the public meetings and anguished over the ruling. "It is impossible to be happy now," she wrote, rededicating herself to abolitionist efforts. Abolitionism was a family tradition. The granddaughter of a prosperous black sailmaker and daughter of a respected abolitionist, she was well educated and well-to-do. Despite her privilege, she saw herself as an African American in a country that dehumanized all black people, and she empathized with slaves who suffered because of their race.

## THE POWER OF STORIES

In her 1987 best-selling novel *Beloved,* Toni Morrison describes a slave who so loves her child that she kills her rather than see her grow up in bondage. Morrison's fictional character was a composite of actual enslaved women who had been driven to this desperate act. In the 1850s, such tragic stories captured the attention of northern and southern audiences. A second wave of writing—often poetry, fiction, and historical accounts—came from northern African

Americans who focused on the struggles of free black people. The writings of white abolitionists, such as William Lloyd Garrison, publisher of *The Liberator,* argued that unless white people destroyed slavery, they risked incurring God's wrath. White Southerners, in contrast, wrote to demonstrate that slavery was better than free labor systems.

## SLAVE NARRATIVES

In the dead of winter in 1848, William and Ellen Craft escaped from Georgia to freedom. William disguised himself as a servant to the light-skinned Ellen, who dressed like a man, posing as a slave owner's son. With the money saved from William's carpentry work, the Crafts traveled as paying customers on steamboats, staying in fine hotels along the way. Who, after all, would look in such places for runaways? The following year, the Crafts toured England, explaining to spellbound audiences that although their master had not treated them harshly, they escaped lest they bear a child who would be sold from them. In 1851, the Crafts published their experiences in a London newspaper, demonstrating the power of stories to move minds and hearts and to enlist British sympathies to the American antislavery cause. These African American–British networks—what one historian has called "an anti-slavery wall"—proved invaluable in coming years.

African American fugitives had dramatic stories to tell. The saga of former slave Henry "Box" Brown, published in 1854, provides an apt example of a slave narrative, a firsthand account that exposed the cruelties of slavery. Five years earlier, Brown had himself packed in a 2-foot-square crate and shipped by boat from Richmond to Philadelphia. As we saw in Chapter 7, Harriet Jacobs's *Incidents in the Life of a Slave Girl* (1861) constituted one of the most gripping stories of the cruelties inflicted on slave women. Sexual abuse and fear for their children often heightened slave women's desperation. Some took huge risks to free or protect themselves and their youngsters; others "freed" their children from bondage by killing them. Frederick Douglass, who had published his autobiography in 1845, released an updated version entitled *My Bondage and My Freedom* in 1855 that included his analysis of the effect of the Fugitive Slave Act. Long silenced, black Americans finally had a voice. They also had an audience hungry for their words.

## NORTHERN BLACK VOICES

Northern African Americans told a different story of slavery and abolition. In 1826, Isabella Van Wageren, born a slave in upstate New York, walked away from an owner who reneged on his promise to free her. There was no daring escape, no long journey, no secrecy, for both slave and master knew that New York's gradual abolition law would free her the next year. Deeply religious, Van Wageren later reported that God had called her and told her to change her name to Sojourner Truth. A sojourner, she explained, is one who travels. She was to take to the road to tell the truth about the evils of slavery and the oppression of women.

*Known best as a stalwart abolitionist and crusader for women's rights, Sojourner Truth was masterful at promoting her concerns. She distributed prints of herself like this one mounted on small cards to spread her reputation and raise money for her cause.*

In 1850, Truth published her life story, *Narrative of Sojourner Truth*. A spellbinding storyteller, Truth began to travel widely on the antislavery lecture circuit. She enjoyed public speaking, she said, because "I wanted to see what God would have me say." Truth emerged as a powerful voice for women's suffrage as well as African American rights. She secured a lasting reputation when she preached that if one woman—the biblical Eve—could turn the world upside down, then a united community of women could put it right again. Truth frequently claimed she could work as hard as any man, yet she challenged her audience, "Ain't I a woman?"

Most black Americans lacked the resources to publicize their plight, but others spoke for them. In 1855, Bostonian William C. Nell, America's first black historian, published two volumes documenting African Americans' participation in the American Revolution and the War of 1812 (downplaying the numbers who fought for the British, who promised them freedom). In 1847 William Wells Brown published the story of his life and escape from slavery. Six years later he published *Clotel,* a novel about Thomas Jefferson's mixed-race daughter that portrayed black Americans as complex human beings rather than as stereotyped slaves and fugitives. In 1857, Frank Webb published *The Garies and Their Friends,* about the social life of Philadelphia's black middle class. Webb's popular novel also helped white Americans put a human face on black men and women.

Francis Ellen Watkins also contributed to this black intellectual movement. Born free in 1825 and orphaned young in the slave city of Baltimore, she was raised by her uncle, an abolitionist shoemaker who was friends with Garrison. The uncle nurtured his precocious niece's writing talent and her strong social conscience. Before she was twenty, Watkins had published *Forest Leaves* (1845), a collection of poems. More volumes followed, including one introduced by Garrison. Lecturing on the antislavery circuit, she encouraged her listeners to boycott products resulting from slave labor.

## WHITE ABOLITIONIST APPEALS

White abolitionists also used stories of slavery's horror to advance the antislavery cause. One involved Margaret Garner, who fled with her family in 1856. When U.S. marshals located them in Ohio, the distraught Garner slit the throat of her infant daughter and struck two of her sons with a shovel to prevent them from being re-enslaved. Then she threw herself and one or perhaps more of her children—accounts vary—into the Ohio River. Still, she was captured before she could kill herself. She was sold into the Lower South, and her remaining children sold to different masters. Within days, abolitionists everywhere had begun recounting Margaret Garner's story.

In 1851, Harriet Beecher Stowe began publishing a serialized novel about slavery. Neither a historian nor an abolitionist, Stowe was a religious woman inflamed by the Fugitive Slave Act. Eventually titled *Uncle Tom's Cabin*, her story was sympathetic to southern slave owners as well as to slaves. Stowe characterized most white Southerners as decent, God-fearing people trapped in an economy supported by a tradition of bondage and cruelty. Only the overseer, Simon Legree, was presented as heartless. Stowe portrayed a tender friendship between Eva, an innocent white child, and Tom, a patient and loving elderly slave who was devoted to his master's family and who took comfort in Christian faith. Stowe contrasted his acceptance of his lot with the rebellious young fugitive Eliza, fleeing to freedom across the icy Ohio River.

*Raised in a slave-owning Kentucky family, Thomas Satterthwaite Noble painted many slave scenes, including this one dramatizing the 1856 event of fugitive Margaret Garner attempting to destroy her children lest they be seized by federal authorities. The painting, done in 1867, several years after slavery's end, demonstrates the story's enduring hold on the public imagination.*

By allowing readers to empathize with most of her characters—black and white, northern and southern—Stowe reached many who had not previously advocated abolition. In 1852, when the serial was published as a novel, it immediately sold 300,000 copies. Quickly translated into several languages, *Uncle Tom's Cabin* became an international best seller, breathing new life into the antislavery movement.

Annoyed by Stowe's passive hero, Martin Delany claimed Stowe "knows nothing about us." In response, he published a novel drawn on his reminiscences of his trip through the South, *Blake; or, The Huts of Africa* (1852). Henry Blake, the protagonist, was the antithesis of Uncle Tom. A rebel who escaped from slavery, Blake had no religious qualms against killing a white man. On his way to Canada, Blake urged other African Americans to contact "one good man or woman on [each] plantation" to incite rebellion.

## SOUTHERN VIEWS OF SLAVERY

For different reasons, Southerners were also enraged by *Uncle Tom's Cabin*. Some Southerners claimed that because Stowe had never visited the South, she had no authority to condemn its ways. Others argued that brutal overseers like Simon Legree were the exception. Southern novelist William Gilmore Simms said his novel, *Woodcraft* (1854), was "probably as good an answer to Mrs. Stowe as has ever been published." Using humor, Simms portrayed a plantation life in which the sense of loyalty and responsibility on the part of slave owners to both the land and slaves created a model society.

Other Southerners joined Simms's defense of slavery. Among the most persuasive was George Fitzhugh, an aristocratic Virginia lawyer. Fitzhugh held that southern slavery offered the most moral and humane system for both white and black Americans. Although Northerners were not slaveholders, he said, their system exploited weak individuals, while southern society protected them. In several works, including *Cannibals All! or, Slaves Without Masters* (1857), Fitzhugh argued that the North had abolished the name of slavery "but not the *thing*."

In Fitzhugh's view, the "thing" that dehumanized the North was the wage system, which made no provisions for workers' illnesses, pregnancy, childrearing, or old age. Industrialism forced owners to cast out all but the most efficient laborers. In contrast, said Fitzhugh, southern planters looked after slaves' welfare, for it was to their economic advantage to do so. Applauding Fitzhugh's publications, which articulated long-held views, many Southerners shifted from a defensive posture to defiance.

# THE CHANGING SOUTH

In 1857, North Carolinian Hinton Rowan Helper's *The Impending Crisis of the South, and How to Meet It* infuriated many Southerners with its assertion that the economy was fundamentally unsound. Helper looked at slavery from a purely economic point of view, arguing that it undermined both the livelihoods of non-slaveholding white people (such as himself) and the southern economy at large. By depressing the employment opportunities and wages of white workers, slavery kept southern industries and ports from expanding. *The Impending Crisis* was banned across the South; southern post offices refused to deliver it. Helper fled to New York, but suppression of his book did nothing to stop the forces transforming the South's society and economy.

## SOUTHERN SOCIETY AND ECONOMY

During the 1850s, about 25 percent of the 8 million white people living in the South owned slaves, and only about 1 percent possessed as many as 300 slaves. A minority of the South's white men controlled almost all the region's slaves, yet they had disproportionate social and political influence. The nearly 55 million bales of cotton they produced annually accounted for more than half of the dollar value of all U.S. exports. Because northern textile mills relied on southern cotton, many northern congressmen sympathized with southern arguments that only slave labor could sustain the U.S. economy.

The South that Helper described was actually becoming several Souths, each with its own economy and social structure. In the Upper South (Virginia, Maryland, and North Carolina), corn and wheat production was replacing tobacco, and the selling of surplus slaves to the Lower South was rapidly reducing the number of African Americans. In contrast, the Lower South (from South Carolina to eastern Texas), where cotton production dominated the economy, the black population swelled rapidly. The forested Appalachian Upcountry remained the preserve of struggling white farmers. In North Carolina, for example, most of the slave-owning planters were in the coastal region, while most white people (70 percent of the white population) living in the hilly western region held no slaves at all, and over two-thirds of those who owned slaves had fewer than ten.

Imbalances in southern demographics worried some white Southerners. The slave count climbed steadily, especially in the Lower South. Meanwhile, the free black population grew slowly—mostly in the Upper South—from 250,000 in 1850 to about 260,000 in 1860. More than one-third of free black people lived in cities, while less than one-quarter of the white population did. Though the birthrate for all black Americans, enslaved and free, decreased slightly, the free black population in the West more than quadrupled as free African Americans left the South. The more than two million European immigrants who arrived during these years settled almost exclusively in the North and West, giving these regions labor alternatives unavailable to the South. Most white Southerners feared losing control of the dependable labor that had once given them an economic advantage over the North.

In *The Impending Crisis,* Helper championed the cause of southern white farmers who struggled to make a living on small plots of land without sufficient labor. He decried their dependence on large planters to market their crops and the injustice of their taxes being used to compensate owners whose slaves were executed for crimes. Using statistics (some exaggerated), Helper argued that slavery deprived the South of funds for schools, roads, libraries, newspapers, and industries. Policies that maintained large planters' dominance kept poor white people

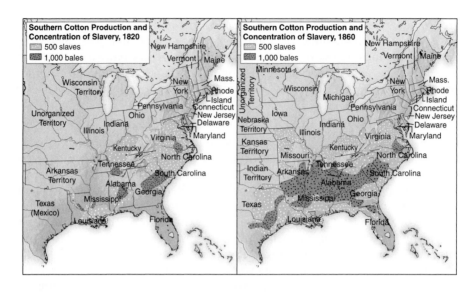

*Map 9.1*
Southern Cotton Production and Concentration of Slavery, 1820 and 1860

*Between 1820 and 1860, as cotton production eclipsed tobacco, the concentration of slaves shifted from the Upper South to the Lower South. Most slaves were now further isolated from the Atlantic coast and from the North.*

isolated, ignorant, and dependent. Railroads built with slave labor, for example, connected cities but did not link to the hinterlands, as railroads in the North did. By retarding the South's industry, transportation, and commerce, Helper claimed, planters forced Southerners to import most finished goods from the North or abroad.

Historians are still debating how prosperous the South really was, but Helper identified real problems with its economy. Much land was mortgaged to banks in England or the North. Planters were often land rich but cash poor, unable to pay for labor. Sometimes the cost of acquiring and maintaining a slave worker exceeded the slave's productivity. Yet most planters were wedded to their way of life, even if it was in crisis.

## "THE WORLD THEY MADE TOGETHER"

With the large black-to-white ratio in many parts of the South, African Americans—including fugitives and even some black slaveholders—exerted surprisingly great influence. In theory, white Southerners controlled black lives, but the interdependence between slaves and owners was so intricate that one historian describes the black-and-white South as "a world they made together."

In the summer of 1855, Lucy Skipwith wrote to her absent master in Virginia: "We keeps up family Prayers every morning. I does the best I can teaching the children but I can never get more than two and sometimes three little ones on week days. My little girl Maria is beginning to write very well and is very anxious to write to you." Through the letters of Lucy Skipwith, who managed a plantation household during the 1850s, we can see the workings of plantation life. Her master, John Hartwell Cocke, was a southern reformer who planned to Christianize his slaves, teach them thrift and temperance, and then free and dispatch them as missionaries to Liberia. To that end, in 1840 he established Hopewell, a cotton plantation in Greene County, Alabama. There he installed Lucy Skipwith's father, George, as head driver, and sometimes as overseer, of four dozen slaves.

George Skipwith, a man of independent spirit, often ignored overseers' authority. Yet Cocke tolerated him because slaves worked efficiently under his supervision. Lucy apparently inherited her father's strong sense of his own mind. Though Cocke set Hopewell's goals, its daily operation lay in the hands of the black Skipwiths. For over a decade, Cocke spent almost half of each year in Virginia. When he was at Hopewell, Lucy Skipwith was his personal servant. But when he was in Virginia, she set her own schedule and household priorities, managing sewing, weaving, cooking, and religious education. Taking advantage of Cocke's instructions to Christianize the slaves, she lobbied for black education and complained when work routines interfered. Thus Cocke's legal authority and power intertwined with the Skipwith's actual authority and power. The power was unequal, but the interdependence was inescapable.

The lives of most black slaves and their masters fell somewhere between what readers found in Harriet Beecher Stowe's meek Uncle Tom and Martin Delany's insurrectionist Henry Blake. White slaveholders believed they controlled their world, but in fact they depended heavily on slaves' ingenuity and loyalty. They had to tolerate countless acts of slave resistance—burned meals, deliberately broken tools, pilfered livestock, or sabotaged crops—even as they wavered between denying and fearing the system's instability. Every law, every policy, every move a master made was shaped by the desire to tighten control over potentially rebellious bondspeople.

## FREE BLACK PEOPLE

By 1850, more than 200,000 free black people lived in the South. Most were clustered in the cities, where they worked as domestic workers or as carpenters, blacksmiths, or clothiers. Some of these African Americans were the children of masters. Others were slaves whose masters had allowed them to hire out their time; they had saved their money and purchased themselves or their families. It was not uncommon for a man to purchase his wife—while himself remaining enslaved—to protect her from sexual exploitation and assure that his children would be born free. But the free black person's life was precarious. If captured by an unscrupulous slave hunter, a free black man or woman might be sold to some distant location. Because black people were usually not allowed to testify in the courts, there was little recourse if a white person claimed a free black person as property.

Yet some southern free African Americans made a comfortable life. Often choosing not to leave the area where relatives were still enslaved, they opened schools or shops or made a living on the docks. A few even acquired substantial property—including slaves. By 1850, a few hundred black slaveholders owned 9,000 bondspeople. To be sure, most southern free African Americans, even those of substantial means, did not traffic in black people. But those who did were as free as their white neighbors to exploit their human property.

A few black planters grew wealthy. South Carolina's William Ellison owned more than five dozen slaves. William Johnson of Natchez left a diary of his career as landlord and farmer. A mixed-race man freed by his master, Johnson was twenty-three when he bought his first slave. When he died, he owned 400 acres. Like his white neighbors, he gambled, traveled, hunted, fished—and whipped his slaves. As he was in a position to lend money to some of his white neighbors, Johnson attained a status that was remarkable in the slave South.

In the weeks following the passage of the 1850 Fugitive Slave Act, Johnson's diary entries remained focused on produce, wool, livestock, and his white overseer and his slaves. However, a cryptic comment from late September suggests local tensions: "Young Jno [Jonathan] Gains shot a Black man that had ran away from Mr. Hutcheons this morning and killed him dead. This was done in the woods." Ironically, Johnson was shot to death in those woods the next year, apparently in a property dispute with another biracial planter. The only witnesses were black men—who were not allowed to testify in the courts. After two years in jail and many trials, Johnson's killer convinced a jury he was white. Because the murder of a black man by a white man was not considered a crime, the killer was acquitted.

Viewing black planters as potential allies in the cause of justifying bondage and suppressing slave insurrection, some white planters encouraged black slaveholding. But there were limits to what black slaveholders could do. They could not vote or escape racial insults, and they had no protection in the courts. Their status and freedom depended on not angering powerful white neighbors.

# BLACK EXILES ABROAD AND AT HOME

The number of hospitable destinations for free black people in the United States shrank quickly during the 1850s. Ohio, for example, imposed a heavy tax on free black immigrants, while a new Illinois law halted black immigration completely. Maryland, long home to thousands of free African Americans, began to allow slave hunters to seize *free* black people entering from other states and sell them into bondage. Virginia laid a poll tax—a tax on voting—on free black residents, intended specifically to create funds to deport them to Africa. Minnesota revoked a long-held black right to vote. Other states followed suit until black men could vote only in Maine, New Hampshire, Rhode Island, Vermont, Wisconsin, and Massachusetts. In response, black leaders debated the best options for free black people, with some advocating that they leave the country that curtailed their freedoms. Some black people went to the American frontier; others left for Canada, Haiti, and Africa.

## THE DEBATE OVER EMIGRATION

The divisions between the Holly brothers exemplified the debates over emigration taking place in free black communities in the 1850s. The son of a shoemaker, James T. Holly studied mathematics and classics in black schools in his native Washington, DC, and in Brooklyn, New York. In 1850, Holly and his older brother Joseph established themselves as bootmakers in Burlington, Vermont. But James Holly dreamed of a better life outside the United States. He was attracted by the argument that black Americans should save money to relocate to Africa or accept offers from groups like the American Colonization Society to help finance such a move. Joseph Holly, James's brother, insisted that expatriates were traitors, as they left enslaved black people without advocates. Expatriates, he said, were manipulated by white schemers intending to send the most talented (and therefore troublesome) black people to places where they could not incite slaves to rebel.

By 1852, James Holly had settled in Ontario, where he met the embittered Martin Delany. Two years earlier, Delany had gained admission to Harvard University's medical school. In 1850, only a few black doctors practiced in the United States, and most had been educated abroad. In 1849, Bowdoin College awarded medical degrees to two African American brothers, Thomas and John White, and Harvard's training would position Delany as the next black American doctor trained in his own country. However, white fellow students forced Delany to withdraw during his first year. Unable to enlist the support of Boston abolitionists, who felt they had more pressing battles to fight, Delany moved to Ontario with his wife and children. There, he became a leader of the black exile community.

Together, Delany and James Holly formed the American Emigration Society. At its annual conventions, its leaders encouraged emigration to Canada, which offered citizenship and all-black communities. They also suggested the West Indies, Liberia, Haiti, and Central America as havens from discrimination.

But in the years before the Civil War, views changed. At first Holly championed Canada, citing its proximity to the United States as ideal for aiding slaves. But influenced by white abolitionist James Redpath, who urged black people to leave "this bastard democracy in the United States," Holly soon recommended Haiti, where he and Redpath persuaded the government to give land to African American settlers. Meanwhile, Martin Delany, fearing the United States would soon annex Canada, recommended Central and South America and the British Caribbean.

## SAFE HAVEN IN CANADA

In 1852, young Mary Ann Shadd touted Canada as a home for free black people. In a pamphlet, "Notes of Canada West," she compared opportunities in the British West Indies and Central America and concluded that the Great Lakes region of southern Canada, a short ferry ride from Detroit, "offers stronger inducements to colored people."

Indeed, Canada's government, hoping new black communities would be a buffer between white Canadians and rebellious Indians, offered citizenship and the vote to black immigrants after just three years' residency. Canada's invitation had wide appeal, and Ontario's black communities grew dramatically, attracting the principal players in the Christiana episode—William and Eliza Parker and some of the fugitive slaves—Martin Delany, and other disaffected African Americans. By 1860, several thousand black immigrants were living in Canada. While grateful for Canadian sanctuary, many resented their exile and their treatment as second-class citizens. Although several hundred black newcomers owned businesses and land, many had trouble finding work, and their wages were often lower than those of white workers.

Unlike Delany and many other Canadian immigrants, Mary Ann Shadd had never experienced slavery. Born in 1823 to free and relatively prosperous parents in Delaware, she had studied at Quaker schools. In the 1840s, the family relocated to Canada. Shadd's father, Abraham, was elected to the town council in Chatham—the first black person to win an elective office in Canada. In the late 1840s, Mary Ann Shadd returned to the United States to teach black children in Pennsylvania, Delaware, and New York. Then passage of the Fugitive Slave Act spurred her to return to Canada to teach fugitive slaves. In 1851 she accepted support from the American Missionary Association (AMA) to open a school. But she always felt uneasy about the AMA, suspecting it cheated black refugees by selling them Canadian land at inflated prices. In 1856, when the AMA withdrew its support from her school, she was relieved to regain her autonomy.

Shadd was mentored by Henry Bibb, a black newspaper publisher who had arrived in Canada with a more harrowing history. It had taken Bibb five attempts before he finally escaped from his master in Kentucky in 1842. Then he spent several years lecturing for the antislavery cause and campaigning for the antislavery Liberty Party. In 1849, settled in Detroit, Bibb published his *Narrative of the Life and Adventures of Henry Bibb, An American Slave, Written by Himself.* When the Fugitive Slave Act made him feel vulnerable in Detroit, Bibb moved to Ontario, where he felt safe enough to write to his former owner celebrating his own "work of self-emancipation." By 1852, Bibb was publishing his own newspaper, *The Voice of the Fugitive.*

Shadd and Bibb parted ways over education for black children, however, reflecting frustrations within black communities over how to carve out lives in a new country. The Canadian government provided schools for black immigrants, but they were inferior to those for white students. Shadd advocated independent schools. Black and white parents alike, she insisted, could pool their resources to educate children of both races. In contrast, Bibb, whose wife's independent school for black children had failed financially, felt African Americans could ill afford private schools and that government-supported all-black schools were better than no schools at all. Bibb had no faith that interracial schools would work.

In 1853, Shadd assumed editorship of the *Provincial Freeman,* an independent black newspaper. She was the first female newspaper editor, black or white, in North America. The paper gave voice to her views about emigration, community life, and education, and to her frustration with Bibb. Their feud over education played out in public, in their respective newspapers.

## THE LURE OF THE FRONTIER

While several thousand African Americans sought refuge in Canada in the 1850s, a small but steady stream went west. During the 1840s, a few fled to

Texas—but by 1860, when some 300 free black Texans were outnumbered by a slave population grown to 183,000, white Texans acted to constrain free black peoples' rights. So black freedom-seekers moved on to the next frontier. By 1860, several thousand reached California. Another hundred made it to the Oregon Territory. In both regions, slavery was outlawed. Though these areas hardly extended a warm welcome, African Americans established themselves as tavern-keepers, laundresses, haulers, and shopkeepers. Others became scouts, cooks, livestock tenders, or gold prospectors.

Among the most colorful black westerners was free-born Mifflin W. Gibbs. As a twenty-two-year-old Philadelphian in 1850, Gibbs was recruited to the anti-slavery lecture circuit by Frederick Douglass and Charles Remond. But soon he was lured to California by the gold rush, where he learned of Biddy Mason, whose master had brought her from Utah to California in 1851. Encouraged by free black leaders, Mason petitioned the California courts for her family's freedom. In 1855, after three days of hearings, the courts declared the Masons free.

The abolitionist spirit in California energized Gibbs, who founded *Mirror of the Times*, the state's first black newspaper. He protested California's poll tax, which was imposed only on black voters. When he voted without paying the tax, officials seized goods from his clothing store, but Gibbs resisted. "With a fervor as cool as the circumstances would permit" he pledged "that the great State of California might annually confiscate our goods, but we would never pay the voters tax." When the courts restored his goods, Gibbs gloated, "No further attempts to enforce the law upon colored men were made."

# REGIONAL CRISIS

"Are we incapable of self-government?" Martin Delany asked black Americans in an 1852 essay. Answering his own question, Delany insisted that only political power, not moral argument, could assure African Americans lives of dignity. Smarting after his humiliation at Harvard, Delany poured out his discouragement at the prospects for equality and justice in the country of his birth. "No people can have political power if they do not constitute a majority," he concluded.

Delany's concern about finding a place where black people could influence government policy mirrored regional concerns about representation. White Southerners despaired the loss of their majority in Congress. Western settlers worried that federal laws would favor easterners. As free black people sought influence, their leadership splintered. Meanwhile, white leaders' attempts to settle the slavery question with the Kansas-Nebraska Act of 1854 took the nation to the precipice of civil war. Regional compromise seemed all but impossible.

## FROM MORAL SUASION TO POLITICAL POWER

While some black Americans chose emigration, others, like Frederick Douglass, began exploring political methods to end slavery and gain citizenship. For more than a decade, he promoted William Lloyd Garrison's concept of "moral suasion"—appealing to American consciences to end slavery. But increasingly convinced that this tactic was naive and unrealistic, Douglass moved toward political action after the 1839 founding of the Liberty Party. He came to believe that the U.S. Constitution—if it could be enforced—guaranteed African Americans citizenship. In 1848, he joined the Free Soil Party, a coalition led by New England abolitionists who wanted any territory gained from Mexico to be non-slave. The Free Soil Party ran an antislavery candidate for president in 1848. Though black men could vote in only a few states, Douglass helped design the party's platform.

Douglass also began to see a value in separate black organizations, and he encouraged black people to work with—but not within—white reform organizations. These ideas drew him away from other black leaders, who still believed biracial cooperation to change the hearts and minds of white Americans was the only way to achieve enduring racial peace. Through these differences in perspective, black leadership splintered in the 1850s.

## THE KANSAS-NEBRASKA ACT

In 1854, Illinois Senator Stephen A. Douglas reopened the question of slavery in the territories. Arguing that local people could best determine their region's needs, Douglas had a further suggestion for helping Americans remember their common interests. A railroad from Chicago to the Pacific, he argued, would benefit the whole nation's economy. For the railroad to succeed, however, white Americans would need to settle Kansas and Nebraska. Why not offer these new settlers popular sovereignty—that is, the right to decide whether to have slavery in their communities? Though some politicians feared the plan would lead to battles over community control, Congress passed the Kansas-Nebraska Act in May 1854.

Despite twenty years of political experience, Douglas had misjudged how Americans' anxieties about slavery could fuel their fears of conspiracies. When fugitive Anthony Burns was apprehended in Boston just two days after passage of the new act, northern reformers accused Douglas of plotting with others in the federal government to stir southern resentment against the North. Radical white abolitionists and even many moderate Northerners also worried that popular sovereignty would undermine the Missouri Compromise, as both Kansas and Nebraska were north of the line where slavery was to have been prohibited. Losing faith in Douglas's integrity, Northerners deserted his Democratic Party. Some switched to the antislavery Republican Party, a new coalition formed in 1854 when remnants of the Liberty Party joined with the Free Soil Party. Others opted for the two-year-old Know-Nothing Party, which condemned abolitionists and proslavery advocates alike to focus its fury on Catholics and recent immigrants who, they feared, would bring religion into America's carefully guarded separation between church and state.

In the wake of the Kansas-Nebraska Act, the opening of new territory, combined with the desire to stake a claim for a slave or non-slave community, sent many from both North and South rushing west. By 1856, the region was poised for confrontation.

## "BLEEDING KANSAS"

The Kansas-Nebraska region soon erupted in violence. Southern settlers, frustrated that the federal government refused full support for slavery, rioted in the antislavery town of Lawrence, Kansas. In retaliation, the New England Emigrant Aid Society sent white radical abolitionists into the area, including John Brown and four of his sons. Brown, who had moved many times to fulfill his self-proclaimed mission for racial justice, killed several Southerners who had brought slaves to Kansas, and two of his sons died in the skirmishes. Newspapers called the area "Bleeding Kansas." Hearing reports from Kansas, Charlotte Forten, the black abolitionist in Boston, recorded both concern and exhilaration. "Mr. [Charles] Remond lectured for us this evening," she wrote. "I particularly liked what he said about Kansas. Everybody has so much sympathy for the [white] sufferers there, and so little for the poor slave, who for centuries has suffered tenfold worse miseries—still I am glad that something has roused the people of the North at last.... A very great political excitement prevails."

Anger over Kansas ignited chaos in Congress. During a debate over Kansas statehood in May 1856, Massachusetts abolitionist senator Charles Sumner passionately denounced the "crime against Kansas," holding Stephen A. Douglas responsible for the policy that precipitated violence. Two days later, South Carolina congressman Preston Brooks, nephew of a senator who had supported Douglas, stormed into the Senate and pounded Sumner with a cane. Disabled, Sumner could not return to Congress, but Massachusetts voters reelected him in 1857 so his empty chair would symbolize abolitionist sacrifice.

## THE *DRED SCOTT* DECISION

As blood spilled in Kansas, the U.S. Supreme Court considered a crucial suit that had been in the courts for more than a decade. The suit centered on Dred Scott, a Missouri slave whose master had taken him from slave territory into Illinois and free Wisconsin Territory in the 1830s, and then back south. When the master died in 1846, his widow's brother, an abolitionist, helped Scott sue for his freedom on the grounds that he had lived on free soil.

Before the Fugitive Slave Act was passed, Missouri's local courts had judged Scott free. But in the post-Act hysteria, the state's supreme court overturned this decision. After five more years of litigation, in March 1857 the U.S. Supreme Court reached its decision. Though there was considerable disagreement among the judges, the majority handed down three important rulings. First, the Court said Scott was not free, because to free him would deprive his owner of property without due process of law. Second, the Court said slaves were not entitled to use the courts, as only citizens had that right. Finally, the Court ruled that neither slaves nor their descendants could ever be citizens. The effect of the ruling was to overturn the Missouri Compromise, which prohibited owners from taking slaves north of the compromise line. No law, said the Court, could deprive a citizen of property anywhere in the United States.

While the ruling did not *enslave* free African Americans, it did encourage free states to strip away their few remaining rights as citizens. New York's radical

The U.S. Supreme Court's ruling on the Dred Scott case evoked a wave of public sympathy for Scott, as this news story highlighting his family suggests.

black *Weekly Anglo-African* promised persistent opposition: "When you repeal the Fugitive Slave Law, reverse the *Dred Scott* decision, and give us the right of citizenship in the free states, and break up the internal slave trade between the slave states, then, and not until then, you may expect us to be silent."

## THE LINCOLN-DOUGLAS DEBATES

Running for reelection in 1858, Stephen Douglas was challenged by Abraham Lincoln, a Republican who accused Douglas of contradictions. The principle of popular sovereignty, said Lincoln, which Douglas had embedded in the Kansas-Nebraska Act, promised power to local residents. But the *Dred Scott* decision, which Douglas supported, gave power to the federal government. Though Douglas was reelected, Lincoln gained popularity for his more moderate approach. While not suggesting that Southerners do "what I would not know how to do,"—that is, abolish slavery—he warned that the nation could not exist "half-slave and half-free."

But Lincoln took contradictory stances as well. He argued both that the Constitution protected African Americans as citizens and that only white people should settle the West. While emphasizing that slavery was morally wrong, he stopped short of suggesting it be abolished. He condemned the *Dred Scott* decision, saying black people should be equal before the law, but he shied away from affirming intellectual or social equality. While contending that discrimination based on race could easily become discrimination based on eye color, height, or other physical characteristics, he offered no solutions. But he did predict a crisis.

## JOHN BROWN AT HARPERS FERRY

The 1850s ended as they began—with bloody confrontation. On October 16, 1859, John Brown, a bent and aging warrior, ordered his twenty-one-man army, "Men, get on your arms; we will proceed to the ferry." The bearded, stooped, intensely religious leader was dedicated to purging society of the sin of slavery. He had spent months preparing for this day.

Brown represented abolitionists who believed violence was the only solution. They advocated direct action, calling slaves to rebellion. Brown began soliciting arms, information, recruits, and money to set up a sanctuary for runaways in the mountains reaching into the South. From this sanctuary, he envisioned a chain-reaction slave revolt penetrating the southern heartland. If they could "conquer Virginia," Brown told his followers, "the other southern states would nearly conquer themselves."

Arriving in Ontario, Canada, in the spring of 1858, Brown had already studied guerrilla warfare and was finalizing his plans. He consulted with Harriet Tubman, an expert on the southern terrain. He received donations from white New Englanders and black New Yorkers who were weary of ineffectual protests. He spoke with Frederick Douglass, who offered guarded encouragement but would not support violence. The Massachusetts State Kansas Committee—mostly Boston abolitionists—agreed to supply money and guns. Using passionate religious arguments to lure them from pacifism, Brown had recruited several young Iowa Quakers. He was ready to fashion an army. Martin Delany, Mary Ann Shadd, James T. Holly, and William Parker were among the Canadian refugees who listened to him with interest. Parker, Holly, and the Shadd family made tentative plans to join him. But Delany, feeling Brown was moving too slowly, turned his attention to emigration to Africa, sailing for Nigeria in the spring of 1859.

That summer, Brown proceeded to Harpers Ferry, Virginia, an industrial village with a federal armory, which Brown planned to raid to for its rifles. Located just east of the Appalachians, where the Shenandoah and Potomac rivers meet, Harpers Ferry seemed well situated as a base from which to launch an attack on the South. It also had a substantial number of free African Americans who might lend their support.

Brown assembled an army of sixteen white men and five black men, recruited from far afield, reflecting the broad reach of abolitionist networks. Only Shields Green had once been a slave. John Anthony Copeland, a North Carolinian studying at Oberlin College, brought along his uncle, Sheridan Leary, a mixed-race Oberlin resident who left behind his wife and baby daughter. Mixed-race Dangerfield Newby also joined the group, hoping to liberate his wife and children from slavery in Virginia.

When the insurrection began, Brown's men managed to seize a local farmer—George Washington's great-grandnephew—as a hostage. But the campaign to seize the arsenal failed. Brown's group had brought the wrong ammunition for the guns they carried. Holly, Parker, and the Shadd family were delayed in arriving from Canada. Reinforcements promised by Harriet Tubman never arrived. Not one local African American joined in. Most of Brown's freedom fighters, including two more of his sons, perished in the fray. Osborne Anderson, the only black man among the five who escaped capture, returned to Canada. Unlike the Christiana confrontation, the raid at Harpers Ferry had no triumphant ending. This time Southerners got their hangings. On December 2, 1859, Brown went to the gallows for treason.

Yet Brown succeeded in stirring up America. Southerners worried the Harpers Ferry raid would spark full-blown war. Because of "a good deal of talk about Harper's Ferry," wrote one slave trader, "everybody nearly wants to volunteer to go to fight." The uncertainty caused slave prices to plummet. When Congress convened on December 5, lawmakers came armed. Hoping for southern support for a presidential bid, Stephen Douglas blamed the Republicans for

John Brown asked that his execution be attended only by the "poor little, dirty, ragged bare headed and barefooted slave boys & girls led by some old grey headed slave mother." But fearing an attempt to rescue Brown, the authorities barred the public from the abolitionist martyr's scaffold. Still, many artists painted the scene Brown had envisioned anyway, some showing him as a Christ-like avenging angel. More than two decades after the event, Thomas Hovenden, who had married an abolitionist, produced this fictional rendition of Brown kissing a black child.

Brown's insurrection. Southern congressmen demanded an investigation to determine if the Republican Party had supported Brown. But when Abraham Lincoln and other white Republicans also condemned Brown, rumors of a plot subsided.

Though Brown's mission failed, William Lloyd Garrison, heretofore a pacifist, conceded the righteousness of the effort. Black and white abolitionists began describing Brown's raid as "noble." John Copeland, Brown's young black Oberlin recruit, wrote to his mother, "Could I die in a more noble cause?" Black poet Frances Ellen Watkins called Brown "the hero of the nineteenth century." Writing to his wife, Watkins said: "Belonging to the race your dear husband reached forth his hand to assist, I thank you. Not in vain has your dear husband periled all. From the prison comes forth a shout of triumph. Enclosed I send you a few dollars as a token of my gratitude, reverence and love." Frederick Douglass eulogized Brown as "a human soul illuminated with divine qualities" who "saw slavery through no mist or cloud but in the light of infinite wisdom" and "loved liberty for all men." Memorials, songs, and poems helped Brown accomplish in death what he could not in life: stirring abolitionists to agree that the only way to end slavery was to "purge the land with blood."

Brown's army died with a dignity and conviction that drew wide admiration, but the day of his execution was a sad one. Hundreds of thousands of black Americans, weeping, lined the tracks as the train carried Brown's remains home from Virginia through Philadelphia to his farm in New York's Adirondack Mountains.

## CONCLUSION

The congressional leaders who had fashioned the Missouri Compromise, the Compromise of 1850 (with its Fugitive Slave Act), and the policy of popular sovereignty struggled to provide political solutions to the slavery problem ripping at the United States. Antislavery advocates sought to accomplish abolition by raising moral outrage. Proslavery forces called on constitutional and legal power to protect their property—and with the *Dred Scott* decision, the U.S. Supreme Court supported their claims. But both Southerners and Northerners knew the matter was far from settled.

The 1850s opened and closed with bloody confrontations over slavery. The slavery issue ignited conflict over the federal government's jurisdiction over states, federal protection of citizens' property, and the moral and religious implications of holding a person in bondage. As new settlement areas opened in the West and in Canada, Americans struggled to define how race related to citizenship and what individuals could do to defend their rights. Throughout the decade, cotton remained the nation's most profitable export crop, and the land and labor required to grow it became the subjects of hot debate and violence.

For black Americans, these developments had mixed implications. On the one hand, the Fugitive Slave Act increased the danger and desperation of slave life. But the same law helped create and publicize black heroes and chroniclers.

Inspired by accounts of courageous actions, more and more white Americans began to perceive slaves' fates as intertwined with their own. Nonetheless, an increasing number of Americans, black and white alike, began to share Abraham Lincoln's foreboding that the country would have to reach a crisis before the controversy could end.

# 10

## CIVIL WAR AND THE PROMISES OF FREEDOM: THE TURBULENT 1860S

### MARTIN DELANY BECOMES FIRST BLACK U.S. ARMY MAJOR

The 1850s left some African Americans despairing of ever seeing an end to slavery in the United States. Abolitionist Martin Delany, who had settled in Canada in search of greater freedom, began to dream of a home in Africa. "Africa for the African race, and black men to rule them," he proclaimed.

In December 1860, Delany returned to America from an eighteen-month visit to England and Africa during which he made plans for a new black settlement. From Africa, following a meeting with Yoruban leaders, he wrote to New York American Methodist Episcopal (AME) minister Henry Highland Garnet, "I am happy to report that I have concluded a treaty . . . by which we secure the right of locating in common with the natives on any part of their territory not otherwise occupied." Pleased, Garnet contacted a "number of men who are willing to embark on this glorious enterprise, and who believe as I do—that there is a glorious future before Africa." But when Delany returned to the United States he found the nation on the brink of a war that delayed his Africa plans for almost two decades.

Like that of thousands of others, Delany's life was redirected by the civil war that erupted in the spring of 1861. After the federal government eventually recruited black troops, Delany petitioned to serve as a surgeon. Receiving no answer, he journeyed to Washington, DC, to propose that northern black leaders help organize slaves into a fighting force. President Abraham Lincoln agreed and issued Delany a commission. Thus, in February 1865, the fifty-two-year-old

# *Chronology*

**1860** Frederick Douglass is attacked by an angry mob.

South Carolina secedes from the Union.

**1861** In February, seven states form the Confederate States of America.

Confederate troops bombard Fort Sumter in Charleston Harbor in April.

By May, Virginia, North Carolina, Tennessee, and Arkansas join the Confederacy.

Union general Benjamin Butler labels fugitive slaves "contraband" and refuses to return them to masters.

**1862** In May, Congress mandates that slaves seized as contraband not be returned to owners.

President Lincoln issues a provisional Emancipation Proclamation.

The Union army's first all-black unit is formed: the First South Carolina Volunteers.

**1863** On January 1, the Emancipation Proclamation ends slavery in the Confederate states.

The Fifty-Fourth Massachusetts Regiment draws black soldiers from across the North.

In June, Virginia's western counties abolish slavery and return to the Union as West Virginia.

After Union victory at Gettysburg, France and Britain withdraw support of the Confederacy.

In New York City, white rioters protest conscription and competition from black workers.

The Fifty-Fourth's performance at Fort Wagner gains the respect of skeptical white soldiers.

**1864** Union general William Sherman begins a campaign from Chattanooga to Savannah.

Congress mandates equity in black troops' pay.

Abraham Lincoln is reelected by a narrow margin.

The Equal Rights League is formed.

**1865** Martin Delany becomes the first black major in the United States Army.

Congress proposes the Thirteenth Amendment to the Constitution.

Congress establishes the Freedmen's Bureau.

Confederate general Robert E. Lee surrenders at Appomattox Court House.

President Abraham Lincoln is assassinated.

The Thirteenth Amendment abolishes slavery throughout the United States.

**1866** Berea College, in Kentucky, opens as an interracial school.

Congress proposes the Fourteenth Amendment.

The Ku Klux Klan is founded in Tennessee.

**1867** The Freedmen's Bureau opens Howard University in Washington, DC.

**1868** The Fourteenth Amendment guarantees citizenship to any man born in the United States, regardless of race.

Delany—who had been driven from Harvard's medical school, had been an expatriate in Canada, and dreamed of life in Africa—became the U.S. Army's first black major.

The Civil War set Northerners to debating whether it was more important to end slavery or to hold the nation together. Initially, they went to war not over slaves or black people, but to preserve the Union. Describing the conflict as "a white man's war," northern (Union) officials turned away free black men who volunteered for the army. President Lincoln envisioned resettling black people outside the United States, and slaves who escaped from the South (the Confederacy) to Union army camps were returned to their masters. But northern free black men and women insisted that the war *had* to be about black people. When the Union government could not raise enough white recruits, African Americans mustered 190,000 black volunteers whose battlefield achievements won their country's admiration.

Gradually, emancipation came to be seen as an effective military strategy by both the Union and the Confederacy, as both sides concluded that offering freedom could secure black people's loyalty. Meanwhile, free black people petitioned the Union for equal military pay, opportunities for education, and the right to vote.

The war signaled dramatic changes for black and white people alike. In the North, it stimulated the economy but also increased political and racial tensions. In the South, white men needed little persuasion to enlist in the Confederate army, as the war ravaged their homelands. White slave owners persuaded many white men who did not own slaves that they should fight to uphold regional and family loyalty. At war's end, African Americans celebrated emancipation and embraced their new "citizenship." But they knew that without the right to vote, they were not yet full citizens. Only changes in the U.S. Constitution would grant them full citizenship.

While federal officials struggled to plan for 4 million freed black men, women, and children, southern states were forced to grant the franchise to black men. But black people's efforts to build a solid political structure in the South were complicated by economic woes and resistance to slaves' emancipation. These circumstances left the majority of black Southerners unable to attain better lives or protection from white violence. By June 1868, southern freedmen could cast a ballot—but most northern African Americans could not. So black people confronted the next hurdle: gaining the franchise for black men in the North.

# "A White Man's War"

On December 10, 1860, while Martin Delany was crossing the Atlantic Ocean, Frederick Douglass was speaking in Boston's Music Hall to commemorate John Brown's martyrdom. Douglass described a meeting the week before that had been "invaded, insulted, captured by a mob of gentlemen." These were antiabolitionists, and though most people assumed they were lower-class ruffians, Douglass knew better. "The leaders of the mob," he said, "were gentlemen . . . who pride themselves upon their respect for law and order." Many were northern

*By war's end, Martin Delany—having spent the first five decades of his life as an outsider in his native United States—achieved as much honor as his government had to offer: the highly dignified rank of major.*

textile manufacturers who profited from slave-produced cotton, and feared that abolition might mean the end of easy and inexpensive cotton supplies. But soon these "gentlemen" would be drawn into a war against their southern suppliers and customers. If slavery was the spark that ignited the war, the election of a new president fanned the flame.

## THE ELECTION OF ABRAHAM LINCOLN

For the 1860 presidential election, the Republicans hoped to appeal to both abolitionists and southern planters. Their platform called for prohibiting slavery in the territories but reaffirmed states' right to control local institutions. The Democratic Party split in two. Southerners called for protecting slavery in the West, while followers of Illinois senator Stephen A. Douglas favored a hands-off policy. With the splintering of the Democrats, Republican Abraham Lincoln won the presidency by a narrow margin—without the support of a single southern state.

Many Southerners thought the newly elected president was an abolitionist, but black Americans knew better. In a February 1860 speech, Lincoln condemned abolition as "extremism." Though he opposed the extension of slavery into the western territories, he also opposed interfering with it where it existed. Black Americans generally distrusted politicians. The usually optimistic Frederick Douglass conceded, "[T]he very best that can be said of [the Republican] party . . . is that it is simply opposed to allowing slavery to go where it is not at all likely to go." In New York's *Weekly Anglo-African* newspaper, publisher Thomas Hamilton explained:

> *The two great political parties . . . entertain the same ideas. . . . [T]he Democratic party would make the white man the master and the black man the slave, and have them thus together occupy every foot of American soil. . . . The Republican party . . . with larger professions for humanity . . . oppose[s] the progress of slavery in the territories, . . . but . . . their opposition to slavery means opposition to the black man—nothing else. . . . We have no hope from either [Democrats or Republicans]. We must rely on ourselves, [and on] the righteousness of our cause.*

Nearly a year after Lincoln's election, New Jersey AME minister Jabez Campbell despaired that "the president is not now, and never was, either an abolitionist or an anti-slavery man. He has no quarrel whatever with the South upon the slavery question."

## SOUTHERN STATES SECEDE

Convinced that Lincoln intended to eradicate slavery, South Carolina's legislators in December 1860 voted to withdraw from a union they felt threatened their right to hold slaves. Many South Carolinians who did not own slaves also voted to secede, as they felt excluded from a political system that could choose a president without a single southern electoral vote. They also worried about how thousands of free black people would fit into their society. Most Americans hoped a compromise would prevent war, but now that possibility vanished.

Cotton was also a catalyst for secession. By 1860, cotton production had expanded by 30 percent over two decades, and its value had more than doubled. Most Southerners could not envision a southern economy without cotton and could not imagine cotton without slaves. South Carolina and Mississippi, which depended heavily on cotton and slaves, were the first to secede.

By February 1861, Florida, Alabama, Georgia, Louisiana, and Texas had joined the Confederacy. Its constitution stressed each state's "sovereign and independent character." The new president was Jefferson Davis of Mississippi, brother of Hurricane Plantation owner Joseph Davis (see Chapter 8). Quickly raising an army, the Confederacy began seizing federal forts, post offices, and arsenals across the South. By April, Fort Sumter, in Charleston Harbor, was one of only three southern forts still under Union control.

In his March 1861 inaugural speech, Lincoln promised not to interfere with slavery, but he refused to accept secession. In early April, informed of supply shortages at Fort Sumter, he determined to send food but no arms or troops. But South Carolinians concluded that provisions would prolong Union control. On April 12, they fired on Fort Sumter and blockaded the harbor. The next day, Union forces, out of ammunition, surrendered.

With the outbreak of war, Virginia seceded. Though its voters had rejected secession early in 1861, Lincoln's call for troops changed their minds. (The western counties, too mountainous for plantation slavery, later broke away to form the new state of West Virginia). The secession of Arkansas, Tennessee, and North Carolina brought the number of Confederate states to eleven.

Four slave states—Delaware, Maryland, Kentucky, and Missouri—did not secede. These states grew tobacco and other crops, mostly on small farms. With relatively few slaves and large free black populations, they accepted Lincoln's claim that he was more interested in maintaining federal authority than ending slavery, a system they were beginning to phase out anyway. They sent thousands of troops to the Union army, but many young men from these states also fought on the Confederate side.

Frederick Douglass welcomed secession. "God be praised," he wrote. "The slaveholders have saved our cause. They have exposed the throat of slavery to the keen knife of liberty." Through the early summer of 1861, he persisted in

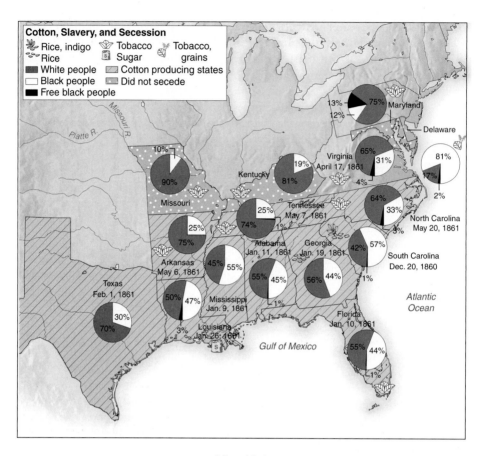

**Map 10.1**
Cotton, Slavery, and Secession

*The greater the investment in slaves and cotton, the more quickly and resoundingly came the vote for secession. In the four states where cotton was unimportant and the free black population high, white soldiers chose to fight on each side. At least 40 percent of Kentucky soldiers served in the Confederate army, as did 30 percent of Maryland volunteers, 25 percent of recruits from Missouri, and about 10 percent from Delaware. More than 13,000 Delaware men fought for the Union.*

believing that the "inexorable logic of events will force it upon them . . . that the war now being waged . . . is a war for and against slavery." But skeptics observed that a federal government willing to allow "loyal" slaveholders to keep their chattel hardly demonstrated a commitment to ending slavery. Yet many African Americans shared Douglass's optimism.

## BLACK VOLUNTEERS REJECTED

Like most Northerners, Lincoln felt certain the South would soon collapse. After all, the North had most of the nation's banks and industry, a better railroad system, and more than twice the South's population. It outpaced the South in firearms and in the resources to repair and replace them. European immigrants, arriving at a rate of nearly 200,000 per year, could replenish men lost to war. Expecting quick victory, Lincoln requested recruits for only three months' duty. Even so, many eligible white men resisted leaving their homes to pursue a war they did not care about in a region they had never seen.

But thousands of free black Americans volunteered for military service— only to be turned away. African Americans sent dozens of petitions to President Lincoln. One proclaimed, "We cherish a strong attachment for the land of our birth and for our Republican Government. We are strong in numbers, in courage, and in patriotism, and . . . we offer to you and to the nation a power and a will sufficient to conquer rebellion." Lincoln ignored them. When African American attorney John Mercer Langston, a member of Ohio's board of education, offered to raise troops, Ohio's governor responded, "Do you not know, Mr. Langston, that this is a white man's government; that white men are able to defend and protect it? When we want you colored men we will notify you." In Cincinnati, police forced a black recruiting station to remove the American flag. "We want you . . . niggers out of this," police officers declared. "This is a white man's war."

# WAR AND FREEDOM

Union leaders hoped that blockading southern ports and seizing southern cities would quickly end the conflict. In July 1861, Union troops marched toward Richmond, the Confederate capital. But on July 21, Confederate soldiers stopped them cold near Manassas Junction, less than 30 miles out of Washington. The Confederacy's success there—known as the Battle of Bull Run—caught Union leaders off guard.

On the heels of this defeat, some black Americans again hoped Lincoln would accept black soldiers, but again they were disappointed. Most white Northerners shared Lincoln's conviction that black soldiers were a bad idea— they were possibly cowardly and undisciplined, probably a threat to white civilians. Not until 1863 would official black Union regiments form, even then under some white officers who doubted black soldiers' courage and ability.

## SLAVES AS CONTRABAND

Within weeks of the firing on Fort Sumter, slaves fleeing to Union-held Fort Monroe, near Hampton Roads, Virginia, were put to work. Commanding general Benjamin Butler declared them "contraband"—enemy property seized in war—arguing that returning them to owners was counterproductive. Butler reasoned that planters who joined the Confederate army had abandoned their human property. "Have [slaves] not assumed the condition [i.e., freedom] which we hold to be the normal one of those made in God's image?" he asked.

Butler was not alone in thinking that war changed the status of slaves. General John C. Frémont, an abolitionist, harbored similar notions. Declaring military law in Missouri in August 1861, Frémont proclaimed that "real and personal property of those who shall take up arms against the United States . . . is declared confiscated, and their slaves are hereby declared free men." Lincoln reversed this policy and promptly removed Frémont from command of the Army of the West. But Congress soon passed the Confiscation Act, authorizing confiscation of "property used for Insurrectionary Purposes." Through the summer of 1861, field commanders followed Frémont's example, liberating thousands of slaves and using them as cooks, laborers, spies, and sometimes as armed soldiers.

Meanwhile, local communities made their own military plans. By the end of 1861, the First Kansas Colored Infantry had organized. Its slaveholding Cherokee commander, at first supporting the Confederacy, soon transferred his loyalties to the Union (which he thought was likely to win) and declared his unit open to "all persons, without reference to color . . . willing to fight for the American flag." In 1862, Union general David Hunter, in charge of captured coastal South Carolina, organized the First South Carolina Volunteers, the Union's first all-black fighting unit comprised primarily of ex-slaves. In Kentucky, a "general stampede" of slaves (as one white officer described it) arrived at Hart County's Camp Nevin. Union officers put many to work building fortifications. When the army moved on, these workers accompanied them and began to move onto the battlefield.

## New Roles for Southern Slaves

In spring 1862, when Joseph Davis heard that Union forces had seized New Orleans, he abandoned Hurricane Plantation near Vicksburg, Mississippi, leaving it in the hands of his trusted slave, Ben Montgomery. Montgomery wrote regularly to Davis, reporting that some slaves had gone to Vicksburg to help build Union fortifications, others had disappeared, but many remained on the plantation. In June, Union forces swept through Hurricane, destroying what remained of the previous year's cotton crop. Montgomery survived by starting a small business, tanning leather and making shoes to sell to neighbors. When Union admiral David D. Porter arrived at Hurricane in the spring of 1863, he set Montgomery and his talented son, Isaiah, to repairing machines on Union boats. But he soon sent them north to Ohio.

Some slaves cast their lot with the Confederacy. Hearing stories of Yankee cruelty, or worried about reprisals if the South won the war, many chose to remain in familiar surroundings, or went to war as servants to masters they knew and trusted. Others were pressed to remain with their masters. By 1865, fearing defeat, some Confederate leaders grew desperate enough to recruit black regiments with the promise of freedom.

Like Ben Montgomery, many black people, free and enslaved, remained in the South but took new roles. In Kentucky in 1862, a free black man known only as Mr. Bradwell organized his slave neighbors to grow and sell livestock and produce. The group raised $700 to erect their own Methodist church building.

But many bondspeople fled their masters. A Georgia slave who escaped recalled how she "had been reading so much about the 'Yankees' and was . . .

anxious to see them. The [southern] whites would tell their colored people not to go to the Yankees, for they would harness them to carts . . . in place of horses." But, she understood, they said "those things to frighten them. . . . I heard that the Yankee was going to set all the slaves free." One Louisiana house servant and his mother stole a mule from their master and "traveled eighteen miles to a plantation . . . where the Yankees had a camp." In May 1862, South Carolina's Robert Smalls, an experienced steamboat pilot, stowed his family aboard the *Planter* and delivered the ship to the Union navy near Charleston. The Union converted the *Planter* to a warship and appointed Smalls captain.

## THE PORT ROYAL EXPERIMENT

Early in 1862, the Union army seized the Sea Islands off the coast of South Carolina. The few white islanders fled, abandoning meals in their kitchens, crops in the fields, and thousands of bewildered slaves. As Union leaders debated whether the slaves were contraband or recruits, northern abolitionists arrived, bringing food, clothing, and volunteer teachers. One was twenty-four-year-old Charlotte Forten, from a free black family in Philadelphia. Arriving at Port Royal in October 1862, she recorded her excitement as she "commenced teaching the children [the song] 'John Brown' . . . [and] felt the full significance of that song being sung here . . . by little negro children . . . whom the glorious old man died to save."

Federal officials encouraged teaching in Port Royal, but they also set black residents to cultivating cotton, which the government could sell abroad and to

*Organizations sponsored by northern philanthropists sent young women into the South to teach black people. Though one black volunteer wrote proudly, "We think it noble work, and will do it nobly," some observers have commented that the black teachers in this photograph seem to be marginalized as the white people take center stage.*

factories in the North. Ex-slaves were angry to discover that "freedom" meant only more of the familiar backbreaking labor. One black woman, hoeing cotton at Port Royal under the new wage system, complained to a Union agent that the New England manager of her plantation gave her *less* clothing, shoes, and food than had her former master.

The system introduced at Port Royal was replicated in numerous places throughout the South as Union forces liberated one area after another. Northerners, both black and white, showed up to help slaves with the transition to freedom. Held to a strict regimen of schooling and manual labor, many former slaves were disappointed in so-called freedom. After the war, the rebuilding of the South became known as "Reconstruction." One historian has described the Port Royal experiment as a "rehearsal for Reconstruction."

Near Hurricane plantation, in the winter of 1863, Admiral Porter set up contraband camps like those at Port Royal. He invited Quaker missionaries to set up schools, and he pressed black refugees into tilling confiscated land, for scanty wages or none. In this Mississippi outpost, more than one-third of the black population died as malnutrition and poor sanitation lowered resistance to pneumonia, smallpox, measles, and malaria.

# EMANCIPATION AS MILITARY AND POLITICAL STRATEGY

In the summer of 1862, Frederick Douglass wrote to Charles Sumner, a white abolitionist and Massachusetts senator, "The events taking place seem like a dream." He was describing a series of federal policies gradually overriding Lincoln's official position that the war was not about ending slavery. As the war dragged on, undermining slavery became both a goal of the war and a strategy for weakening the South. Congressional leaders agreed with General Butler: Returning slaves to their masters only aided the enemy. In the spring of 1862, Congress forbade commanders to return captured or fugitive slaves.

## EMANCIPATION POSSIBILITIES

As the war unfolded, Union leaders confronted thorny issues. How would they mount a long-distance campaign to retake the rebellious South? How would they maintain Northerners' confidence in federal authority? How would they keep foreign nations—some dependent on southern cotton—from aiding the Confederacy? By 1862, Union officials concluded that African Americans could have immense strategic value in dealing with these challenges.

Throughout 1862, Lincoln tried to strike a balance between keeping northern abolitionists' support and persuading the South to cease hostilities—all while trying to avoid alienating slave states loyal to the Union. Many northern white Americans who opposed slavery made it clear they did not want black people as social or political equals. Walking a tightrope, Lincoln proposed that the federal government free slaves and compensate their masters. Congress voted him down.

With Southerners absent and reformist Republicans dominant, Congress set out to define black Americans as people rather than property. In a symbolic move, it abolished slavery in the District of Columbia—the only area of the United States where it had the power to do so. With similar symbolism, Congress established diplomatic relations with Haiti and Liberia, two black nations ruled by former slaves. Then the secretary of state made a public event of issuing a passport to Henry Highland Garnet as a "*citizen* of the United States." A well-known black Bostonian, William C. Nell, was made a postal clerk, becoming the first African American to hold a federal civilian appointment. Lincoln even signed a second Confiscation Act, freeing any slave entering Union-held territory and allowing Union soldiers to seize "all property"—including slaves—in areas they captured. Though each step was a token, each also eroded slavery and elevated free African Americans. Black hopes were raised. When slavery was banned in the nation's capital, the editor of New York's *Anglo-African* exulted, "Henceforth, whatever betide the nation, its physical heart is freed from the presence of slavery."

Lincoln made clumsy overtures toward African Americans, reiterating his abhorrence of slavery but insisting that his goal was holding the nation together, not ending slavery. Frederick Douglass described the Lincoln administration as "fighting the war with only one hand" in refusing to allow black troops. In August, inviting Douglass and other black leaders to the White House, Lincoln suggested relocating slaves—and any interested free black people—to Central America. Feeling betrayed, Douglass reflected, "Abraham Lincoln is . . . the miserable tool of traitors and rebels. . . . [He] seems to possess an ever increasing passion for making himself appear silly and ridiculous." But Douglass's son Lewis became one of several hundred African Americans who volunteered to relocate to Chiriqui, in today's Panama.

Some black Americans grew increasingly skeptical of all federal policy. They suspected that Garnet had been recognized as a citizen because he endorsed Lincoln's plan to remove black people from the United States, and that Nell got a postal clerkship only because Massachusetts had an abolitionist governor. Disillusioned and frustrated, a few prominent African Americans insisted black people should not fight in a war that would not free slaves. Others imagined opportunities abroad. Uncharacteristically, Frederick Douglass considered moving to Haiti. But Martin Delany, declaring Haiti "a small island, with no prospect of additional territory," favored "Africa . . . a vast continent peopled by one of the great, enduring . . . absorbing races of the earth." Hoping to gather recruits for African resettlement, Delany crisscrossed the North and West, and found support for emigration. "If this war should result in the abolition of slavery, as we hope it may," wrote a black New Yorker in the *Weekly Anglo African,* "it will not ameliorate the condition of the free black man one iota. . . . The scanty pittance of social toleration which is here and there grudgingly doled out to us ... illustrat[es] the more strikingly the rule which everywhere excludes us."

But most black people yearned to fight for justice in the America of their birth. In a black newspaper, Isaiah Wears of Philadelphia explained: "To be asked, after so many years of oppression ... by a [white] people who have been so largely enriched by the black man's toil, to pull up stakes ... and go ... is unreasonable and anti-Christian." Douglass agreed, publicly stating he would stay in the United States. Sarah Remond, fiery sister of Charles Remond, campaigned to keep Britain from aiding the South. "Let no diplomacy of statesmen," she implored, "no intimidation of slaveholders, no scarcity of cotton, no fear of slave insurrections, prevent the people of Great Britain from maintaining their position as the friend of the oppressed negro."

*Table 10.1*
### The Federal Power Struggle, 1861–1865

*During the Civil War, a federal power struggle ensued among the military, Congress, president, and Supreme Court on the status of slaves and Confederate lands.*

| DATE | MILITARY | CONGRESS | PRESIDENCY | SUPREME COURT |
|------|----------|----------|------------|---------------|
| 1861 | General Benjamin Butler accepts freed slaves at Union army post in Hampton Roads, Virginia, declaring them "contraband."  General Benjamin Butler declares fugitive slaves in Georgia, Florida, and South Carolina to be free. | Congressional Confiscation Act seizes Confederate farms, and frees all slaves employed by Confederate military; abolishes slavery in District of Columbia. | Lincoln reverses Butler's emancipation order. | Supreme Court rules that wartime exigency allows the president to institute a blockade of southern ports, and that the president and military can suspend the right of *habeas corpus*. |
| 1862 | Over Lincoln's disapproval, General David Hunter organizes freemen into First South Carolina volunteers.  In response to Lincoln's Constitutional concerns, Congress amends Confiscation Act, allowing confiscated land to revert to heirs of Confederates. | | Lincoln objects to congressional plan to confiscate land, on grounds that it would deprive heirs of their rightful inheritance. | |

*Table 10.1 (continued)*

| DATE | MILITARY | CONGRESS | PRESIDENCY | SUPREME COURT |
|------|----------|----------|------------|---------------|
| 1863 | General John Frémont frees slaves of Missouri residents who are in rebellion. | | Lincoln reverses General Frémont's order freeing Missouri slaves. | |
| | | | Lincoln issues Emancipation Proclamation, abolishing slavery in states still in rebellion, but promises amnesty to southern states where 10% of citizens take loyalty oaths, and state agrees to free slaves. | |
| | | | Lincoln offers amnesty to states that comply with loyalty-oath requirements; Arkansas and Louisiana comply. | |
| | | Congress refuses to seat Arkansas and Louisiana representatives pardoned by Lincoln. | | |
| 1864 | Sherman's "Field Order #15" designates 80,000 acres of confiscated land in South Carolina for rent or purchase by freedmen.<br><br>Military field officers claim right to try civilians. | Congress passes Wade-Davis Bill, requiring that, for readmission, a majority of a Confederate states' citizens must swear allegiance to Union. | Lincoln pocket-vetoes Wade-Davis Bill. | In *Ex Parte Vallandighan,* Supreme Court refuses to rule on whether military has wartime jurisdiction in civilian offenses. |
| 1865 | | Congress establishes Freedmen's Bureau.<br><br>Congress refuses to seat ex-Confederates who have not sworn allegiance to the Union.<br><br>Congress passes Thirteenth Amendment, abolishing slavery in *all* states and territories. It is ratified by 27 states. | Andrew Johnson grants "amnesty and pardon" to most Confederate citizens, restoring their confiscated land, and exiling thousands of black farmers from their land. | |

## THE EMANCIPATION PROCLAMATION

The Battle of Antietam finally prompted Lincoln to stop waffling on the fate of slaves. By mid-1862, the Union navy had blockaded southern seaports and captured Memphis and New Orleans. With Union commanders poised to control the Mississippi River, Confederate general Robert E. Lee tried to push the war into the North to disrupt railroad lines that supplied Washington, DC. On September 17, Lee's troops met General George McClellan, at Sharpsburg, on Antietam Creek. The bloodiest one-day battle of the war ensued; more than 22,000 soldiers perished or suffered injuries.

Lee retreated to Virginia. Had McClellan pursued Lee, he might have won a decisive victory. But the Union general, characteristically timid and slow to act, missed his chance. Nonetheless, as Antietam was a southern defeat, England and France began to doubt the South could win. More significantly, the battle moved the cautious Lincoln to action. First, he removed McClellan from duty. Second, on September 22, the president surprised the nation by offering a provisional promise of freedom to slaves in the Confederate states.

In this preliminary emancipation proclamation, Lincoln chose his words carefully. Emphasizing that he was not planning to free slaves in states loyal to the Union, he promised that any Confederate state that rejoined the Union by January 1, 1863 would also be allowed to retain slavery. The effect was to free slaves only in areas where the Union had no control. Moreover, the order would be void if the war ended before that date. Though aware of its limitations, Frederick Douglass made the best of the promise: "We shout for joy that we live to record this righteous decree." Everywhere, Lincoln's emancipation promise lifted black spirits. In New Orleans, where the newspaper L'Union served a vibrant mixed-race community, an editorial urged readers to drop "the craven behavior of bondage" and to "stand up under the noble flag of the union." One black observer recalled that in Washington, DC, "men squealed, women fainted, dogs barked, songs were sung, and cannons began to fire at the navy yard." Philadelphia's Christian Recorder thanked "God and President Lincoln" even while the editor expressed his hope that "Congress will do something for those poor souls [slaves] who will still remain in degradation."

In December 1862, when Union troops tried again to capture Richmond, they were stopped at Fredericksburg, Virginia. As the year ended, southern leaders declared that the Confederate states would not return to the Union.

So on January 1, 1863, as promised, Lincoln declared that any slave living in Confederate territory was "then, thenceforward, and forever free." One Virginia slave remembered the day: "It was wintertime and mighty cold, but we danced and sang right out in the cold . . . then we [left] the plantation, carrying blankets and pots and pans and chickens piled on our backs." In Port Royal, where black Americans jubilantly read aloud the new order, Charlotte Forten called this "the most glorious day this nation has yet seen." She wrote, "I was in such a state of excitement. It all seemed . . . like a brilliant dream." The news traveled throughout the slave South: Lincoln might finally liberate slaves—if the North could win the war.

# "Men of Color, To Arms!"

Martin Delany responded to the Emancipation Proclamation by proposing the "Corps D'Afrique," a private black army to aid Union forces. But before he could organize it, Lincoln authorized Massachusetts governor John Andrew to raise the first northern black regiment—the Massachusetts Fifty-fourth. Andrew sent a team of black leaders to recruit in other Union states. With renewed hope, Delany joined the team.

But many white Northerners doubted black men would be good soldiers. One northern reformer at Port Royal, appalled at General Hunter's plans for a southern black regiment, wrote, "Plantation negroes will never make soldiers.... Five white men could put a [black] regiment to flight." But Colonel Thomas Wentworth Higginson disagreed. A white Massachusetts abolitionist and Unitarian minister, he ignored his West Point comrades' warning that commanding black troops would ruin his career. "It needs but a few days," he insisted, "to show the absurdity of doubting the equal military availability of these people, as compared with whites. There is quite as much . . . courage . . . as much previous knowledge of the gun, & there is readiness of the ear."

After the Emancipation Proclamation, black leaders buried their philosophical differences. Instead they united to recruit black soldiers. Posters proclaimed: "Men of Color, To Arms!" Sarah Woodson, sister of reformer Lewis Woodson, urged listeners "to accept the means which God has placed in your power." New York minister J. W. C. Pennington exhorted: "The only wise and safe course is to [join the army and] press rapidly into the heart of the slave country, and [secure] the Proclamation of freedom." While a few thought black Americans should withhold support until they got citizenship, the rhetoric of the New York *Anglo-African* is representative: "Should we not with two centuries of cruel wrong stirring our heart's blood, be but too willing to embrace any chance to settle accounts with the slaveholders? . . . Can you ask any more than a chance to drive bayonet or bullet into the slaveholders' hearts?"

Black communities sent more than 190,000 black enlisted men and over 7,000 officers to Union service—constituting 10 percent of the North's total fighting force. Most volunteers came from unremarkable circumstances, but sons of renowned black leaders also enlisted. Alongside Martin Delany's seventeen-year-old son, Toussaint L'Ouverture Delany, marched with Frederick Douglass's sons Lewis and Charles. Sojourner Truth sent off her grandson James Caldwell, observing wryly that this was yet another example of how "the niggers always have to clean up after the white folks." Even as they worried that if captured they would be immediately killed, black men volunteered in record numbers.

## Colored Troops

At Camp Meigs near Boston, the Massachusetts Fifty-fourth received just two months' training before heading south in July 1863 to launch a night attack on Fort Wagner, in the Charleston harbor. Led by their young white colonel, Robert Gould Shaw, the regiment withstood relentless shelling that left Shaw and many

*These pictures show the transformation of a slave into a freedman. After Contraband Jackson fled to the Union army, he was mustered into the 79th U.S. Colored Troops as Drummer Jackson. Abolitionists produced such visual renditions to show how changes in clothing and occupation transformed African Americans' posture, facial expression, and confidence.*

others dead or wounded. Toussaint L'Ouverture Delany received injuries from which he never recovered. Though its objective was not won, the Massachusetts Fifty-fourth earned wide recognition for its battlefield performance. For bravery at Fort Wagner, Sergeant William Carney was the first black serviceman to be awarded the Congressional Medal of Honor, the military's new medal. Poet Frances Ellen Watkins Harper captured the moment in a poem: "Bearers of a high commission; To break each brother's chain; With hearts aglow for freedom, They bore the toil and pain." The *New York Tribune* wrote that the regiment "made Fort Wagner such a name to the colored race as Bunker Hill has been for ninety years to the white Yankees."

Other black regiments showed similar bravery and discipline. Louisiana's First and Third Native Guards helped establish Union control at Port Hudson, near Vicksburg, in May 1863, and at nearby Milliken's Bend, three black regiments held off a division of Texans. One black observer wrote, "The bravery displayed before Port Hudson by the colored troops was applaudingly received here by persons who have not been looked upon as friendly to the movement [of raising black troops]."

By summer 1863, support for black units came from surprising places. Sidestepping her pacifism, white Quaker abolitionist Lucretia Mott offered her farm near Philadelphia as a training camp for black recruits. In Ohio, the governor who had rebuffed John Mercer Langston's offer of aid now requested his help in recruiting.

Northern black soldiers took great pride in their regiments. Before setting off into battle, the Sixth Colored Infantry dedicated its regimental flag. "Soldiers," the speaker urged, "under this flag let your rallying cry be 'for God, for freedom, and our country.' If for this you must fall, you fall the country's patriots, heroes, and martyrs." The Sixth carried its flag at Petersburg, Dutch Gap, and New Market Heights in Virginia; at Fort Fisher in Wilmington, North Carolina; and at the Battle of Olustee in the Florida swamps. Not just a battlefield marker, the flag had a symbolic meaning that extended beyond the

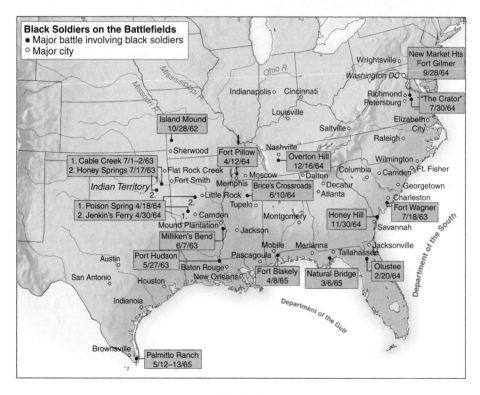

*Map 10.2*
**Black Soldiers on the Battlefields**

*This map shows some of the more than two hundred Civil War engagements in which black soldiers participated. In all, black soldiers served in battles as far north as Maryland, as far south as Florida, and as far west as the Indian Territory. A number of black men rose to the rank of sergeant during the Civil War, and more than a dozen received the Congressional Medal of Honor.*

*This lithograph, produced thirty years after the Battle of Olustee, attests to the conflict's enduring symbolic importance.*

battlefield and even beyond the war. When the Sixth disbanded at war's end, its banner was in tatters. Still, Sergeant Major Thomas Hawkins, a Congressional Medal of Honor winner, was honored to receive it from his comrades. The flag dropped from public view but now resides in a museum, where it helps Americans remember the part played by African American patriots and heroes in the preservation of the Union.

Yet military service did not necessarily bring glory. Black soldiers often got the toughest assignments and longest guard duty. Some were relegated to building fortifications, growing food, or tending livestock. For them, war continued the drudgery of slavery. For those captured in battle, death might follow, as the Confederate army labeled black soldiers "insurrectionists." The worst incident occurred at Fort Pillow, Mississippi, where, on April 12, 1864, more than 300 black prisoners were massacred.

## THE FIGHT FOR EQUAL PAY

Black recruits often earned less than half the pay of white soldiers. In August 1863, Frederick Douglass beseeched President Lincoln to end this blatant inequity. As Douglass later recalled, Lincoln explained that black soldiers were "a serious offense to popular prejudice" so unequal pay "seemed a necessary concession to smooth the way to their employment at all as soldiers."

Meanwhile, black soldiers at the front petitioned Secretary of War Edwin Stanton. In the fall of 1863, the Massachusetts Fifty-fourth refused to accept any pay until it matched that of white soldiers. One regiment member remembered, "Four months we have been working night and day under fire . . . patiently, waiting for justice." After more than a year of pressure from northern abolitionists and the horror of black sacrifice at Fort Pillow, Congress passed legislation equalizing pay in June 1864.

## BLACK WOMEN AND WAR

Black women also advanced the cause of black freedom. Dozens of black women labored alongside Clara Barton, nursing wounded soldiers in Baltimore. Fugitive slave leader Harriet Tubman returned to the South as both nurse and spy, her information helping to secure a Union victory at the Combahee River. Tubman reported that one slave woman rejoiced, "Oh! Praise de Lord! I'd prayed seventy-three years, and now he's come and we's all free." Mary Elizabeth Bowser, a literate servant in the Confederate presidential mansion, feigned mental illness to gain access to Jefferson Davis's military secrets, which she passed to Union officers. In Washington, DC, Elizabeth Keckley, a free black seamstress employed by Mrs. Lincoln, helped raise relief money for southern black people. "If the white people can give festivals to raise funds for the relief of suffering soldiers, why should not the well-to-do colored people . . . do something for . . . suffering blacks? The next Sunday I made a suggestion in the colored church," Keckley said, "and in two weeks the 'Contraband Relief Association' was organized, with forty working members." This was one of dozens of black groups that raised money for southern contraband camps.

But in the South, as the Civil War disrupted households, many black women and children were set adrift. Unlike black men, they were not thought useful to the Union army in the war effort. Yet as large numbers of black women, some with children, arrived at Union camps, white troops sometimes put them to work in the fields alongside black men and assigned them to heavy labor. Other women worked as cooks, nurses, or livestock tenders, seldom receiving the pay they were promised. Learning they might be separated from husbands or assigned to housekeeping for white people, some black women collected their families and traveled to nearby towns, where Confederates paid for such services.

Single or widowed women often accepted help from northern relief agencies, or tried to fend for themselves. Nearly 6,000 Natchez, Mississippi, black women were dependent on American Missionary Association philanthropy or on funds raised by northern black women for relief and education. Other women huddled in camps outside towns, vulnerable to Confederate raids and to Union officers who might coerce them into field labor. One woman, probably typical of many, reported trading sex for pay because "we women had to make a living." Still, some newly freed women were able to find paid work, save money, and buy a home, even during the war.

# 1863: The Tide Turns

After losses to the Confederates in 1862, in May 1863 Union general Ulysses Grant won five battles in three weeks at Vicksburg. Union victory seemed within reach, but a draft met surprisingly strong resistance in the North.

## Victory at Gettysburg

At first, as Confederates marched north into Pennsylvania, Lincoln's call for volunteers got a quick response. In a three-day clash at Gettysburg in July 1863, northern troops led by General George Meade shot down more than half of the Confederate troops sent into the battle. By the time Confederate forces retreated from this bloodiest battle of the war, more than 23,000 Union soldiers and 28,000 Confederates had perished or been injured.

The Union victory at Gettysburg proved a turning point. Now European nations definitively withdrew their support from the South. Britain canceled contracts to build warships for the Confederacy, as British dependence on northern wheat outweighed its need for southern cotton, now imported from India and Egypt. British popular opinion, massaged into abolitionist sympathies by dozens of black abolitionists, helped solidify this decision. France, too, distanced itself from the Confederacy.

President Lincoln bestowed symbolic importance on this battle by traveling to Gettysburg in November 1863 to deliver his memorable address dedicating the battlefield as a cemetery. Before a somber audience, he declared that the Gettysburg victory foretold "a new birth of freedom" in a nation that had been "conceived in liberty and dedicated to the proposition that all men are created equal."

## Anti-Draft Riots

Along with Union gains came setbacks, especially the difficulty in finding new recruits. In the spring of 1863, Congress enacted a draft law requiring three years military service for every man between ages twenty and forty-five. (Those who could pay a fee or find a substitute were exempted.) Shortly after the Gettysburg victory, when New York newspapers printed a list of draftees, hundreds of young white men rioted in New York City. Convinced that black men would take their jobs while they were off fighting, the white draftees stormed a building where a draft lottery was taking place. For more than a week mobs vandalized factories and shipyards where war supplies were manufactured or transported. Black workers were randomly attacked on the streets, and black neighborhoods were ravaged.

Why such resistance to the draft? Many of the rioters were poor immigrants who resented the provision allowing wealthier men to avoid service. Falling wages also provoked the outbursts. Military purchasing had inflated prices, but earnings had not kept pace. Thus, poorly paid white factory workers, seeing their standard of living decline, were frustrated and viewed black workers as the source of the troubles. Black workers lowered wages, claimed the protesters, by settling for less money than white workers. Moreover, the rioters resented black men and women who carved out successful lives. As black New Yorkers struggled to defend themselves, more than one hundred black and white people died. Troops were called from the battlefield to crush the uprising. In the end, Union draft officers looked the other way while fully 10 percent of young white men ignored their call or deserted after entering the army. In Detroit, Philadelphia, and other cities, as the Democratic press fanned fears of job competition, white workers replayed the New York riots, resisting the draft by attacking black Americans.

## GRANT AND SHERMAN LEAD UNION VICTORIES

By early 1864, victories at Vicksburg and Gettysburg had solidified the North's advantage. Now black troops were under Union general Ulysses S. Grant's command in Virginia when he confronted Confederate general Robert E. Lee. "By arming the negro we have added a powerful ally," Grant told Lincoln. "They make good soldiers, and taking them from the enemy weakens [the South] as it strengthens us." In June 1864, when Lee's forces stopped Grant's at the outskirts of Petersburg, Virginia, both sides suffered high casualties in a siege that lasted nine months.

African American soldiers also accompanied Union general William T. Sherman in May 1864 as he began his march from Tennessee through Georgia to the sea and north into South Carolina. One black Rhode Island recruit described the southern white people he encountered: "We could see signs of smothered hate [for] both our color and [our] present character as Union soldiers. But, for once [I] walked fearlessly and boldly through the streets of a southern city, without being required to take off my hat at every step, or to give all the side-walks to the planters' sons." During this eight-month campaign, Union troops systematically destroyed everything in their path: bridges, railroads, factories, warehouses, barns, crops, and homes all went up in flames. By the time Sherman reached Savannah in December 1864, he had severed the South's transportation and supply routes.

While Sherman swept through the South, the 1864 presidential election revealed a precarious political situation as politicians and federal officials in Washington clashed over the management of the war, of slaves, and of procedures for reunification. The Democrats called for an immediate end to the war. Weary of war, Republicans could not unite behind Lincoln. The Radical faction nominated Frémont and the Republican (National Union) faction nominated Lincoln, with Andrew Johnson, a Democrat from Tennessee, for vice president. Only Sherman's victories in Georgia assured Lincoln's reelection. He won by a mere 40,000 votes out of 4 million cast, revealing that Northerners (Southerners did not vote) had mixed feelings about the war.

## "FORTY ACRES AND A MULE"

Sherman's success marked another turning point for former slaves. In January 1865, after he took Savannah, black ministers petitioned Sherman for land on which they and their people could raise food for their families. The general responded with Special Field Order No. 15, granting thousands of acres of confiscated land along the Florida, Georgia, and South Carolina coast to black families in 40-acre plots. Sherman also gave them mules to work the acreage.

News of Field Order No. 15 spread quickly. Many ex-slaves and northern reformers concluded the government should provide *all* freed people with "40 acres and a mule." But some white leaders doubted the legality of confiscating and redistributing property, and black leaders who had worked their way up the economic ladder worried that free land might foster laziness and undermine the capitalist economy they now embraced. Both black and white leaders also feared that, at war's end, white resentment of land grants might spark riots. South Carolina's Alonzo Ransier, an African American soon to win election to the U.S. House of Representatives, advised people to "buy lands by saving their money, and not to expect confiscation or the possession of lands that were not theirs."

But most ex-slaves disagreed. Some suggested the states buy land at tax auction, then resell it to freedmen at reduced costs if they would improve it with a dwelling and farm it. Modeled after the 1862 Homestead Act, this plan never saw the light of day. One landless South Carolinian concluded: "At the close of the war [we] were set free without a dollar, and without a foot of land [or] the wherewithal to get the next meal even. The labor of these people had for two hundred years cleared away the forests and produced crops that brought millions of dollars annually. . . . Did they get any portion of it? Not a cent. . . . Four million people turned loose without a dollar . . . [by those] whose duty it was to feed them. My opinion is that the government should have done it."

## AN INCOMPLETE VICTORY

By the time Major Martin Delany arrived in Charleston on April 3, 1865 to organize a black fighting force, the war was nearly over. On April 9, Confederate general Lee surrendered at Virginia's Appomattox Court House.

Across the nation, black people rejoiced. Local black soldiers hurried home with the news to West Chester, Pennsylvania, to ring the courthouse bell. Black residents in New York celebrated with a parade. Thomas Morris Chester, the black war correspondent for African American newspapers, sent word to Philadelphia: "The colored population was wild with enthusiasm. Old men thanked God in a very boisterous manner, and old women shouted upon the pavement as high as they ever had done at a religious revival."

On April 14, ex-slave Robert Smalls sailed into Charleston Harbor on the steamship *Planter*, which he had stolen for the Union early in the war. Now a gunboat captain, Smalls joined the Union flag-raising celebration at Fort Sumter—four years, almost to the day, after its fall. William Lloyd Garrison, and the son of slave rebel Denmark Vesey, were among the veteran abolitionists there when Martin Delany recorded the buoyant mood: "The Union flag," he said, "now symbolizes freedom for all, without distinction of race or color."

In Texas, the Union army arrived on June 19 to announce victory ("Juneteenth" celebrations still mark the day). One black woman who had fled slavery and survived in the wild for several years now had, it was told, "freedom not of the swamp, but of the world." At a New Orleans Fourth of July parade in 1865, a black military officer "declared that slavery was dead and will be buried so deep that the judgment will not find it!"

But the idea of freedom proved more exhilarating than the reality. Freed slaves had few resources with which to provide for or protect themselves—and no power to acquire them. Across the South, state governments were in disarray, local economies broken, and cities and farms in shambles. Black and white families alike desperately needed food, shelter, medical care, and reassurance. One black Floridian wrote, "Nobody had his bearings. The freed people had no homes and no names except such as they inherited from their owners. They [did not know] whether to rejoice because they were free or to be cast down at their new condition of . . . responsibility and homelessness." In New Orleans, Frank Bell recalled his experience: "When war am over [the master] won't free me, says I'm valuable to him in his trade. He say, 'Nigger, you's supposed to be free but I'll pay you a dollar a week and iffen you runs off I'll kill you.'" In South Carolina, Nancy Johnson repeatedly sent her four hungry children back to her former master for food. "I might as well stayed where I was. It 'pears we can't be free, no-how," said another black South Carolinian. "The rebs [Confederates] won't let us alone. If they can't kill us, they'll kill all our frien's."

## THE ASSASSINATION OF PRESIDENT LINCOLN

Within days of the South's surrender, Confederate sympathizer John Wilkes Booth killed Abraham Lincoln in a theater. Setting aside earlier disappointments with Lincoln, Martin Delany eulogized him as "the humane, the benevolent, the philanthropic, the generous, the beloved, the able, the wise, great and good President of the United States." Delany suggested a fitting memorial would be a statue depicting a kneeling African woman with tear-filled eyes cast to heaven, to be funded by a penny from every African American man, woman, and child. The work was never erected.

Other black Americans also memorialized Lincoln as their savior, creating a legend that remained untarnished for more than a century. The black New Orleans *Tribune,* having criticized the living Lincoln, now linked him with the most radical abolitionist: "Lincoln and John Brown are two martyrs. . . . Both have willingly jeopardized their lives for the sacred cause of freedom." Black people in the Sea Islands, where the Port Royal system still tied black people to the land, passed a resolution praising "the wisdom and Christian patriotism [Lincoln] displayed" in the "most memorable act proclaiming Liberty to our race."

## THE THIRTEENTH AMENDMENT

In February 1865 the Thirteenth Amendment to the U.S. Constitution, ending slavery everywhere in the United States and its territories, was passed by

Congress. By December 18, 1865, twenty-seven states (including eight in the South) had ratified the premise that "neither slavery nor involuntary servitude, except as a punishment for crime, shall exist within the United States." Once again, celebrations followed. In Boston, black and white abolitionists crowded into Music Hall, where William Lloyd Garrison reported being moved by the "deeply religious and moral significance" of outlawing slavery.

But the Thirteenth Amendment did not include the franchise. Even as black people celebrated, Delany urged them to organize for the right to vote. Augusta, Georgia's *Colored American* reported that a black convention in South Carolina called for "equal suffrage [to] be conferred in common with white men as a protection from hostility, and because all free governments derive their power from the consent of the governed." In the North and South, Equal Rights Leagues, many led by black veterans of antebellum abolitionism, took up the franchise battle. Only the vote could safeguard the freedom promised by the Thirteenth Amendment.

## REUNITING BLACK FAMILIES

With slavery vanquished, thousands of liberated black Americans sought lost family members. Northern and southern black newspapers published notices like this one: "I have a mother somewhere in the world. I know not where. She used to belong to Philip Mathias in Elbert County, Georgia, and she left four of her children there about twenty-three years ago. . . . I ask all who read this to inquire for her. Her name was Martha and I heard that she was carried off to Mississippi by speculators."

Similar heart-wrenching appeals testified to African Americans' longing to be reunited with loved ones. Some had been separated by slave sales or war. Others hoped to locate relatives who had escaped to the North or were returning from exile. Fugitive slave James Davis, heading home from Canada, yearned to hear from his family. "Write me word how Johnny is getting on," implored his notice. "I am in East Boston but I feel very lonesome. I don't see any colored ladies & gentlemens." From Cincinnati, Ben Montgomery and his family returned home to Hurricane Plantation in 1865. They reopened their old store but now served the free black farmers who leased confiscated land from the government.

## THE FREEDMEN'S BUREAU

In 1865, Congress established a Freedmen's Bureau to allocate work, supplies, and abandoned and confiscated southern lands among freed black people. Bureau agents also delivered medical, educational, and legal services and helped set up hospitals, schools, and stores. The bureau assigned Martin Delany a post in South Carolina.

The federal government sent troops to impose political order in the South, but the Freedmen's Bureau was charged with repairing the region's social and economic order. It encouraged white planters to revive their farms, urged black workers to accept jobs, monitored contracts between landowners and workers, and pressed both to treat each other as employers and employees, not owners and property. Bureau agents followed the Port Royal model in blending education, philanthropy, and paid labor.

As the extent of the South's devastation became clear, Congress renewed the Freedmen's Bureau charter in 1866. Bureau agents now expanded their reach, working to reunite families and helping black refugees write or read letters and newspaper notices for lost kin. Reuniting families sometimes involved legal battles with local and national courts, as local governments tried to replace slavery with other forms of servitude. Maryland's oppressive apprentice system was a typical example, finally overturned by the Supreme Court in 1868. In the process, the bureau established African Americans' right to seek justice in the Maryland courts.

## BLACK CODES AND SHARECROPPING

Maryland's system of separate laws for black people was part of a larger southern legal pattern known as Black Codes. After the Civil War, the federal government restored citizenship privileges and statehood to former Confederate states whose white leaders swore allegiance to the United States. By 1869, many southern states had elected new officials and reorganized law enforcement to restrict black people's movement, economic and social prospects, and access to legal recourse. Alabama gave former slave owners the right of first refusal for black apprentices. Georgia banned interracial marriage. North Carolina required the death penalty if a black man raped a white woman (in all other instances, rapists were fined).

Many contracts promoted by the Freedmen's Bureau bound black workers to repetitive tasks, long hours, low wages, or compensation in produce rather than cash. When the dream of "40 acres and a mule" evaporated, the Bureau pressured black freedmen to accept an owner-tenant relationship known as *sharecropping*. In such arrangements, a landowner provided about forty acres and some of the seeds and supplies to plant cotton, corn, wheat, oats, or rice. In return, the tenant gave the landlord a percentage, or share, of the resulting crop.

Viewed by the Freedmen's Bureau as suppressing vagrancy, sharecropping encouraged blatant exploitation. Many landowners manipulated the cost of supplies so it exceeded the tenant's share of crop production. This ploy kept the tenant perpetually indebted to the owner and, therefore, tied to the land. Other landowners found excuses to dismiss tenants just before their compensation was due. Such incidents made black people wary of entering into contracts. "I am opposed to working under a contract," wrote one black South Carolinian. "I expect to stay in the South . . . but not to hire myself to a planter. . . . I have seen some men hired who were turned off [of the land] without being paid."

"Times are very hard, and hard to get money," wrote South Carolina ex-slave Celia Johnson in 1868, resigning herself to a farming contract. As often as men, women suffered their employers' violent resentment of the postwar changes. One Georgia county agent reported that a landowner had "cursed and abused" a freedwoman working for him "when she told him she was as free as he. On this he kicked her in the head and knocked her down seriously hurting her."

By 1869, sharecropping was supported by Black Codes. Black adults who failed to enter into contracts, or who broke them, could be arrested for vagrancy and imprisoned. Prisoners, in turn, were leased to farmers or commercial concerns, and the wages from their labor went to state coffers. A ball and chain attached to the ankle kept prisoners from escaping as they toiled on county roads and private railroads. Freedmen's Bureau agents declined to interfere with such practices, believing they brought order by preventing black vagrancy. But few black Southerners described their new conditions as free.

## BLACK EDUCATION

The Freedmen's Bureau was overwhelmed by land and labor issues, but it did a better job of providing other services. Between 1866 and 1872, it distributed more than 21 million food rations and widespread medical care to distressed Southerners, both black and white. But its most enduring influence was on black education. In its sixteen years, it established more than 4,000 schools for former slaves, many of which survive today.

Private organizations often helped develop black schools. In 1868, Samuel Chapman Armstrong organized a black boarding school near Hampton Roads, Virginia. The curriculum at Hampton focused on self-discipline, hygiene, and manual skills, and aimed to produce skilled, responsible workers. Other schools aimed to develop black leaders. Established by the Freedmen's Bureau in 1867 and named for Bureau director and Union general Oliver O. Howard, Howard University in Washington, DC, offered a rigorous and varied curriculum, including degrees in law and medicine. Lincoln University in Pennsylvania and Wilberforce in Ohio, supported by the American Missionary Association, shared Howard University's focus on liberal education.

So, too, did the innovative Berea College in Kentucky. Opened in 1858, Berea was suspended during wartime but reopened in 1866 with a program similar to Hampton's. Students put their manual training to use in maintaining the school's buildings and grounds. Berea's abolitionist founder, Reverend John Fee, welcomed black and white students and hired an integrated faculty. To this day, tuition is free at Berea, and graduates are expected to commit their lives to social reform ideals.

## THE RISE OF THE KU KLUX KLAN

Even while black Southerners pursued self-improvement, they remained aware of white Southerners' bitterness over the war, the demise of slavery, and the federal military presence in the South. In Tennessee in 1866, angry white Southerners formalized their hatred in an organization known as the Ku Klux Klan. Billing itself as the protector of the Old South's noble traditions, the Klan united resentful Confederates from many walks of life. Led by a former Confederate general, the Klan used hoods and fiery crosses, secret codes, and night raids to stop black Americans from taking advantage of new opportunities. Thousands of so-called night riders systematically threatened, maimed, or killed to keep black people out of politics. Nevertheless, between 1867 and 1870, southern black men gained the right to vote, while most of their northern counterparts could not legally cast a ballot. They were determined to leverage this power.

## THE FOURTEENTH AMENDMENT

Race-based hatred showed black Southerners what black Northerners had long understood: True equality comes from political power only. As early as February 1862, Frederick Douglass laid out his vision of the war's outcome: "No war but an Abolition war; no peace but an Abolition peace; liberty for all, chains for none; the black man a soldier in war, a laborer in peace; a voter at the South as well as at the North; America his permanent home, and all Americans his fellow countrymen. [Then] our glory as a nation will be complete."

Following Douglass's lead, black Northerners began organizing for the right to vote during the war. In 1864, more than a hundred African Americans from eighteen states (including states still in the Confederacy) gathered in Syracuse, New York, to create the National Equal Rights League. They insisted the war was about citizenship as well as slavery.

To secure citizenship rights for black people, the Republican Congress in 1866 proposed the Fourteenth Amendment, aimed at overriding the Supreme Court's 1857 *Dred Scott* ruling that African Americans were not citizens. The amendment, stating that "no state shall make or enforce any law which shall abridge the privileges or immunities of citizens in the United States," protected citizens' rights from violation by state governments. It also promised that "when the right to vote at any election is denied to any of the male inhabitants of such state . . . the representation [in Congress] shall be reduced in proportion." To regain representation in Congress, Confederate states had to ratify the Fourteenth Amendment. As they did, federal troops began to leave, and the Freedmen's Bureau began to close down.

But black Americans did not consider the job done until black men had the right to vote everywhere. The National Equal Rights League expanded rapidly, linking New York, Michigan, Pennsylvania, and Ohio with Tennessee, Louisiana, and North Carolina. Proclaiming that "it is the duty of every colored citizen to obtain a repeal of [any state] law which disfranchises him on the soil on which he was born," members repeatedly petitioned state legislatures for the franchise implied under the Fourteenth Amendment.

Thus, securing the right to vote became paramount in the postwar years. The black editor of the Atlanta paper *Loyal Georgian* spoke for many when he wrote, "The colored man owes it to the martyrs who have fallen to procure his right to—upon their graves reared to liberty—*vote* and vote *right*. Let the Republicans of the North know the strength and character of the colored voter in the South." The *Arkansas Freeman* agreed: "The colored voters hold the power to strike out for themselves" and "demand their rights." In Mississippi, black planter P. B. S. Pinchback told African Americans that voting was essential "if they wanted to be men." For decades to come, black people equated manhood with the right to vote.

# CONCLUSION

What began as a "white man's war" in 1861 evolved over four years into a conflict where black men fought to end slavery. Former slaves assumed leadership positions in the military, and a president who wanted to deport black people issued the Emancipation Proclamation freeing them. Congress followed with the Thirteenth Amendment to the Constitution, finally eradicating slavery. Federal soldiers, the Freedmen's Bureau, and private agencies moved into the South to build a new society that included African Americans as free people, not slaves.

Postwar freedom brought black Southerners real advances—reunited families, increased land ownership (in some regions), and rising literacy rates. The Fourteenth Amendment guaranteed citizenship to anyone born in the United States. But these advances came only in the South, and only under pressure from Congress. Moreover, black freedom sparked white hate groups in the South, bent on restricting black progress.

In Washington, meanwhile, the struggle over ending slavery and defining new roles for black Americans highlighted rivalries among the legislative, judicial, and executive branches of the federal government, as well as between these units and the military. For African Americans, the struggle did not end with the war's conclusion. As we'll see in the next chapter, the federal government gradually concluded that black citizens in the North should also have the right to vote. In February 1869, when Congress proposed the Fifteenth Amendment, giving the franchise to all black men, African Americans' hopes stirred again. Nonetheless, it required intense pressure from the federal government to ratify the amendment that made the African American man a voter, finally fulfilling Frederick Douglass's dream.

# 11

POST-CIVIL WAR
RECONSTRUCTION:
A NEW NATIONAL ERA

## EMANUEL FORTUNE TESTIFIES
## BEFORE CONGRESS

**"T**hey always spoke very bitterly against it," said Florida Republican Emanuel Fortune, describing his white neighbors' reaction to the idea of black people voting. Those neighbors told Fortune, "The damned Republican party has put niggers to rule us, and we will not suffer it." Fortune was testifying before a congressional committee investigating Ku Klux Klan threats and violence against black Southerners. After the Civil War, when anger in many southern white communities erupted in violence, some white Southerners targeted black men like Fortune who organized voters or ran for office. "I got information that I would be missing some day and no one would know where I was, on account of my being a leading man in politics," Fortune recalled.

Emanuel Fortune's story typified the experience of black political leaders who emerged in the postwar period. Relatively young—Fortune was thirty-nine in 1871—these leaders were new to politics. Just a few years earlier, they had been outsiders—many of them slaves. Now they had a political voice. Fortune, for example, had participated in the 1868 constitutional convention that qualified Florida—part of the Confederacy during the war—to reenter the Union by guaranteeing black suffrage and ratifying the Fourteenth Amendment, which defined citizens as anyone born in the United States, guaranteed them the equal protection of the laws, and provided for a reduction in congressional representation for any state that denied the vote to some of its citizens. The fact that a black man could run for office and get elected by a black constituency demonstrated those new rights. But the threats Fortune received also highlighted the risks run by southern black men who dared to claim seats at the political table. He described Jackson County, Florida, in 1869 as being in "such a state of lawlessness that my life was in danger at all times."

Fortune was prepared to fight back. He was remembered by friends as a "dead shot, and he *would* shoot." Despites threats, he never relinquished his political commitment. Over the next ten years, he served as city marshal, Republican national convention delegate, county commissioner, clerk of the city market, and state congressman.

Fortune's testimony before Congress reveals the realities of the postwar South. White Southerners complained bitterly about what they called "black rule" as African Americans took positions as sheriffs, justices of the peace, county clerks, and school superintendents. Even so, only a few dozen black Americans occupied positions of real authority. Few actually ran for office, and many black voters, intimidated by threats or actual violence in the open southern polls, where a vote was public knowledge, supported white politicians.

With the South's return to the Union after the Civil War, race relations in that embattled region took center stage. For the first dozen years after the war—a period that became known as Reconstruction—the federal government sent troops and agents to restore order and aid slaves' transition to freedom. Federal and private agencies opened schools, distributed food and medicine, and intervened in legal disputes between freed people and their white neighbors. In what many Northerners considered a new national era, the federal government aimed to heal the war-torn South and make it more like the North, physically, economically, socially, and politically. While repairing fields, roads, and homes was foremost, many Northerners hoped the South would soon have new railroads, factories, banks, and wage laborers as well.

Reconstruction extended to the national level, as black men were elected to Congress and Republican presidents appointed African Americans to positions of authority. During this era, black leaders made access to the polls their highest priority, believing African Americans could vote into office leaders who supported their goals, such as farm ownership and jobs that would allow them to be independent of white landowners. They also wanted education for their children, as literacy would, in turn, provide opportunities for entrepreneurship and political power that would lift people out of poverty.

But most northern and southern white Americans hoped to "reconstruct" a system that tied black Americans to menial roles. A few white Americans envisioned former bondspeople becoming successful landowners or entrepreneurs, although certainly not equal members of society. Though slavery had been outlawed, persuasion, local statutes, intimidation, and widespread prejudice kept black people tied to agricultural and service jobs in both the South and the North.

As we saw in Chapter 10, resentful southern planters also began instituting Black Codes to keep black people subservient. These laws were backed by violence, threats, or economic reprisals, such as dismissing black farm workers who

## *Chronology*

**1865** In March, Congress charters the Freedmen's Bureau and the Freedmen's Savings and Trust Bank.

In December, the Thirteenth Amendment, ratified in twenty-seven states, abolishes slavery throughout the United States.

**1866** Over President Andrew Johnson's veto, Congress passes the Civil Rights Act granting citizenship and civil rights to African Americans.

In Pulaski, Tennessee, the secretive Ku Klux Klan is formed.

**1868** Congress carries out impeachment proceedings against President Andrew Johnson. Johnson is acquitted in May, when the Senate fails, by one vote, to reach the two-thirds vote necessary for conviction.

The Fourteenth Amendment is ratified, guaranteeing citizenship to African Americans and requiring southern states to approve it before gaining readmission to the Union.

**1869** Congress proposes the Fifteenth Amendment to protect "the right of citizens of the United States to vote."

Mary Ann Shadd Cary tries to register to vote in Washington, DC, and petitions Congress when officials deny her.

Over the issue of black civil and voting rights, the women's rights movement splits into two rival organizations.

**1870** The Fifteenth Amendment is ratified.

Seven southern legislators become the first black men elected to the United States Congress.

Congress passes the Ku Klux Klan Act to protect voting rights, also known as the Enforcement Act, making it a federal offense to interfere with franchise rights guaranteed by the Fifteenth Amendment.

**1871** The District of Columbia is granted self-rule.

After holding a series of hearings on Ku Klux Klan violence, Congress enacts a second Ku Klux Klan Act.

**1872** At the National Colored Men's Labor Convention in Washington, DC, Frederick Douglass and Mary Ann Shadd Cary champion manual laborers' rights.

The Freedmen's Bureau is dismantled.

Black leaders endorse the reelection of Republican presidential candidate Ulysses S. Grant for president, pleased that he advocates annexing the Dominican Republic, with its majority black population.

**1873** Beginning in September, the Panic of 1873 plunges the United States into economic depression.

In *Slaughterhouse Cases*, Supreme Court narrows the scope of the Fourteenth Amendment.

**1874** The Freedmen's Savings and Trust Bank fails.

The Virginia legislature reorganizes election districts to dilute the black vote.

**1875** Congress passes the Civil Rights Act, guaranteeing black Americans access to public accommodations.

*(continued on next page)*

## Chronology (continued)

1876 Harriet Purvis is elected first black president of the American Woman Suffrage Association.

1877 A compromise between Congress and the Republican Party over the disputed presidential election results in complete withdrawal of federal troops from the South.

The Republican Party establishes a separate Black and Tan Party, segregating black Americans from the mainstream Republican Party.

A nationwide railroad workers' strike in July elevates Peter Clark, the first known African American socialist, to leadership.

1878 The Liberia Exodus Joint Stock Company sends the ship *Azor* to Africa.

1879 The Kansas Exodus Joint Stock Company sends emigrants west to Kansas.

tried to vote or who encouraged others to do so. The presence of the federal Freedmen's Bureau in the South, which aimed to help former slaves become full citizens, infuriated many white Southerners. These planters hoped to reconstruct the old agricultural system in which wealthy white men made the laws, leaving both white and black poor people powerless.

But black Americans had sweeping ambitions: strengthening their communities economically, reassembling their families, and protecting themselves from violence and intimidation. All these goals hinged on acquiring and protecting political rights, navigating the shifting and sometimes treacherous tides of southern and federal politics. Washington, DC—seat of the national government—symbolized the complexities of the new era. From across the nation, black Americans seeking employment and federal protection streamed into the capital city.

But federal sympathy toward freedmen and freedwomen waned after a decade of Reconstruction efforts, and federal promises went unfulfilled. Discouraged by slow progress, some black Americans again directed their hopes elsewhere—to African or western frontiers.

# POSTWAR RECONSTRUCTION

On February 25, 1870, an ambitious, urbane Southerner arrived in Washington, DC with a mission: to ensure that the federal government treated black people as full citizens. That man was Hiram Revels—African Methodist Episcopal Church (AME) minister, former Union recruitment officer, and advocate of education for black people. The first black American to be elected to Congress, Revels soon discovered how fervently white congressmen resented his presence. His public service career—beginning before the Civil War and continuing until his death in 1901—reveals much about how emancipation transformed black people and about the complexities of Reconstruction.

## RADICAL RECONSTRUCTION

Revels found Congress dominated by a coalition of northern representatives known as Radical Republicans. These politicians aimed to protect and promote

*Hiram Revels helped recruit the first black Civil War regiments in Maryland and Missouri. After his U.S. Senate service, he returned to Mississippi and became president of Alcorn, a Reconstruction-era black college. This photo of Revels with his wife and five daughters was taken in about 1870.*

the interests of black Southerners and to punish white Southerners for the Civil War. Simultaneously, Congress clashed with the president over how to define and protect black rights. Though the war had ended, sectional tensions remained. Until black Southerners could not yet vote, southern white aristocrats returned to the congressional seats they had vacated with secession. Radical Republicans, still in the majority, asserted Congress's right to refuse to seat southern congressmen who had not yet sworn Union allegiance. Led by Pennsylvania representative Thaddeus Stevens and Massachusetts senator Charles Sumner (who returned to the Senate in 1860), they strategized on how to get southern black candidates seated in Congress in order to drive southern white men from the legislature.

Radical Republicans pounded the South with new policies. In early 1867, Congress passed three new Reconstruction acts. The first divided the South into five military districts, sending federal troops to maintain order and protect freed people. The second required former Confederate states to draft constitutions guaranteeing black male suffrage. The third stipulated that former Confederate states could send congressmen to Washington only after state legislatures had ratified the Fourteenth Amendment. This amendment, ratified in 1868, was the most important product of the Reconstruction era. It affirmed black people's citizenship, removing any ambiguity left from the *Dred Scott* case of 1857. It also denied former slave owners' claims that they should be compensated for their lost "property." Emanuel Fortune, a delegate to Florida's constitutional convention, helped pass these provisions. To build support for punishing Southerners, Congress also established a committee to investigate southern anti-black violence.

## PRESIDENTIAL RECONSTRUCTION

Black people across the nation hoped the Fourteenth Amendment would secure them a place in their nation's economic, political, and social life. However, a milder form of Reconstruction proposed by President Abraham Lincoln and fa-vored by his successor, Andrew Johnson, enabled the white South to resist. Hoping to heal sectional bitterness, Lincoln and some Northerners favored a non-punitive approach. The South, they contended, did not possess the authority to leave the United States. Hence, southern states had always remained in the Union, and thus technically did not need to rejoin.

When Lincoln was assassinated in April 1865, the presidency fell to Vice President Andrew Johnson. A former Democratic senator from Tennessee, Johnson also favored a lenient Reconstruction policy. Reversing Congress's Confiscation Act of 1862, which had allowed the federal government to seize Confederates' property without compensation, Johnson offered to pardon and to restore the property of former Confederates who took an oath of allegiance to the Constitution. He also promised to restore their confiscated land. He ac-knowledged North Carolina's new constitution, which, following Republican guidelines, gave black men the vote, and encouraged other Confederate states to reestablish state governments.

Thus, black rights became the focus of Johnson's power struggle with Congress in the postwar era. He vetoed Congress's Civil Rights Act of 1866, which gave limited legal rights to African Americans, as well as a bill to renew the Freedmen's Bureau. But Radical Republicans overrode both vetoes and passed both bills. Johnson still opposed the Fourteenth Amendment because he felt it violated southern states' rights to control their citizenship. During the 1866 midterm campaign, he urged southern states not to ratify it.

Tension between Johnson and Congress reached a climax when the President tried to remove Secretary of War Edwin Stanton, who was encouraging military officers stationed in the South to ignore communications from the president. Seeking to undermine Johnson's authority, Congress passed the Tenure of Office Act, which blocked Johnson from firing Stanton and guaranteed tenure of office to anyone appointed with the Senate's approval. When Johnson dismissed Stanton anyway, Republicans promptly called for the president's impeachment on the grounds that he had violated the Tenure of Office Act and other charges. A three-month impeachment trial failed to remove Johnson, however, because the two-thirds majority required in the Senate fell one vote short. Once more, the contest for power between the South and branches of the federal government—ostensibly about black issues—only diverted federal attention from black peo-ple's needs.

## THE FIFTEENTH AMENDMENT

The Fourteenth Amendment should have secured black freedom everywhere, but even as congressional policies gave southern black men the franchise, northern black men with political ambitions had to head south to fulfill them. In a bitter irony, southern black men, so recently liberated from slavery, had more opportunities for political leadership than did black Northerners. Many northern states still banned black men from voting. The *New York Tribune* put the matter bluntly: "They who desire the Right of Suffrage for Blacks of the South oppose the extension of the same right to Blacks of the North." Across the North, Equal Rights Leagues advocated for full political equality.

By 1868 elections, northern voters had enough of the tug-of-war in Washington. They elected moderate Republicans who distanced themselves from the Radicals' platform and supported the new president: military hero Ulysses S. Grant. With conservative governments victorious in Virginia by 1869 and in North Carolina and Georgia by 1871, aggressively pro-black Reconstruction all but vanished.

Now that Congress had a conservative southern contingent, even moderate Republicans—most of whom had rejected a black suffrage amendment—began to see that northern black voters could be useful. So in February 1869, moderate Republicans proposed the Fifteenth Amendment, prohibiting federal and state governments from limiting the franchise because of "race, color, or previous condition of servitude." To return to the Union, former Confederate states had to ratify this amendment. Mississippi was among the first to comply. Upon its readmission, black voters sent state senator Hiram Revels to Washington to finish out the Senate term vacated by Jefferson Davis in 1861. As a black Pittsburgh teacher commented, "The Republican party had done the Negro good [in passing the Fifteenth Amendment], but they were doing themselves good at the same time." When Revels took his seat in Congress, he was as much a symbol as a politician. To black Americans and Radical Republicans, he embodied black enfranchisement and the South's defeat. To moderate Republicans, he represented a concession to Radical Republican schemes that would preserve the Republican majority in Congress.

## BLACK SUFFRAGE AND WOMAN SUFFRAGE

The passage of the Fourteenth and Fifteenth amendments exposed the fragility of the northern white and black reformer alliance. With Emancipation, war's end, and the Thirteenth Amendment, many white abolitionists, satisfied that black rights would come in due course, diverted some of their energies to promoting full citizenship for women. This connection between black rights and women's rights had been marked since Frederick Douglass attended the 1848 Women's Rights Convention at Seneca Falls, New York. Douglass and Elizabeth Cady Stanton had long been friends, as Douglass backed Stanton's claim that "the power to choose rulers and make laws was the right by which all others could be secured."

During the war, Stanton had circulated petitions supporting the Thirteenth Amendment outlawing slavery. When it was ratified, she expected antislavery

## Table 11.1
## The Federal Power Struggle 1865–1877

*Black newspapers recognized that often white Americans' interest in Reconstruction involved a power struggle among the three branches of government rather than the best interests of black people or the South. African American concerns frequently faded into the background. Below are some of the battles that took place during the Reconstruction years.*

| DATE | CONGRESS | PRESIDENCY | SUPREME COURT |
|---|---|---|---|
| 1865 | Establishes Freedmen's Bureau. | Andrew Johnson grants "amnesty and pardon" to most Confederates, restoring confiscated land, and exiling thousands of black farmers from their land. | |
| 1866 | Passes Thirteenth Amendment, abolishing slavery in all states and territories; ratified by 27 states.<br><br>Expands Freedmen's Bureau authority and over Johnson's veto empowers it to try civil cases for freedmen.<br><br>Over Johnson's veto, passes three Civil Rights Acts, including one that vacates 1857 *Dred Scott* decision and grants citizenship to black Americans.<br><br>Passes Fourteenth Amendment, guaranteeing citizenship and requiring Confederate states' approval; ratified in 1868. | Johnson vetoes two-year extension for Freedmen's Bureau.<br><br>Johnson vetoes Civil Rights Acts. | In *Ex Parte Milligan*, rules that neither the president nor Congress has legal power to allow other agencies to try civilian cases, except in theater of war. |
| 1867 | | Enforces provisions of Civil Rights Acts. | In *Cummings* v. *Missouri*, rules that government may not require voters to take oaths of past loyalty. |
| 1868 | Passes Tenure of Office Act, forbidding president to remove Secretary of War Edwin Stanton.<br><br>Impeaches Johnson; conviction fails by one vote. | Removes military officers from duty, including Secretary of War Edwin Stanton. | Agrees to hear a southern state's case regarding the constitutionality of Reconstruction Acts.<br><br>Outlaws Maryland's race-based apprentice system. |

*Table 11.1 (continued)*

| DATE | CONGRESS | PRESIDENCY | SUPREME COURT |
|------|----------|------------|---------------|
| 1869 | Passes Fifteenth Amendment guaranteeing suffrage, requiring Confederate states to ratify; ratified in 1870. | | Upholds congressional authority to shape Reconstruction.<br><br>In *Texas* v. *White*, rules that Confederate officials had never left Union, since secession was illegal. |
| 1870–71 | Passes Ku Klux Klan Acts.<br><br>Moderate Republicans refuse to seat black Louisiana Senator P. B. S. Pinchback. | | |
| 1872 | Passes Amnesty Act<br><br>Dismantles Freedmen's Bureau. | | |
| 1873 | | | In *Slaughterhouse Cases*, rules that only the rights of federal citizenship are protected under Fourteenth Amendment; other rights at state discretion. |
| 1875 | Passes Civil Rights Act guaranteeing freedmen access to public accommodations. | | |
| 1877 | Compromise installs Rutherford B. Hayes as president; federal troops withdrawn from South. | | |

leaders like Wendell Phillips to support her women's agenda in return. At issue for her was the word *male* in the Fourteenth Amendment. Previously, women had assumed they were citizens. The new amendment, which specified voters as "male inhabitants," underscored women's exclusion from the political process. Furious, Stanton refused to support the Fourteenth and Fifteenth amendments. "My question is," she challenged Phillips, "do you believe the African race is composed entirely of males?" Stanton's friendship with Douglass also soured, as Douglass argued that the right to vote was more crucial for black men than for women. "The government of this country loves women," he contended, "but the Negro is loathed." Douglass feared a bill giving women the vote could not pass, even in a Radical Republican Congress.

The question of whether women had as much right to vote as freedmen found few sympathizers, even among Radical Republicans. Most reformers adopted a "black men first" strategy. By opposing the Fourteenth and later the Fifteenth amendments, Stanton found herself linked to anti-black forces. The issue split the women's movement. Remaining true to her abolitionist principles that black male suffrage was more important than women's suffrage, Lucy Stone founded the interracial American Woman Suffrage Association (AWSA). She was soon joined by Harriet Purvis, who became its first black president in 1876. Other reformers sought to promote the cause of women *and* African Americans equally. "If colored men get their rights, and not colored women theirs, colored men will be masters over the women. . . . I am glad to see that men are getting their rights, but I want women to get theirs," said Sojourner Truth in an 1867 speech. Frances Ellen Watkins Harper and Mary Ann Shadd Cary agreed. They joined Stanton and Susan B. Anthony in the National Woman Suffrage Association in 1869. Cary, who shared Anthony's interest in divorce reform and support for women entrepreneurs, drafted a woman-suffrage statement to the House of Representatives and led a group of women who attempted to register to vote in the District of Columbia elections in 1869.

But soon Cary and other black women were put off by Stanton's and Anthony's impulsive rhetoric about "black [male] beasts" gaining the ballot before white women. In 1871, Cary broke away, establishing the Colored Woman's Progressive Franchise Association, which aimed to "take an aggressive stand against the assumption that men only [should vote]." Thus, in one of the nation's greatest ironies, enfranchisement for African Americans severed alliances between black leaders and white female reformers. When the Fifteenth Amendment

*A woman who made her living by words, Frances Ellen Watkins Harper (1835–1911) often canonized black heroes in poetry. A staunch advocate of temperance and the franchise for women, she agonized over the tensions tearing at reformers' alliances as rival groups argued about the Fourteenth and Fifteenth Amendments.*

was ratified in 1870, Douglass resumed his advocacy of women's suffrage and slowly rebuilt his friendship with Stanton. But the contest between race progress and gender reform continued into the twenty-first century.

## ELECTED BLACK LEADERS

Hiram Revels's election as the first black man to serve in the U.S. Senate was a mixed victory, as northern and southern congressmen questioned his eligibility: Had he been a citizen of the United States for the required nine years? After all, the Fourteenth Amendment granting citizenship had been ratified only two years before. By arguing that he had some white ancestors and therefore had been at least *partly* a citizen before 1868, Senator Revels succeeded in taking his seat.

Within months, six other African Americans joined Revels in Congress, thanks to the rising number of southern black voters. To represent South Carolina, Georgia, Alabama, and Mississippi came former slaves and free men born in the North and the South. All seven knew their fellow congressmen would feel—at best—ambivalent about their presence. Yet they set out to help maintain a Republican majority in Congress and to sustain its commitment to African Americans. Black Americans celebrated what promised to be a new national era. Frederick Douglass, who had long argued that the black man must be "a voter at

*This popular portrait of the seven black congressmen, from spring of 1873, includes several who were ending their term and several just arriving. Missing is Pinckney Benton Stewart Pinchback, elected to the Senate from Louisiana in 1872.*

the South as well as at the North," envisioned a day when black Northerners would have the voting strength to elect black representatives.

Black congressmen were pragmatic about the limits of their new power. Familiar with the ways of white Southerners, they recognized the need for compromise to accomplish their goals. Revels reassured those white Americans who feared politically powerful black men: "The white race has no better friend than I. I am true to my own race. I wish to see all done that can be done . . . to assist [black men] in acquiring property, in becoming intelligent, enlightened . . . citizens . . . but at the same time, I would not have anything done which would harm the white race." Yet Revels lobbied for integrated schools. Segregation, he said, "is wicked. . . . I hold it to be the duty of this nation to discourage it, because it is wicked, because it is wrong." Recognizing the atmosphere of violence in which black politicians operated, he recommended self-defense. "We all have to go armed in the South," he reported, "ready at a moment's warning to sell our lives if it is necessary." Delicately balancing humility, resolution, and self-protection, Revels worked for political progress.

Blanche K. Bruce, also from Mississippi, hoped compromise with white Southerners could spur black progress. A well-educated man who had held local offices, Bruce was elected to the Senate in 1874. Even as he joined southern white senators lobbying for federal funds to improve Mississippi's ports, he advocated full citizenship for Chinese and Native Americans—groups that, he figured, would then support the Republican Party.

Many black congressmen looked for ways to gain white allies. Revels and Alabama's Benjamin Turner were among those African Americans voting for the Amnesty Act of 1872, which would end restrictions on former Confederates' political participation. Revels explained to his constituency that accommodating white Southerners "got colored mechanics in the United States Navy Yard for the first time." With compromise and accommodation, Bruce negotiated alliances that brought black people jobs in post offices, customs offices, and Freedmen's Bureau offices across the South. Black representatives in Washington also cut deals that brought black cadets to West Point and the Naval Academy. Maneuvering through Washington's corridors of power, black politicians understood that their constituents were vulnerable and their own positions fragile. They sought issues on which they could negotiate with white allies without trading away too many black political gains. The balancing act demanded constant attention and vigilance.

Some black congressmen refused to compromise or negotiate. "In my state, since emancipation there have been over five hundred loyal men shot down by the disloyal men there, and not one of those men who took part in committing those outrages has ever been brought to justice," said Congressman Jefferson Long of Georgia. "Those disloyal people still hate this Government, [and] when loyal men dare to carry the 'stars and stripes' through our streets, they are turned out of employment." But outspoken black congressmen like Long found it hard to push their agenda. Too few in number and too new to politics, they struggled to represent their constituents' concerns. Sometimes simply being heard was all they could hope for. For example, Long voted against the Amnesty Act, knowing

### Table 11.2
### The Black Men Who Went to Congress in 1870

*Most African American congressmen were young, ambitious, and outspoken. All represented the South, though some were born in the North. Some brought prestigious educational credentials; others brought a wisdom born of life experience. Here is a look at the first seven black men who were elected to Congress. Most went on to fruitful careers following their terms in Congress.*

| NAME/STATE/ AGE IN 1870 | BACKGROUND | PRIOR EXPERIENCE | SERVICE IN CONGRESS | POST-CONGRESS EXPERIENCE |
|---|---|---|---|---|
| Blanche K. Bruce (1841–1898) Mississippi 29 years old | Born slave in Virginia to master and slave woman. | Studied at Oberlin College; Mississippi tax assessor, superintendent of education, alderman, sheriff. | Senate, 1875–1881. Supported seating of P. B. S. Pinchback, Mississippi River flood control and port development, citizenship for Chinese and Native Americans, dissolving all-black regiments. | 1881–1893: Register of the Treasury and DC Recorder of Deeds; trustee of Howard University. |
| Richard H. Cain (1825–1887) South Carolina 45 years old | Born free in western Virginia to black mother, Cherokee father. | Studied at Wilberforce College; delegate to SC state constitutional convention; served in SC state senate. | House of Representatives 1873–1874; 1877–79. Opposed Amnesty Act; supported woman suffrage, education, and land. | 1878: Encouraged South Carolinians to support Liberia exodus. |
| Robert DeLarge (1842–1874) South Carolina 28 years old | Born free in Virginia. | SC constitutional convention (1868) and state legislature. | House of Representatives, 1871–1873. Removed from office 2 months before his term expired because white opponent won contested election. Supported Amnesty Act, black land ownership. | Magistrate in Charleston. |
| Robert Brown Elliott (1842–1884) South Carolina 28 years old | Born in South Carolina to free black parents. | Passed SC bar in 1867; editor of black Republican newspaper, the *South Carolina Leader*; SC constitutional convention; assistant adjutant-general of SC. | House of Representatives, 1871–1875. Supported suppression of Ku Klux Klan, protection of black vote. | Lawyer in New Orleans, Louisiana. |

*(continued on next page)*

## Table 11.2 (continued)

| NAME/STATE/ AGE IN 1870 | BACKGROUND | PRIOR EXPERIENCE | SERVICE IN CONGRESS | POST-CONGRESS EXPERIENCE |
|---|---|---|---|---|
| Jefferson Long (1836–1900) Georgia 34 years old | Born a slave in Georgia to slave mother and white father. | Tailor. | House of Representatives, 1871–1873. Supported Ku Klux Klan Acts, opposed amnesty for ex-Confederates. | Tailoring business suffered because of his continued organizing for Republican Party. |
| John Roy Lynch (1847–1939) Mississippi 23 years old | Louisiana slave, freed when Union army seized Natchez, 1863. | Elected justice of the peace; Mississippi legislature speaker of the house. | House of Representatives, 1872–1876. Supported civil rights legislation. | Delegate to four national Republican conventions; appointed by President Benjamin Harrison to be auditor of the U.S. Treasury for the Navy Department. |
| Pinckney Benton Stewart Pinchback (1837–1921) Louisiana 33 years old | Born free to Georgia planter and an emancipated slave. | Louisiana state senator; lieutenant governor; acting governor. | Senate: elected in 1872, but never allowed to assume office. Advocated education, women's suffrage. | U.S. Customs inspector; cotton planter; owner of Mississippi riverboat company; admitted to Louisiana bar in 1886; helped found Southern Normal School. |

this would further isolate him in a Congress bent on reconciliation. Richard Cain, a representative from South Carolina, also voted no. "I want to see a change in this country," said Cain, a northern-born minister whose calling had taken him South to fight for black justice. "Instead of colored people being always penniless, I want to see them coming in with their mule teams and ox teams, with their corn and potatoes to exchange for silks and satins. I want to see children coming to enjoy life as it ought to be enjoyed." Cain doubted that reinstating political rights to Confederates would help realize this vision. Several other black congressmen also voted no on amnesty. Even red-inked letters from the Ku Klux Klan warning of "doom sealed in blood" could not deter these men from speaking out—knowing their arguments fell on deaf ears.

Young black congressmen sought counsel from seasoned political activists like Douglass. The esteemed black leader befriended them, often hosting them at his home. Yet even Douglass misread the political realities of Reconstruction. In the 1872 presidential race, he supported Republican President Ulysses S. Grant's bid for reelection. When Grant suggested annexing the Dominican Republic as a haven for African Americans, Douglass believed in Grant's goodwill. But others did not. Douglass's abolitionist friend Senator Charles Sumner, who chaired the Senate Foreign Relations Committee, suspected that annexation was a scheme to enrich white land speculators. Even when Grant refused to include black representatives at a White House dinner discussion on annexation, Douglass continued to support him. With support from the black voters Douglass helped deliver, Grant won reelection—but neither annexation of the Dominican Republic nor a federal appointment for Douglass materialized. Black people now had another reminder that their vote wielded little influence unless they could enlist support from powerful white allies.

## LOCAL POLITICS IN THE SOUTH

"When we opened the school a party of armed men came to my house, seized me, carried me out and threw me in Thompson's Creek after they had belabored me with the muzzles of their revolvers . . . [saying] they 'did not want . . . any damned nigger school in that town and were not going to have it,'" Texas state senator George Ruby recalled in testimony about obstacles facing southern black politicians at the state and local levels. These politicians often had to craft political strategies and alliances simply to ensure constituents' safety, and in the South, black politicians had few white allies. Nor did Radical Republicans intercede on their behalf. Even the presence of federal troops could not deter threats such as those Ruby endured merely for opening a school.

Ruby quickly learned the Texas political terrain. Born in New York and educated in New England, he had lived for a while in Haiti but returned to the United States to work for the Freedmen's Bureau. Assigned to build schools in Texas, he also represented Galveston County at the 1868 Texas constitutional convention, where he gained enough visibility to be elected to the State Senate. One of only two black state senators in Texas, Ruby had a constituency mainly of black voters and the minority of white politicians who sought federal assistance for rebuilding the state's infrastructure, refurbishing the Galveston port, and establishing an educational system benefiting poor Texans of all races.

Like Revels and other black leaders at the national level, Ruby used compromise and negotiation. He supported white Texans as well as black for patronage positions, and he tolerated the new state laws segregating public travel, parks, and even Republican political events. In return, he hoped to gain white support for laws that would restrain the Klan, give citizenship and the franchise to Native Americans, and promote schools and other services for freed people. He also hoped to limit Black Codes, those state or local laws restricting African Americans' employment choices, land ownership, mobility, and other opportunities.

Ruby's strategy reflected his understanding of southern political realities. In the postwar era, southern politics took one of three forms: the political middle (the vast majority of white Southerners), the political right, and the radical left. The political middle, or "moderates," included entrepreneurs, professionals, and farmers who had concluded even before the war that the South needed to modernize—to diversify its economy, develop technology and industry, and gain federal subsidies for geological surveys, railroads, factories, and ports.

Moderate white Southerners were not much interested in economic advancement for African Americans, but they envisioned black laborers as part of the new South, working in factories as well as in fields. They welcomed alliances with black leaders who could help persuade black communities to meet moderate white people's goals. As long as leaders like Ruby stayed "in their place" and were deferential to white people, white moderates supported black education and voting rights.

South Carolina planter Wade Hampton exemplified white moderates. Hampton believed black and white southern leaders should unite in rebuilding the South. "Does not that glorious southern sun above us shine alike for both of us?" he asked. But Hampton and other moderates made no overtures toward social integration, viewing class and racial divisions as natural for society.

Black leaders like Ruby knew white moderates could help black people obtain access to education and jobs in agriculture or factories. Martin Delany was another who advocated black-white alliances. Filling in as editor for South Carolina's *Missionary Record*, he developed a blueprint for black-white cooperation. He felt certain that "the black man and the white man must work together . . . [to] bring about the redemption of the state and prosperity and happiness for the whole people." "The black men of this state are dependent on the whites, just as the whites are dependent on them," he wrote in 1873. Thus he advised black Southerners to relinquish "hatred and resentment" and to be "polite, pleasant, agreeable, ever ready and obliging." Persuaded by Hampton's argument that "when all our troubles and trials are over, [black and white Southerners] will sleep in that same soil in which we first drew breath," Delany supported Hampton's successful bid for governor of South Carolina in 1876.

At the political right stood what some might call radical reactionaries, a small but significant group of white Southerners. These included dislocated plantation owners who had lost their economic system and a few struggling white farmers emotionally invested in the South's old way of life, which had given even poor white people a higher status than black people. Their anger at the ravages of war prevented them from embracing any part of a new order that enabled African Americans to progress beyond a servile role. Intent on reviving the prewar agricultural economy, radical reactionaries needed laborers to work the land, and they wanted freed slaves to do the job. They had little interest in modernizing the South. They were most often the instigators of violence against black people, and black politicians did their best to avoid them.

The South's radical left—the third political group—argued that poor black people had more in common with poor white people than with wealthy black ones. That is, class was more important than race in working to achieve goals. Seeking unity among poor people regardless of race, they were concerned with universal education, more equitable land policies, better contracts for renters, and the rights of the poor. Some of their ideas were rooted in socialism, a political belief that government should distribute wealth equally among all its citizens. This philosophy, which defined economic circumstance as more important than race or ethnicity, gained favor with many of the world's poor in the late nineteenth century.

As steel and mining industries began to modernize southern cities like Birmingham and Atlanta, a black laborers' movement, allied with white radicals, gathered momentum. A small but vocal minority of southern white labor organizers embraced black radicals like Lucy Parsons, an organizer of Texas's Socialist Workingmen's Party, which advocated interracial labor unions, and Peter Clark of Cincinnati, who urged industrial workers to put class unity above racial division. Parsons, married to a white Texas socialist, exemplified what conservative white Southerners feared: miscegenation, or sexual liaison between black and white people. Though such "race-mixing" was common under slavery, white planters feared that in post-slavery times, mixed-race people would feel entitled to the privileges of white Americans.

Only the most optimistic of black Americans joined the socialist ranks. Most soon recognized that white socialists had little power to effect real change. However, the idea of political parties that subordinated racial differences to class loyalty remained alive for decades. In the 1890s, when the Populist Party emerged to put many of these concerns on the national agenda, poor black Southerners were among its strongest supporters.

## WHITE BACKLASH

Even outside the South, white Americans found many ways to keep black people "in their place." Immediately after Congress introduced the Thirteenth Amendment abolishing slavery, white-on-black violence intensified in the North. The same night President Abraham Lincoln was assassinated, an Ohio mob torched the main building of the black Wilberforce University. The blaze destroyed all of Martin Delany's correspondence, manuscripts, and African art collections. "The hand that placed the torch," wrote Delany, was "leagued in sentiment with the same dastardly villains who struck down the greatest Chief Magistrate [Lincoln] of the present age."

Indeed, that hand had a broad span. In Philadelphia and San Francisco, in the late 1860s, white trolley riders shoved black people off when they tried to board. In Rochester, New York, in the winter of 1867, Frederick Douglass's son-in-law was so badly menaced by white drivers that he quit the taxi trade. That same winter, in the Freedmen's Bureau offices in Washington, DC, General Oliver O. Howard had to threaten to fire his white clerks to get them to accept black coworkers.

In the South, members of the Ku Klux Klan, cloaked in white hoods, galloped on horseback to the homes of black political leaders and their supporters who tried to vote, or those who had become economically comfortable, or supposedly did not show due deference to whites. The attackers often dragged black people out of their homes and whipped or tortured them. Sometimes they killed them, mutilated them, set them on fire, or hanged them from trees—a practice that became known as *lynching*.

Between 1868 and 1876, while an estimated 20,000 black people were murdered by the Klan, southern officials looked the other way. Many victims had been active in local politics. One Alabama woman said the Klan had murdered her husband because "he just would hold up his head and say he was a strong Radical." Klan members beat people who, like Ruby, did nothing more radical than build a school or exude confidence. Another woman reported that the "Ku Klux came to my house and took us out and whipped us, and then said 'don't lets hear any big talk from you, and don't sass any white ladies.'"

Klan tactics helped end Republican Party control in Georgia in 1870, as terrified black voters stayed away from the polls. The following year, Mississippi Klansmen burned dozens of black churches and schools, torturing and killing the ministers and teachers. Klansmen also harassed and murdered the few poor or idealistic southern white citizens who supported socialist groups and advocated racial equality. Still, many black Southerners refused to be intimidated. Exclaimed one black Alabaman: "The Republican party freed me, and I will die on top of it. I vote every time."

## THE ENFORCEMENT ACTS

The Fifteenth Amendment gave all black American men the right to vote—but securing that right in practical terms presented an entirely separate challenge. Affirming the federal commitment to the Fourteenth and Fifteenth Amendments, Congress passed two Enforcement Acts in 1870 and 1871—also known as the Klan Acts because they attempted to protect black voters from Klan violence. Both acts defined interference with a person's right to vote as a federal offense punishable by fine or imprisonment. In the summer of 1871, responding to Freedmen's Bureau reports of continued attacks against black Southerners, Congress collected testimony from Emanuel Fortune and hundreds of others to learn whether southern voters indeed were still unable to express their political views safely. The hearings produced thirteen volumes of testimony.

*After Emanuel Fortune's death in 1903, his son, journalist Timothy Thomas Fortune, reported, "It was natural [for him] to take the leadership in any independent movement of Negroes."*

But the Enforcement Acts did not stop the violence. In Louisville, Kentucky, white people pummeled black residents who exercised their court-won right to ride the trolley cars. In Colfax, Louisiana, long-simmering racial hatred led local black men to arm themselves and patrol the town. In a confrontation on Easter Sunday, 1873, when the black militia and a white posse exchanged fire, more than a dozen white men were killed or wounded and two dozen black men injured. About three dozen black men were arrested and executed without a trial. Frederick Douglass's *New National Era* reported that in the wake of the incident, the local White League, with guns and cannons from neighboring states, randomly shot, stabbed, and beat black citizens. They intended, they said, to set an example for "every parish in the State [so] we shall begin to have some quiet and niggers will know their place."

Racial violence also broke out in the North. A white mob murdered Octavius Catto, a Union major and beloved school principal, at his Philadelphia polling place. Catto's leadership in the Pennsylvania Equal Rights League had made him a target. A friend lamented, "The Ku Klux of the South are not by any means the lower classes of society. The same may be said of the Ku Klux of the North. Both are industriously engaged in trying to break us down." Black Americans experienced yet another instance of their government's inability to protect them.

## THE FREEDMEN'S BANK

If reconstructing the nation politically posed daunting challenges, establishing a firm economic foundation for African Americans proved even more difficult. In 1865, Congress chartered the Freedmen's Savings and Trust Company to offer black people the chance to save money and purchase land and farm equipment. In 1870, the *New National Era* gave glowing reports of the bank's progress. Though Congress did not monitor the bank's operations, thousands of black depositors in Washington, Baltimore, New York, and other cities trusted it. Year by year, coin by coin, they accumulated nest eggs they hoped would give them financial autonomy.

But the bank soon fell on hard times. In its first years, well-known white bankers—along with Freedmen's Bureau director Oliver Howard and a national board of four dozen trustees—oversaw operations. They upheld the congressional mandate of investing depositors' money in government securities. But in 1870, during a postwar building boom and railroad expansion, Congress amended the bank's charter, enabling the managers to invest deposits in real estate and railroads. In the next few years, several white members of the bank's board made speculative loans in these enterprises. By the time the enterprises failed, these white board members had resigned, leaving mostly black trustees to repair the damage.

Desperate to maintain black people's confidence in the bank, the trustees called on Frederick Douglass to replace the white bank president. Douglass did so, even investing $10,000 of his own money. Yet he could not salvage the bank and had to preside over its closing in July 1874. As the savings of thousands of African Americans evaporated, some blamed the bank's failure on Douglass, and his reputation was seriously tarnished. Discouraged that Congress had offered no assistance, many African Americans also lost their faith in the federal government, convinced it had abandoned them yet again.

# WASHINGTON, DC, IN THE NEW NATIONAL ERA

The seat of both hope and disappointment, Washington, DC, became a magnet for black Americans. By 1870, they constituted more than 30 percent of the city's population of 132,000, up from 10 percent just ten years before. Due in part to its proximity to the South, the city's black population soon eclipsed even that of Philadelphia and Baltimore, in both absolute numbers and proportion. The nation's capital offered black people greater economic and social opportunities than any other city. Along with federal protection and political power came black organizations and businesses and plentiful jobs in the federal bureaucracy.

## THE BLACK ELITE

Drawn by the federal government and Howard University, many accomplished African Americans settled in the capital city. Frederick Douglass moved to Washington during the 1870s, working with his sons to publish the *New National Era,* which chronicled the political progress of the Republican Party and its new black constituency. Douglass himself launched what would be a quarter-century-long career in government service as the District of Columbia Recorder of Deeds and as director of U.S. diplomatic relations with Haiti. John Mercer Langston, the Oberlin-educated lawyer and Equal Rights League activist, came to Washington from Ohio to direct the law curriculum at Howard University. Langston also served as counsel to the city Board of Health, collecting vital statistics and monitoring the city's health measures.

Douglass and Langston were central figures in a growing cadre of Washington intellectuals. Anticipating ties with well-read companions and sophisticated conversation with like-minded colleagues and friends, they encouraged those with similar tastes to join them. Black poets, essayists, novelists, and public speakers responded to the call. Literate women such as Frances Ellen Watkins Harper, Maria Stewart, and Charlotte Forten were among them. Harper became a frequent lecturer, while Stewart taught in the public schools and served as a matron at the Freedmen's Hospital, established by the Freedmen's Bureau to provide medical care for Washington's black population. Though long retired from public speaking, she kept her feminist drive, publishing her speeches on women's rights in 1878. Charlotte Forten arrived in Washington from the South Carolina Sea Islands in 1864, exhausted and ill after eighteen months of teaching. In the capital city, she became one of fifteen black female clerks employed in the Treasury Department.

The black elite of Washington—around 2 percent of the city's black population—included lawyers, doctors, teachers, publishers, and business owners. Many were of mixed-race background, and their families, free a generation or more, had been able to educate themselves and establish businesses or professions that gave them influence far beyond their small numbers. They provided employment for many black newcomers. For example, James Wormley's hotel near the White House drew praise from guests even as it provided a handsome living to its black proprietor and steady employment for black workers. These individuals led black social clubs, churches, schools, and social service agencies.

Some even lived in integrated neighborhoods. They sent their children to the growing number of African American colleges and universities. A few young people attended the small number of white colleges—including Bowdoin, Amherst, Oberlin, and the University of Pennsylvania—that accepted black students. Thus the black people in these wealthy, educated circles prepared their children and grandchildren to become Washington's future leaders.

Shopkeepers and service workers formed the core of Washington's black middle class. They enjoyed the chance to associate with Washington's black politicians and intellectuals and with renowned social activists such as Sojourner Truth. In 1874, Truth became the first African American to take communion at the white Metropolitan Methodist Church. She also spoke before the white congregation of First Congregational Church, where General Oliver Howard called for desegregation. She focused her attention, however, on the desperate situation of black people outside in the streets. Seeing black "men and women taking dry bread from the government to keep from starving," she set out to get "land for these people, where they can work and earn their own living." She had the ear of General Howard, who offered money and moral support for her plan to help freedmen obtain farmland in the West under the 1862 Homestead Act. Truth also assisted Freedmen's Bureau agents in relocating refugees from Washington to Ohio and Michigan.

## THE BLACK WORKING CLASS AND POOR

Like Sojourner Truth, Mary Ann Shadd Cary was concerned with the plight of ordinary black people. Widowed in 1860 with two children to raise, Cary moved to Washington permanently in 1869. Believing black people needed their own legal counseling, she became Howard University's first female law student. Encouraged by her family, Cary also assumed leadership in other areas where she felt black communities needed to make progress. She left Howard University in 1871 to go on the lecture circuit, speaking out about the need to ensure that young African Americans gained access to education and employment opportunities—a notion that became a theme for black leaders in the century ahead. In 1873 she and Douglass spoke before the National Colored Men's Labor Convention, stressing the need for programs that would teach black youth job skills such as blacksmithing, dressmaking, and carpentry.

That year, a panic brought economic depression. Over-inflated railroad speculation, reduced European demand for American farm products, and the failure of

*A woman of strong opinions, Mary Ann Shadd Cary caught the attention of outspoken white women, including fellow Washington lawyer Belva Lockwood. Throwing her energies into Lockwood's 1872 presidential campaign, Cary hoped to show her support not only for black rights but also for women's leadership.*

powerful American banks cut job opportunities for all Americans, especially un-skilled black workers. In 1874, Cary wrote two articles to provoke black par-ents' thinking about employment for their sons: "We have members of State Legislatures . . . [and] aspirants in the field of letters, all of which is enjoyably rose-tinted and gilded as compared to the past; but we, no more than others, can afford to build at the top of the house only. . . . [T]he craftsman, the architect, the civil engineer must all come through the door opened to us by the mechanic." Cary believed most young black workers would be more able to benefit from training in—and finding work in—manual trades than in intellectual or political leadership roles. In succeeding years, many black leaders shared her concern for the fate of the average worker.

Cary's views on the lack of economic opportunities for African Americans deepened when she saw the widespread poverty in the nation's capital. More than three-quarters of Washington's black families lived in alleys near to large houses where they served as laundresses, porters, handymen, and domestic ser-vants. In the crowded alleys around the Capitol and along the Potomac River lived those who worked in government service. In many of these black house-holds, teeming with family members and boarders, conditions were as bleak as those under slavery. Malnutrition, poor health, violence, and alcoholism plagued them. Fish from local rivers and lakes and vegetables from urban gardens helped ward off starvation, but some black people resorted to prostitution and petty theft in order to survive. Others returned home to the familiar rural South. As black historian John Hope Franklin observed, "It was one thing to provide tem-porary relief for freedmen, and another to guide them along the road to eco-nomic stability and independence."

Despite these difficulties, many freed people built vibrant communities in the capital city. The streets of Washington's poor black neighborhoods rang with the shouts of children playing games, adults performing music, and residents regal-ing each other with stories. But there was typically a large gap between these people and black political leaders, who were often economically well off, at least comparatively. Some black leaders—both social advocates and politicians—lost touch with the needs of ordinary black people. While they took seriously their role as advocates for racial and economic justice, their own lives came to include second homes at summer resorts, international travel, and interracial marriages. Many seemed to forget the impact of slavery on the present generation. Cary was one leader who never forgot; she dedicated herself to working for economic sta-bility and independence for the poor.

## POLITICAL PATRONAGE AND POLITICS

In 1871, Congress established a local government for the District of Columbia consisting of a governor, eleven commissioners appointed by the president, and twenty-two delegates, elected by popular vote, with the power to make local laws. Though the District had no voice in Congress or in national politics, as the states did, respected black leaders—including Frederick Douglass and AME bishop James A. Handy—were elected as delegates and hence had a say in local politics. The new structure was seen by many northern leaders as an improvement over the charter that had expired in 1870.

Though African Americans were in a minority in this interracial governing group, the restructured District government signaled a friendly attitude toward black residents, and dozens of loyal black Republican supporters were rewarded with political patronage jobs in such agencies as the Board of Health and the Recorder of Deeds Office, Patent Office, Treasury Department, Post Office, public schools, and municipal utilities. Hundreds more found employment as government clerks and service workers. Local ordinances outlawed racial segregation in public services, and operators of hotels, restaurants, concert halls, and theaters paid fines and had licenses suspended if they did not comply. The Civil Rights Act of 1875, though soon to be overturned by the Supreme Court, reinforced open access to public accommodations.

Steady cash wages—a first for most black people—allowed for middle-class lifestyles for some, and elevated others to elite status. Black service workers were sometimes able to save money and buy property of their own. A government salary allowed Frederick Douglass to move to Cedar Hill, an estate in nearby Anacostia. Even as she railed against segregated schools, Mary Ann Shadd Cary's position of principal at the American Missionary Association's Lincoln School placed her in Washington's professional class. These developments mirrored a phenomenon unfolding across the nation. In staggering numbers, African Americans left the countryside, relocating to urban areas where some made economic progress and began participating in local politics. They headed for Detroit and Cincinnati, for New York, Philadelphia and Pittsburgh. Black communities flourished in Baltimore, Charleston, Galveston, Richmond, and Jacksonville. Many cities had enough black residents to support a black press, and black newspapers proliferated.

# THE END OF RECONSTRUCTION

Radical Reconstruction brought important gains to black Southerners: schools, varied economic possibilities, and the franchise. Efforts to diversify the economy, increase access to the polls and leadership positions, and reunite families separated by slavery also improved black lives. In 1867, in New Orleans, African Americans won the right to ride the public trolley cars. Through protests and negotiations, they persuaded the car companies to admit "our citizens into all the cars, without any distinction as to color." In many southern states, Radical Republican governments passed laws granting black people access to soda fountains, opera houses, railroads, and steamboats. In 1875, Congress certified these gains in a Civil Rights Act banning discrimination in public places across the country. But the act constituted the last piece of civil rights legislation until the 1950s.

## WANING FEDERAL SYMPATHY

Even as the Civil Rights Act was passed, many reformers pulled back from the enormous effort required to remake a former slave society. The same 1870 elections that brought black congressmen to power also swept away the Republican majority in the House of Representatives. With the crumbling of Republican power, African American progress began to disintegrate as well. In the South, as federal troops were gradually withdrawn, black political organizations withered away. In 1869, Mississippi had 87,000 registered black voters; eleven years later, it had just half that number. Radical Republican governments in southern states gave way to conservative white Democratic ones. White Southerners called these developments "redemption." A black Louisianan saw it differently in 1877: "The whole South—every state in the South—had got into the hands of the very men that held us slaves."

The Supreme Court encouraged the retreat from black causes by limiting the scope of the Fourteenth Amendment. In the *Slaughterhouse Cases* (1873), it distinguished between citizenship of the United States and citizenship of a state, saying that the amendment applied only to the former and that states had the right to define citizenship and its accompanying rights for their residents. In 1883, the Court heard several cases in the course of which it overturned the 1875 Civil Rights Act. In their rulings, the justices distinguished between political rights (guaranteed by the Constitution) and social rights (pertaining to public accommodations), which involved citizens' private lives. The Court declared the federal government had no authority over social rights. The stage was now set for the so-called Jim Crow laws, which limited the rights of African Americans for the next seventy-five years.

## The Compromise of 1877

The 1876 presidential contest was so close that it fell to the House of Representatives to adjudicate disputed electoral votes. The agreement Republicans and Democrats worked out became known as the Compromise of 1877: Southern congressmen agreed to concede the presidency to Republican candidate Rutherford B. Hayes, while Republicans agreed to allow white Southerners to control local elections and local ordinances on black employment contracts and racial separation. The few remaining federal troops were withdrawn from the South, federal intervention in southern state affairs ceased, and the U.S. government agreed to appoint at least one Southerner to the president's cabinet. Across the South, state governments now lay firmly in the hands of the white "redeemers," who regained local power to deny true citizenship privileges—such as the vote—to thousands of African Americans. The national Republican Party distanced itself from black interests, entrenching segregated "Black and Tan" parties in an increasingly segregated South. For white Americans, the era of Reconstruction had ended.

## African Americans on the Move

"I made the outside box [for Julia Haven] and her coffin, in Smith County, Tennessee. And another young colored lady . . . they committed an outrage on her and then shot her, and I helped to make her coffin." In the spring of 1880, seventy-year-old Benjamin "Pap" Singleton used these examples of women who had been raped and killed to help a Senate committee understand why black people were fleeing the South. The investigation was launched after both Democrats and Republicans claimed the other was conspiring to provoke black people to migrate. Republicans accused Democrats of wanting to gain control of the South by expelling black voters; Democrats said Republicans wanted to spread their influence outside the South. Singleton knew better: Black people were fleeing the South to avoid rape, murder, and mutilation.

## THE EXODUSTERS

Benjamin Singleton, a former Tennessee slave who had escaped via the Underground Railroad through Detroit into Canada, returned to his home state after the war. Like many black Americans, Singleton soon took advantage of the 1862 Homestead Act, which offered 160 acres of government land free to anyone who would live on it, improve it, and pay a small registration fee. With other black Tennesseeans, he started the Edgfield Real Estate and Homestead Association to establish a new black settlement in Kansas. Several families who had visited Kansas, he said, "brought back favorable reports.... Three or four hundred ... went into Southern Kansas ... and formed a colony there, and bought about a thousand acres of ground." Comparing their projects to the exodus of the biblical Hebrews from Egyptian bondage, the thousands of black Americans who went west with groups such as the Kansas Exodus Joint Stock Company in the late 1870s called themselves *Exodusters*.

The town of Nicodemus in Graham County, Kansas, on the Solomon River typifies these new African American frontier communities. By 1880, 700 black settlers had moved to Nicodemus, but many encountered stiff resistance even as they left home. To retain the South's cheap labor force, white Southerners tried to sabotage the planned black exodus. Singleton told Congress how armed white men blocked Mississippi River crossings to black travelers, seizing them

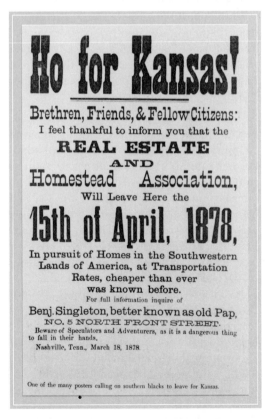

One of the many posters calling on southern blacks to leave for Kansas.

*Recruiters for the new black settlements took posters such as this one to local meetings across both North and South.*

and even hacking off their hands. "Now see if you can go to Kansas and work," they said. White sheriffs arrested black travelers for breach of contract (if they were contracted to a planter) or for vagrancy (if they were not). Despite these tactics, black people continued to head west. Between 1870 and 1880, the African American population in Kansas doubled to more than 40,000.

At first white Kansans welcomed the Exodusters. Eager to increase the population of farmers and defend themselves from belligerent Native Americans, some Kansas communities raised money to help black newcomers pay land fees. But black homesteaders, with few tools or work animals, found independent farming hard. Discouraged, many Exodusters ended up in Topeka, where they hunted for work. But this city was also home to displaced white Southerners also seeking jobs. Racial intimidation and lynchings became so common that the Republican mayor of Topeka, once sympathetic to African Americans, suggested the money raised for black relief might better go to returning black refugees to the South—especially agitators "who were always talking politics."

Some black leaders like Frederick Douglass urged black families to stay in the South. Only with large numbers, they contended, could black voters exert power and influence. But Douglass wrote from the relative safety and comfort of Washington. It was people like Singleton who experienced the southern predicament firsthand: "We don't want to leave the South," he wrote in 1881, "and just as soon as we have confidence in the South I am going to . . . persuade every man to go back, because that is the best country; . . . we love that country . . . but [by leaving] we are going to learn the South a lesson."

## THE WESTERN FRONTIER

Beyond Kansas, numerous African Americans found adventure and fortune in Nebraska, Colorado, North Dakota, and along the Pacific coast. Closed out of northern and southern economy and politics, black families headed for these new frontiers. Nancy Lewis told how she and her husband, a Civil War veteran, established their Nebraska farm in the 1870s. By 1880, they counted among 2,000 black Nebraskans. Virginia-born Barney Ford, a one-time barber and ship's steward, journeyed to Denver and by 1874 had opened a prosperous hotel. Two of Frederick Douglass's sons were also among Denver's thousand African Americans. Cowboy Nat Love's prowess in an 1876 rodeo in Deadwood City, North Dakota, gained him the nickname "Deadwood Dick." His autobiography, *The Life & Adventures of Nat Love, Better Known in the Cattle Country As Deadwood Dick* (1876), promoted the escapades of black cowboys. But when the book was later published as one of many mass-market stories of the West, Love's African heritage was omitted.

Some black Americans got all the way to California. By 1880, as many as 6,000 were there, and several hundred had settled in each of the other western states and territories. These pioneers included cowboys, farmers, shopkeepers, prospectors, and service workers such as barbers, laundresses, and domestic servants. Biddy Mason, who remained in California after the courts declared her free, purchased property, ran a grocery store and boardinghouse, supported black schools, and helped establish the West's first AME church.

*Finishing a term as a forager (raider) for the Confederate army, Isom Dart was among the cowboys who drifted west. Joining a group of cattle thieves, he was arrested in Texas, Colorado, and Wyoming. Legend has it that he was never imprisoned.*

## To Africa

Driven by the same hope and frustration that motivated western migration, other black Americans looked east to Africa. In the postwar years, Martin Delany revived his dream of claiming a black nationality there. "We have no chance to rise from beggars," he argued. "Men own the capital that we work who believe that my race have no more right to any of the profits of their labor than one of their mules." Richard Cain, a disillusioned ex-congressman, echoed Delany's despair: "The colored people of the South are tired of the constant struggle for life and liberty and prefer going where [there are] no obstacles ... to ... their liberty." Partnering with AME minister Henry McNeal Turner, Delany recruited settlers for Liberia. Turner had been born free in South Carolina in 1834, studied in the North, and served as pastor for a Washington, DC, church before the Civil War. After a stint as an army chaplain, he stayed in Georgia, working for the Republican Party and the AME church. By 1877, he shared Delany's dismay at the federal government's abandonment of black Southerners.

In the spring of 1878, thousands of black Americans watched the launching of the *Azor* from Charleston's wharf. Led by Delany and Turner, and with support from Cain, the Liberian Exodus Joint Stock Company had raised more than $6,000 to purchase the ship, which now carried some 200 settlers to Africa. Other black families invested thousands more. But expenses exceeded the company's capital, and the Exodus Company soon lay in financial shambles. After delivering its first settlers, it collapsed without establishing a permanent community. Though the effort represented yet another failed dream, the image of an African homecoming remained in the black imagination. Future generations would try again.

# CONCLUSION

Emanuel Fortune's testimony in 1871 before the congressional committee investigating the Ku Klux Klan revealed the violence underlying post-Civil War southern politics. The politics of this war-torn region was no longer merely a regional concern of Southerners and a few abolitionist Northerners. The challenges facing African Americans now dominated the national agenda.

The federal government had outlawed slavery, extended equal rights to all citizens, and mandated that all black men could vote, but the law had little to do with reality. Though Hiram Revels and other black men represented southern states in Congress, white supremacist groups such as the Ku Klux Klan used threats, torture, and murder to scare southern black voters away from the polls. Still, many black politicians sought common ground to negotiate compromises with southern white politicians. Sometimes they urged their black followers to accommodate some aspect of racial oppression in return for economic gains or political representation. At the far margin of the political spectrum, radicals tried to bridge the gap between the wealthy and the disaffected by envisioning a society that transcended divisions of race and class. All these strategies aimed to enable black people to move toward economic and social equality.

By 1877, African Americans seemed destined to be shunted aside again. With the Compromise of 1877, the federal government withdrew from helping freed slaves gain political rights and economic security. In the postwar era, black politicians had seats in Congress and in state legislatures. But with the end of Reconstruction, black politicians began returning to the South to manage their personal lives and to try to forge working relationships with white neighbors. Most white people in the North and the South expected black Americans to stay in the South, resigning themselves to menial jobs, limited political power, and continued deference to white people. Indeed, in the coming decades, southern black laborers seemed doomed to jobs that ensured only subordination and debt, and black leaders understood these as the limitations within which they must operate.

Though Washington, DC, the federal capital, continued to attract black people seeking jobs and a strong black community, the American frontier and Africa lured others who dreamed of better opportunities and fresh ideas. By 1879, with the passing of many antebellum black leaders, the black cause desperately needed new energy and direction. The ratification of the Thirteenth, Fourteenth, and Fifteenth Amendments had promised African Americans access to political participation. Now, with Black Codes, poverty, and violence circumscribing those promises, black Americans needed new leadership.

# APPENDIX

The Declaration of Independence

The Constitution of the United States of America

Amendments to the Constitution

*Dred Scott* v. *Sandford* (1857)

The Emancipation Proclamation

*Plessy* v. *Ferguson* (1896)

*Brown* v. *Board of Education of Topeka* (1954)

Key Provisions of the Civil Rights Act of 1964

Key Provisions of the Voting Rights Act of 1965

# The Declaration of Independence

## In Congress, July 4, 1776

## The Unanimous Declaration
## of the Thirteen United States of America,

When, in the course of human events, it becomes necessary for one people to dissolve the political bonds which have connected them with another, and to assume, among the powers of the earth, the separate and equal station to which the laws of nature and of nature's God entitle them, a decent respect to the opinions of mankind requires that they should declare the causes which impel them to the separation.

We hold these truths to be self-evident: That all men are created equal; that they are endowed by their Creator with certain unalienable rights; that among these are life, liberty, and the pursuit of happiness; that, to secure these rights, governments are instituted among men, deriving their just powers from the consent of the governed; that whenever any form of government becomes destructive of these ends, it is the right of the people to alter or to abolish it, and to institute new government, laying its foundation on such principles, and organizing its powers in such form, as to them shall seem most likely to effect their safety and happiness. Prudence, indeed, will dictate that governments long established should not be changed for light and transient causes; and accordingly all experience hath shown that mankind are more disposed to suffer, while evils are sufferable, than to right themselves by abolishing the forms to which they are accustomed. But when a long train of abuses and usurpations, pursuing invariably the same object, evinces a design to reduce them under absolute despotism, it is their right, it is their duty, to throw off such government, and to provide new guards for their future security. Such has been the patient sufferance of these colonies; and such is now the necessity which constrains them to alter their former systems of government. The history of the present King of Great Britain is a history of repeated injuries and usurpations, all having in direct object the establishment of an absolute tyranny over these states. To prove this, let facts be submitted to a candid world.

He has refused his assent to laws, the most wholesome and necessary for the public good.

He has forbidden his governors to pass laws of immediate and pressing importance, unless suspended in their operation till his assent should be obtained; and, when so suspended, he has utterly neglected to attend to them.

He has refused to pass other laws for the accommodation of large districts of people, unless those people would relinquish the right of representation in the legislature, a right inestimable to them, and formidable to tyrants only.

He has called together legislative bodies at places unusual, uncomfortable, and distant from the depository of their public records, for the sole purpose of fatiguing them into compliance with his measures.

He has dissolved representative houses repeatedly, for opposing, with manly firmness, his invasions on the rights of the people.

He has refused for a long time, after such dissolutions, to cause others to be elected; whereby the legislative powers, incapable of annihilation, have returned to the people at large for their exercise; the state remaining, in the mean time, exposed to all the dangers of invasions from without and convulsions within.

He has endeavored to prevent the population of these states; for that purpose obstructing the laws for naturalization of foreigners; refusing to pass others to encourage their migration hither, and raising the conditions of new appropriations of lands.

He has obstructed the administration of justice, by refusing his assent to laws for establishing judiciary powers.

He has made judges dependent on his will alone, for the tenure of their offices, and the amount and payment of their salaries.

He has erected a multitude of new offices, and sent hither swarms of officers to harass our people and eat out their substance.

He has kept among us, in times of peace, standing armies, without the consent of our legislatures.

He has affected to render the military independent of, and superior to, the civil power.

He has combined with others to subject us to a jurisdiction foreign to our constitution, and unacknowledged by our laws, giving his assent to their acts of pretended legislation:

For quartering large bodies of armed troops among us;

For protecting them, by a mock trial, from punishment for any murder which they should commit on the inhabitants of these states;

For cutting off our trade with all parts of the world;

For imposing taxes on us without our consent;

For depriving us, in many cases, of the benefits of trial by jury;

For transporting us beyond seas, to be tried for pretended offenses;

For abolishing the free system of English laws in a neighboring province, establishing therein an arbitrary government, and enlarging its boundaries, so as to render it at once an example and fit instrument for introducing the same absolute rule into these colonies;

For taking away our charters, abolishing our most valuable laws, and altering fundamentally the forms of our governments;

For suspending our own legislatures, and declaring themselves invested with power to legislate for us in all cases whatsoever.

He has abdicated government here, by declaring us out of his protection and waging war against us.

He has plundered our seas, ravaged our coasts, burned our towns, and destroyed the lives of our people.

He is at this time transporting large armies of foreign mercenaries to complete the works of death, desolation, and tyranny already begun with circumstances of cruelty and perfidy scarcely paralleled in the most barbarous ages, and totally unworthy the head of a civilized nation.

He has constrained our fellow-citizens, taken captive on the high seas, to bear arms against their country, to become the executioners of their friends and brethren, or to fall themselves by their hands.

He has excited domestic insurrection among us, and has endeavored to bring on the inhabitants of our frontiers the merciless Indian savages, whose known rule of warfare is an undistinguished destruction of all ages, sexes, and conditions.

In every stage of these oppressions we have petitioned for redress in the most humble terms; our repeated petitions have been answered only by repeated injury. A prince, whose character is thus marked by every act which may define a tyrant, is unfit to be the ruler of a free people.

Nor have we been wanting in our attentions to our British brethren. We have warned them, from time to time, of attempts by their legislature to extend an unwarrantable jurisdiction over us. We have reminded them of the circumstances of our emigration and settlement here. We have appealed to their native justice and magnanimity; and we have conjured them, by the ties of our common kindred, to disavow these usurpations, which would inevitably interrupt our connections and correspondence. They, too, have been deaf to the voice of justice and of consanguinity. We must, therefore, acquiesce in the necessity which denounces our separation, and hold them, as we hold the rest of mankind, enemies in war, in peace friends.

We, therefore, the representatives of the United States of America, in General Congress assembled, appealing to the Supreme Judge of the world for the rectitude of our intentions, do, in the name and by the authority of the good people of these colonies, solemnly publish and declare, that these United Colonies are, and of right ought to be, FREE AND INDEPENDENT STATES; that they are absolved from all allegiance to the British crown, and that all political connection between them and the state of Great Britain is, and ought to be, totally dissolved; and that, as free and independent states, they have full power to levy war, conclude peace, contract alliances, establish commerce, and do all other acts and things which independent states may of right do. And for the support of this declaration, with a firm reliance on the protection of Divine Providence, we mutually pledge to each other our lives, our fortunes, and our sacred honor.

## JOHN HANCOCK

| | | |
|---|---|---|
| Button Gwinnett | Thos. Nelson, Jr. | Richd. Stockton |
| Lyman Hall | Francis Lightfoot Lee | Jno. Witherspoon |
| Geo. Walton | Carter Braxton | Fras. Hopkinson |
| Wm. Hooper | Robt. Morris | John Hart |
| Joseph Hewes | Benjamin Rush | Abra. Clark |
| John Penn | Benja. Franklin | Josiah Bartlett |
| Edward Rutledge | John Morton | Wm. Whipple |
| Thos. Heyward, Junr. | Geo. Clymer | Saml. Adams |
| Thomas Lynch, Junr. | Jas. Smith | John Adams |
| Arthur Middleton | Geo. Taylor | Robt. Treat Paine |
| Samuel Chase | James Wilson | Elbridge Gerry |
| Wm. Paca | Geo. Ross | Step. Hopkins |
| Thos. Stone | Caesar Rodney | William Ellery |
| Charles Carroll of | Geo. Read | Roger Sherman |
| Carrollton | Tho. M'Kean | Sam'el Huntington |
| George Wythe | Wm. Floyd | Wm. Williams |
| Richard Henry Lee | Phil. Livingston | Oliver Wolcott |
| Th. Jefferson | Frans. Lewis | Matthew Thornton |
| Benj. Harrison | Lewis Morris | |

# The Constitution of the United States of America

## PREAMBLE

We the People of the United States, in Order to form a more perfect Union, establish Justice, insure domestic Tranquility, provide for the common defence, promote the general Welfare, and secure the Blessings of Liberty to ourselves and our Posterity, do ordain and establish this Constitution for the United States of America.

## ARTICLE 1

### Section 1

All legislative Powers herein granted shall be vested in a Congress of the United States, which shall consist of a Senate and House of Representatives.

### Section 2

The House of Representatives shall be composed of Members chosen every second Year by the People of the several States, and the Electors in each State shall have the Qualifications requisite for Electors of the most numerous Branch of the State Legislature.

No Person shall be a Representative who shall not have attained to the Age of twenty five Years, and been seven Years a Citizen of the United States, and who shall not, when elected, be an inhabitant of that State in which he shall be chosen.

Representatives and direct Taxes shall be apportioned among the several States which may be included within this Union, according to their respective Numbers, *which shall be determined by adding to the whole Number of free Persons, including those bound to Service for a Term of Years, and excluding Indians not taxed, three fifths of all other Persons.* * The actual Enumeration shall be made within three Years after the first Meeting of the Congress of the United States, and within every subsequent Term of ten Years, in such Manner as they shall by Law direct. The Number of Representatives shall not exceed one for every thirty Thousand, but each State shall have at Least one Representative; *and until such enumeration shall be made, the State of New Hampshire shall be entitled to chuse three, Massachusetts eight, Rhode-Island and Providence Plantations one, Connecticut five, New York six, New Jersey four, Pennsylvania eight, Delaware one, Maryland six, Virginia ten, North Carolina five, South Carolina five, and Georgia three.*

When vacancies happen in the Representation from any State, the Executive Authority thereof shall issue Writs of Election to fill such Vacancies.

The House of Representatives shall chuse their Speaker and other Officers; and shall have the sole Power of Impeachment.

## Section 3

The Senate of the United States shall be composed of two Senators from each State, *chosen by the Legislature thereof,* for six Years; and each Senator shall have one Vote.

*Immediately after they shall be assembled in Consequence of the first Election, they shall be divided as equally as may be into three Classes. The Seats of the Senators of the first Class shall be vacated at the Expiration of the second Year, of the second Class at the Expiration of the fourth Year, and of the third Class at the Expiration of the sixth Year so that one third may be chosen every second Year; and if Vacancies happen by Resignation, or otherwise, during the Recess of the Legislature of any state, the Executive thereof may make temporary Appointments until the next Meeting of the Legislature, which shall then fill such Vacancies.*

No Person shall be a Senator who shall not have attained to the Age of thirty Years, and been nine Years a Citizen of the United States, and who shall not, when elected, be an Inhabitant of that State for which he shall be chosen.

The Vice President of the United States shall be President of the Senate, but shall have no Vote, unless they be equally divided.

The Senate shall chuse their other Officers, and also a President *pro tempore,* in the Absence of the Vice President, or when he shall exercise the Office of President of the United States.

The Senate shall have the sole Power to try all Impeachments. When sitting for that Purpose, they shall be on Oath or Affirmation. When the President of the United States is tried the Chief Justice shall preside: And no Person shall be convicted without the Concurrence of two thirds of the Members present.

Judgment in Cases of Impeachment shall not extend further than to removal from Office, and disqualification to hold and enjoy any Office of honor, Trust or Profit under the United States: but the Party convicted shall nevertheless be liable and subject to Indictment, Trial, Judgment and Punishment, according to Law.

## Section 4

The Times, Places and Manner of holding Elections for Senators and Representatives, shall be prescribed in each State by the Legislature thereof; but the Congress may at any time by Law make or alter such Regulations, except as to the Places of chusing Senators.

The Congress shall assemble at least once in every Year, *and such Meeting shall be on the first Monday in December, unless they shall by Law appoint a different Day.*

## Section 5

Each House shall be the Judge of the Elections, Returns and Qualifications of its own Members, and a Majority of each shall constitute a Quorum to do Business; but a smaller Number may adjourn from day to day, and may be authorized to compel the Attendance of absent Members, in such Manner, and under such Penalties as each House may provide.

Each House may determine the Rules of its Proceedings, punish its Members for disorderly Behaviour, and, with the Concurrence of two thirds, expel a Member.

*\*Passages no longer in effect are printed in italic type.*

Each House shall keep a Journal of its Proceedings, and from time to time publish the same, excepting such Parts as may in their Judgment require Secrecy; and the Yeas and Nays of the Members of either House on any question shall, at the Desire of one fifth of those Present, be entered on the Journal.

Neither House, during the Session of Congress, shall, without the Consent of the other, adjourn for more than three days, nor to any other Place than that in which the two Houses shall be sitting.

## Section 6

The Senators and Representatives shall receive a Compensation for their Services, to be ascertained by Law, and paid out of the Treasury of the United States. They shall in all Cases, except Treason, Felony and Breach of the Peace, be privileged from Arrest during their Attendance at the Session of their respective Houses, and in going to and returning from the same; and for any Speech or Debate in either House, they shall not be questioned in any other Place.

No Senator or Representative shall, during the Time for which he was elected, be appointed to any civil Office under the Authority of the United States, which shall have been created, or the Emoluments whereof shall have been encreased during such time, and no Person holding any Office under the United States, shall be a Member of either House during his Continuance in Office.

## Section 7

All Bills for raising Revenue shall originate in the House of Representatives; but the Senate may propose or concur with Amendments as on other Bills.

Every Bill which shall have passed the House of Representatives and the Senate, shall, before it become a Law, be presented to the President of the United States; If he approve he shall sign it, but if not he shall return it, with his Objections to the House in which it shall have originated, who shall enter the Objections at large on their Journal, and proceed to reconsider it. If after such Reconsideration two thirds of that House shall agree to pass the Bill, it shall be sent, together with the Objections, to the other House, by which it shall likewise be reconsidered, and if approved by two thirds of that House, it shall become a Law. But in all such Cases the Votes of both Houses shall be determined by Yeas and Nays, and the Names of the Persons voting for and against the Bill shall be entered on the Journal of each House respectively. If any Bill shall not be returned by the President within ten Days (Sundays excepted) after it shall have been presented to him, the Same shall be a Law, in like Manner as if he had signed it, unless the Congress by their Adjournment prevent its Return, in which Case it shall not be a Law.

Every Order, Resolution, or Vote to which the Concurrence of the Senate and House of Representatives may be necessary (except on a question of Adjournment) shall be presented to the President of the United States; and before the Same shall take Effect, shall be approved by him, or being disapproved by him, shall be repassed by two thirds of the Senate and House of Representatives, according to the Rules and Limitations prescribed in the Case of a Bill.

## Section 8

The Congress shall have Power To lay and collect Taxes, Duties, Imposts and Excises, to pay the Debts and provide for the common Defence and general Welfare of the United States; but all Duties, Imposts and Excises shall be uniform throughout the United States;

To borrow Money on the credit of the United States;

To regulate Commerce with foreign Nations, and among the several States, and with the Indian Tribes;

To establish an uniform Rule of Naturalization, and uniform Laws on the subject of Bankruptcies throughout the United States;

To coin Money, regulate the Value thereof, and of foreign Coin, and fix the Standard of Weights and Measures;

To provide for the Punishment of counterfeiting the Securities and current Coin of the United States;

To establish Post Offices and post Roads;

To promote the Progress of Science and useful Arts, by securing for limited Times to Authors and Inventors the exclusive Right to their respective Writings and Discoveries;

To constitute Tribunals inferior to the supreme Court;

To define and punish Piracies and Felonies committed on the high Seas, and Offences against the Law of Nations;

To declare War, grant Letters of Marque and Reprisal, and make Rules concerning Captures on Land and Water;

To raise and support Armies, but no Appropriation of Money to that Use shall be for a longer Term than two Years;

To provide and maintain a Navy;

To make Rules for the Government and Regulation of the land and naval Forces;

To provide for calling forth the Militia to execute the Laws of the Union, suppress Insurrections and repel Invasions;

To provide for organizing, arming, and disciplining, the Militia, and for governing such Part of them as may be employed in the Service of the United States, reserving to the States respectively, the Appointment of the Officers, and the Authority of training the Militia according to the discipline prescribed by Congress;

To exercise exclusive Legislation in all Cases whatsoever, over such District (not exceeding ten Miles square) as may, by Cession of particular States, and the Acceptance of Congress, become the Seat of the Government of the United States, and to exercise like Authority over all Places purchased by the Consent of the Legislature of the State in which the Same shall be, for the Erection of Forts, Magazines, Arsenals, dock-Yards, and other needful Buildings;—And

To make all Laws which shall be necessary and proper for carrying into Execution the foregoing Powers, and all other Powers vested by this Constitution in the Government of the United States, or in any Department of Officer thereof.

## Section 9

*The Migration or Importation of such Persons as any of the States now existing shall think proper to admit, shall not be prohibited by the Congress prior to the Year one thousand eight hundred and eight, but a Tax or duty may be imposed on such Importation, not exceeding ten dollars for each Person.*

The Privilege of the Writ of Habeas Corpus shall not be suspended, unless when in Cases of Rebellion or Invasion the public Safety may require it.

No Bill of Attainder or ex post facto Law shall be passed.

No Capitation, or other direct, Tax shall be laid, unless in Proportion to the Census or Enumeration herein before directed to be taken.

No Tax or Duty shall be laid on Articles exported from any State.

No Preference shall be given by any Regulation of Commerce or Revenue to the Ports of one State over those of another: nor shall Vessels bound to, or from, one State, be obliged to enter, clear, or pay Duties in another.

No Money shall be drawn from the Treasury, but in Consequence of Appropriations made by Law; and a regular Statement and Account of the Receipts and Expenditures of all public Money shall be published from time to time.

No Title of Nobility shall be granted by the United States: And no Person holding any Office of Profit or Trust under them, shall, without the Consent of the Congress, accept of any present, Emolument, Office, or Title, of any kind whatever, from any King, Prince, or foreign State.

## Section 10

No State shall enter into any Treaty, Alliance, or Confederation; grant Letters of Marque and Reprisal; coin Money; emit Bills of Credit; make any Thing but gold and silver Coin a Tender in Payment of Debts; pass any Bill of Attainder, ex post facto Law, or Law impairing the obligation of Contracts, or grant any Title of Nobility.

No State shall, without the Consent of the Congress, lay any Imposts or Duties on Imports or Exports, except what may be absolutely necessary for executing its inspection Laws: and the net

Produce of all Duties and Imposts, laid by any State on Imports or Exports, shall be for the Use of the Treasury of the United States; and all such Laws shall be subject to the Revision and Controul of the Congress.

No State shall, without the Consent of Congress, lay any Duty of Tonnage, keep Troops, or Ships of War in time of Peace, enter into any Agreement or Compact with another State, or with a foreign Power, or engage in War, unless actually invaded, or in such imminent Danger as will not admit of delay.

# ARTICLE II

## Section 1

The executive Power shall be vested in a President of the United States of America. He shall hold his Office during the Term of four Years, and, together with the Vice President, chosen for the same Term, be elected, as follows:

Each State shall appoint, in such Manner as the Legislature thereof may direct, a Number of Electors, equal to the whole Number of Senators and Representatives to which the State may be entitled in the Congress: but no Senator or Representative, or Person holding an Office of Trust or Profit under the United States, shall be appointed an Elector.

*The Electors shall meet in their respective States, and vote by Ballot for two Persons, of whom one at least shall not be an Inhabitant of the same State with themselves. And they shall make a List of all the Persons voted for, and of the Number of Votes for each; which List they shall sign and certify, and transmit sealed to the Seat of the Government of the United States, directed to the President of the Senate. The President of the Senate shall, in the Presence of the Senate and House of Representatives, open all the Certificates, and the Votes shall then be counted. The Person having the greatest Number of Votes shall be the President, if such Number be a Majority of the whole number of Electors appointed; and if there be more than one who have such Majority, and have an equal Number of Votes, then the House of Representatives shall immediately chuse by Ballot one of them for President; and if no Person have a Majority, then from the five highest on the List the said House shall in like Manner chuse the President. But in chusing the President, the Votes shall be taken by States, the Representation from each State having one Vote; A quorum for this Purpose shall consist of a Member or Members from two thirds of the States, and a Majority of all the States shall be necessary to a Choice. In every Case, after the Choice of the President, the Person having the greatest Number of Votes of the Electors shall be the Vice President. But if there should remain two or more who have equal Votes, the Senate shall chuse from them by Ballot the Vice President.*

The Congress may determine the time of chusing the Electors, and the Day on which they shall give their Votes; which Day shall be the same throughout the United States.

No person except a natural born Citizen, *or a Citizen of the United States, at the time of the Adoption of this Constitution,* shall be eligible to the Office of President; neither shall any Person be eligible to that Office who shall not have attained to the Age of thirty five Years, and been fourteen Years a Resident within the United States.

In Case of the Removal of the President from Office, or of his Death, Resignation, or Inability to discharge the Powers and Duties of the said Office, the Same shall devolve on the Vice President, and the Congress may by Law provide for the Case of Removal, Death, Resignation or Inability, both of the President and Vice President, declaring what Officer shall then act as President, and such Officer shall act accordingly, until the Disability be removed, or a President shall be elected.

The President shall, at stated Times, receive for his Services, a Compensation, which shall neither be encreased nor diminished during the Period for which he shall have been elected, and he shall not receive within that period any other Emolument from the United States, or any of them.

Before he enter on the Execution of his Office, he shall take the following Oath or Affirmation:—"I do solemnly swear (or affirm) that I will faithfully execute the Office of President of the United States, and will to the best of my Ability, preserve, protect and defend the Constitution of the United States."

## Section 2

The President shall be Commander in Chief of the Army and Navy of the United States, and of the Militia of the several States, when called into the actual Service of the United States; he may require the Opinion, in writing, of the principal Officer in each of the executive Departments, upon any Subject relating to the Duties of their respective Offices, and he shall have Power to grant Reprieves and Pardons for Offences against the United States, except in Cases of Impeachment.

He shall have Power, by and with the Advice and Consent of the Senate, to make Treaties, provided two thirds of the Senators present concur; and he shall nominate, and by and with the Advice and Consent of the Senate, shall appoint Ambassadors, other public Ministers and Consuls, Judges of the supreme Court, and all other Officers of the United States, whose Appointments are not herein otherwise provided for, and which shall be established by Law: but the Congress may by Law vest the Appointment of such inferior Officers, as they think proper in the President alone, in the Courts of Law, or in the Heads of Departments.

The President shall have Power to fill up all Vacancies that may happen during the Recess of the Senate, by granting Commissions which shall expire at the End of their next Session.

### Section 3

He shall from time to time give to the Congress Information of the State of the Union, and recommend to their Consideration such Measures as he shall judge necessary and expedient; he may, on extraordinary Occasions, convene both Houses, or either of them, and in Case of disagreement between them, with Respect to the Time of Adjournment, he may adjourn them to such Time as he shall think proper; he shall receive Ambassadors and other public Ministers; he shall take Care that the Laws be faithfully executed, and shall Commission all the officers of the United States.

### Section 4

The President, Vice President and all civil Officers of the United States, shall be removed from Office on Impeachment for, and Conviction of, Treason, Bribery or other high Crimes and Misdemeanors.

## ARTICLE III
### Section 1

The judicial Power of the United States, shall be vested in one supreme Court, and in such inferior Courts as the Congress may from time to time ordain and establish. The Judges, both of the supreme and inferior Courts, shall hold their offices during good Behaviour, and shall, at stated Times, receive for their Services, a Compensation, which shall not be diminished during their Continuance in Office.

### Section 2

The judicial Power shall extend to all Cases, in Law and Equity, arising under this Constitution, the Laws of the United States, and Treaties made, or which shall be made, under their Authority;—to all Cases affecting Ambassadors, other public Ministers and Consuls;—to all Cases of admiralty and maritime Jurisdiction;—to Controversies to which the United States shall be a Party;—to Controversies between two or more States;—between a State and Citizens of another State;—*between Citizens of different States;*—between Citizens of the same State claiming Lands under Grants of different States, and between a State, or the Citizens thereof, and foreign States, Citizens or Subjects.

In all Cases affecting Ambassadors, other public Ministers and Consuls, and those in which a State shall be Party, the supreme Court shall have original Jurisdiction. In all the other Cases before mentioned, the supreme Court shall have appellate Jurisdiction, both as to Law and Fact, with such Exceptions, and under such Regulations as the Congress shall make.

The Trial of all Crimes, except in Cases of Impeachment, shall be by Jury; and such Trial shall be held in the State where the said Crimes shall have been committed, but when not committed within any State, the Trial shall be at such Place or Places as the Congress may by Law have directed.

### Section 3

Treason against the United States, shall consist only in levying War against them, or in adhering to their Enemies, giving them Aid and Comfort. No person shall be convicted of Treason unless on the Testimony of two Witnesses to the same overt Act, or on Confession in open Court.

The Congress shall have Power to declare the Punishment of Treason, but no Attainder of Treason shall work Corruption of Blood, or Forfeiture except during the Life of the Person attainted.

# Article IV

## Section 1

Full Faith and Credit shall be given in each State to the public Acts, Records, and judicial Proceedings of every other State. And the Congress may by general Laws prescribe the Manner in which such Acts, Records and Proceedings shall be proved, and the Effect thereof.

## Section 2

The Citizens of each State shall be entitled to all Privileges and Immunities of Citizens in the several States.

A Person charged in any State with Treason, Felony, or other Crime, who shall flee from Justice, and be found in another State, shall on Demand of the executive Authority of the State from which he fled, be delivered up, to be removed to the State having Jurisdiction of the Crime.

*No Person held to Service or Labour in one State, under the Laws thereof, escaping into another, shall, in Consequence of any Law or Regulation therein, be discharged from such Service or Labour, but shall be delivered up on Claim of the Party to whom such Service or Labour may be due.*

## Section 3

New States may be admitted by the Congress into this Union; but no new State shall be formed or erected within the Jurisdiction of any other State; nor any State be formed by the Junction of two or more States, or Parts of States, without the Consent of the Legislatures of the States concerned as well as of the Congress.

The Congress shall have Power to dispose of and make all needful Rules and Regulations respecting the Territory or other Property belonging to the United States; and nothing in this Constitution shall be so construed as to Prejudice any Claims of the United States, or of any particular States.

## Section 4

The United States shall guarantee to every State in this Union a Republican Form of Government, and shall protect each of them against Invasion; and on Application of the Legislature, or of the Executive (when the Legislature cannot be convened) against domestic violence.

# Article V

The Congress, whenever two thirds of both Houses shall deem it necessary, shall propose Amendments to this Constitution, or, on the Application of the Legislatures of two thirds of the several States, shall call a Convention for proposing Amendments, which, in either Case, shall be valid to all Intents and Purposes, as Part of this Constitution, when ratified by the Legislatures of three fourths of the several States, or by Conventions in three fourths thereof, as the one or the other Mode of Ratification may be proposed by the Congress; Provided *that no Amendment which may be made prior to the Year One thousand eight hundred and eight shall in any Manner affect the first and fourth Clauses in the Ninth Section of the first Article;* and that no State, without its Consent, shall be deprived of its equal Suffrage in the Senate.

# Article VI

All Debts contracted and Engagements entered into, before the Adoption of this Constitution, shall be as valid against the United States under this Constitution, as under the Confederation.

This Constitution, and Laws of the United States which shall be made in Pursuance thereof; and all Treaties made, or which shall be made, under the Authority of the United States, shall be the supreme Law of the Land; and the Judges in every State shall be bound thereby, any Thing in the Constitution or Laws of any State to the Contrary notwithstanding.

The Senators and Representatives before mentioned, and the Members of the several State Legislatures, and all executive and Judicial Officers, both of the United States and of the several States, shall be bound by Oath or Affirmation, to support this Constitution; but no religious Test shall ever be required as a Qualification to any Office of public Trust under the United States.

## ARTICLE VII

The Ratification of the Conventions of nine States, shall be sufficient for the Establishment of this Constitution between the States so ratifying the Same.

Done in Convention by the Unanimous Consent of the States present the Seventeenth Day of September in the Year of our Lord one thousand seven hundred and Eighty seven and of the Independence of the United States of America the Twelfth.* IN WITNESS whereof We have hereunto subscribed our Names,

### GEORGE WASHINGTON
*President and Deputy from Virginia*

*Delaware*
GEORGE READ
GUNNING BEDFORD, JR.
JOHN DICKINSON
RICHARD BASSETT
JACOB BROOM

*Maryland*
JAMES MCHENRY
DANIEL OF ST. THOMAS JENIFER
DANIEL CARROLL

*Virginia*
JOHN BLAIR
JAMES MADISON, JR.

*North Carolina*
WILLIAM BLOUNT
RICHARD DOBBS SPRAIGHT
HUGH WILLIAMSON

*South Carolina*
JOHN RUTLEDGE
CHARLES COTESWORTH PINCKNEY
CHARLES PINCKNEY
PIERCE BUTLER

*Georgia*
WILLIAM FEW
ABRAHAM BALDWIN

*New Hampshire*
JOHN LANGDON
NICHOLAS GILMAN

*Massachusetts*
NATHANIEL GORHAM
RUFUS KING

*Connecticut*
WILLIAM SAMUEL JOHNSON
ROGER SHERMAN

*New York*
ALEXANDER HAMILTON

*New Jersey*
WILLIAM LIVINGSTON
DAVID BREARLEY
WILLIAM PATERSON
JONATHAN DAYTON

*Pennsylvania*
BENJAMIN FRANKLIN
THOMAS MIFFLIN
ROBERT MORRIS
GEORGE CLYMER
THOMAS FITZSIMONS
JARED INGERSOLL
JAMES WILSON
GOUVERNEUR MORRIS

---

*The Constitution was submitted on September 17, 1787, by the Constitutional Convention, was ratified by the Convention of several states at various dates up to May 29, 1790, and became effective on March 4, 1789.*

# Amendments to the Constitution

## AMENDMENT I

Congress shall make no law respecting an establishment of religion, or prohibiting the free exercise thereof; or abridging the freedom of speech, or of the press; or the right of the people peaceably to assemble, and to petition the Government for a redress of grievances.

## AMENDMENT II

A well regulated Militia being necessary to the security of a free State, the right of the people to keep and bear Arms, shall not be infringed.

## AMENDMENT III

No Soldier shall, in time of peace be quartered in any house, without the consent of the Owner, nor in time of war, but in a manner to be prescribed by law.

## AMENDMENT IV

The right of the people to be secure in their persons, houses, papers, and effects, against unreasonable searches and seizures, shall not be violated, and no Warrants shall issue, but upon probable cause, supported by Oath or affirmation, and particularly describing the place to be searched, and the persons or things to be seized.

## AMENDMENT V

No person shall be held to answer for a capital, or otherwise infamous crime, unless on a presentment or indictment of a Grand Jury, except in cases arising in the land or naval forces, or in the Militia, when in actual service in time of War or public danger; nor shall any person be subject for the same offense to be twice put in jeopardy of life or limb; nor shall be compelled in any criminal case to be a witness against himself, nor be deprived of life, liberty, or property, without due process of law; nor shall private property be taken for public use, without just compensation.

## AMENDMENT VI

In all criminal prosecutions, the accused shall enjoy the right to a speedy and public trial, by an impartial jury of the State and district wherein the crime shall have been committed, which district shall have been previously ascertained by law, and to be informed of the nature and cause of the accusation; to be confronted with the witnesses against him; to have compulsory process for obtaining witnesses in his favor, and to have the Assistance of Counsel for his defence.

## AMENDMENT VII

In Suits at common law, where the value in controversy shall exceed twenty dollars, the right of trial by jury shall be preserved, and no fact tried by a jury, shall be otherwise re-examined in any Court of the United States, than according to the rules of the common law.

## AMENDMENT VIII

Excessive bail shall not be required, nor excessive fines imposed, nor cruel and unusual punishments inflicted.

## AMENDMENT IX

The enumeration in the Constitution, of certain rights, shall not be construed to deny or disparage others retained by the people.

## AMENDMENT X*

The powers not delegated to the United States by the Constitution, nor prohibited by it to the States, are reserved to the States respectively, or to the people.

## AMENDMENT XI
## [ADOPTED 1798]

The Judicial power of the United States shall not be construed to extend to any suit in law or equity, commenced or prosecuted against one of the United States by Citizens of another State, or by Citizens or Subjects of any Foreign State.

## AMENDMENT XII
## [ADOPTED 1804]

The Electors shall meet in their respective states, and vote by ballot for President and Vice President, one of whom, at least, shall not be an inhabitant of the same state with themselves; they shall name in their ballots the person voted for as President, and in distinct ballots the person voted for as Vice President, and they shall make distinct lists of all persons voted for as President, and of all persons voted for as Vice President, and of the number of votes for each, which lists they shall sign and certify, and transmit sealed to the seat of the government of the United States, directed to the President of the Senate;—The President of the Senate shall, in the presence of the Senate and House of Representatives, open all the certificates and the votes shall then be counted;—The person having the greatest number of votes for President, shall be the President, if such number be a majority of the whole number of Electors appointed; and if no person have such majority, then from the persons having the highest numbers not exceeding three on the list of those voted for as President, the House of Representatives shall choose immediately, by ballot, the President. But in choosing the President, the votes shall be taken by states, the representation from each state having one vote; a quorum for this purpose shall consist of a member or members from two-thirds of the states, and a majority of all the states shall be necessary to a choice. And if the House of Representatives shall not choose a President whenever the right of choice shall devolve upon them, before *the fourth day of March* next following, then the Vice President shall act as President, as in the case of the death or other constitutional disability of the President.—The person having the greatest number of votes as Vice President, shall be the Vice President, if such number be a majority of the whole number of Electors appointed, and if no person have a majority, then from the two highest numbers on the list, the Senate shall choose the Vice President; a quorum for the purpose shall consist of two-thirds of the whole number of Senators, and a majority of the whole number shall be necessary to a choice. But no person constitutionally ineligible to the office of President shall be eligible to that of Vice President of the United States.

## AMENDMENT XIII
## [ADOPTED 1865]

### Section 1

Neither slavery nor involuntary servitude, except as a punishment for crime whereof the party shall have been duly convicted, shall exist within the United States, or any place subject to their jurisdiction.

### Section 2

Congress shall have power to enforce this article by appropriate legislation.

---

*The first ten amendments (the Bill of Rights) were ratified, and their adoption was certified, on December 15, 1791.*

# AMENDMENT XIV
# [ADOPTED 1868]

## Section 1

All persons born or naturalized in the United States, and subject to the jurisdiction thereof, are citizens of the United States and of the State wherein they reside. No State shall make or enforce any law which shall abridge the privileges or immunities of citizens of the United States; nor shall any State deprive any person of life, liberty, or property, without due process of law; nor deny to any person within its jurisdiction the equal protection of the laws.

## Section 2

Representatives shall be apportioned among the several States according to their respective numbers, counting the whole number of persons in each State, excluding Indians not taxed. But when the right to vote at any election for the choice of electors for President and Vice President of the United States, Representatives in Congress, the Executive and Judicial officers of a State, or the members of the Legislature thereof, is denied to any of the male inhabitants of such State, being twenty-one years of age, and citizens of the United States, or in any way abridged, except for participation in rebellion, or other crime, the basis of representation therein shall be reduced in the proportion which the number of such male citizens shall bear to the whole number of male citizens twenty-one years of age in such State.

## Section 3

No person shall be a Senator or Representative in Congress, or elector of President and Vice President, or hold any office, civil or military, under the United States, or under any State, who, having previously taken an oath, as a member of Congress, or as an officer of the United States, or as a member of any State legislature, or as an executive or judicial officer of any State, to support the Constitution of the United States, shall have engaged in insurrection or rebellion against the same, or given aid or comfort to the enemies thereof. But Congress may by a vote of two-thirds of each House, remove such disability.

## Section 4

The validity of the public debt of the United States, authorized by law, including debts incurred for payment of pensions and bounties for services in suppressing insurrection or rebellion, shall not be questioned. But neither the United States nor any State shall assume or pay any debt or obligation incurred in aid of insurrection or rebellion against the United States, or any claim for the loss or emancipation of any slave; but all such debts, obligations and claims shall be held illegal and void.

## Section 5

The Congress shall have power to enforce, by appropriate legislation, the provisions of this article.

# AMENDMENT XV
# [ADOPTED 1870]

## Section 1

The right of citizens of the United States to vote shall not be denied or abridged by the United States or by any State on account of race, color, or previous condition of servitude.

## Section 2

The Congress shall have power to enforce this article by appropriate legislation.

## AMENDMENT XVI
## [ADOPTED 1913]

The Congress shall have power to lay and collect taxes on incomes, from whatever source derived, without apportionment among the several States, and without regard to any census or enumeration.

## AMENDMENT XVII
## [ADOPTED 1913]

The Senate of the United States shall be composed of two Senators from each State, elected by the people thereof, for six years; and each Senator shall have one vote. The electors in each State shall have the qualifications requisite for electors of the most numerous branch of the State legislatures.

When vacancies happen in the representation of any State in the Senate, the executive authority of such State shall issue writs of election to fill such vacancies: *Provided,* That the legislature of any State may empower the executive thereof to make temporary appointments until the people fill the vacancies by election as the legislature may direct.

This amendment shall not be so construed as to affect the election or term of any Senator chosen before it becomes valid as part of the Constitution.

## AMENDMENT XVIII
## [ADOPTED 1919, REPEALED 1933]

### Section 1

*After one year from the ratification of this article the manufacture, sale, or transportation of intoxicating liquors within, the importation thereof into, or the exportation thereof from the United States and all territory subject to the jurisdiction thereof for beverage purposes is hereby prohibited.*

### Section 2

*The Congress and the several States shall have concurrent power to enforce this article by appropriate legislation.*

### Section 3

*This article shall be inoperative unless it shall have been ratified as an amendment to the Constitution by the legislatures of the several States, as provided in the Constitution, within seven years from the date of the submission hereof to the States by the Congress.*

## AMENDMENT XIX
## [ADOPTED 1920]

The right of citizens of the United States to vote shall not be denied or abridged by the United States or by any State on account of sex.

Congress shall have power to enforce this article by appropriate legislation.

## AMENDMENT XX
## [ADOPTED 1933]

### Section 1

The terms of the President and Vice President shall end at noon on the 20th day of January, and the terms of Senators and Representatives at noon on the 3d day of January, of the years in which such terms would have ended if this article had not been ratified and the terms of their successors shall then begin.

### Section 2

The Congress shall assemble at least once in every year, and such meeting shall begin at noon on the 3d day of January, unless they shall by law appoint a different day.

### Section 3

If, at the time fixed for the beginning of the term of the President, the President elect shall have died, the Vice President elect shall become President. If a President shall not have been chosen before the time fixed for the beginning of his term, or if the President elect shall have failed to qualify, then the Vice President elect shall act as President until a President shall have qualified; and the Congress may by law provide for the case wherein neither a President elect nor a Vice President elect shall have qualified, declaring who shall then act as President, or the manner in which one who is to act shall be selected, and such person shall act accordingly until a President or Vice President shall have qualified.

### Section 4

The Congress may by law provide for the case of the death of any of the persons from whom the House of Representatives may choose a President whenever the right of choice shall have devolved upon them, and for the case of the death of any of the persons from whom the Senate may choose a Vice President whenever the right of choice shall have devolved upon them.

### Section 5

Sections 1 and 2 shall take effect on the 15th day of October following the ratification of this article.

### Section 6

This article shall be inoperative unless it shall have been ratified as an amendment to the Constitution by the legislatures of three fourths of the several States within seven years from the date of its submission.

## AMENDMENT XXI
## [ADOPTED 1933]

### Section 1

The eighteenth article of amendment to the Constitution of the United States is hereby repealed.

### Section 2

The transportation or importation into any State, Territory, or possession of the United States for delivery or use therein of intoxicating liquors in violation of the laws thereof, is hereby prohibited.

### Section 3

This article shall be inoperative unless it shall have been ratified as an amendment to the Constitution by conventions in the several States, as provided in the Constitution, within seven years from the date of the submission hereof to the States by the Congress.

## AMENDMENT XXII
## [ADOPTED 1951]

### Section 1

No person shall be elected to the office of the President more than twice, and no person who has held the office of President, or acted as President, for more than two years of a term to which some other person was elected President shall be elected to the office of the President more than once. But this Article shall not apply to any person holding the office of President when this Article was proposed by the Congress, and shall not prevent any person who may be holding the office of President, or acting as President, during the term within which this Article becomes operative from holding the office of President or acting as President during the remainder of such term.

### Section 2

This article shall be inoperative unless it shall have been ratified as an amendment to the Constitution by the legislatures of three-fourths of the several States within seven years from the date of its submission to the States by the Congress.

# Amendment XXIII
## [Adopted 1961]

### Section 1

The District constituting the seat of Government of the United States shall appoint in such manner as the Congress shall direct:

A number of electors of President and Vice President equal to the whole number of Senators and Representatives in Congress to which the District would be entitled if it were a State, but in no event more than the least populous State; they shall be in addition to those appointed by the States, but they shall be considered, for the purposes of the election of President and Vice President, to be electors appointed by a State; and they shall meet in the District and perform such duties as provided by the twelfth article of amendment.

### Section 2

The Congress shall have power to enforce this article by appropriate legislation.

# Amendment XXIV
## [Adopted 1964]

### Section 1

The right of citizens of the United States to vote in any primary or other election for President or Vice President, for electors for President or Vice President, or for Senator or Representative in Congress, shall not be denied or abridged by the United States or any state by reason of failure to pay any poll tax or other tax.

### Section 2

The Congress shall have the power to enforce this article by appropriate legislation.

# Amendment XXV
## [Adopted 1967]

### Section 1

In case of the removal of the President from office or his death or resignation, the Vice President shall become President.

### Section 2

Whenever there is a vacancy in the office of the Vice President, the President shall nominate a Vice President who shall take the office upon confirmation by a majority vote of both houses of Congress.

### Section 3

Whenever the President transmits to the President pro tempore of the Senate and the Speaker of the House of Representatives his written declaration that he is unable to discharge the powers and duties of his office, and until he transmits to them a written declaration to the contrary, such powers and duties shall be discharged by the Vice President as Acting President.

### Section 4

Whenever the Vice President and a majority of either the principal officers of the executive departments or of such other body as Congress may by law provide, transmit to the President pro tempore of the Senate and the Speaker of the House of Representatives their written declaration that the President is unable to discharge the powers and duties of his office, the Vice President shall immediately assume the powers and duties of the office as Acting President.

Thereafter, when the President transmits to the President pro tempore of the Senate and the Speaker of the House of Representatives his written declaration that no inability exists, he shall resume the powers and duties of his office unless the Vice President and a majority of either the principal officers of the executive department or of such other body as Congress may by law provide, transmit within four days to the President pro tempore of the Senate and the Speaker of the House of Representatives their written declaration that the President is unable to discharge the powers and duties of his office. Thereupon Congress shall decide the issue, assembling within 48 hours for that purpose if not in session. If the Congress, within 21 days after receipt of the latter written declaration, or, if Congress is not in session, within 21 days after Congress is required to assemble, determines by two-thirds vote of both houses that the President is unable to discharge the powers and duties of his office, the Vice President shall continue to discharge the same as Acting President; otherwise, the President shall resume the powers and duties of his office.

## Amendment XXVI
## [Adopted 1971]

### Section 1

The right of citizens of the United States, who are 18 years of age or older, to vote shall not be denied or abridged by the United States or any state on account of age.

### Section 2

The Congress shall have the power to enforce this article by appropriate legislation.

## Amendment XXVII
## [Adopted 1992]

No law, varying the compensation for the services of the Senators and Representatives shall take effect, until an election of Representatives shall have intervened.

# Dred Scott v. Sandford (1857)

*With the help of abolitionist lawyers, Dred Scott spent twenty years trying to convince local, state, and national courts that he should be entitled to freedom because his master had taken him to live for a time in a northern territory where slavery had been outlawed by Congress. When the Supreme Court ruled against him, it also took the opportunity to declare that no African American could either be an American citizen or use the court system.*

Chief Justice Taney delivered the opinion of the Court.

The question is simply this: Can a negro, whose ancestors were imported into this country, and sold as slaves, become a member of the political community formed and brought into existence by the Constitution of the United States, and as such become entitled to all the rights, and privileges, and immunities, guarantied by that instrument to the citizen? One of which rights is the privilege of suing in a court of the United States in the cases specified in the constitution. . . .

The words "people of the United States" and "citizens" are synonymous terms, and mean the same thing. They both describe the political body who, according to our republican institutions, form the sovereignty, and who hold the power and conduct the government through their representatives. They are what we familiarly call the "sovereign people," and every citizen is one of this people, and a constituent member of this sovereignty. The question before us is, whether the class of persons described in the plea in abatement compose portion of this people, and are constituent members of this sovereignty? We think they are not, and that they are not included, and were not intended to be included, under the word "citizens" in the constitution, and can therefore claim none of the rights and privileges which that instrument provides for and secures to citizens of the United States. On the contrary, they were at that time considered as a subordinate and inferior class of beings, who had been subjugated by the dominant race, and, whether emancipated or not, yet remained subject to their authority, and had no rights or privileges but such as those who held the power and the government might choose to grant them.

It is not the province of the court to decide upon the justice or injustice, the policy or impolicy, of these laws. The decision of that question belonged to the political or law-making power; to those who formed the sovereignty and framed the constitution. The duty of the court is to interpret the instrument they have framed, with the best lights we can obtain on the subject, and to administer it as we find it, according to its true intent and meaning when it was adopted.

In discussing this question, we must not confound the rights of citizenship which a State may confer within its own limits, and the rights of citizenship as a member of the Union. It does not by any means follow, because he has all the rights and privileges of a citizen of a State, that he must be a citizen of the United States. He may have all of the rights and privileges of the citizen of a State, and yet not be entitled to the rights and privileges of a citizen in any other State. For, previous to the adoption of the constitution of the United States, every State had the undoubted right to confer on whomsoever it pleased the character of citizen, and to endow him with all its rights. But this character of course was confirmed to the boundaries of the State, and gave him no rights or privileges in other States beyond those secured to him by the laws of nations and the comity of States. Nor have the several States surrendered the power of conferring these rights and privileges by adopting the constitution of the United States. . . .

It is very clear, therefore, that no State can, by any actor law of its own, passed since the adoption of the constitution, introduce a new member into the political community created by the constitution of the United States. It cannot make him a member of this community by making him a member of its own. And for the same reason it cannot introduce any person, or description of persons, who were not intended to be embraced in this new political family, which the constitution brought into existence, but were intended to be excluded from it.

The question then arises, whether the provisions of the constitution, in relation to the personal rights and privileges to which the citizen of a State should be entitled, embraced the negro African race, at that time in this country, or who might afterwards be imported, who had then or should afterwards be made free in any State; and to put it in the power of a single State to make him a citizen of the United States, and endue him with the full rights of citizenship in every other State without their consent? Does the constitution of the United States act upon him whenever he shall be made free under the laws of a State, and raised there to the rank of a citizen, and immediately clothe him with all the privileges of a citizen in every other State, and in its own courts?

The court thinks the affirmative of these propositions cannot be maintained. And if it cannot, the plaintiff in error could not be a citizen of the State of Missouri, within the meaning of the constitution of the United States, and, consequently, was not entitled to sue in its courts.

It is true, every person, and every class and description of persons, who were at the time of the adoption of the constitution recognized as citizens in the several States, became also citizens of this new political body; but none other; it was formed by them, and for them and their posterity, but for no one else. And the personal rights and privileges guaranteed to citizens of this new sovereignty were intended to embrace those only who were then members of the several State communities, or who should afterwards by birthright or otherwise become members, according to the provisions of the constitution and the principles on which it was founded. It was the union of those who were at that time members of distinct and separate political communities into one political family, whose power, for certain specified purposes, was to extend over the whole territory of the United States. And it gave to each citizen rights and privileges outside of his State which he did not before possess, and placed him in every other State upon a perfect equality with its own citizens as to rights of person and rights of property; it made him a citizen of the United States. . . .

In the opinion of the court, the legislation and histories of the times, and the language used in the declaration of independence, show, that neither the class of persons who had been imported as slaves, nor their descendants, whether they had become free or not, were then acknowledged as a part of the people, nor intended to be included in the general words used in that memorable instrument. . . .

It is too clear for dispute, that the enslaved African race were not intended to be included, and formed no part of the people who framed and adopted this declaration; for if the language, as understood in that day, would embrace them, the conduct of the distinguished men who framed the declaration of independence would have been utterly and flagrantly inconsistent with the principles they asserted; and instead of the sympathy of mankind, to which they so confidently appealed, they would have deserved and received universal rebuke and reprobation. . . .

But there are two clauses in the constitution which point directly and specifically to the negro race as a separate class of persons, and show clearly that they were not regarded as a portion of the people or citizens of the government then formed.

One of these clauses reserves to each of the thirteen States the right to import slaves until the year 1808, if it thinks proper. . . . And by the other provision the States pledge themselves to each other to maintain the right of property of the master, by delivering up to him any slave who may have escaped from his service, and be found within their respective territories. . . .

The only two provisions which point to them and include them, treat them as property, and make it the duty of the government to protect it; no other power, in relation to this race, is to be found in the constitution; and as it is government of special, delegated powers, no authority beyond these two provisions can be constitutionally exercised. The government of the United States had no right to interfere for any other purpose but that of protecting the rights of the owner, leaving it altogether with the several States to deal with this race, whether emancipated or not, as each State may think justice, humanity, and the interests and safety of society, require. The States evidently intended to reserve this power exclusively to themselves. . . . Upon a full and careful consideration of the subject, the court is of opinion, that, upon the facts stated . . . Dred Scott was not a citizen of Missouri within the meaning of the constitution of the United States, and not entitled as such to sue in its courts; and, consequently, that the circuit court had no jurisdiction of the case, and that the judgment on the plea in abatement is erroneous. . . .

We proceed . . . to inquire whether the facts relied on by the plaintiff entitled him to his freedom. . . .

The act of Congress, upon which the plaintiff relies, declares that slavery and involuntary servitude, except as a punishment for crime, shall be forever prohibited in all that part of the territory ceded by France, under the name of Louisiana, which lies north of thirty-six degrees thirty minutes north latitude and not included within the limits of Missouri. And the difficulty which meets us at the threshold of this part of the inquiry is whether Congress was authorized to pass this law under any of the powers granted to it by the Constitution; for, if the authority is not given by that instrument, it is the duty of this Court to declare it void and inoperative and incapable of conferring freedom upon anyone who is held as a slave under the laws of any one of the states.

The counsel for the plaintiff has laid much stress upon that article in the Constitution which confers on Congress the power "to dispose of and make all needful rules and regulations respecting the territory or other property belonging to the United States"; but, in the judgment of the Court, that provision has no bearing on the present controversy, and the power there given, whatever it may be, is confined, and was intended to be confined, to the territory which at that time belonged to, or was claimed by, the United States and was within their boundaries as settled by the treaty with Great Britain and can have no influence upon a territory afterward acquired from a foreign government. It was a special provision for a known and particular territory, and to meet a present emergency, and nothing more. . . .

We do not mean, however, to question the power of Congress in this respect. The power to expand the territory of the United States by the admission of new states is plainly given; and in the construction of this power by all the departments of the government, it has been held to authorize the acquisition of territory, not fit for admission at the time, but to be admitted as soon as its population and situation would entitle it to admission. . . .

It may be safely assumed that citizens of the United States who migrate to a territory belonging to the people of the United States cannot be ruled as mere colonists, dependent upon the will of the general government, and to be governed by any laws it may think proper to impose. The principle upon which our governments rest, and upon which alone they continue to exist, is the union of states, sovereign and independent within their own limits in their internal and domestic concerns, and bound together as one people by a general government, possessing certain enumerated and restricted powers, delegated to it by the people of the several states, and exercising supreme authority within the scope of the powers granted to it, throughout the dominion of the United States. A power, therefore, in the general government to obtain and hold colonies and dependent territories, over which they might legislate without restriction, would be inconsistent with its own existence in its present form. Whatever it acquires, it acquires for the benefit of the people of the several states who created it. It is their trustee acting for them and charged with the duty of promoting the interests of the whole people of the Union in the exercise of the powers specifically granted. . . .

But the power of Congress over the person or property of a citizen can never be a mere discretionary power under our Constitution and form of government. The powers of the government and the rights and privileges of the citizen are regulated and plainly defined by the Constitution itself. And, when the territory becomes a part of the United States, the federal government enters into possession in the character impressed upon it by those who created it. It enters upon it with its powers over the citizen strictly defined and limited by the Constitution, from which it derives its own existence, and by virtue of which alone it continues to exist and act as a government and sovereignty. It has no power of any kind beyond it; and it cannot, when it enters a territory of the United States, put off its character and assume discretionary or despotic powers which the Constitution has denied to it. It cannot create for itself a new character separated from the citizens of the United States and the duties it owes them under the provisions of the Constitution. The territory, being a part of the United States, the government and the citizen both enter it under the authority of the Constitution, with their respective rights defined and marked out; and the federal government can exercise no power over his person or property, beyond what that instrument confers, nor lawfully deny any right which it has reserved. . . .

These powers, and others, in relation to rights of person, which it is not necessary here to enumerate, are, in express and positive terms, denied to the general government; and the rights of private property have been guarded with equal care. Thus the rights of property are united with the rights of person and placed on the same ground by the Fifth Amendment to the Constitution, which provides that no person shall be deprived of life, liberty, and property without due process of law. And an act of Congress which deprives a citizen of the United States of his liberty or property, without due process of law, merely because he came himself or brought his property into a particular territory of the United States, and who had committed no offense against the laws, could hardly be dignified with the name of due process of law. . . .

It seems, however, to be supposed that there is a difference between property in a slave and other property and that different rules may be applied to it in expounding the Constitution of the United States. And the laws and usages of nations, and the writings of eminent jurists upon the relation of master and slave and their mutual rights and duties, and the powers which governments may exercise over it, have been dwelt upon in the argument.

But, in considering the question before us, it must be borne in mind that there is no law of nations standing between the people of the United States and their government and interfering with their relation to each other. The powers of the government and the rights of the citizen under it are positive and practical regulations plainly written down. The people of the United States have delegated to it certain enumerated powers and forbidden it to exercise others. It has no power over the person or property of a citizen but what the citizens of the United States have granted. And no laws or usages of other nations, or reasoning of statesmen or jurists upon the relations of master and slave, can enlarge the powers of the government or take from the citizens the rights they have reserved. And if the Constitution recognizes the right of property of the master in a slave, and makes no distinction between that description of property and other property owned by a citizen, no tribunal, acting under the authority of the United States, whether it be legislative, executive, or judicial, has a right to draw such a distinction or deny to it the benefit of the provisions and guaranties which have been provided for the protection of private property against the encroachments of the government.

Now, as we have already said in an earlier part of this opinion, upon a different point, the right of property in a slave is distinctly and expressly affirmed in the Constitution. The right to traffic in it, like an ordinary article of merchandise and property, was guaranteed to the citizens of the United States, in every state that might desire it, for twenty years. And the government in express terms is pledged to protect it in all future time if the slave escapes from his owner. That is done in plain words—too plain to be misunderstood. And no word can be found in the Constitution which gives Congress a greater power over slave property or which entitles property of that kind to less protection than property of any other description. The only power conferred is the power coupled with the duty of guarding and protecting the owner in his rights.

Upon these considerations it is the opinion of the Court that the act of Congress which prohibited a citizen from holding and owning property of this kind in the territory of the United States north of the line therein mentioned is not warranted by the Constitution and is therefore void; and that neither Dred Scott himself, nor any of his family, were made free by being carried into this territory; even if they had been carried there by the owner with the intention of becoming a permanent resident.

# The Emancipation Proclamation
## By the President of the United States of America:

*On January 1, 1863, when President Abraham Lincoln decreed that slaves within Confederate states would be free, black communities across the country gathered to read aloud the proclamation.*

Whereas, on the twenty-second day of September, in the year of our Lord one thousand eight hundred and sixty-two, a proclamation was issued by the President of the United States, containing, among other things, the following, to wit:

*That on the first day of January, in the year of our Lord one thousand eight hundred and sixty-three, all persons held as slaves within any State or designated part of a State, the people whereof shall then be in rebellion against the United States, shall be then, thenceforward, and forever free; and the Executive Government of the United States, including the military and naval authority thereof, will recognize and maintain the freedom of such persons, and will do no act or acts to repress such persons, or any of them, in any efforts they may make for their actual freedom.*

*That the Executive will, on the first day of January aforesaid, by proclamation, designate the States and parts of States, if any, in which the people thereof, respectively, shall then be in rebellion against the United States; and the fact that any State, or the people thereof, shall on that day be, in good faith, represented in the Congress of the United States by members chosen thereto at elections wherein a majority of the qualified voters of such State shall have participated, shall, in the absence of strong countervailing testimony, be deemed conclusive evidence that such State, and the people thereof, are not then in rebellion against the United States.*

Now, therefore I, Abraham Lincoln, President of the United States, by virtue of the power in me vested as Commander-in-Chief, of the Army and Navy of the United States in time of actual armed rebellion against the authority and government of the United States, and as a fit and necessary war measure for suppressing said rebellion, do, on this first day of January, in the year of our Lord one thousand eight hundred and sixty-three, and in accordance with my purpose so to do publicly proclaimed for the full period of one hundred days, from the day first above mentioned, order and designate as the States and parts of States wherein the people thereof respectively, are this day in rebellion against the United States, the following, to wit:

Arkansas, Texas, Louisiana, (except the Parishes of St. Bernard, Plaquemines, Jefferson, St. John, St. Charles, St. James Ascension, Assumption, Terrebonne, Lafourche, St. Mary, St. Martin, and Orleans, including the City of New Orleans), Mississippi, Alabama, Florida, Georgia, South Carolina, North Carolina, and Virginia, (except the forty-eight counties designated as West Virginia, and also the counties of Berkley, Accomac, Northampton, Elizabeth City, York, Princess Ann, and Norfolk, including the cities of Norfolk and Portsmouth), and which excepted parts, are for the present, left precisely as if this proclamation were not issued.

And by virtue of the power, and for the purpose aforesaid, I do order and declare that all persons held as slaves within said designated States, and parts of States, are, and henceforward shall be free; and that the Executive government of the United States, including the military and naval authorities thereof, will recognize and maintain the freedom of said persons.

And I hereby enjoin upon the people so declared to be free to abstain from all violence, unless in necessary self-defense; and I recommend to them that, in all cases when allowed, they labor faithfully for reasonable wages. And I further declare and make known, that such persons of suitable condition, will be received into the armed service of the United States to garrison forts, positions, stations, and other places, and to man vessels of all sorts in said service.

And upon this act, sincerely believed to be an act of justice, warranted by the Constitution, upon military necessity, I invoke the considerate judgment of mankind, and the gracious favor of Almighty God.

In witness whereof, I have hereunto set my hand and caused the seal of the United States to be affixed. Done at the City of Washington, this first day of January, in the year of our Lord one thousand eight hundred and sixty-three, and of the Independence of the United States of America the eighty-seventh.

By the President: Abraham Lincoln
William H. Seward, Secretary of State.

# Plessy v. Ferguson (1896)

*When Homer Plessy led a challenge to Louisiana's segregated trains, he started a series of events that led the Supreme Court, in 1896, to conclude that the races may be separated, as long as public facilities—such as trains and schools—were "equal."*

Mr. Justice Brown, after stating the case, delivered the opinion of the court.

This case turns upon the constitutionality of an act of the General Assembly of the State of Louisiana passed in 1890, providing for separate railway carriages for the white and colored races. Acts 1890, No. 111, p. 152. . . .

The constitutionality of this act is attacked upon the ground that it conflicts both with the Thirteenth Amendment of the Constitution, abolishing slavery, and the Fourteenth Amendment, which prohibits certain restrictive legislation on the part of the States. . . .

A statute which implies merely a legal distinction between the white and colored races—a distinction which is founded in the color of the two races, and which must always exist so long as white men are distinguished from the other race by color—has no tendency to destroy the legal equality of the two races, or re-establish a state of involuntary servitude. Indeed, we do not understand that the Thirteenth Amendment is strenuously relied upon by the plaintiff in error in this connection. . . .

The object of the [Fourteenth] amendment was undoubtedly to enforce the absolute equality of the two races before the law, but in the nature of things it could not have been intended to abolish distinctions based upon color, or to enforce social, as distinguished from political equality, or a commingling of the two races upon terms unsatisfactory to either. Laws permitting, and even requiring, their separation in places where they are liable to be brought into contact do not necessarily imply the inferiority of either race to the other, and have been generally, if not universally, recognized as within the competency of the state legislatures in the exercise of their police power. The most common instance of this is connected with the establishment of separate schools for white and colored children, which has been held to be a valid exercise of the legislative power even by courts of States where the political rights of the colored race have been longest and most earnestly enforced. . . .

... Legislation is powerless to eradicate racial instincts or to abolish distinctions based upon physical differences, and the attempt to do so can only result in accentuating the difficulties of the present situation. If the civil and political rights of both races be equal one cannot be inferior to the other civilly or politically. If one race be inferior to the other socially, the Constitution of the United States cannot put them upon the same plane. . . .

*Affirmed.*

Mr. Justice Harlan dissenting.

. . . However apparent the injustice of such legislation may be, we have only to consider whether it is consistent with the Constitution of the United States. . . .

I am of opinion that the statute of Louisiana is inconsistent with the personal liberty of citizens, white and black, in that State, and hostile to both the spirit and letter of the Constitution of the United States. If laws of like character should be enacted in the several States of the Union, the effect would be in the highest degree mischievous. Slavery, as an institution tolerated by law would, it is true, have disappeared from our country, but there would remain a power in the States, by sinister legislation, to interfere with the full enjoyment of the blessings of freedom; to regulate civil rights, common to all citizens, upon the basis of race; and to place in a condition of legal inferiority a large body of American citizens, now constituting a part of the political community called the People of the United States, for whom, and by whom through representatives, our government is administered. Such a system is inconsistent with the guarantee given by the Constitution to each State of a republican form of government, and may be stricken down by Congressional action, or by the courts in the discharge of their solemn duty to maintain the supreme law of the land, anything in the constitution or laws of any State to the contrary notwithstanding.

For the reasons stated, I am constrained to withhold my assent from the opinion and judgment of the majority.

# Brown v. Board of Education of Topeka (1954)

Brown *comprised five different lawsuits aimed at school desegregation. Thurgood Marshall and other NAACP attorneys argued that segregation in public schools was psychologically harmful. In May, 1954, the Supreme Court unanimously overturned the* Plessy *decision and ruled that educational facilities were "inherently unequal" and thus unconstitutional under the Fourteenth Amendment.*

Mr. Chief Justice Warren delivered the opinion of the Court.

These cases come to us from the States of Kansas, South Carolina, Virginia, and Delaware. They are premised on different facts and different local conditions, but a common legal question justifies their consideration together in this consolidated opinion. . . .

Today, education is perhaps the most important function of state and local governments. Compulsory school attendance laws and the great expenditures for education both demonstrate our recognition of the importance of education to our democratic society. It is required in the performance of our most basic public responsibilities, even service in the armed forces. It is the very foundation of good citizenship. Today it is a principal instrument in awakening the child to cultural values, in preparing him for later professional training, and in helping him to adjust normally to his environment. In these days, it is doubtful that any child may reasonably be expected to succeed in life if he is denied the opportunity of an education. Such an opportunity, where the state has undertaken to provide it, is a right which must be made available to all on equal terms.

We come then to the question presented: Does segregation of children in public schools solely on the basis of race, even though the physical facilities and other "tangible" factors may be equal, deprive the children of the minority group of equal education opportunities? We believe that it does. . . .

We conclude that in the field of public education the doctrine of "separate but equal" has no place. Separate educational facilities are inherently unequal. Therefore, we hold that the plaintiffs and others similarly situated for whom the actions have been brought are, by reason of the segregation complained of, deprived of the equal protection of the laws guaranteed by the Fourteenth Amendment. . . .

# Key Provisions of the Civil Rights Act of 1964

*The Civil Rights Act of 1964 outlawed racial discrimination in schools, restaurants, theaters, and other public places where Jim Crow laws had long reigned. The Act also prohibited large employers from discriminating against racial and religious minorities as well as women.*

## AN ACT

To enforce the constitutional right to vote, to confer jurisdiction upon the district courts of the United States to provide injunctive relief against discrimination in public accommodations, to authorize the Attorney General to institute suits to protect constitutional rights in public facilities and public education, to extend the Commission on Civil Rights, to prevent discrimination in federally assisted programs, to establish a Commission on Equal Employment Opportunity, and for other purposes.

Be it enacted by the Senate and House of Representatives of the United States of America in Congress assembled, that this Act may be cited as the "Civil Rights Act of 1964."

### Title I—Voting Rights

***Section 101.*** . . . (2) No person acting under color of law shall—

(a) In determining whether any individual is qualified under State law or laws to vote in any Federal election, apply any standard, practice, or procedure different from the standards, practices, or procedures applied under such law or laws to other individuals within the same county, parish, or similar political subdivision who have been found by State officials to be qualified to vote;

(b) deny the right of any individual to vote in any Federal election because of an error or omission on any record or paper relating to any application, registration, or other act requisite to voting, if such error or omission is not material in determining whether such individual is qualified under State law to vote in such election;

(c) employ any literacy test as a qualification for voting in any Federal election unless (i) such test is administered to each individual and is conducted wholly in writing, and (ii) a certified copy of the test and of the answers given by the individual is furnished to him within twenty-five days of the submission of his request made within the period of time during which records and papers are required to be retained and preserved pursuant to title III of the Civil Rights Act of 1960 (42 U.S.C. 1974–74e; 74 Stat. 88): Provided, however, That the Attorney General may enter into agreements with appropriate State or local authorities that preparation, conduct, and maintenance of such tests in accordance with the provisions of applicable State or local law, including such special provisions as are necessary in the preparation, conduct, and maintenance of such tests for persons who are blind or otherwise physically handicapped, meet the purposes of this subparagraph and constitute compliance therewith.

## Title II—Injunctive Relief Against Discrimination in Places of Public Accommodation

*Section 201.* (a) All persons shall be entitled to the full and equal enjoyment of the goods, services, facilities, and privileges, advantages and accommodations of any place of public accommodation, as defined in this section, without discrimination or segregation on the ground of race, color, religion, or national origin. (b) Each of the following establishments which serves the public is a place of public accommodation within the meaning of this title if its operations effect commerce, or if discrimination or segregation by it is supported by State action:

(1) any inn, hotel, motel, or other establishment which provides lodging to transient guests, other than an establishment located within a building which contains not more than five rooms for rent or hire and which is actually occupied by the proprietor of such establishment as his residence;

(2) any restaurant, cafeteria, lunchroom, lunch counter, soda fountain, or other facility principally engaged in selling food for consumption on the premises, including, but not limited to, any such facility located on the premises of any retail establishment; or any gasoline station;

(3) any motion picture house, theater, concert hall, sports arena, stadium or other place of exhibition or entertainment;

(4) any establishment (A) (i) which is physically located within the premises of any establishment otherwise covered by this subsection, or (ii) within the premises of which is physically located any such covered establishment, and (B) which holds itself out as serving patrons of such covered establishment. . . .

(d) Discrimination or segregation by an establishment is supported by State action within the meaning of this title if such discrimination or segregation

(1) is carried on under color of any law, statute, ordinance, or regulation; or

(2) is carried on under color of any custom or usage required or enforced by officials of the State or political subdivision thereof; or

(3) is required by action of the State or political subdivision thereof. . . .

*Section 202.* All persons shall be entitled to be free, at any establishment or place, from discrimination or segregation of any kind on the ground of race, color, religion, or national origin, if such discrimination or segregation is or purports to be required by any law, statute, ordinance, regulation, rule, or order of a State or any agency or political subdivision thereof.

*Section 203.* No person shall (a) withhold, deny, or attempt to withhold or deny, or deprive or attempt to deprive, any person of any right or privilege secured by section 201 or 202, or (b) intimidate, threaten, or coerce, or attempt to intimidate, threaten, or coerce any person with the purpose of interfering with any right or privilege secured by section 201 or 202, or (c) punish or attempt to punish any person for exercising or attempting to exercise any right or privilege secured by section 201 or 202.

*Section 204.* (a) Whenever any person has engaged or there are reasonable grounds to believe that any person is about to engage in any act or practice prohibited by section 203, a civil action for preventive relief, including an application for a permanent or temporary injunction, restraining order, or other order, may be instituted by the person aggrieved and, upon timely application, the court may, in its discretion, permit the Attorney General to intervene in such civil action if he certifies that the case is of general public importance. Upon application by the complainant and in such circumstances as the court may deem just, the court may appoint an attorney for such complainant and may authorize the commencement of the civil action without the payment of fees, costs, or security. . . .

*Section 206.* (a) Whenever the Attorney General has reasonable cause to believe that any person or group of persons is engaged in a pattern or practice of resistance to the full enjoyment of any of the rights secured by the title, and that the pattern or practice is of such a nature and is intended to deny the full exercise of the rights herein described, the Attorney General may bring a civil action in the appropriate district court of the United States by filing with it a complaint

(1) signed by him (or in his absence the Acting Attorney General),

(2) setting forth facts pertaining to such pattern or practice, and

(3) requesting such preventive relief, including an application for a permanent or temporary injunction, restraining order or other order against the person or persons responsible for such pattern or practice, as he deems necessary to insure the full enjoyment of the rights herein described. . . .

## Title III—Desegregation of Public Facilities

**Section 301.** (a) Whenever the Attorney General receives a complaint in writing signed by an individual to the effect that he is being deprived of or threatened with the loss of his right to the equal protection of the laws, on account of his race, color, religion, or national origin, by being denied equal utilization of any public facility which is owned, operated, or managed by or on behalf of any State or subdivision thereof, other than a public school or public college as defined in section 401 of title IV hereof, and the Attorney General believes the complaint is meritorious and certifies that the signer or signers of such complaint are unable, in his judgment, to initiate and maintain appropriate legal proceedings for relief and that the institution of an action will materially further the orderly progress of desegregation in public facilities, the Attorney General is authorized to institute for or in the name of the United States a civil action in any appropriate district court of the United States against such parties and for such relief as may be appropriate. And such court shall have and shall exercise jurisdiction of proceedings instituted pursuant to this section. The Attorney General may implead as defendants such additional parties as are or become necessary to the grant of effective relief hereunder. . . .

## Title IV—Desegregation of Public Education

Definitions
**Section 401.** As used in this title—. . . .

(b) "Desegregation" means the assignment of students to public schools and within such schools without regard to their race, color, religion, or national origin, but "desegregation" shall not mean the assignment of students to public schools in order to overcome racial imbalance. . . .

Survey and Report of Educational Opportunities
**Section 402.** The Commissioner shall conduct a survey and make a report to the President and the Congress, within two years of the enactment of this title, concerning the lack of availability of equal educational opportunities for individuals by reason of race, color, religion, or national origin in public educational institutions at all levels in the United States, its territories and possessions, and the District of Columbia. . . .

## Title V—Commission on Civil Rights . . .

Duties of the Commission

**Section 104.** (a) The Commission shall—

(1) investigate allegations in writing under oath or affirmation that certain citizens of the United States are being deprived of their right to vote and have that vote counted by reason of their color, race, religion, or national origin; which writing, under oath or affirmation, shall set forth the facts upon which such belief or beliefs are based;

(2) study and collect information concerning legal developments constituting a denial of equal protection of the laws under the Constitution because of race, color, religion, or national origin or in the administration of justice;

(3) appraise the laws and policies of the Federal Government with respect to denials of equal protection of the laws under the Constitution because of race, color, religion, or national origin or in the administration of justice;

(4) serve as a national clearinghouse for information in respect to denials of equal protection of the laws because of race, color, religion, or national origin, including but not limited to the fields of voting, education, housing, employment, the use of public facilities, and transportation, or in the administration of justice;

(5) investigate allegations, made in writing and under oath or affirmation, that citizens of the United States are unlawfully being accorded or denied the right to vote, or to have their votes properly counted, in any election of presidential electors, Members of the United States Senate, or of the House of Representatives, as a result of any patterns or practice of fraud or discrimination in the conduct of such election. . . .

## Title VI—Nondiscrimination in Federally Assisted Programs

**Section 601.** No person in the United States shall, on the ground of race, color, religion, or national origin, be excluded from participation in, be denied the benefits of, or be subjected to discrimination under any program or activity receiving Federal financial assistance.

**Section 602.** Each Federal department and agency which is empowered to extend Federal financial assistance to any program or activity, by way of grant, loan, or contract other than a contract of insurance or guaranty, is authorized and directed to effectuate the provisions of section 601 with respect to such program or activity by issuing rules, regulations, or orders of general applicability which shall be consistent with achievement of the objectives of the statue authorizing the financial assistance in connection with which the action is taken. No such rule, regulation, or order shall become effective unless and until approved by the President. Compliance with any requirement adopted pursuant to this section may be effected

(1) by the termination of or refusal to grant or to continue assistance under such program or activity to any recipient as to whom there has been an express finding on the record, after opportunity for hearing, of a failure to comply with such requirement, but such termination or refusal shall be limited to the particular political entity, or part thereof, or other recipient as to whom such a finding has been made and, shall be limited in its effect to the particular program, or part thereof, in which such non-compliance has been so found, or

(2) by any other means authorized by law:

Provided, however, that no such action shall be taken until the department or agency concerned has advised the appropriate person or persons of the failure to comply with the requirement and has determined that compliance cannot be secured by voluntary means. In the case of any action terminating, or refusing to grant or continue, assistance because of failure to comply with a requirement imposed pursuant to this section, the head of the federal department or agency shall file with the committees of the House and Senate having legislative jurisdiction over the program or activity involved a full written report of the circumstances and the grounds for such action. No such action shall become effective until thirty days have elapsed after the filing of such report. . . .

## Title VII—Equal Employment Opportunity . . .

Discrimination Because of Race, Color, Religion, Sex, or National Origin
**Section 703.** (a) It shall be an unlawful employment practice for an employer—

(1) to fail or refuse to hire or to discharge any individual, or otherwise to discriminate against any individual with respect to his compensation, terms, conditions, or privileges of employment, because of such individual's race, color, religion, sex, or national origin; or

(2) to limit, segregate, or classify his employees in any way which would deprive or tend to deprive any individual of employment opportunities or otherwise adversely affect his status as an employee, because of such individual's race, color, religion, sex, or national origin.

(b) It shall be an unlawful employment practice for an employment agency to fail or refuse to refer for employment, or otherwise to discriminate against, any individual because of his race, color, religion, sex, or national origin, or to classify or refer for employment any individual on the basis of his race, color, religion, sex, or national origin.

(c) It shall be an unlawful employment practice for a labor organization—

(1) to exclude or to expel from its membership, or otherwise to discriminate against, any individual because of his race, color, religion, sex, or national origin;

(2) to limit, segregate, or classify its membership, or to classify or fail or refuse to refer for employment any individual, in any way which would deprive or tend to deprive any individual of employment opportunities, or would limit such employment opportunities or otherwise adversely affect his status as an employee or as an applicant for employment, because of such individual's race, color, religion, sex, or national origin; or

(3) to cause or attempt to cause an employer to discriminate against an individual in violation of this section.

(d) It shall be an unlawful employment practice for any employer, labor organization, or joint labor-management committee controlling apprenticeship or other training or retraining, including on-the-job training programs, to discriminate against any individual because of his race, color, religion, sex, or national origin in admission to, or employment in, any program established to provide apprenticeship or other training. . . .

Other Unlawful Employment Practices

**Section 704.** (a) It shall be an unlawful employment practice for an employer to discriminate against any of his employees or applicants for employment, for an employment agency to discriminate against any individual, or for a labor organization to discriminate against any member thereof or applicant for membership, because he has opposed any practice made an unlawful employment practice by this title, or because he has made a charge, testified, assisted, or participated in any manner in an investigation, proceeding, or hearing under this title.

(b) It shall be an unlawful employment practice for an employer, labor organization, or employment agency to print or publish or cause to be printed or published any notice or advertisement relating to employment by such an employer or membership in or any classification or referral for employment by such a labor organization, or relating to any classification or referral for employment by such an employment agency, indicating any preference, limitation, specification, or discrimination, based on race, color, religion, sex, or national origin, except that such a notice or advertisement may indicate a preference, limitation, specification, or discrimination based on religion, sex, or national origin when religion, sex, or national origin is a bona fide occupational qualification for employment.

Equal Employment Opportunity Commission

**Section 705.** (a) There is hereby created a Commission to be known as the Equal Employment Opportunity Commission, which shall be composed of five members, not more than three of whom shall be members of the same political party, who shall be appointed by the President by and with the advice and consent of the Senate. One of the original members shall be appointed for a term of one year, one for a term of two years, one for a term of three years, one for a term of four years, and one for a term of five years, beginning from the date of enactment of this title, but their successors shall be appointed for terms of five years each, except that any individual chosen to fill a vacancy shall be appointed only for the unexpired term of the member whom he shall succeed. The President shall designate one member to serve as Chairman of the Commission, and one member to serve as Vice Chairman. The Chairman shall be responsible on behalf of the Commission for the administrative operations of the Commission, and shall appoint, in accordance with the civil service laws, such officers, agents, attorneys, and employees as it deems necessary to assist it in the performance of its functions and to fix their compensation in accordance with Classification Act of 1949, as amended. . . .

## Title VIII—Registration and Voting Statistics

**Section 801.** The Secretary of Commerce shall promptly conduct a survey to compile registration and voting statistics in such geographic areas as may be recommended by the Commission on Civil Rights. Such a survey and compilation shall, to the extent recommended by the Commission on Civil Rights, only include a count of persons of voting age by race, color, and national origin, and determination of the extent to which such persons are registered to vote, and have voted in any statewide primary or general election in which the Members of the United States House of Representatives are nominated or elected, since January 1, 1960. Such information shall also be collected and compiled in connection with the Nineteenth Decennial Census, and at such other times as the Congress may prescribe. The provisions of section 9 and chapter 7 of title 13, United States Code, shall apply to any survey, collection, or compilation of registration and voting statistics carried out under this title: Provided, however, that no person shall be compelled to disclose his race, color, national origin, or questioned about his political party affiliation, how he voted, or the reasons therefore, nor shall any penalty be imposed for his failure or refusal to make such disclosure. Every person interrogated orally, by written survey or questionnaire or by any other means with respect to such information shall be fully advised with respect to his right to fail or refuse to furnish such information.

# Key Provisions of the Voting Rights Act of 1965

*The Voting Rights Act of 1965 forced the South to give up literacy tests, poll taxes, and other methods used to prevent black people from voting. It also empowered federal officials to register voters in areas with a history of denying black voter rights.*

## An Act

To enforce the fifteenth amendment to the Constitution of the United States, and for other purposes.

Be it enacted by the Senate and House of Representatives of the United States of America in Congress assembled, That this Act shall be known as the "Voting Rights Act of 1965." . . .

**Section 2.** No voting qualification or prerequisite to voting, or standard, practice, or procedure shall be imposed or applied by any State or political subdivision to deny or abridge the right of any citizen of the United States to vote on account of race or color.

**Section 3.** (a) Whenever the Attorney General institutes a proceeding under any statute to enforce the guarantees of the fifteenth amendment in any State or political subdivision the court shall authorize the appointment of Federal examiners by the United States Civil Service Commission in accordance with section 6 to serve for such period of time and for such political subdivisions as the court shall determine is appropriate to enforce the guarantees of the fifteenth amendment (1) as part of any interlocutory order if the court determines that the appointment of such examiners is necessary to enforce such guarantees or (2) as part of any final judgment if the court finds that violations of the fifteenth amendment justifying equitable relief have occurred in such State or subdivision: Provided, That the court need not authorize the appointment of examiners if any incidents of denial or abridgment of the right to vote on account of race or color (1) have been few in number and have been promptly and effectively corrected by State or local action, (2) the continuing effect of such incidents has been eliminated, and (3) there is no reasonable probability of their recurrence in the future.

(b) If in a proceeding instituted by the Attorney General under any statute to enforce the guarantees of the fifteenth amendment in any State or political subdivision the court finds that a test or device has been used for the purpose or with the effect of denying or abridging the right of any citizen of the United States to vote on account of race or color, it shall suspend the use of tests and devices in such State or political subdivisions as the court shall determine is appropriate and for such period as it deems necessary. . . .

**Section 4.** (a) To assure that the right of citizens of the United States to vote is not denied or abridged on account of race or color, no citizen shall be denied the right to vote in any Federal, State, or local election because of his failure to comply with any test or device in any State with respect to which the determinations have been made under subsection (b). . . .

(b) The provisions of subsection (a) shall apply in any State or in any political subdivision of a state which (1) the Attorney General determines maintained on November 1, 1964, any test or device, and with respect to which (2) the Director of the Census determines that less than 50 per centum of the persons of voting age residing therein were registered on November 1, 1964, or that less than 50 per centum of such persons voted in the presidential election of November 1964. . . .

(c) The phrase "test or device" shall mean any requirement that a person as a prerequisite for voting or registration of voting (1) demonstrate the ability to read, write, understand, or interpret any matter, (2) demonstrate any educational achievement or his knowledge of any particular subject, (3) possess good moral character, or (4) prove his qualifications by the voucher of registered voters or members of any other class. . . .

**Section 6.** Whenever (a) a court has authorized the appointment of examiners pursuant to the provisions of section 3 (a), or (b) unless a declaratory judgment has been rendered under section 4 (a), the Attorney General certifies with respect to any political subdivision named in, or included within the scope of, determinations made under section 4 (b) that (1) he has received complaints in writing from twenty or more residents of such political subdivision alleging that they have been denied the right to vote under color of law on account of race or color, and that he believes such complaints to be meritorious, or (2) that in his judgment (considering, among other factors, whether the ratio of nonwhite persons to white persons registered to vote within such subdivision appears to him to be reasonably attributable to violations of the fifteenth amendment or whether substantial evidence exists that bona fide efforts are being made within such subdivision to comply with the fifteenth amendment), the appointment of examiners is otherwise necessary to enforce the guarantees of the fifteenth amendment, the Civil Service Commission shall appoint as many examiners for such subdivision as it may deem appropriate to prepare and maintain lists of persons eligible to vote in Federal, State, and local elections. . . . Examiners and hearing officers shall have the power to administer oaths. . . .

**Section 10.** (a) The Congress finds that the requirement of the payment of a poll tax as a precondition to voting (i) precludes persons of limited means from voting or imposes unreasonable financial hardship upon such persons as a precondition to their exercise of the franchise, (ii) does not bear a reasonable relationship to any legitimate State interest in the conduct of elections, and (iii) in some areas has the purpose or effect of denying persons the right to vote because of race or color. Upon the basis of these findings, Congress declares that the constitutional right of citizens to vote is denied or abridged in some areas by the requirement of the payment of a poll tax as a precondition to voting.

(b) In the exercise of the powers of Congress under section 5 of the fourteenth amendment and section 2 of the fifteenth amendment, the Attorney General is authorized and directed to institute forthwith in the name of the United States such actions, including actions against States or political subdivisions, for declaratory judgment or injunctive relief against the enforcement of any requirement of the payment of a poll tax as a precondition to voting, or substitute thereof enacted after November 1, 1964, as will be necessary to implement the declaration of subsection (a) and the purposes of this section. . . .

**Section 11.** (a) No person acting under color of law shall fail or refuse to permit any person to vote who is entitled to vote under any provision of this Act or is otherwise qualified to vote, or willfully fail or refuse to tabulate, count, and report such person's vote.

(b) No person, whether acting under color of law or otherwise, shall intimidate, threaten, or coerce, or attempt to intimidate, threaten, or coerce any person for voting or attempting to vote, or intimidate, threaten, or coerce, or attempt to intimidate, threaten, or coerce any person for urging or aiding any person to vote or attempt to vote, or intimidate, threaten, or coerce any person for exercising any powers or duties under section 3 (a), 6, 8, 9, 10, or 12 (e).

# PHOTO CREDITS

# INDEX

Page numbers followed by *f, t,* and *m* refer to figures, tables and maps respectively.

# ADDITONAL TITLES
## OF INTEREST

*Note to Instructors: Any of these Penguin titles can be packaged with this book at a special discount.*

Frederick Douglass, *My Bondage and My Freedom*
Frederick Douglass, *Narrative of the Life of Frederick Douglass* (Penguin Classics Edition)
Frederick Douglass, *Narrative of the Life of Frederick Douglass*
W.E.B. Du Bois, *The Souls of Black Folk*
Olaudah Equiano, *The Interesting Narrative and Other Writings*
Nelson George, *The Death of Rhythm & Blues*
John Howard Griffin, *Black Like Me* (Penguin Classics Edition)
John Howard Griffin, *Black Like Me* (Signet Edition)
Lorraine Hansberry, *A Raisin in the Sun: The Unfilmed Original Screenplay*
Joel Chandler Harris, *Nights with Uncle Remus*
Joseph Harris, *Africans and Their History*
Harriet Jacobs, *Incidents in the Life of a Slave Girl*
James Weldon Johnson, *The Autobiography of an Ex-Colored Man*
Martin Luther King Jr., *Why We Can't Wait*
Nella Larsen, *Passing*
Julius Lester, *From Slave Ship to Freedom Road*
Ellen Levine, *Freedom's Children*
James McBride, *The Color of Water: A Black Man's Tribute to His Mother*
Toni Morrison, *The Bluest Eye*
Rosa Parks, *Rosa Parks: My Story*
Patricia Raybon, *My First White Friend: Confessions of Love, Race, and Forgiveness*
Randall Robinson, *The Debt*
Harriet Beecher Stowe, *Uncle Tom's Cabin*
Clinton L. Taulbert, *Once Upon a Time When We Were Colored*
Sojourner Truth, *The Narrative of Sojourner Truth*
Mark Twain, *The Adventures of Huckleberry Finn*
Various, *Against Slavery*
Various, *The Classic Slave Narratives*
Various, *The Portable Harlem Renaissance Reader*
Rebecca Walker, *Black, White, and Jewish*
Booker T. Washington, *Up from Slavery*
Phillis Wheatley, *The Complete Writings*
Juan Williams, *Eyes on the Prize: America's Civil Rights Years 1954–65*
Harriet L. Wilson, *Our Nig*
August Wilson, *Fences*
August Wilson, *Joe Turner's Come and Gone*
*The Koran*

For more information about these and other Penguin titles, visit us online at
**www.ablongman.com/historyvaluepacks.**